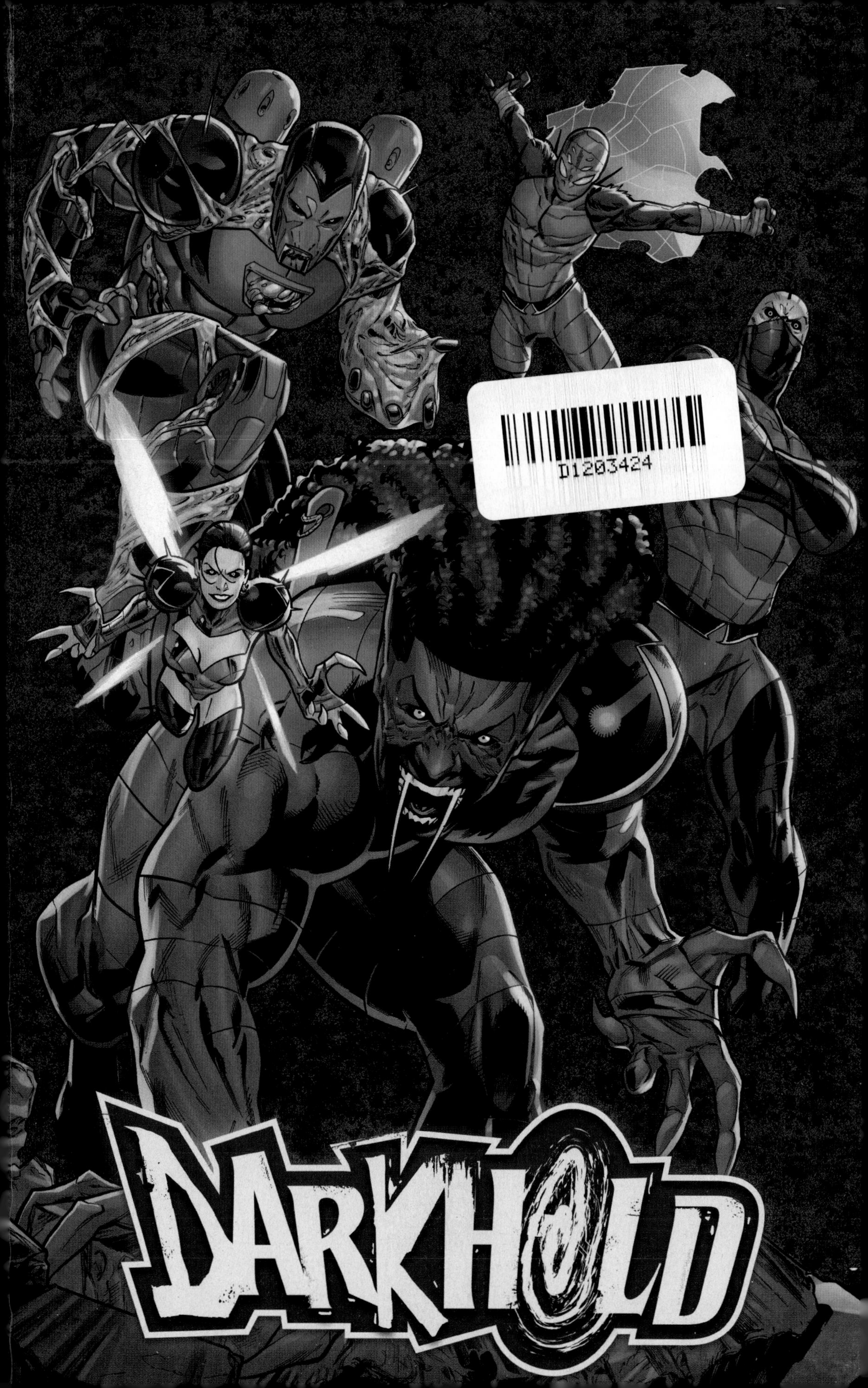
DARKHOLD

THE DARKHOLD ALPHA

WRITER **STEVE ORLANDO**
ARTIST **CIAN TORMEY**
COLOR ARTIST **JESUS ABURTOV**
COVER ART **GREG SMALLWOOD**

THE DARKHOLD: IRON MAN

WRITER **RYAN NORTH**
ARTIST **GUILLERMO SANNA**
COLOR ARTIST **IAN HERRING**
COVER ART **VALERIO GIANGIORDANO**
        & ROMULO FAJARDO JR.

THE DARKHOLD: BLADE

WRITER **DANIEL KIBBLESMITH**
ARTIST **FEDERICO SABBATINI**
COLOR ARTIST **RICO RENZI**
COVER ART **JUAN FERREYRA**

THE DARKHOLD: WASP

WRITER/COLOR ARTIST **JORDIE BELLAIRE**
ARTIST **CLAIRE ROE**
COVER ART **PAUL RENAUD**

THE DARKHOLD. Contains material originally published in magazine form as THE DARKHOLD ALPHA (2021) #1, THE DARKHOLD: BLADE (2021) #1, THE DARKHOLD: WASP (2021) #1, THE DARKHOLD: IRON MAN (2021) #1, THE DARKHOLD: BLACK BOLT (2021) #1, THE DARKHOLD: SPIDER-MAN (2021) #1 and THE DARKHOLD OMEGA (2020) #1. First printing 2021. ISBN 978-1-302-92584-0. Published by MARVEL WORLDWIDE, INC., a subsidiary of MARVEL ENTERTAINMENT, LLC. OFFICE OF PUBLICATION: 1290 Avenue of the Americas, New York, NY 10104. © 2021 MARVEL No similarity between any of the names, characters, persons, and/ or institutions in this book with those of any living or dead person or institution is intended, and any such similarity which may exist is purely coincidental. **Printed in the U.S.A.** KEVIN FEIGE, Chief Creative Officer; DAN BUCKLEY, President, Marvel Entertainment; JOE QUESADA, EVP & Creative Director; DAVID BOGART, Associate Publisher & SVP of Talent Affairs; TOM BREVOORT, VP, Executive Editor; NICK LOWE, Executive Editor, VP of Content, Digital Publishing; DAVID GABRIEL, VP of Print & Digital Publishing; JEFF YOUNGQUIST, VP of Production & Special Projects; ALEX MORALES, Director of Publishing Operations; DAN EDINGTON, Managing Editor; RICKEY PURDIN, Director of Talent Relations; JENNIFER GRÜNWALD, Senior Editor, Special Projects; SUSAN CRESPI, Production Manager; STAN LEE, Chairman Emeritus. For information regarding advertising in Marvel Comics or on Marvel.com, please contact Vit DeBellis, Custom Solutions & Integrated Advertising Manager, at vdebellis@marvel.com. For Marvel subscription inquiries, please call 888-511-5480. **Manufactured between 12/3/2021 and 1/5/2022 by** FRY COMMUNICATIONS, MECHANICSBURG, PA, USA.

10 9 8 7 6 5 4 3 2 1

THE DARKHOLD: BLACK BOLT

WRITER **MARK RUSSEL**
PENCILER **DAVID CUTLER**
INKER **ROBERTO POGGI**
COLORIST **MATT MILLA**
COVER ART **TRAVEL FOREMAN & DAN BROWN**

THE DARKHOLD: SPIDER-MAN

WRITER **ALEX PAKNADEL**
ARTIST **DIO NEVES**
COLOR ARTIST **JIM CHARALAMPIDIS**
COVER ART **JAMES HARREN & DAVE STEWART**

THE DARKHOLD OMEGA

WRITER **STEVE ORLANDO**
PENCILER **CIAN TORMEY**
INKERS **ROBERTO POGGI** WITH **MARC DEERING & WALDEN WONG**
COLOR ARTIST **JESUS ABURTOV**
COVER ART **CHRIS BACHALO**

LETTERER **VC's CLAYTON COWLES**

ASSISTANT EDITOR **KAITLYN LINDTVEDT**
ASSOCIATE EDITOR **ALANNA SMITH**
EDITORS **WIL MOSS & SARAH BRUNSTAD**

COLLECTION EDITOR **DANIEL KIRCHHOFFER**
ASSISTANT MANAGING EDITOR **MAIA LOY**
ASSISTANT MANAGING EDITOR **LISA MONTALBANO**
SENIOR EDITOR, SPECIAL PROJECTS **JENNIFER GRÜNWALD**

VP PRODUCTION & SPECIAL PROJECTS **JEFF YOUNGQUIST**
BOOK DESIGNERS **STACIE ZUCKER** WITH **VC's CLAYTON COWLES**
SVP PRINT, SALES & MARKETING **DAVID GABRIEL**
EDITOR IN CHIEF **C.B. CEBULSKI**

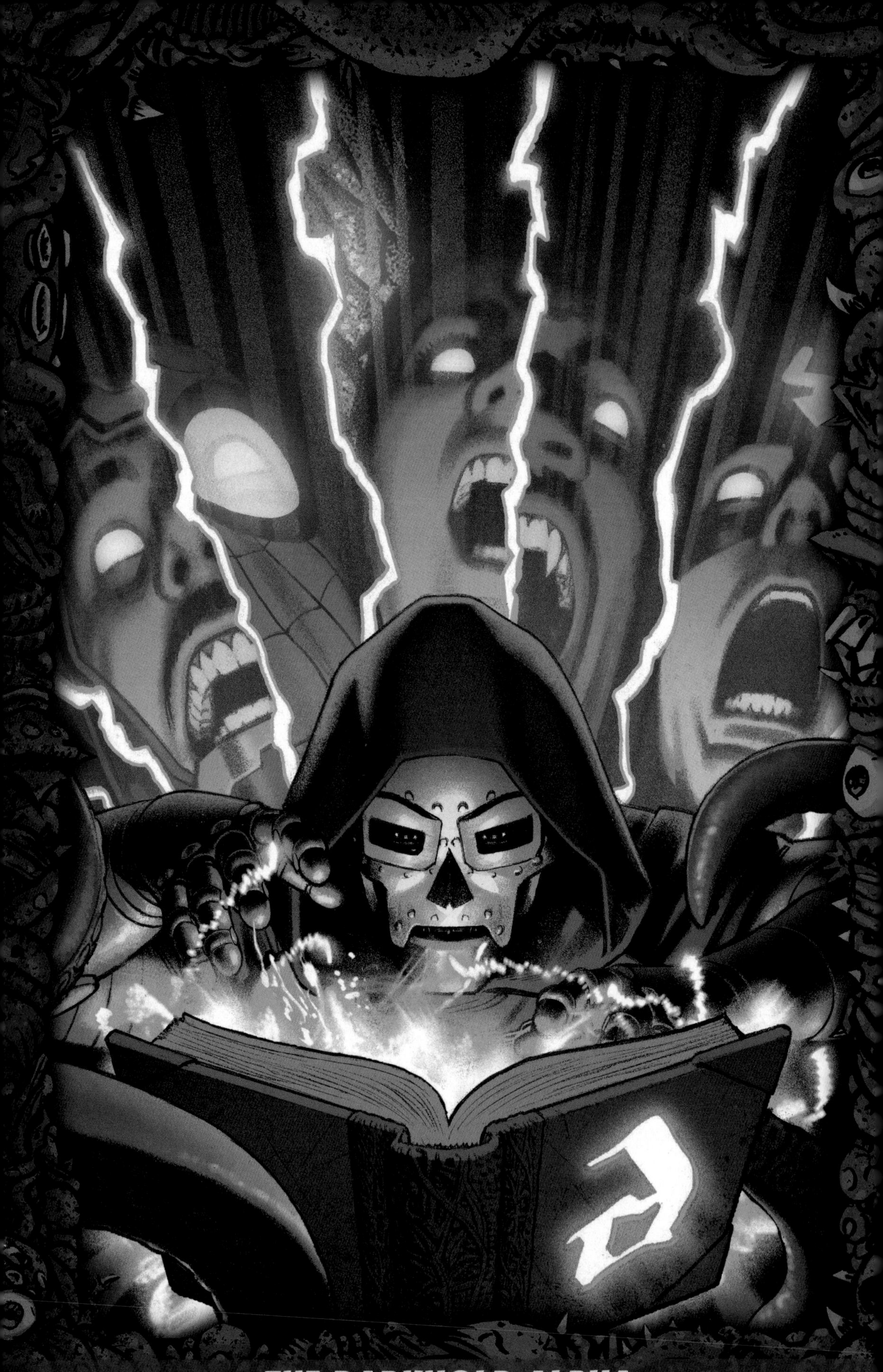

THE DARKHOLD ALPHA

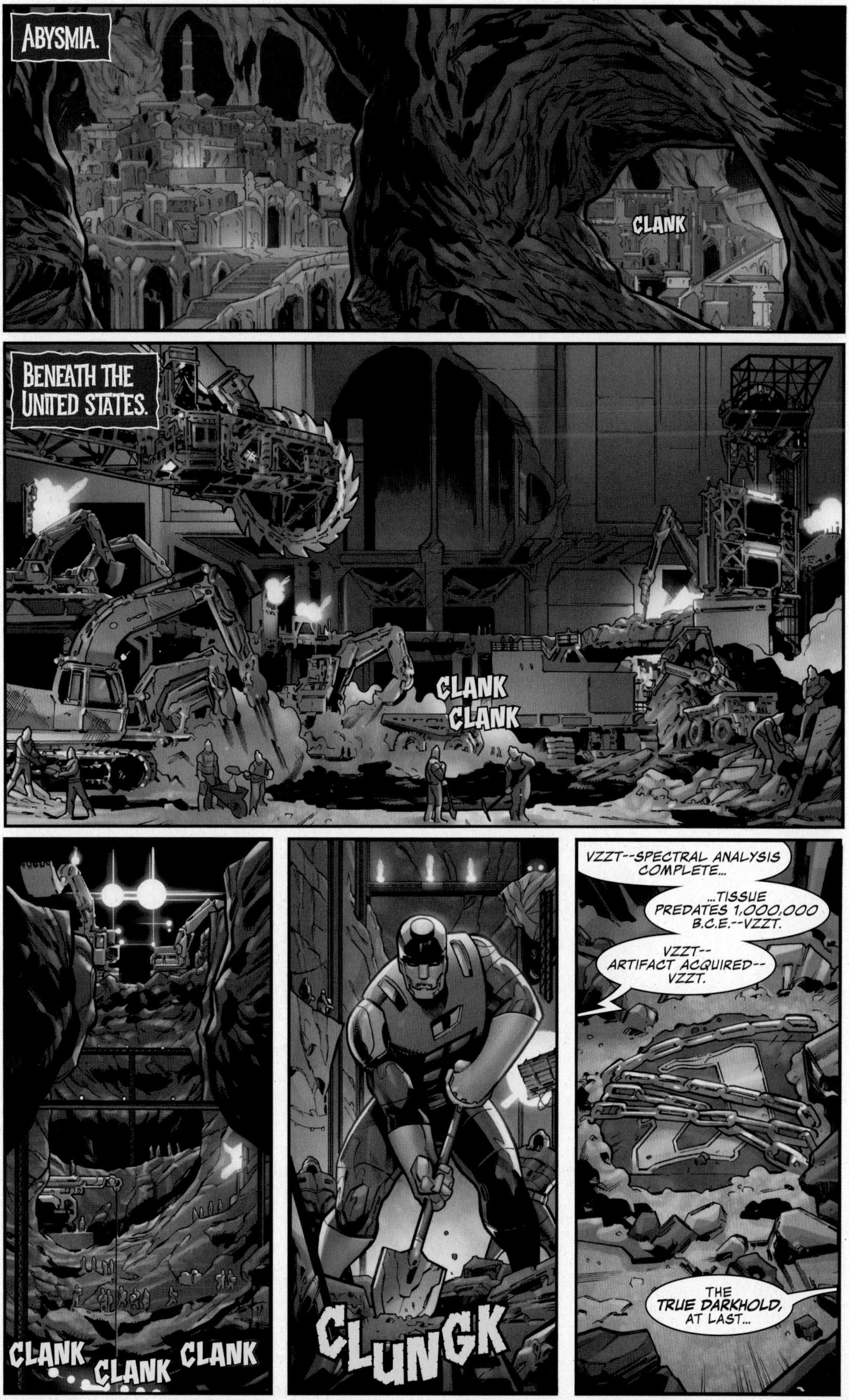
ABYSMIA.
CLANK
BENEATH THE UNITED STATES.
CLANK
CLANK
CLANK
CLANK
CLANK
CLUNGK
VZZT--SPECTRAL ANALYSIS COMPLETE...
...TISSUE PREDATES 1,000,000 B.C.E.--VZZT.
VZZT-- ARTIFACT ACQUIRED-- VZZT.
THE TRUE DARKHOLD, AT LAST...

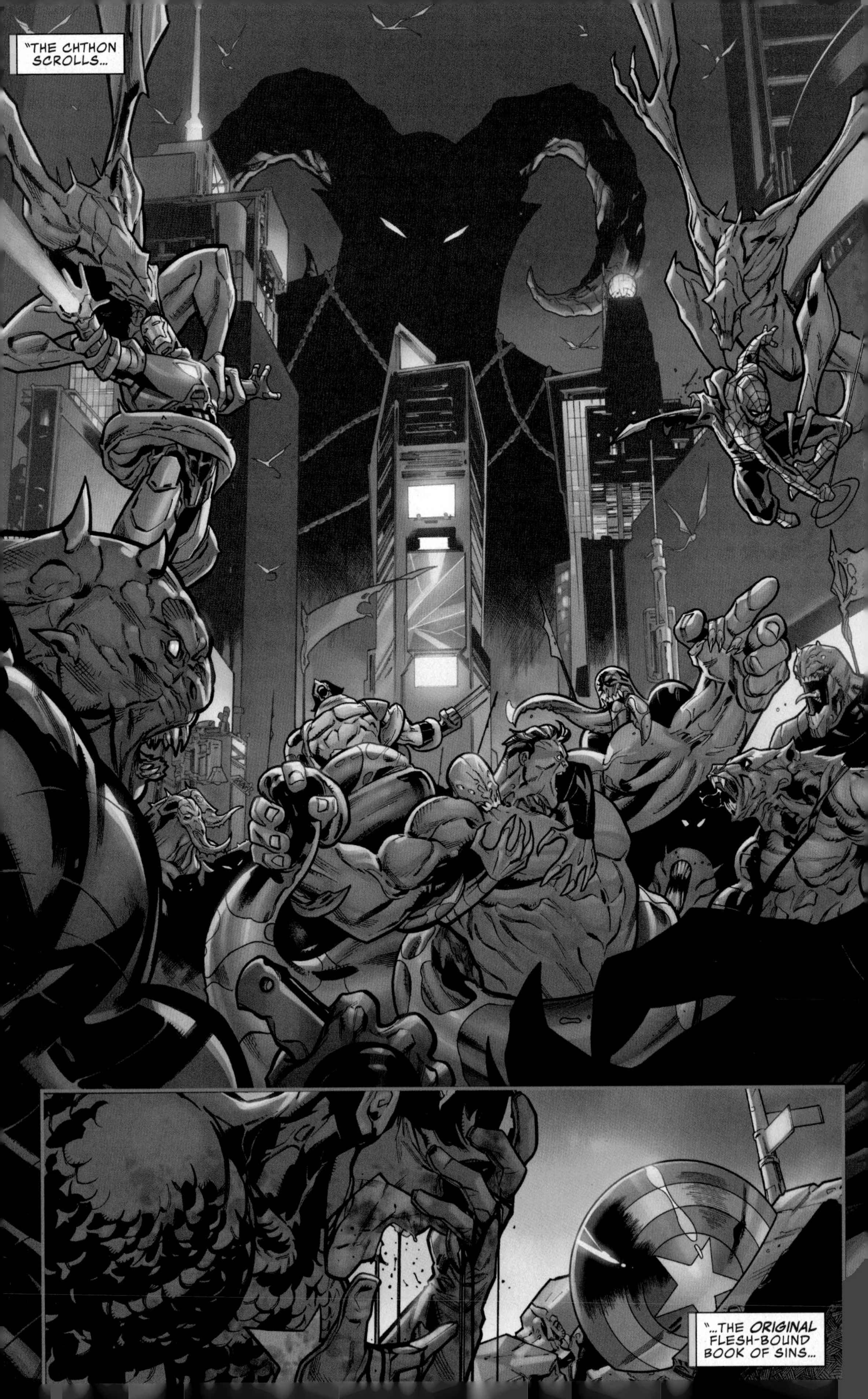
"THE CHTHON SCROLLS...
"...THE ORIGINAL FLESH-BOUND BOOK OF SINS...

"...IN THE HANDS OF ITS *RIGHTFUL OWNER.*"

FRANKLIN!

CHTHON'S *INVASION* IS *CONTAGIOUS!* SEEING, HEARING... EVEN SMELLING THESE CREATURES SPREADS MADNESS EXPONENTIALLY!

BUT I'VE GOT THE *SHAPE* OF IT! THIS IS JUST *EXTRADIMENSIONAL* ENERGY! I CAN *STOP* IT--I CAN!

IF WE CAN JUST--

IRGK!

YOU *COULD* STOP IT, VALERIA...

...AND WE CAN'T HAVE THAT.

CAN WE, *SIS?*

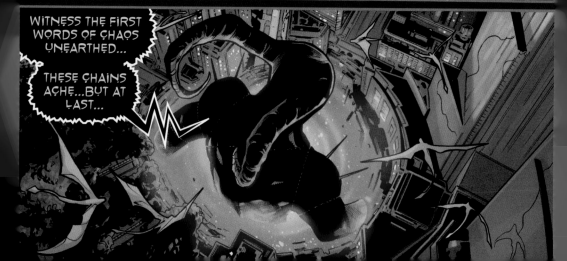

WITNESS THE FIRST WORDS OF CHAOS UNEARTHED...

THESE CHAINS ACHE...BUT AT LAST...

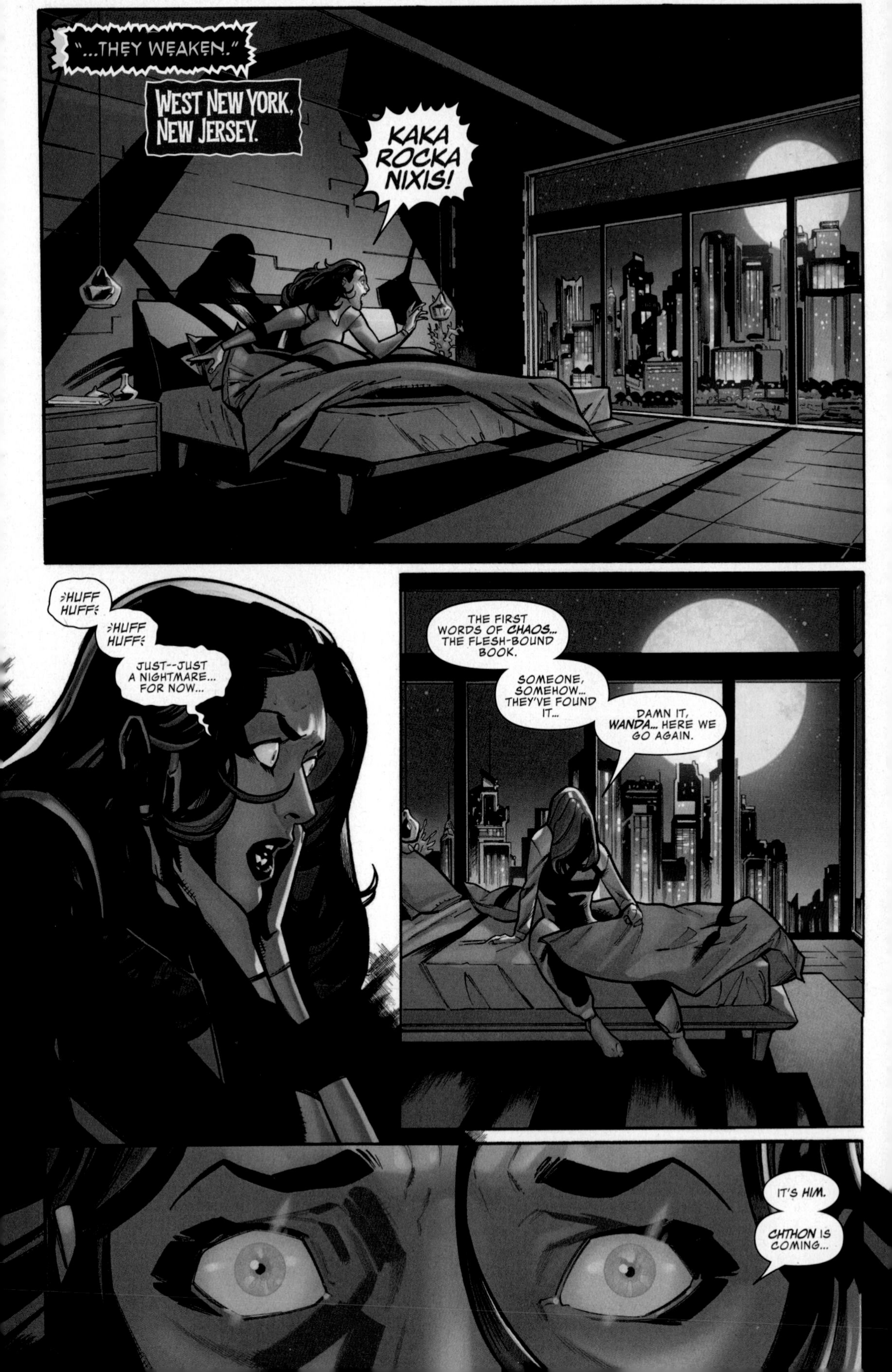
"...THEY WEAKEN."
WEST NEW YORK, NEW JERSEY.
KAKA ROCKA NIXIS!
HUFF HUFF
HUFF HUFF
JUST--JUST A NIGHTMARE... FOR NOW...
THE FIRST WORDS OF CHAOS... THE FLESH-BOUND BOOK.
SOMEONE, SOMEHOW... THEY'VE FOUND IT...
DAMN IT, WANDA... HERE WE GO AGAIN.
IT'S HIM.
CHTHON IS COMING...

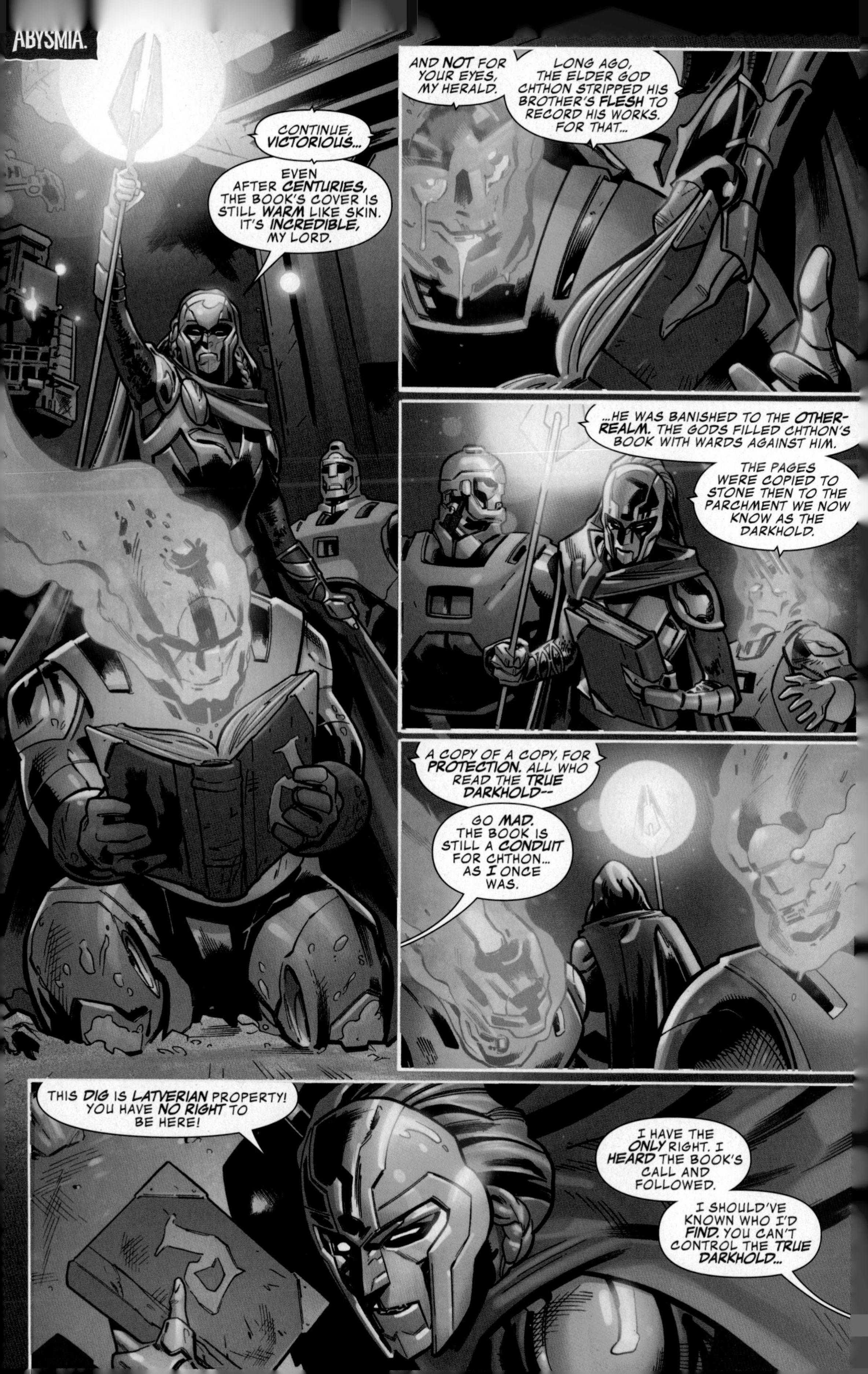
ABYSMIA.
CONTINUE, VICTORIOUS...
EVEN AFTER CENTURIES, THE BOOK'S COVER IS STILL WARM LIKE SKIN. IT'S INCREDIBLE, MY LORD.
AND NOT FOR YOUR EYES, MY HERALD.
LONG AGO, THE ELDER GOD CHTHON STRIPPED HIS BROTHER'S FLESH TO RECORD HIS WORKS. FOR THAT...
...HE WAS BANISHED TO THE OTHER-REALM. THE GODS FILLED CHTHON'S BOOK WITH WARDS AGAINST HIM.
THE PAGES WERE COPIED TO STONE THEN TO THE PARCHMENT WE NOW KNOW AS THE DARKHOLD.
A COPY OF A COPY, FOR PROTECTION. ALL WHO READ THE TRUE DARKHOLD--
GO MAD. THE BOOK IS STILL A CONDUIT FOR CHTHON... AS I ONCE WAS.
THIS DIG IS LATVERIAN PROPERTY! YOU HAVE NO RIGHT TO BE HERE!
I HAVE THE ONLY RIGHT. I HEARD THE BOOK'S CALL AND FOLLOWED.
I SHOULD'VE KNOWN WHO I'D FIND. YOU CAN'T CONTROL THE TRUE DARKHOLD...

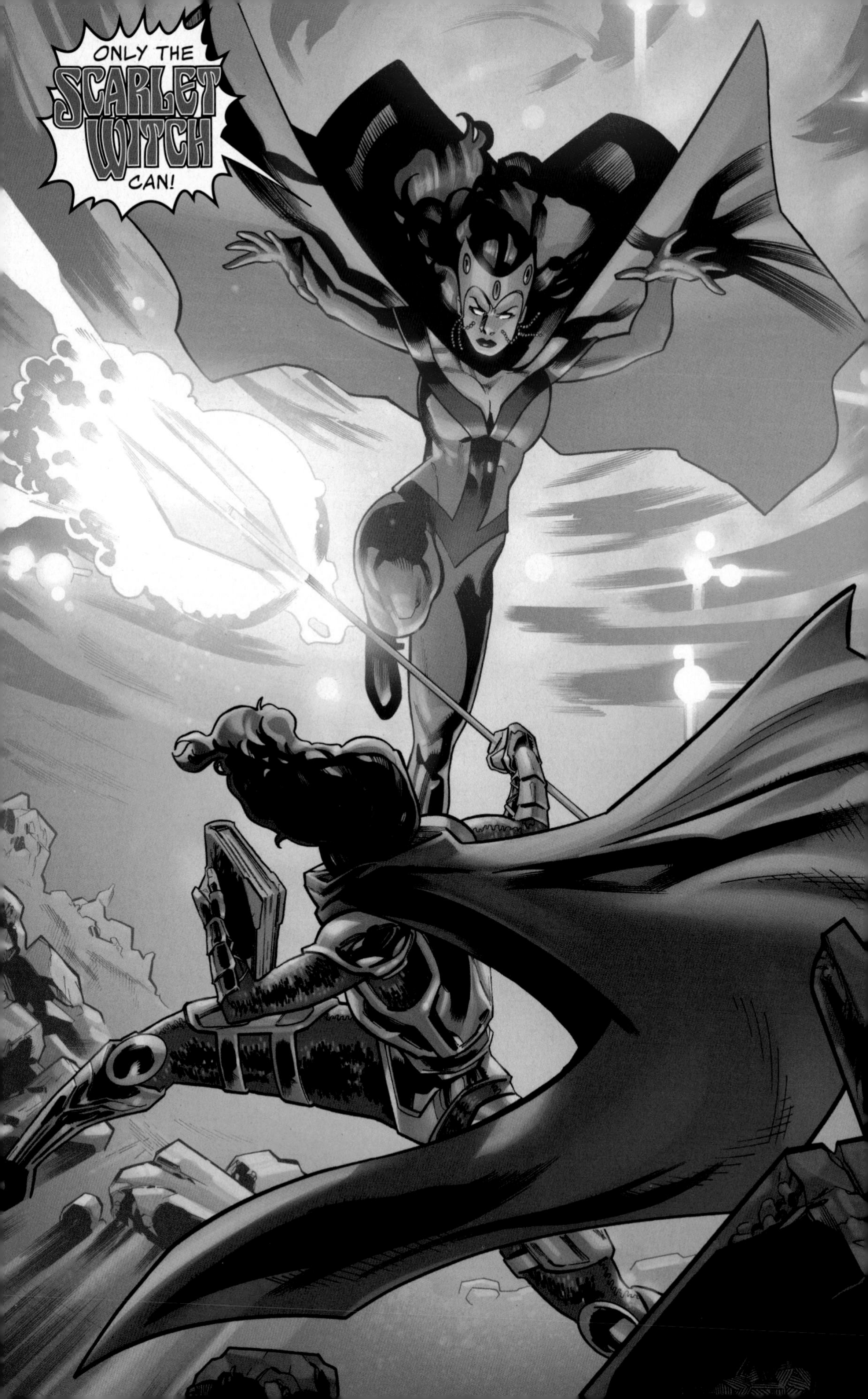
ONLY THE
SCARLET WITCH
CAN!

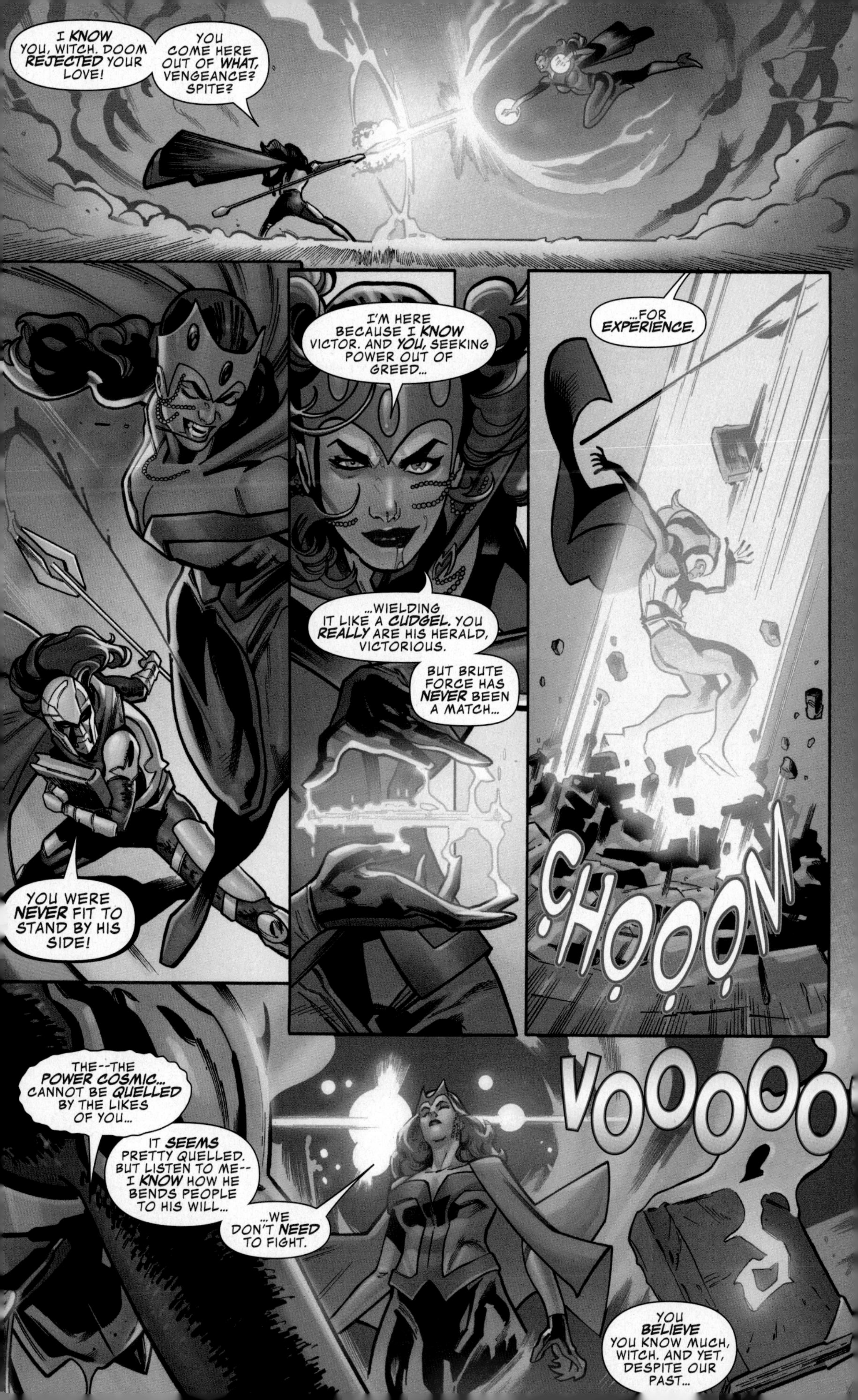
I KNOW YOU, WITCH. DOOM REJECTED YOUR LOVE!
YOU COME HERE OUT OF WHAT, VENGEANCE? SPITE?
I'M HERE BECAUSE I KNOW VICTOR. AND YOU, SEEKING POWER OUT OF GREED...
...WIELDING IT LIKE A CUDGEL. YOU REALLY ARE HIS HERALD, VICTORIOUS.
BUT BRUTE FORCE HAS NEVER BEEN A MATCH...
YOU WERE NEVER FIT TO STAND BY HIS SIDE!
...FOR EXPERIENCE.
CHOOOM
THE--THE POWER COSMIC... CANNOT BE QUELLED BY THE LIKES OF YOU...
IT SEEMS PRETTY QUELLED. BUT LISTEN TO ME-- I KNOW HOW HE BENDS PEOPLE TO HIS WILL...
...WE DON'T NEED TO FIGHT.
VOOOOOO
YOU BELIEVE YOU KNOW MUCH, WITCH. AND YET, DESPITE OUR PAST...

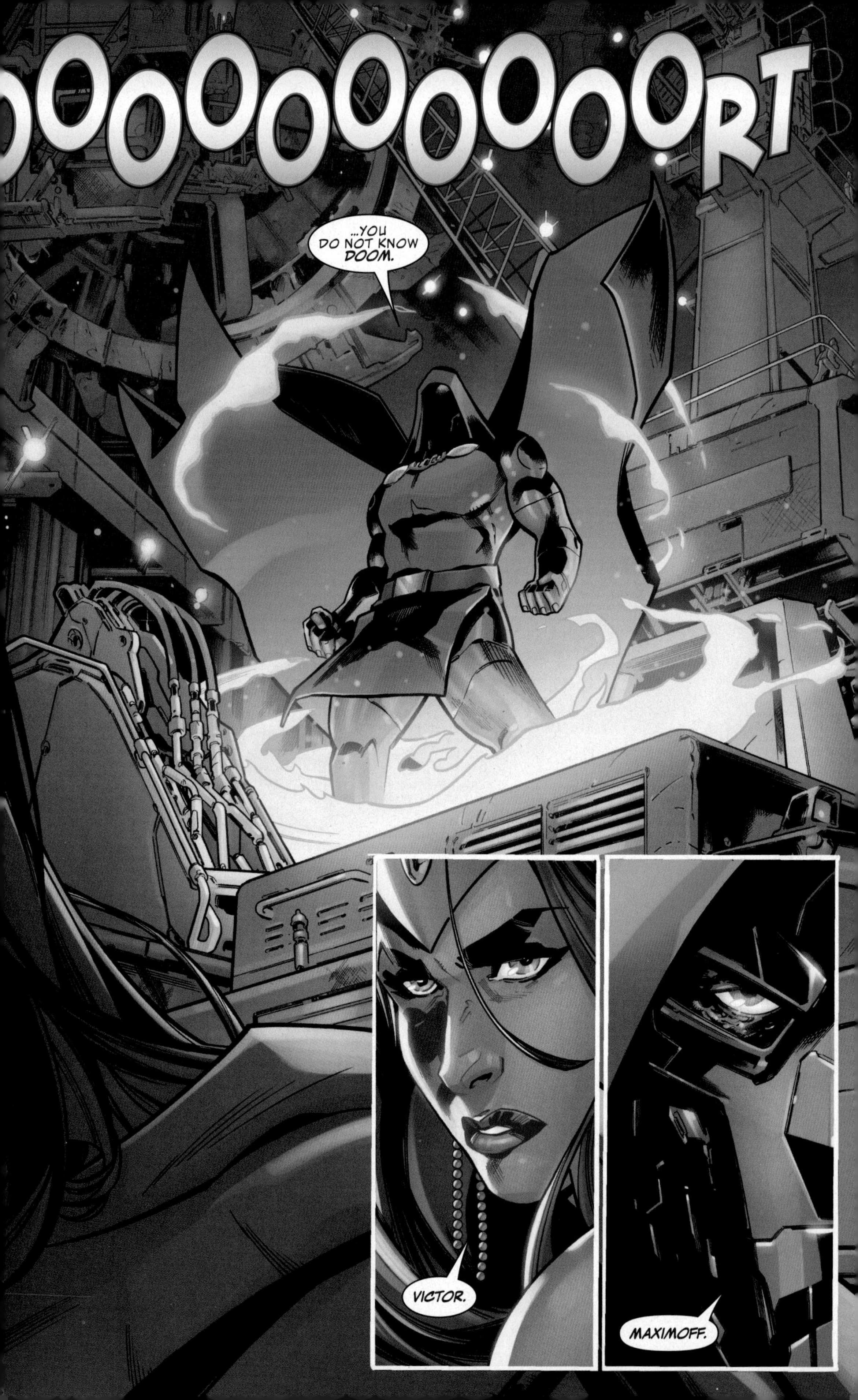
OOOOOOOOOOOOORT
...YOU DO NOT KNOW DOOM.
VICTOR.
MAXIMOFF.

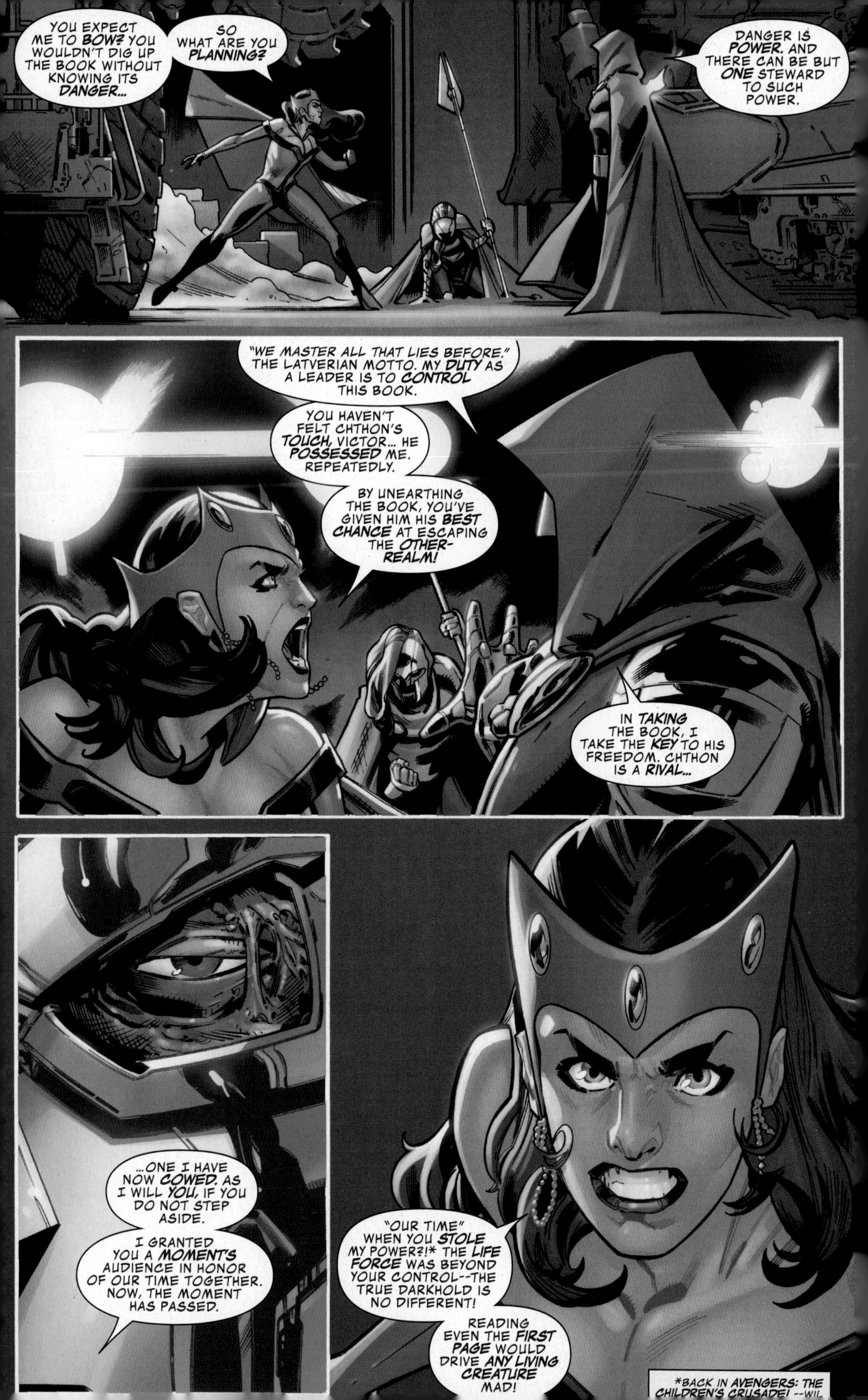
YOU EXPECT ME TO BOW? YOU WOULDN'T DIG UP THE BOOK WITHOUT KNOWING ITS DANGER...
SO WHAT ARE YOU PLANNING?
DANGER IS POWER. AND THERE CAN BE BUT ONE STEWARD TO SUCH POWER.
"WE MASTER ALL THAT LIES BEFORE." THE LATVERIAN MOTTO. MY DUTY AS A LEADER IS TO CONTROL THIS BOOK.
YOU HAVEN'T FELT CHTHON'S TOUCH, VICTOR... HE POSSESSED ME. REPEATEDLY.
BY UNEARTHING THE BOOK, YOU'VE GIVEN HIM HIS BEST CHANCE AT ESCAPING THE OTHER-REALM!
IN TAKING THE BOOK, I TAKE THE KEY TO HIS FREEDOM. CHTHON IS A RIVAL...
...ONE I HAVE NOW COWED. AS I WILL YOU, IF YOU DO NOT STEP ASIDE.
I GRANTED YOU A MOMENT'S AUDIENCE IN HONOR OF OUR TIME TOGETHER. NOW, THE MOMENT HAS PASSED.
"OUR TIME" WHEN YOU STOLE MY POWER?!* THE LIFE FORCE WAS BEYOND YOUR CONTROL--THE TRUE DARKHOLD IS NO DIFFERENT!
READING EVEN THE FIRST PAGE WOULD DRIVE ANY LIVING CREATURE MAD!
*BACK IN AVENGERS: THE CHILDREN'S CRUSADE! --WIL

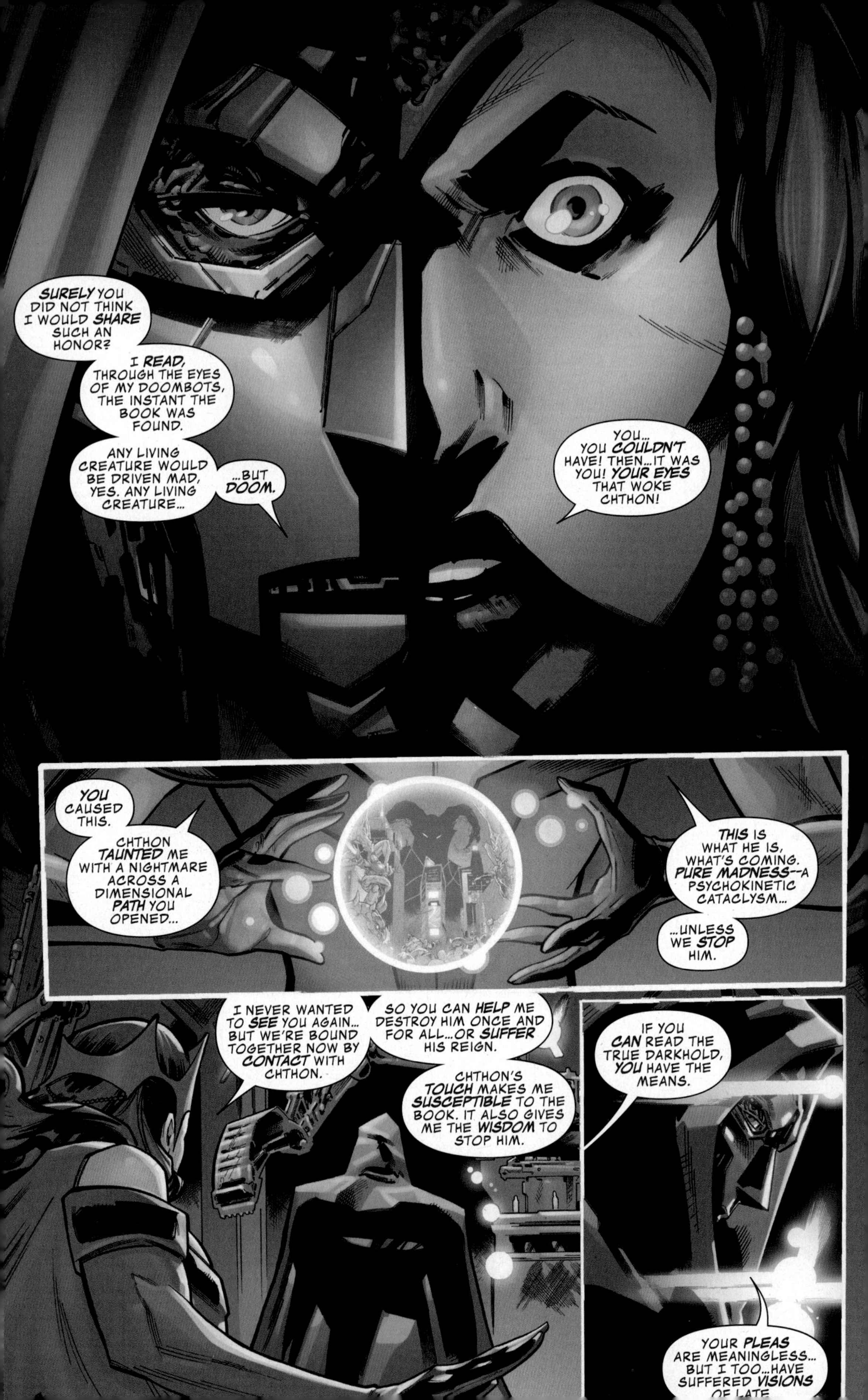
SURELY YOU DID NOT THINK I WOULD SHARE SUCH AN HONOR?
I READ, THROUGH THE EYES OF MY DOOMBOTS, THE INSTANT THE BOOK WAS FOUND.
ANY LIVING CREATURE WOULD BE DRIVEN MAD, YES. ANY LIVING CREATURE...
...BUT DOOM.
YOU... YOU COULDN'T HAVE! THEN...IT WAS YOU! YOUR EYES THAT WOKE CHTHON!
YOU CAUSED THIS.
CHTHON TAUNTED ME WITH A NIGHTMARE ACROSS A DIMENSIONAL PATH YOU OPENED...
THIS IS WHAT HE IS, WHAT'S COMING. PURE MADNESS--A PSYCHOKINETIC CATACLYSM...
...UNLESS WE STOP HIM.
I NEVER WANTED TO SEE YOU AGAIN... BUT WE'RE BOUND TOGETHER NOW BY CONTACT WITH CHTHON.
SO YOU CAN HELP ME DESTROY HIM ONCE AND FOR ALL...OR SUFFER HIS REIGN.
CHTHON'S TOUCH MAKES ME SUSCEPTIBLE TO THE BOOK. IT ALSO GIVES ME THE WISDOM TO STOP HIM.
IF YOU CAN READ THE TRUE DARKHOLD, YOU HAVE THE MEANS.
YOUR PLEAS ARE MEANINGLESS... BUT I TOO...HAVE SUFFERED VISIONS OF LATE.

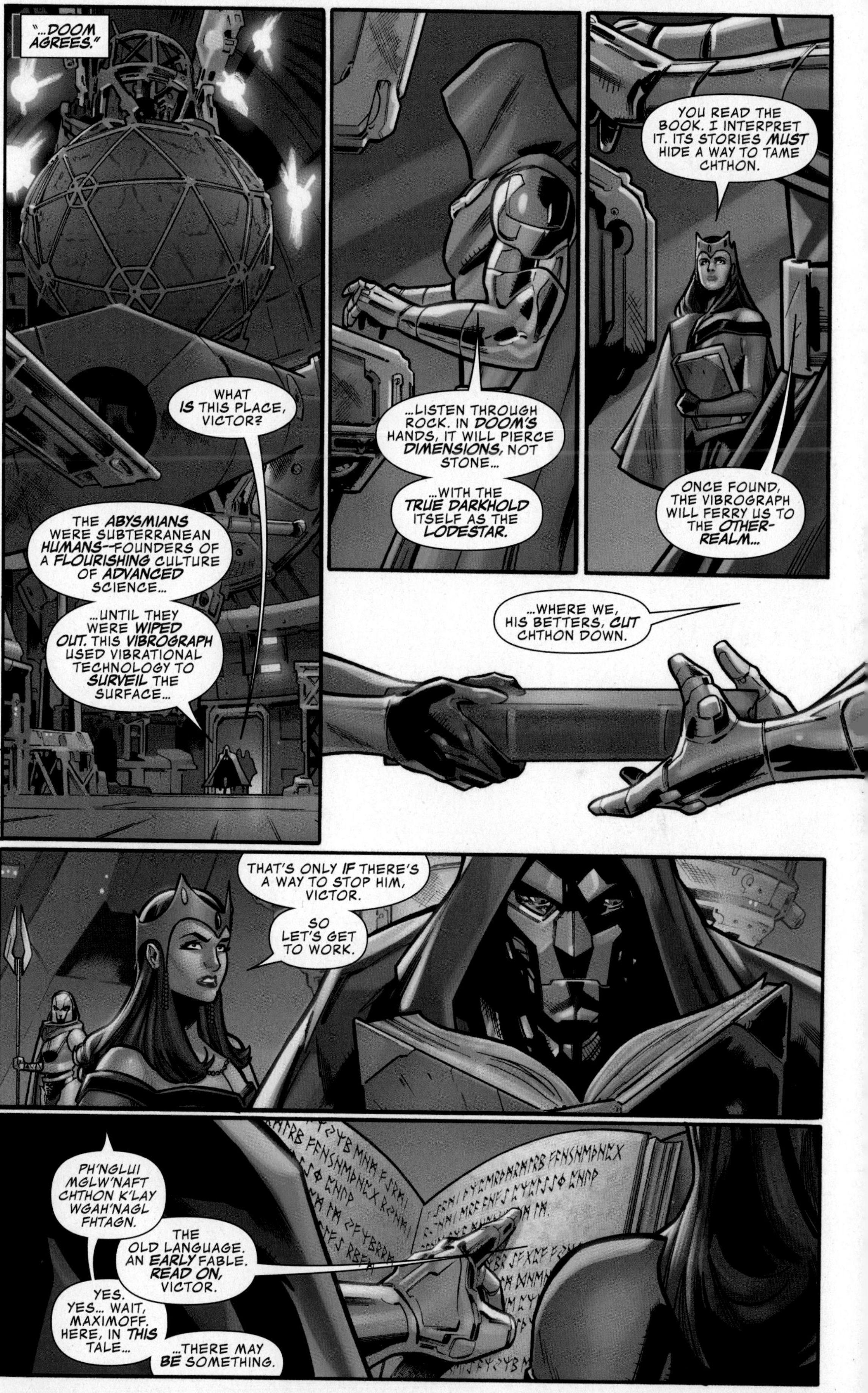

"...DOOM AGREES."
WHAT IS THIS PLACE, VICTOR?
THE ABYSMIANS WERE SUBTERRANEAN HUMANS--FOUNDERS OF A FLOURISHING CULTURE OF ADVANCED SCIENCE...
...UNTIL THEY WERE WIPED OUT. THIS VIBROGRAPH USED VIBRATIONAL TECHNOLOGY TO SURVEIL THE SURFACE...
...LISTEN THROUGH ROCK. IN DOOM'S HANDS, IT WILL PIERCE DIMENSIONS, NOT STONE...
...WITH THE TRUE DARKHOLD ITSELF AS THE LODESTAR.
YOU READ THE BOOK. I INTERPRET IT. ITS STORIES MUST HIDE A WAY TO TAME CHTHON.
ONCE FOUND, THE VIBROGRAPH WILL FERRY US TO THE OTHER-REALM...
...WHERE WE, HIS BETTERS, CUT CHTHON DOWN.
THAT'S ONLY IF THERE'S A WAY TO STOP HIM, VICTOR.
SO LET'S GET TO WORK.
PH'NGLUI MGLW'NAFT CHTHON K'LAY WGAH'NAGL FHTAGN.
THE OLD LANGUAGE. AN EARLY FABLE. READ ON, VICTOR.
YES. YES... WAIT, MAXIMOFF. HERE, IN THIS TALE...
...THERE MAY BE SOMETHING.

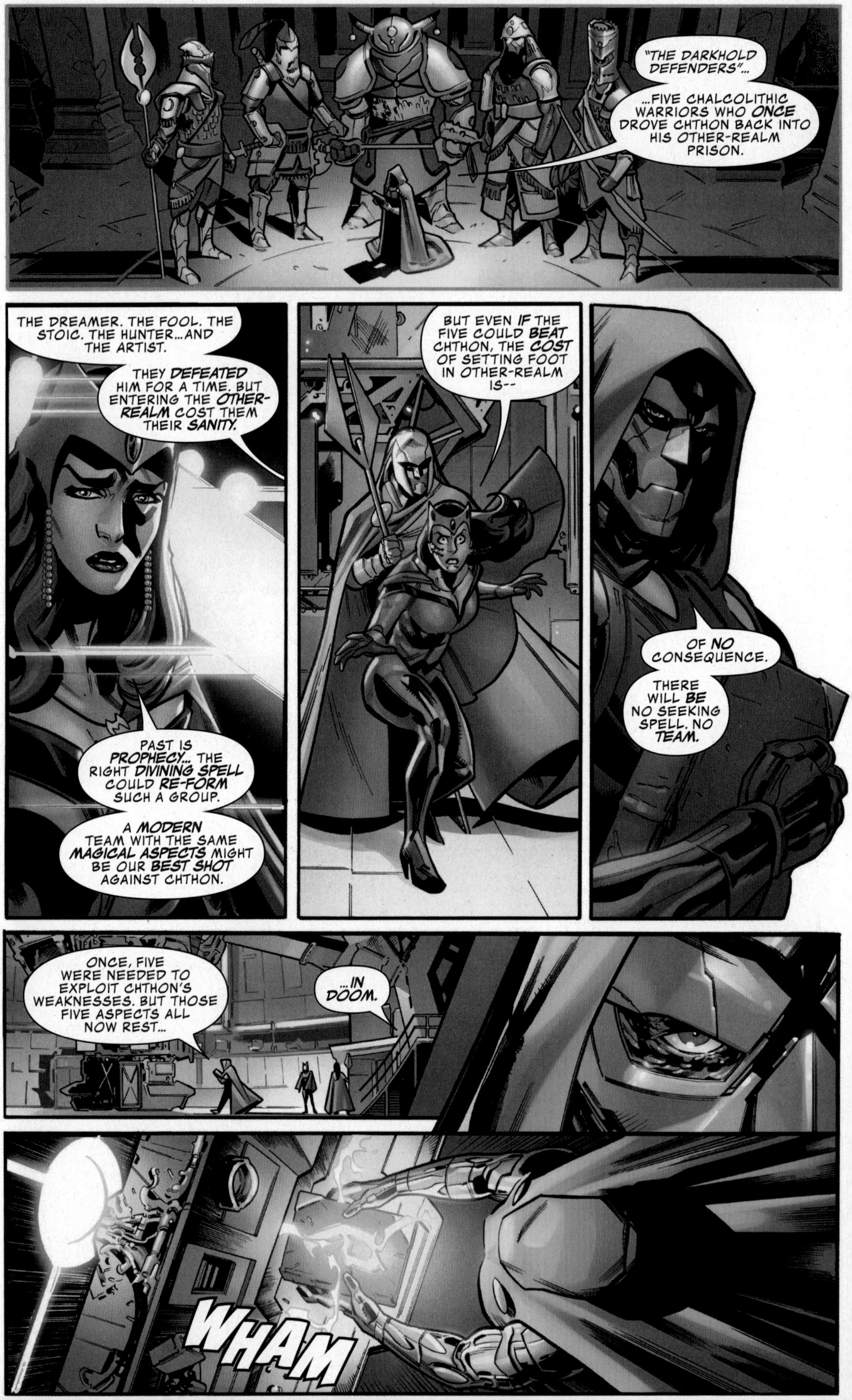
"THE DARKHOLD DEFENDERS"...
...FIVE CHALCOLITHIC WARRIORS WHO ONCE DROVE CHTHON BACK INTO HIS OTHER-REALM PRISON.
THE DREAMER. THE FOOL. THE STOIC. THE HUNTER...AND THE ARTIST.
THEY DEFEATED HIM FOR A TIME. BUT ENTERING THE OTHER-REALM COST THEM THEIR SANITY.
PAST IS PROPHECY... THE RIGHT DIVINING SPELL COULD RE-FORM SUCH A GROUP.
A MODERN TEAM WITH THE SAME MAGICAL ASPECTS MIGHT BE OUR BEST SHOT AGAINST CHTHON.
BUT EVEN IF THE FIVE COULD BEAT CHTHON, THE COST OF SETTING FOOT IN OTHER-REALM IS--
OF NO CONSEQUENCE.
THERE WILL BE NO SEEKING SPELL. NO TEAM.
ONCE, FIVE WERE NEEDED TO EXPLOIT CHTHON'S WEAKNESSES. BUT THOSE FIVE ASPECTS ALL NOW REST...
...IN DOOM.
WHAM

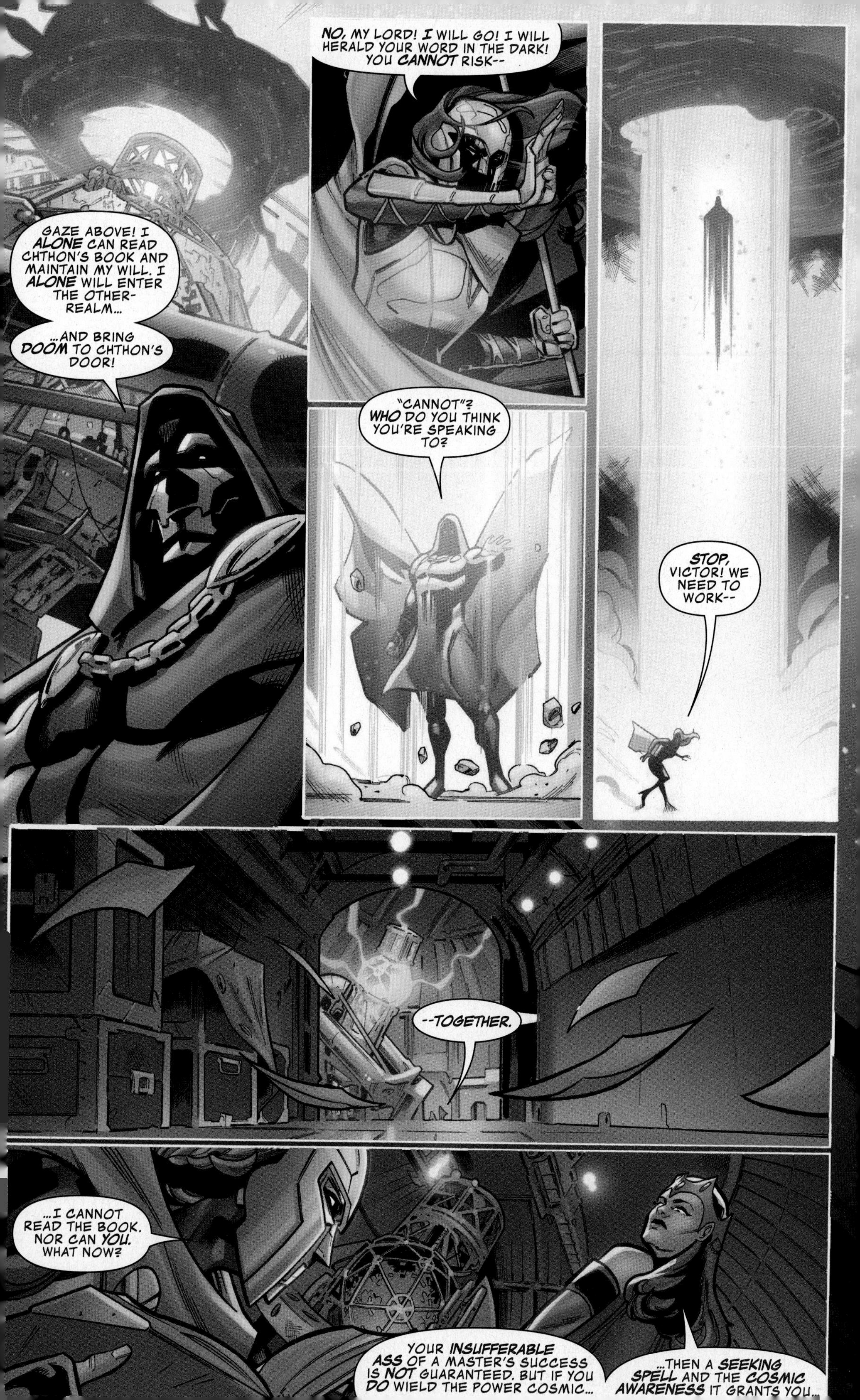

GAZE ABOVE! I ALONE CAN READ CHTHON'S BOOK AND MAINTAIN MY WILL. I ALONE WILL ENTER THE OTHER-REALM...
...AND BRING DOOM TO CHTHON'S DOOR!
NO, MY LORD! I WILL GO! I WILL HERALD YOUR WORD IN THE DARK! YOU CANNOT RISK--
"CANNOT"? WHO DO YOU THINK YOU'RE SPEAKING TO?
STOP, VICTOR! WE NEED TO WORK--
--TOGETHER.
...I CANNOT READ THE BOOK. NOR CAN YOU. WHAT NOW?
YOUR INSUFFERABLE ASS OF A MASTER'S SUCCESS IS NOT GUARANTEED. BUT IF YOU DO WIELD THE POWER COSMIC...
...THEN A SEEKING SPELL AND THE COSMIC AWARENESS IT GRANTS YOU...

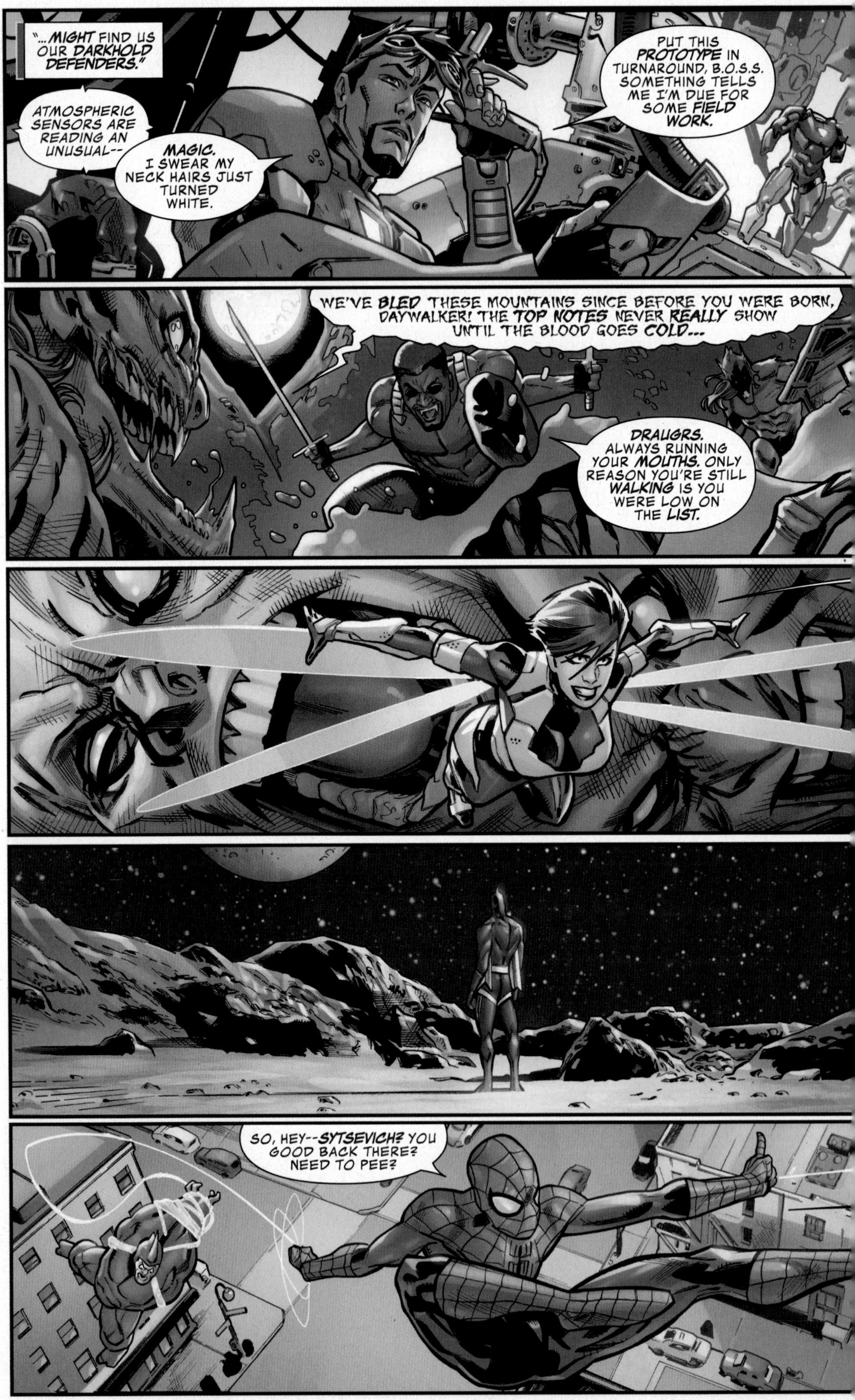
"...MIGHT FIND US OUR DARKHOLD DEFENDERS."
ATMOSPHERIC SENSORS ARE READING AN UNUSUAL--
MAGIC. I SWEAR MY NECK HAIRS JUST TURNED WHITE.
PUT THIS PROTOTYPE IN TURNAROUND, B.O.S.S. SOMETHING TELLS ME I'M DUE FOR SOME FIELD WORK.
WE'VE BLED THESE MOUNTAINS SINCE BEFORE YOU WERE BORN, DAYWALKER! THE TOP NOTES NEVER REALLY SHOW UNTIL THE BLOOD GOES COLD...
DRAUGRS. ALWAYS RUNNING YOUR MOUTHS. ONLY REASON YOU'RE STILL WALKING IS YOU WERE LOW ON THE LIST.
SO, HEY--SYTSEVICH? YOU GOOD BACK THERE? NEED TO PEE?

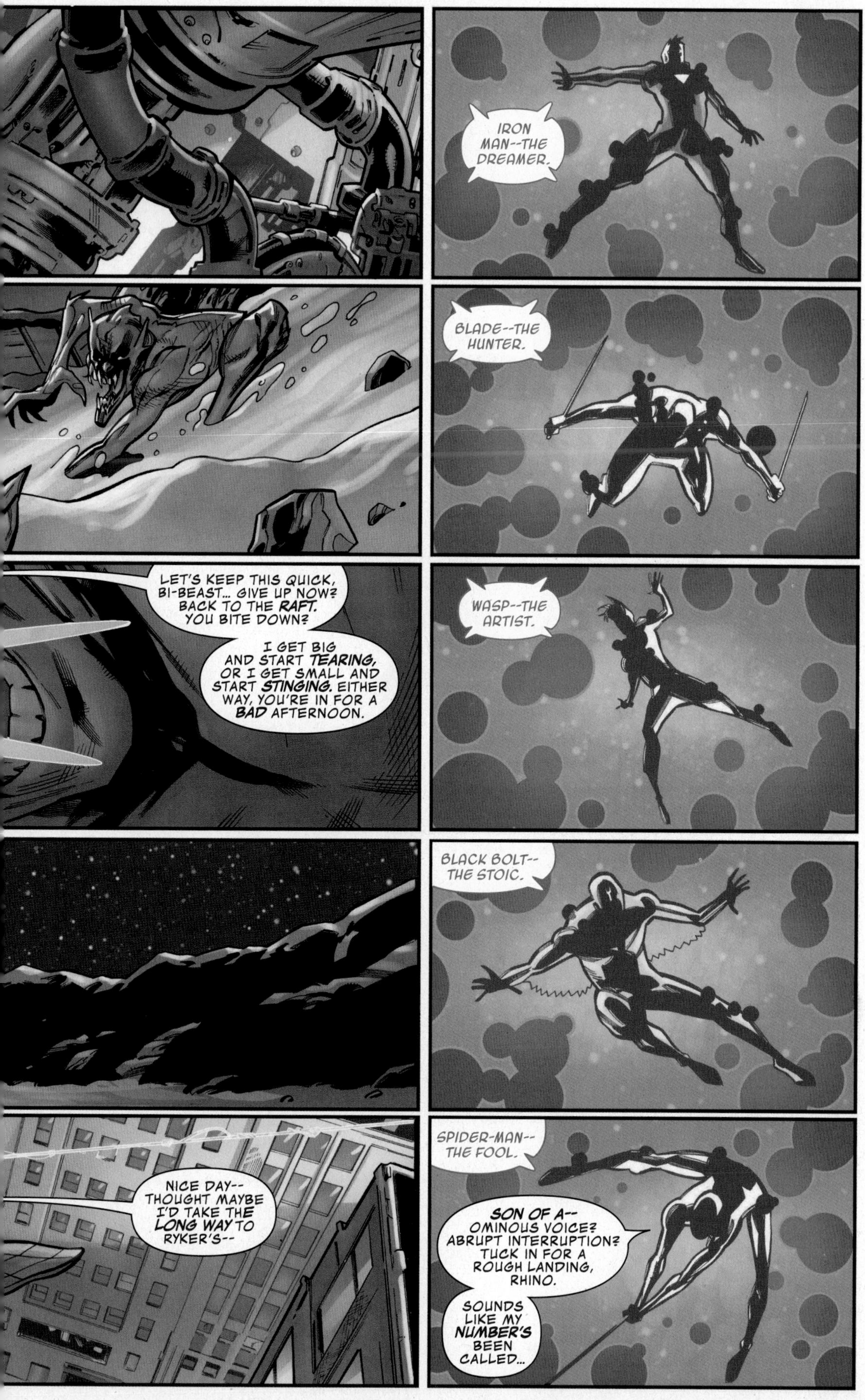
IRON MAN--THE DREAMER.
BLADE--THE HUNTER.
LET'S KEEP THIS QUICK, BI-BEAST... GIVE UP NOW? BACK TO THE RAFT. YOU BITE DOWN?
I GET BIG AND START TEARING, OR I GET SMALL AND START STINGING. EITHER WAY, YOU'RE IN FOR A BAD AFTERNOON.
WASP--THE ARTIST.
BLACK BOLT--THE STOIC.
NICE DAY--THOUGHT MAYBE I'D TAKE THE LONG WAY TO RYKER'S--
SPIDER-MAN--THE FOOL.
SON OF A-- OMINOUS VOICE? ABRUPT INTERRUPTION? TUCK IN FOR A ROUGH LANDING, RHINO.
SOUNDS LIKE MY NUMBER'S BEEN CALLED...

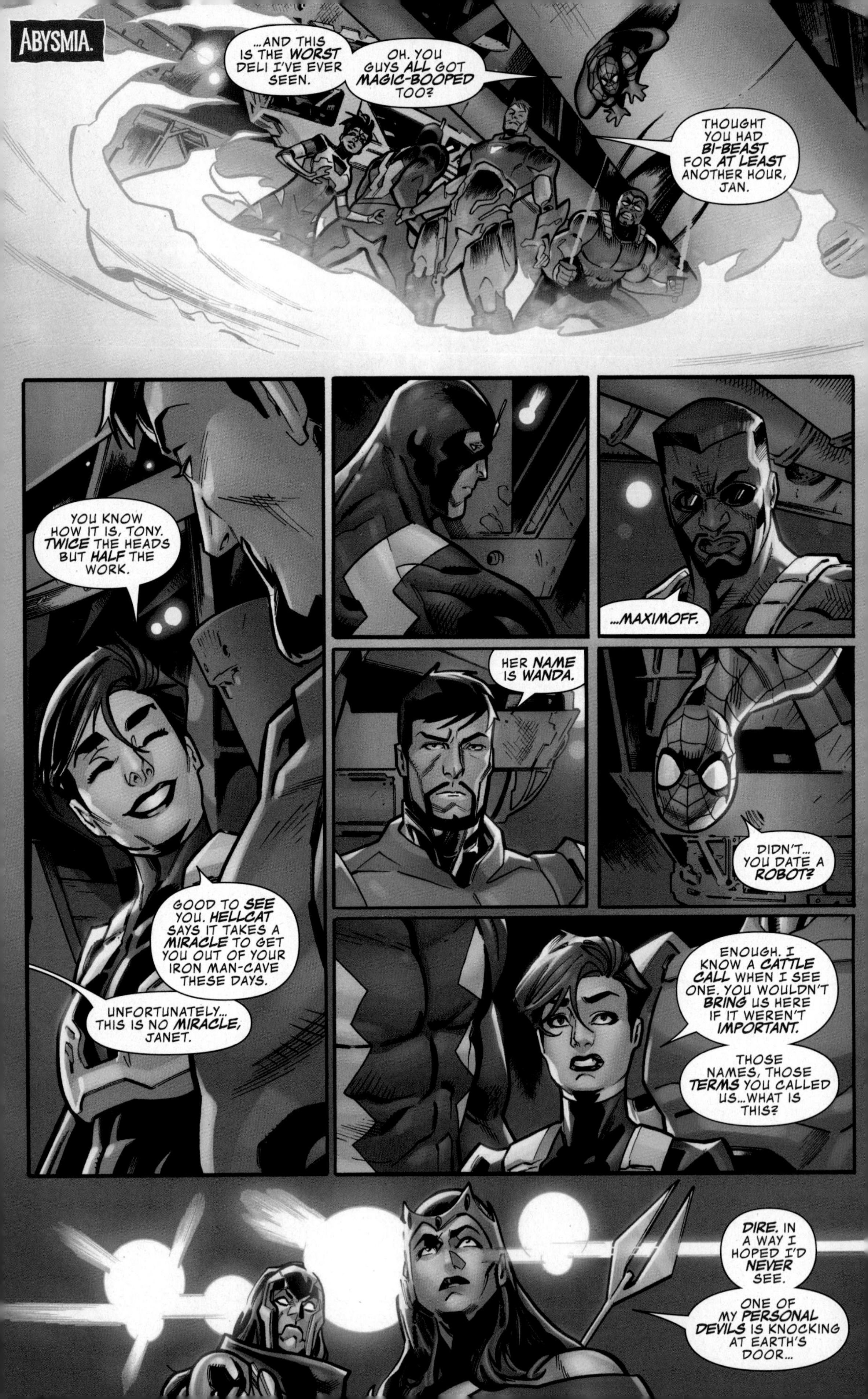
ABYSMIA.
...AND THIS IS THE WORST DELI I'VE EVER SEEN.
OH. YOU GUYS ALL GOT MAGIC-BOOPED TOO?
THOUGHT YOU HAD BI-BEAST FOR AT LEAST ANOTHER HOUR, JAN.
YOU KNOW HOW IT IS, TONY. TWICE THE HEADS BUT HALF THE WORK.
...MAXIMOFF.
HER NAME IS WANDA.
DIDN'T... YOU DATE A ROBOT?
GOOD TO SEE YOU. HELLCAT SAYS IT TAKES A MIRACLE TO GET YOU OUT OF YOUR IRON MAN-CAVE THESE DAYS.
UNFORTUNATELY... THIS IS NO MIRACLE, JANET.
ENOUGH. I KNOW A CATTLE CALL WHEN I SEE ONE. YOU WOULDN'T BRING US HERE IF IT WEREN'T IMPORTANT.
THOSE NAMES, THOSE TERMS YOU CALLED US...WHAT IS THIS?
DIRE. IN A WAY I HOPED I'D NEVER SEE.
ONE OF MY PERSONAL DEVILS IS KNOCKING AT EARTH'S DOOR...

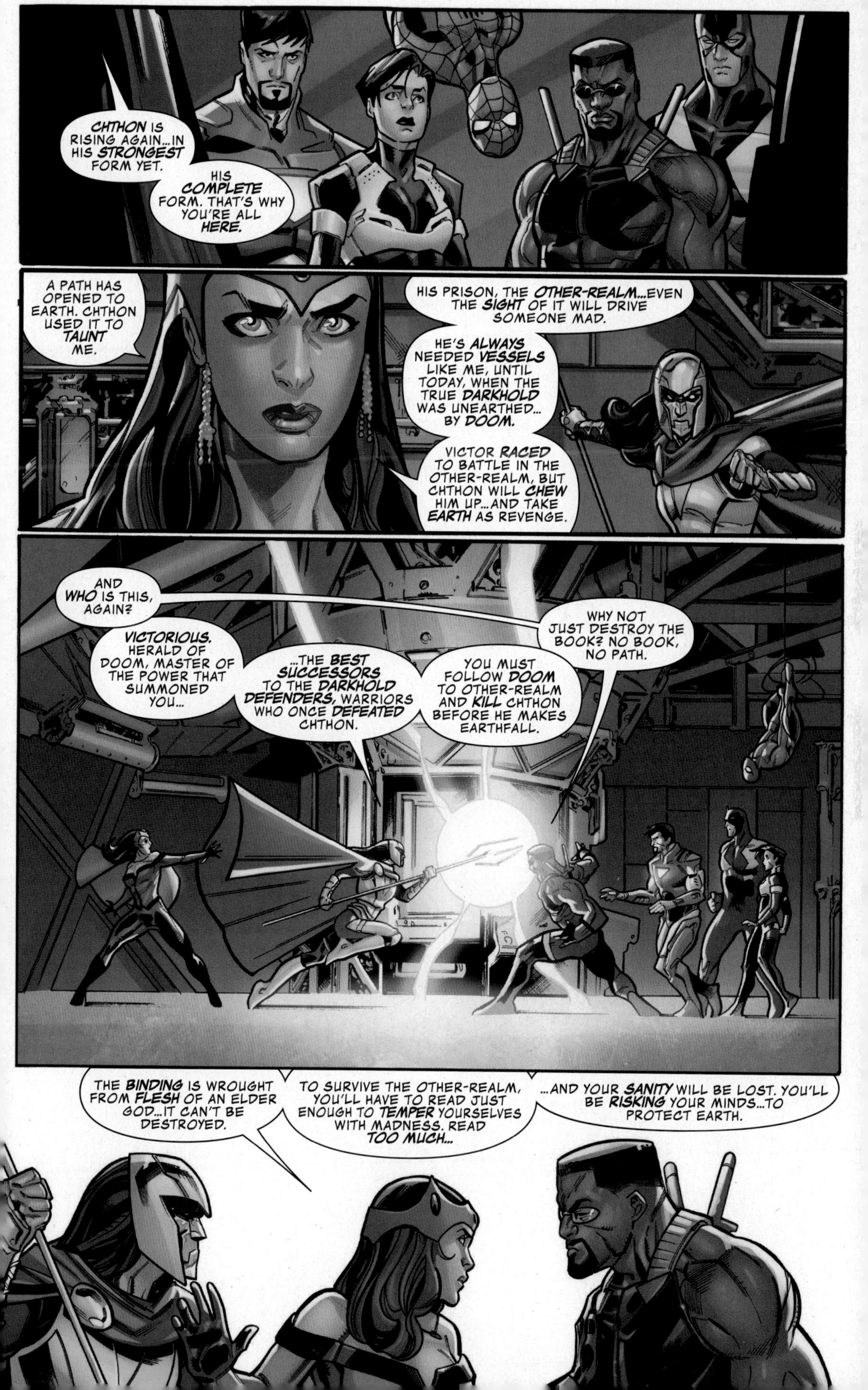
CHTHON IS RISING AGAIN...IN HIS STRONGEST FORM YET.
HIS COMPLETE FORM. THAT'S WHY YOU'RE ALL HERE.
A PATH HAS OPENED TO EARTH. CHTHON USED IT TO TAUNT ME.
HIS PRISON, THE OTHER-REALM...EVEN THE SIGHT OF IT WILL DRIVE SOMEONE MAD.
HE'S ALWAYS NEEDED VESSELS LIKE ME, UNTIL TODAY, WHEN THE TRUE DARKHOLD WAS UNEARTHED... BY DOOM.
VICTOR RACED TO BATTLE IN THE OTHER-REALM, BUT CHTHON WILL CHEW HIM UP...AND TAKE EARTH AS REVENGE.
AND WHO IS THIS, AGAIN?
VICTORIOUS. HERALD OF DOOM, MASTER OF THE POWER THAT SUMMONED YOU...
...THE BEST SUCCESSORS TO THE DARKHOLD DEFENDERS, WARRIORS WHO ONCE DEFEATED CHTHON.
WHY NOT JUST DESTROY THE BOOK? NO BOOK, NO PATH.
YOU MUST FOLLOW DOOM TO OTHER-REALM AND KILL CHTHON BEFORE HE MAKES EARTHFALL.
THE BINDING IS WROUGHT FROM FLESH OF AN ELDER GOD...IT CAN'T BE DESTROYED.
TO SURVIVE THE OTHER-REALM, YOU'LL HAVE TO READ JUST ENOUGH TO TEMPER YOURSELVES WITH MADNESS. READ TOO MUCH...
...AND YOUR SANITY WILL BE LOST. YOU'LL BE RISKING YOUR MINDS...TO PROTECT EARTH.

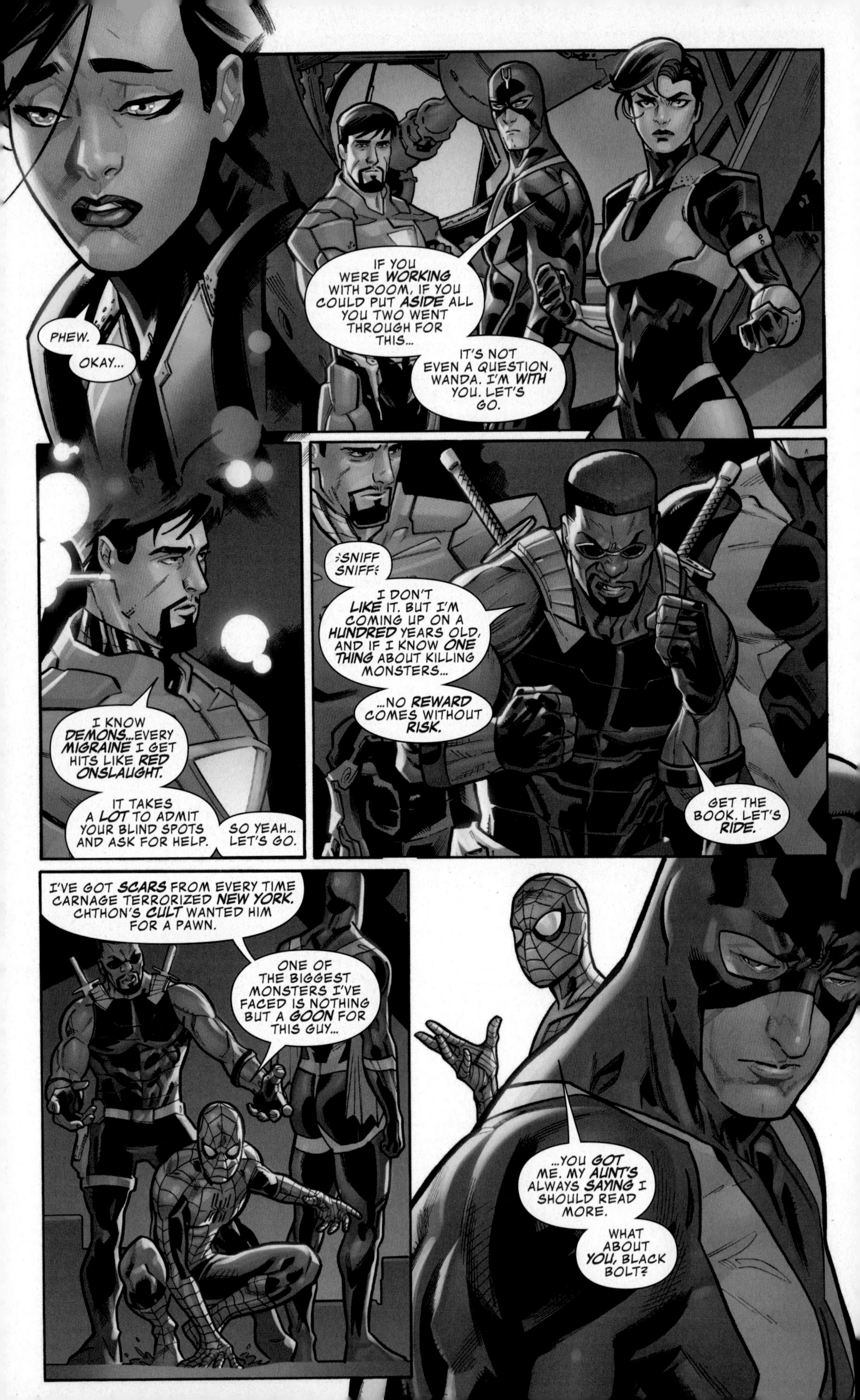
IF YOU WERE WORKING WITH DOOM, IF YOU COULD PUT ASIDE ALL YOU TWO WENT THROUGH FOR THIS...
PHEW.
OKAY...
IT'S NOT EVEN A QUESTION, WANDA. I'M WITH YOU. LET'S GO.
I KNOW DEMONS...EVERY MIGRAINE I GET HITS LIKE RED ONSLAUGHT.
IT TAKES A LOT TO ADMIT YOUR BLIND SPOTS AND ASK FOR HELP.
SO YEAH... LET'S GO.
SNIFF SNIFF
I DON'T LIKE IT. BUT I'M COMING UP ON A HUNDRED YEARS OLD, AND IF I KNOW ONE THING ABOUT KILLING MONSTERS...
...NO REWARD COMES WITHOUT RISK.
GET THE BOOK. LET'S RIDE.
I'VE GOT SCARS FROM EVERY TIME CARNAGE TERRORIZED NEW YORK. CHTHON'S CULT WANTED HIM FOR A PAWN.
ONE OF THE BIGGEST MONSTERS I'VE FACED IS NOTHING BUT A GOON FOR THIS GUY...
...YOU GOT ME. MY AUNT'S ALWAYS SAYING I SHOULD READ MORE.
WHAT ABOUT YOU, BLACK BOLT?

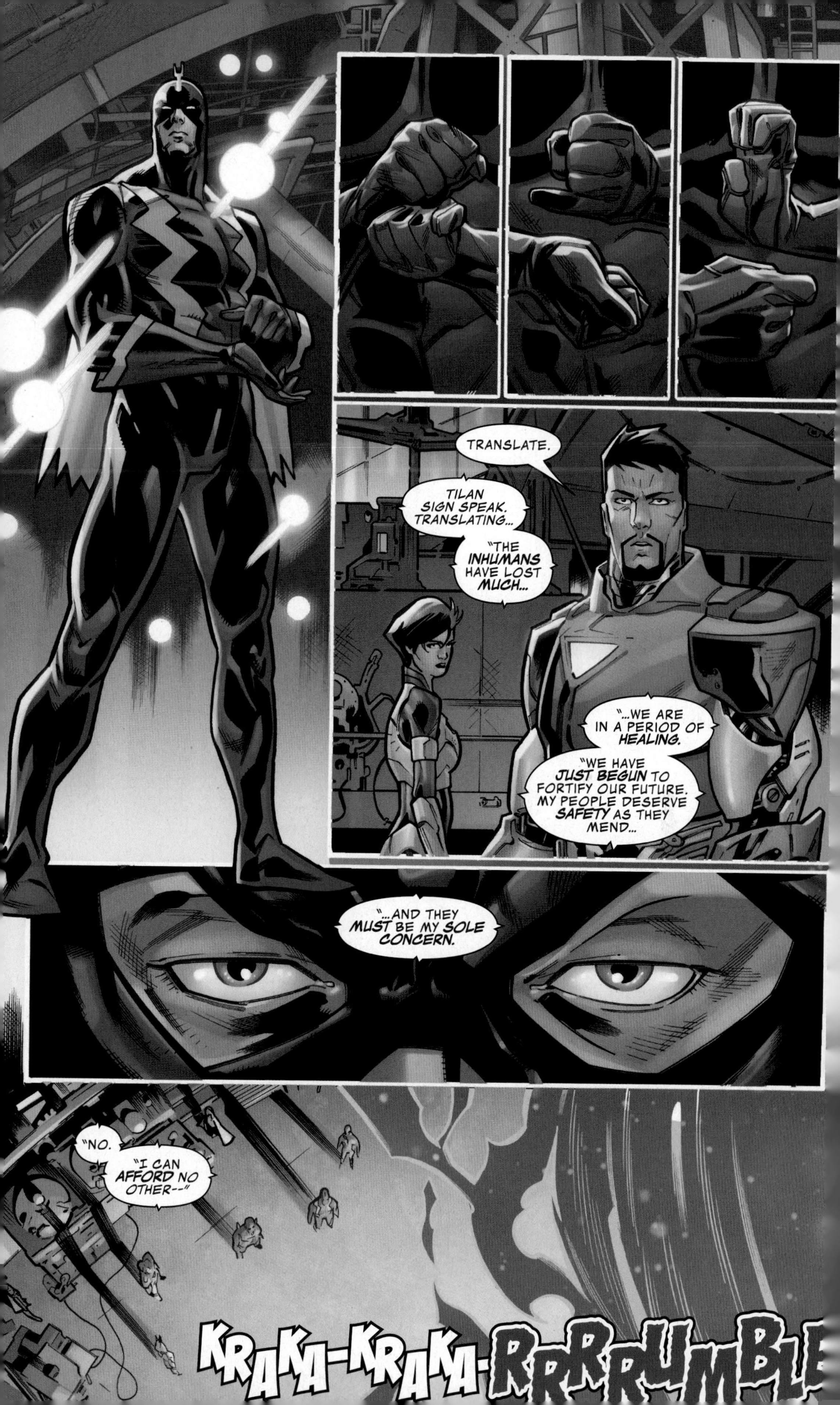
TRANSLATE.
TILAN SIGN SPEAK. TRANSLATING...
"THE INHUMANS HAVE LOST MUCH...
"...WE ARE IN A PERIOD OF HEALING.
"WE HAVE JUST BEGUN TO FORTIFY OUR FUTURE. MY PEOPLE DESERVE SAFETY AS THEY MEND...
"...AND THEY MUST BE MY SOLE CONCERN.
"NO.
"I CAN AFFORD NO OTHER--"
KRAKA-KRAKA-RRRRUMBLE

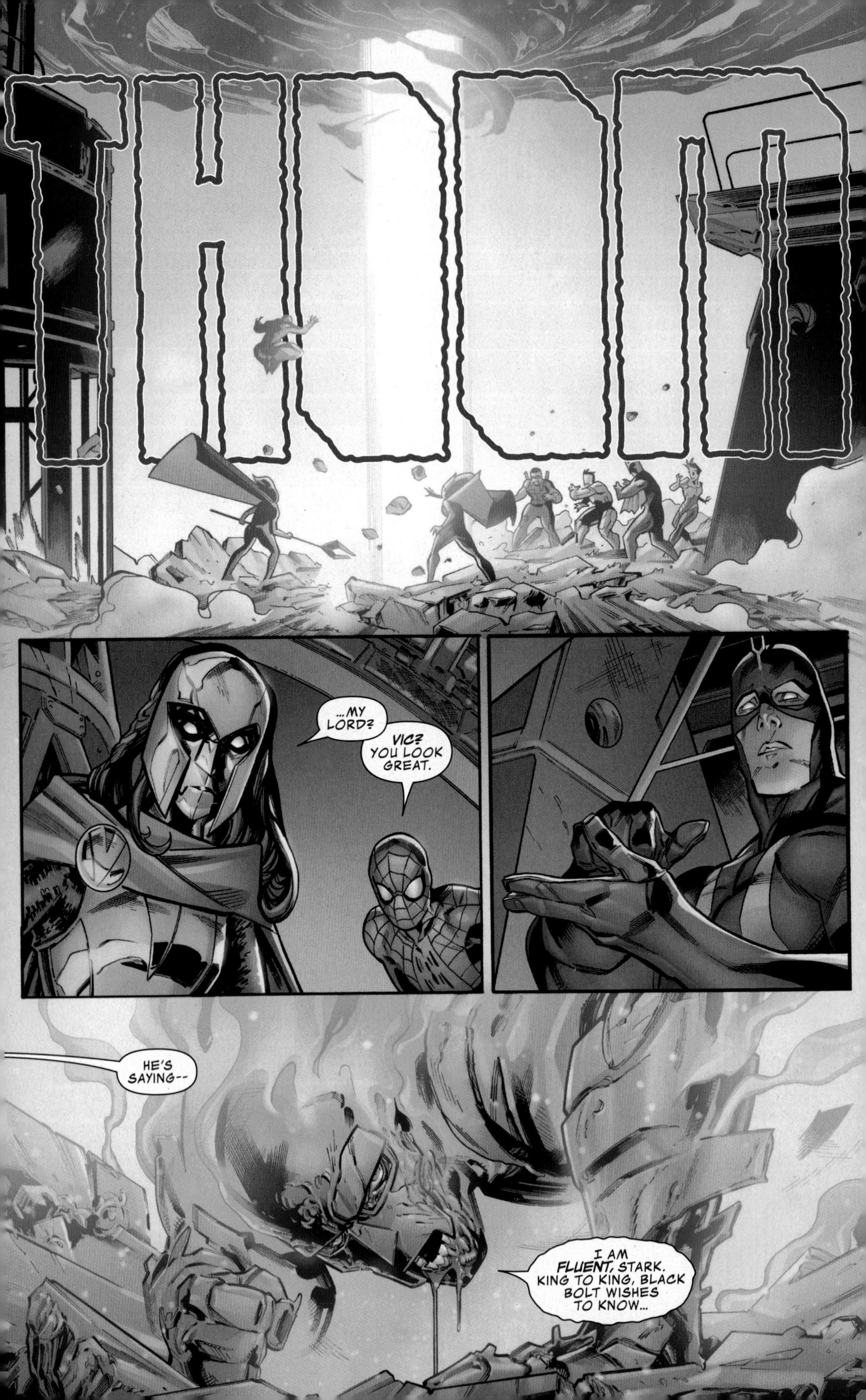
THOOM
...MY LORD?
VIC? YOU LOOK GREAT.
HE'S SAYING--
I AM FLUENT, STARK. KING TO KING, BLACK BOLT WISHES TO KNOW...

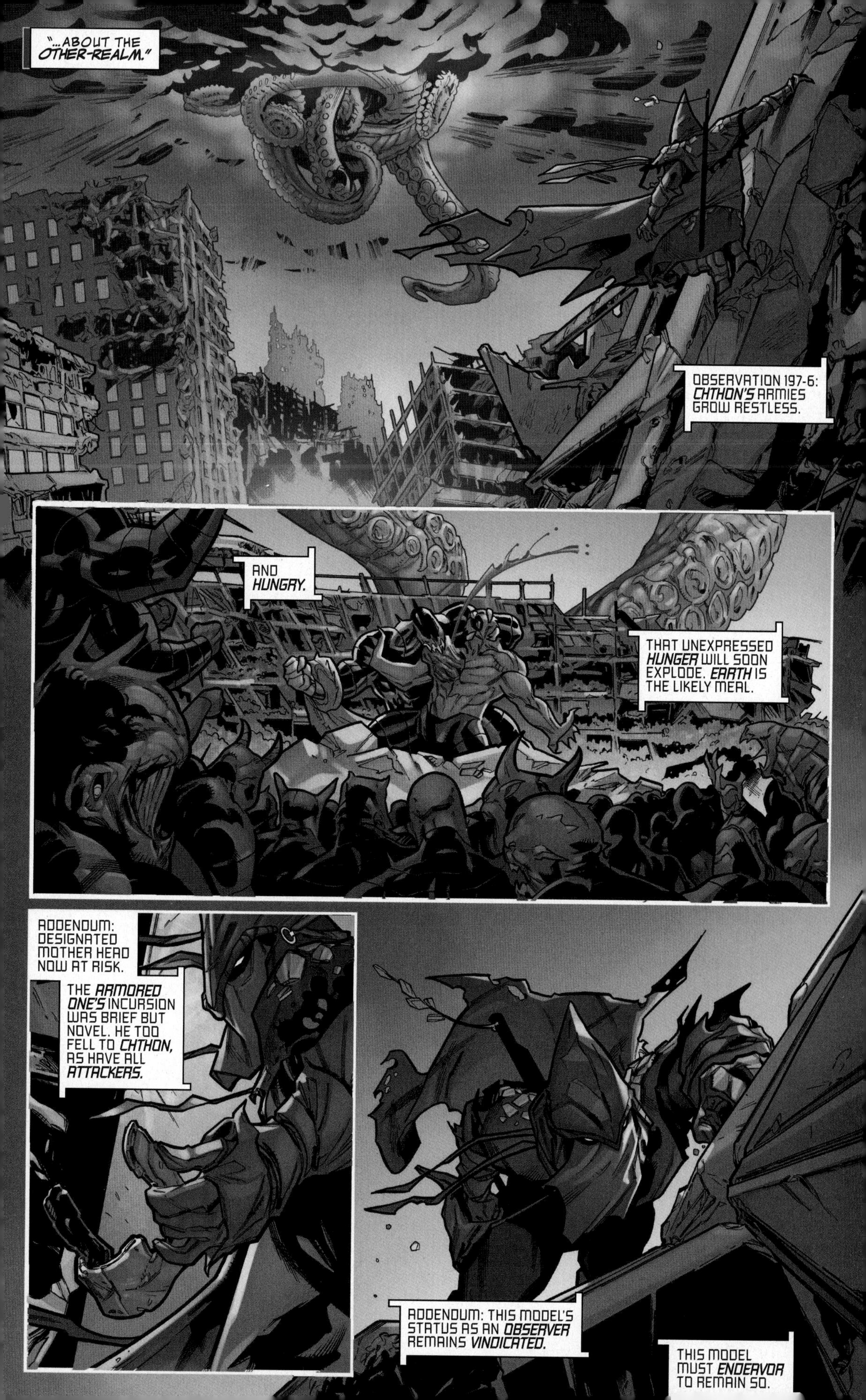
"...ABOUT THE OTHER-REALM."
OBSERVATION 197-6: CHTHON'S ARMIES GROW RESTLESS.
AND HUNGRY.
THAT UNEXPRESSED HUNGER WILL SOON EXPLODE. EARTH IS THE LIKELY MEAL.
ADDENDUM: DESIGNATED MOTHER HEAD NOW AT RISK.
THE ARMORED ONE'S INCURSION WAS BRIEF BUT NOVEL. HE TOO FELL TO CHTHON, AS HAVE ALL ATTACKERS.
ADDENDUM: THIS MODEL'S STATUS AS AN OBSERVER REMAINS VINDICATED.
THIS MODEL MUST ENDEAVOR TO REMAIN SO.

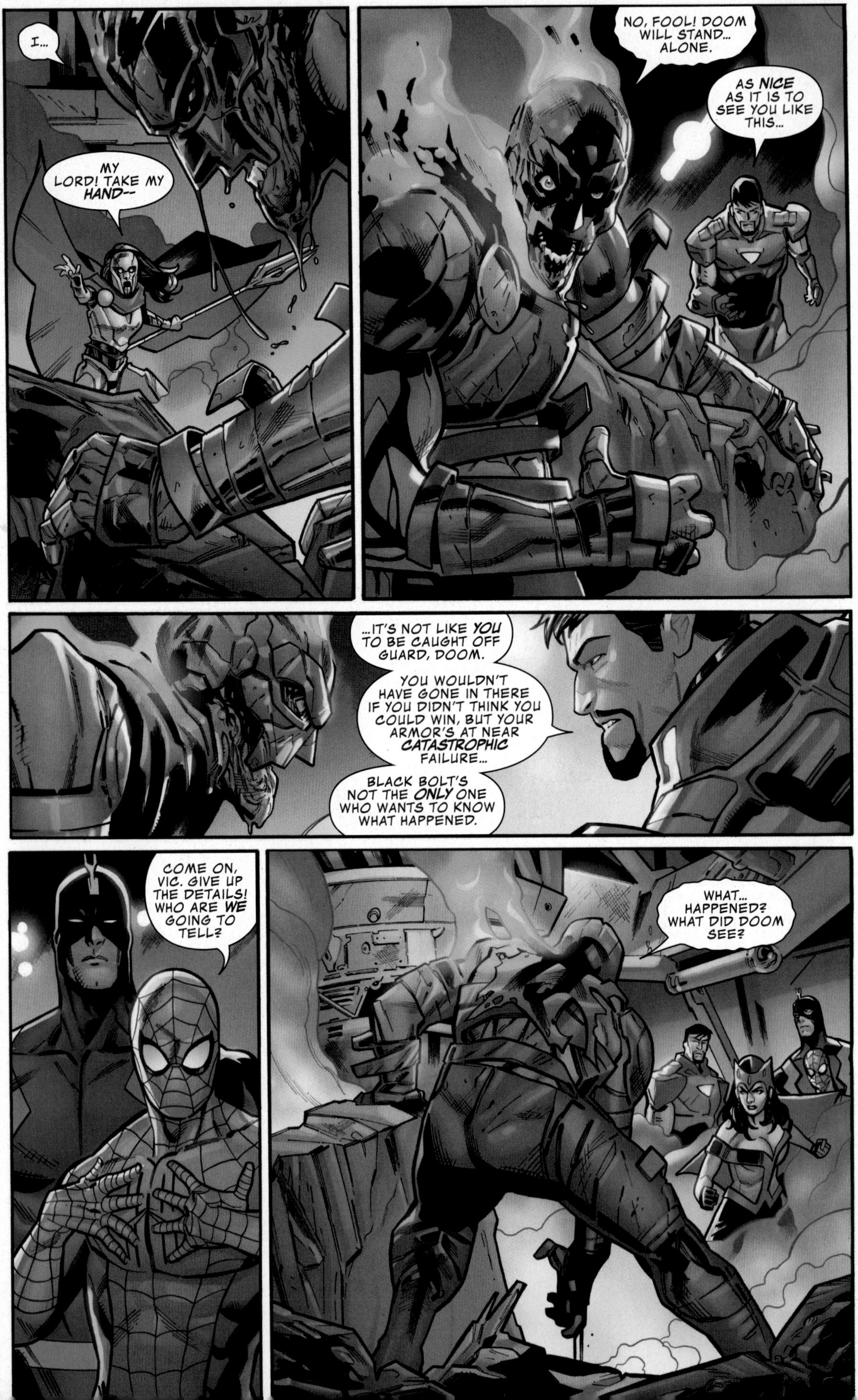
I...
MY LORD! TAKE MY HAND--
NO, FOOL! DOOM WILL STAND... ALONE.
AS NICE AS IT IS TO SEE YOU LIKE THIS...
...IT'S NOT LIKE YOU TO BE CAUGHT OFF GUARD, DOOM.
YOU WOULDN'T HAVE GONE IN THERE IF YOU DIDN'T THINK YOU COULD WIN, BUT YOUR ARMOR'S AT NEAR CATASTROPHIC FAILURE...
BLACK BOLT'S NOT THE ONLY ONE WHO WANTS TO KNOW WHAT HAPPENED.
COME ON, VIC. GIVE UP THE DETAILS! WHO ARE WE GOING TO TELL?
WHAT... HAPPENED? WHAT DID DOOM SEE?

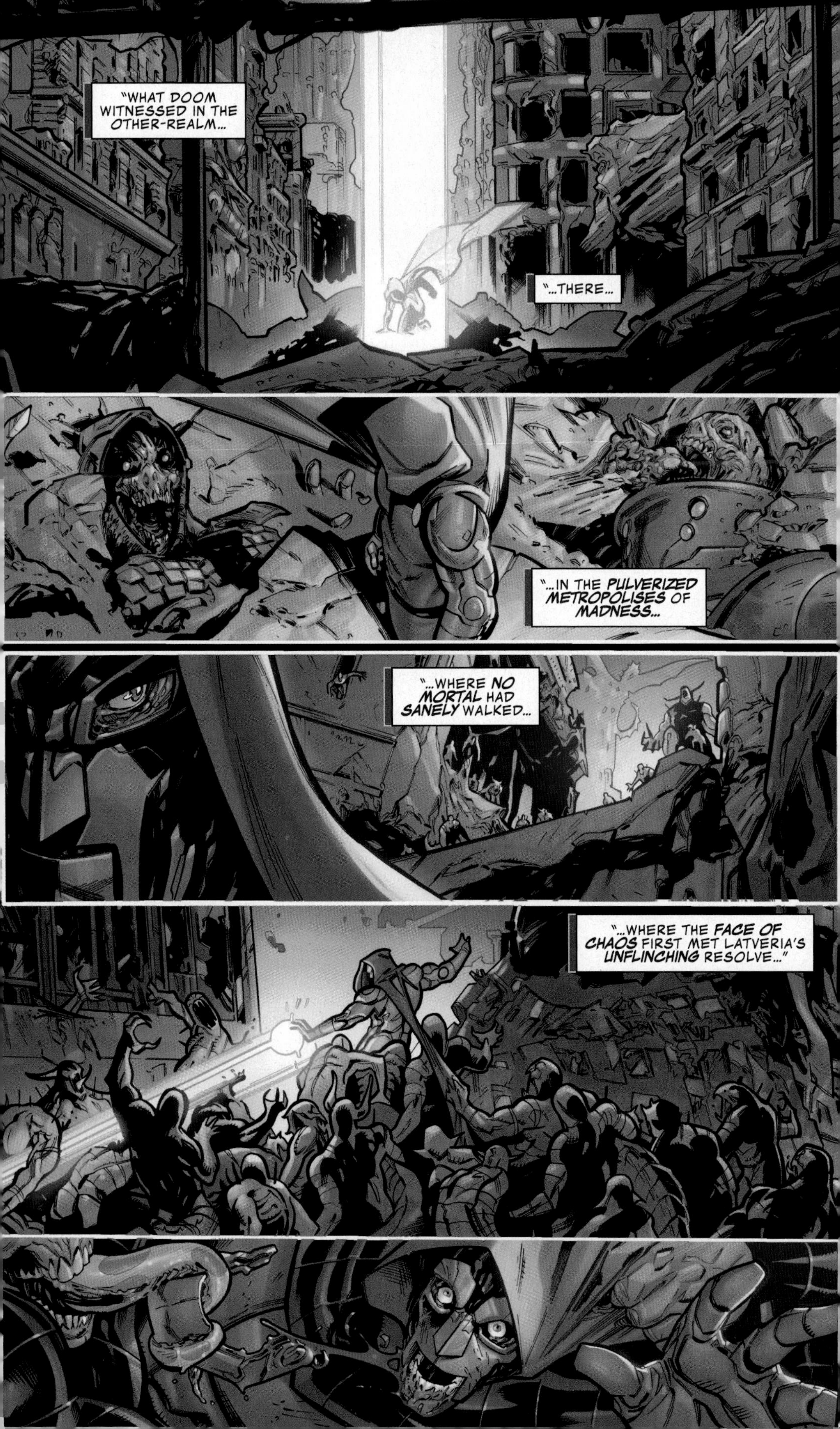
"WHAT DOOM WITNESSED IN THE OTHER-REALM...
"...THERE...
"...IN THE PULVERIZED METROPOLISES OF MADNESS...
"...WHERE NO MORTAL HAD SANELY WALKED...
"...WHERE THE FACE OF CHAOS FIRST MET LATVERIA'S UNFLINCHING RESOLVE..."

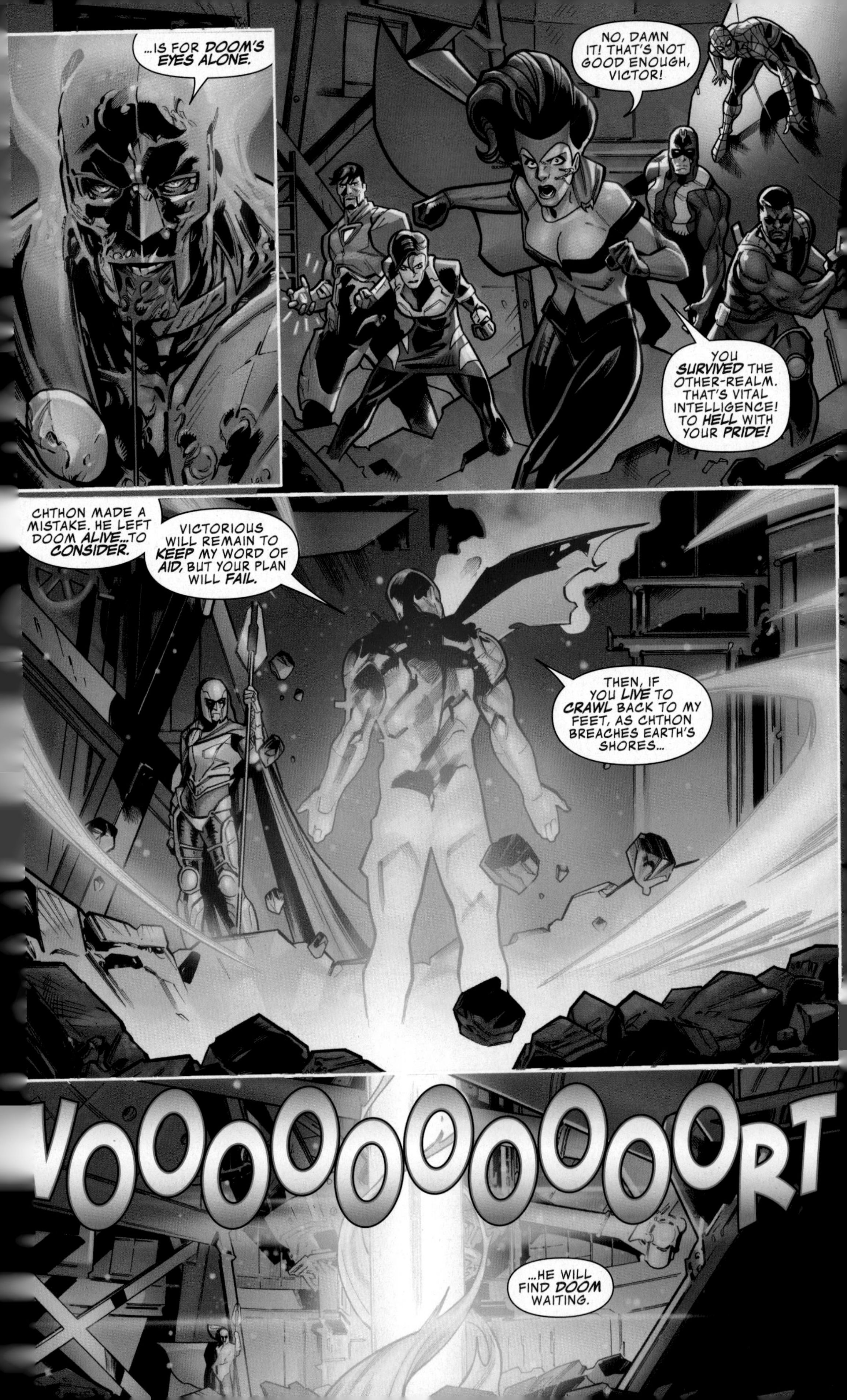
...IS FOR DOOM'S EYES ALONE.
NO, DAMN IT! THAT'S NOT GOOD ENOUGH, VICTOR!
YOU SURVIVED THE OTHER-REALM. THAT'S VITAL INTELLIGENCE! TO HELL WITH YOUR PRIDE!
CHTHON MADE A MISTAKE. HE LEFT DOOM ALIVE...TO CONSIDER.
VICTORIOUS WILL REMAIN TO KEEP MY WORD OF AID, BUT YOUR PLAN WILL FAIL.
THEN, IF YOU LIVE TO CRAWL BACK TO MY FEET, AS CHTHON BREACHES EARTH'S SHORES...
VOOOOOOOOOORT
...HE WILL FIND DOOM WAITING.

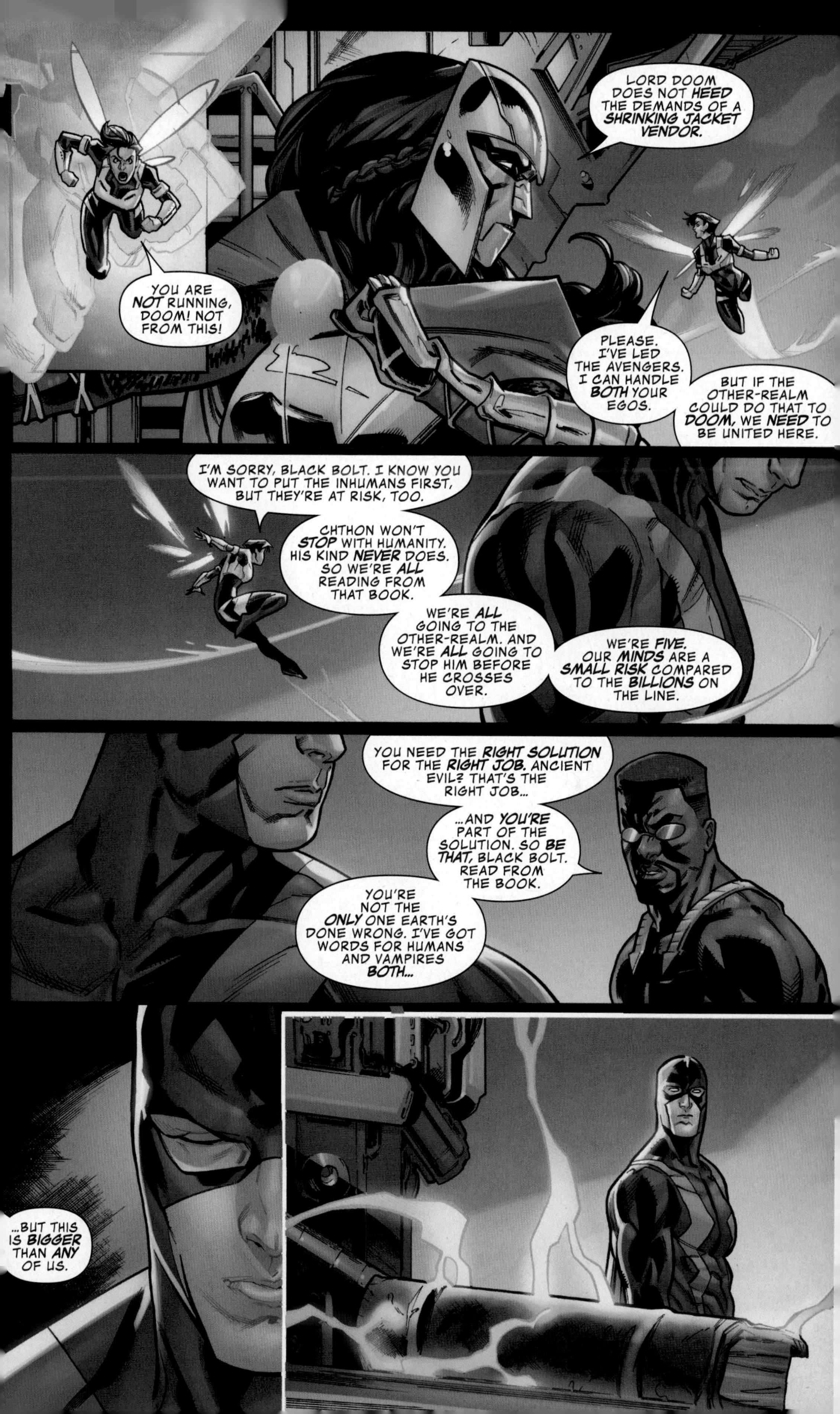
YOU ARE NOT RUNNING, DOOM! NOT FROM THIS!
LORD DOOM DOES NOT HEED THE DEMANDS OF A SHRINKING JACKET VENDOR.
PLEASE. I'VE LED THE AVENGERS. I CAN HANDLE BOTH YOUR EGOS.
BUT IF THE OTHER-REALM COULD DO THAT TO DOOM, WE NEED TO BE UNITED HERE.
I'M SORRY, BLACK BOLT. I KNOW YOU WANT TO PUT THE INHUMANS FIRST, BUT THEY'RE AT RISK, TOO.
CHTHON WON'T STOP WITH HUMANITY. HIS KIND NEVER DOES. SO WE'RE ALL READING FROM THAT BOOK.
WE'RE ALL GOING TO THE OTHER-REALM. AND WE'RE ALL GOING TO STOP HIM BEFORE HE CROSSES OVER.
WE'RE FIVE. OUR MINDS ARE A SMALL RISK COMPARED TO THE BILLIONS ON THE LINE.
YOU NEED THE RIGHT SOLUTION FOR THE RIGHT JOB. ANCIENT EVIL? THAT'S THE RIGHT JOB...
...AND YOU'RE PART OF THE SOLUTION. SO BE THAT, BLACK BOLT. READ FROM THE BOOK.
YOU'RE NOT THE ONLY ONE EARTH'S DONE WRONG. I'VE GOT WORDS FOR HUMANS AND VAMPIRES BOTH...
...BUT THIS IS BIGGER THAN ANY OF US.

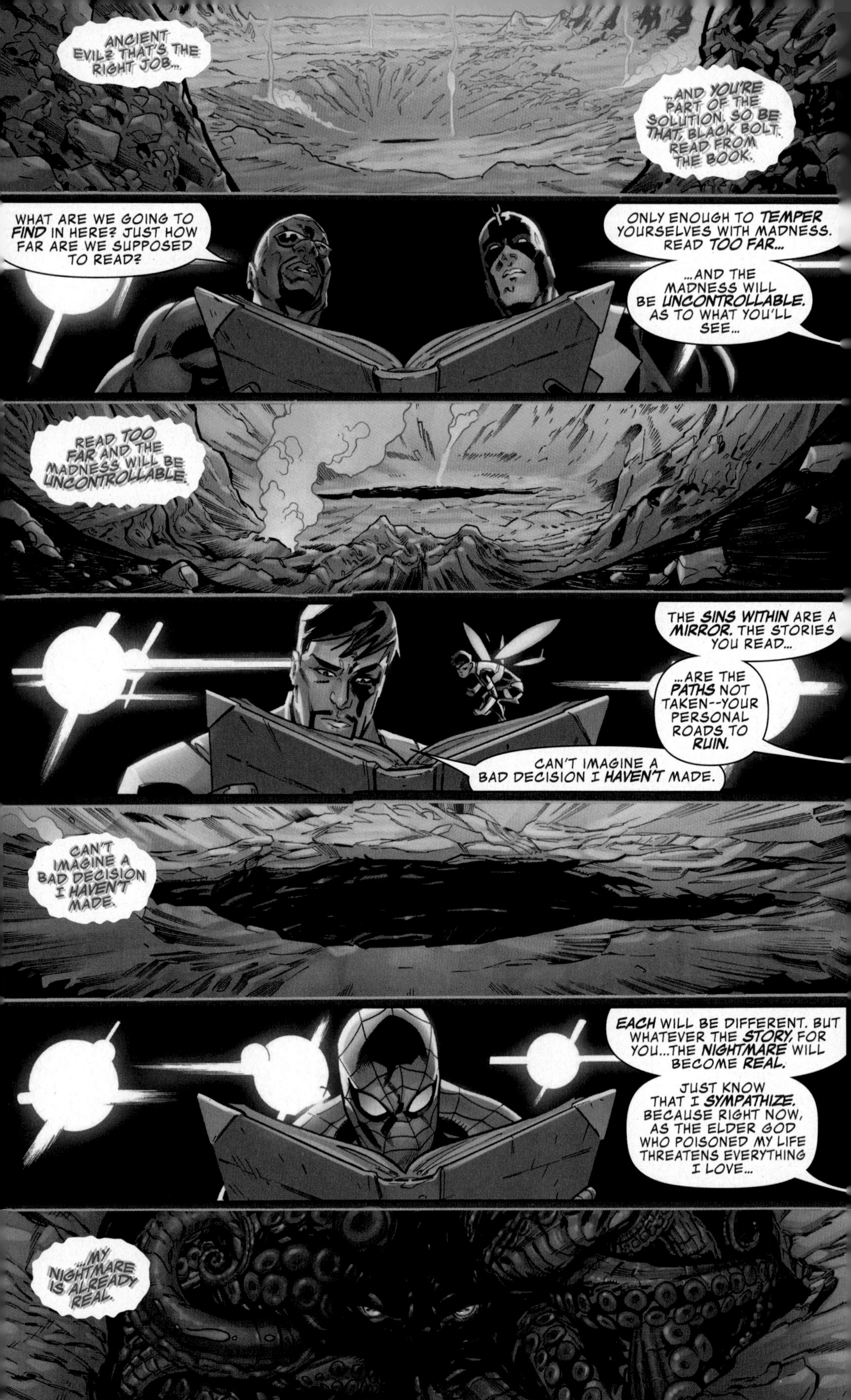

ANCIENT EVIL? THAT'S THE RIGHT JOB...
...AND YOU'RE PART OF THE SOLUTION. SO BE THAT, BLACK BOLT. READ FROM THE BOOK.
WHAT ARE WE GOING TO FIND IN HERE? JUST HOW FAR ARE WE SUPPOSED TO READ?
ONLY ENOUGH TO TEMPER YOURSELVES WITH MADNESS. READ TOO FAR...
...AND THE MADNESS WILL BE UNCONTROLLABLE. AS TO WHAT YOU'LL SEE...
READ TOO FAR AND THE MADNESS WILL BE UNCONTROLLABLE.
THE SINS WITHIN ARE A MIRROR. THE STORIES YOU READ...
...ARE THE PATHS NOT TAKEN--YOUR PERSONAL ROADS TO RUIN.
CAN'T IMAGINE A BAD DECISION I HAVEN'T MADE.
CAN'T IMAGINE A BAD DECISION I HAVEN'T MADE.
EACH WILL BE DIFFERENT. BUT WHATEVER THE STORY, FOR YOU...THE NIGHTMARE WILL BECOME REAL.
JUST KNOW THAT I SYMPATHIZE. BECAUSE RIGHT NOW, AS THE ELDER GOD WHO POISONED MY LIFE THREATENS EVERYTHING I LOVE...
...MY NIGHTMARE IS ALREADY REAL.

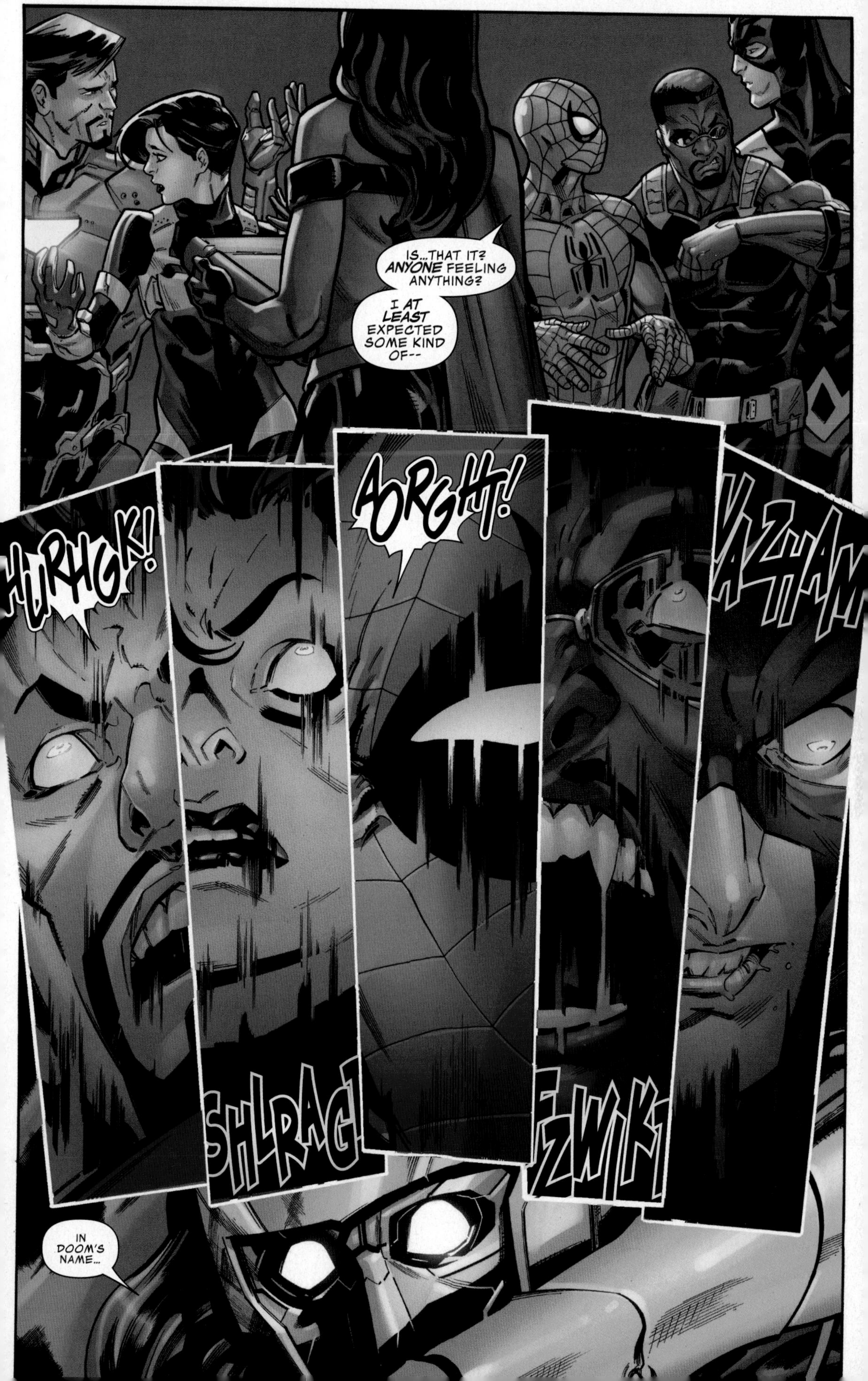

IS...THAT IT? *ANYONE* FEELING ANYTHING?
I AT *LEAST* EXPECTED SOME KIND OF--
HURHGK!
SHLRAG
AORGHT!
ZWIK
AZHAM
IN DOOM'S NAME...

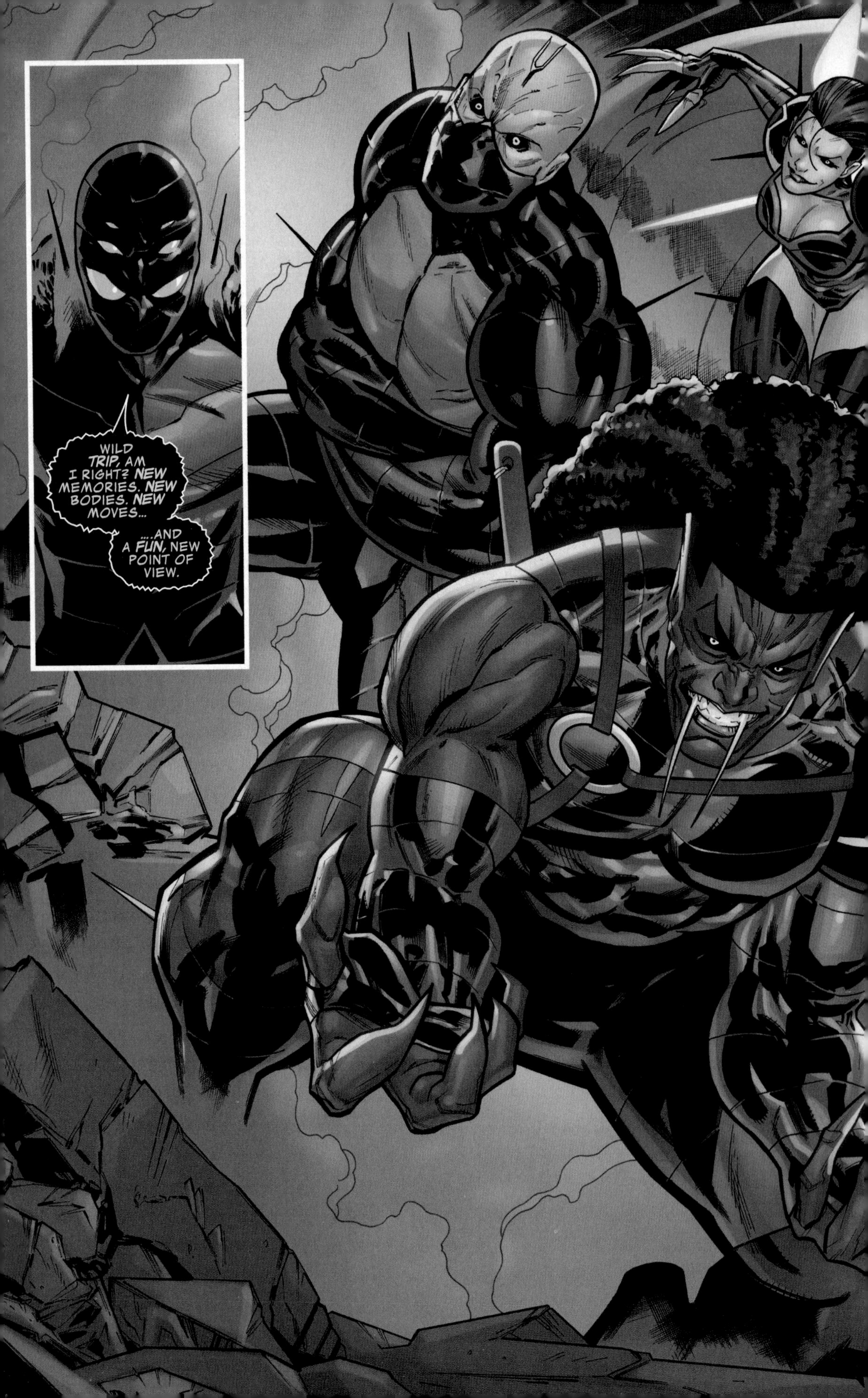
WILD TRIP, AM I RIGHT? NEW MEMORIES. NEW BODIES. NEW MOVES...
...AND A FUN, NEW POINT OF VIEW.

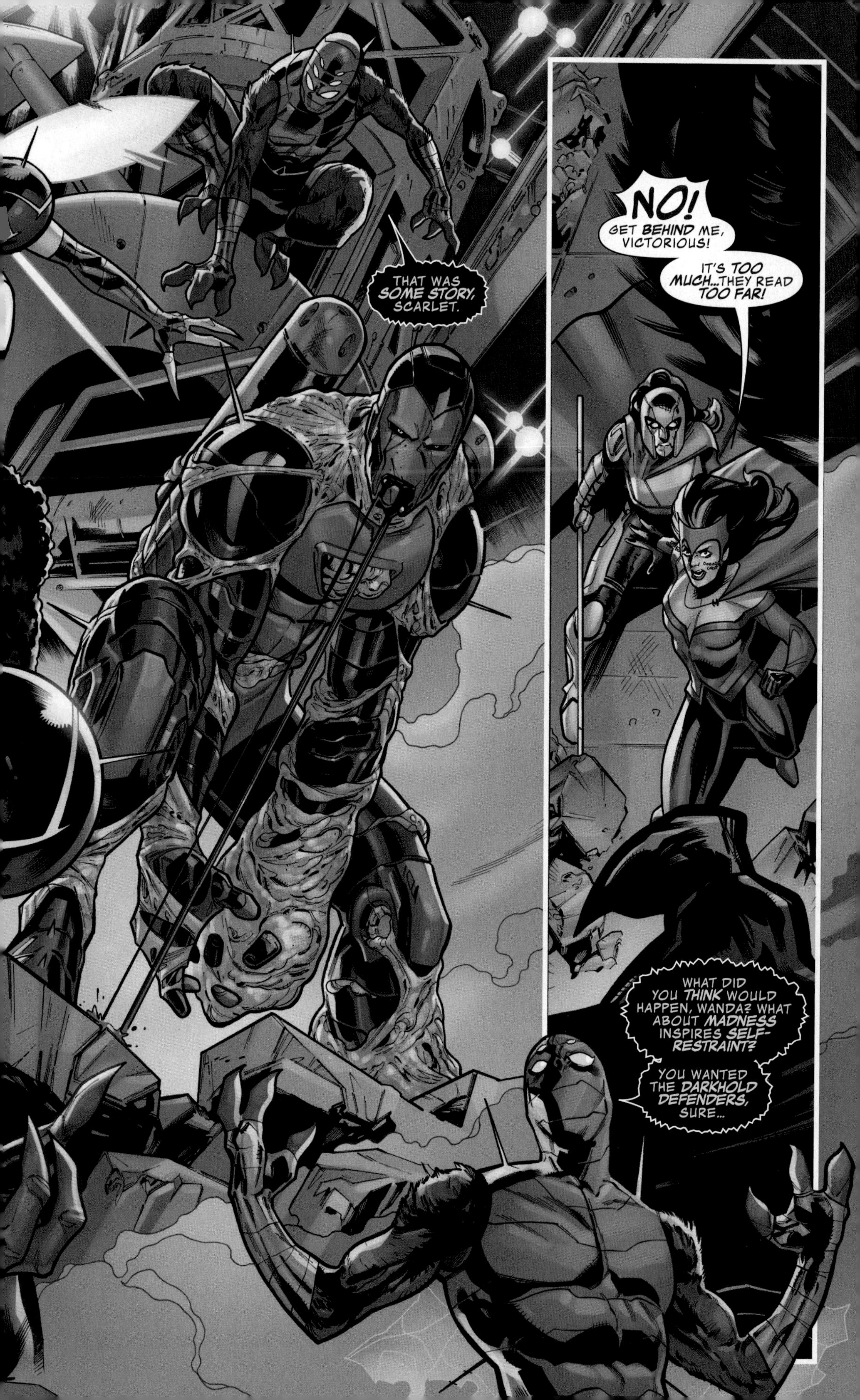
THAT WAS SOME STORY, SCARLET.
NO! GET BEHIND ME, VICTORIOUS!
IT'S TOO MUCH...THEY READ TOO FAR!
WHAT DID YOU THINK WOULD HAPPEN, WANDA? WHAT ABOUT MADNESS INSPIRES SELF-RESTRAINT?
YOU WANTED THE DARKHOLD DEFENDERS, SURE...

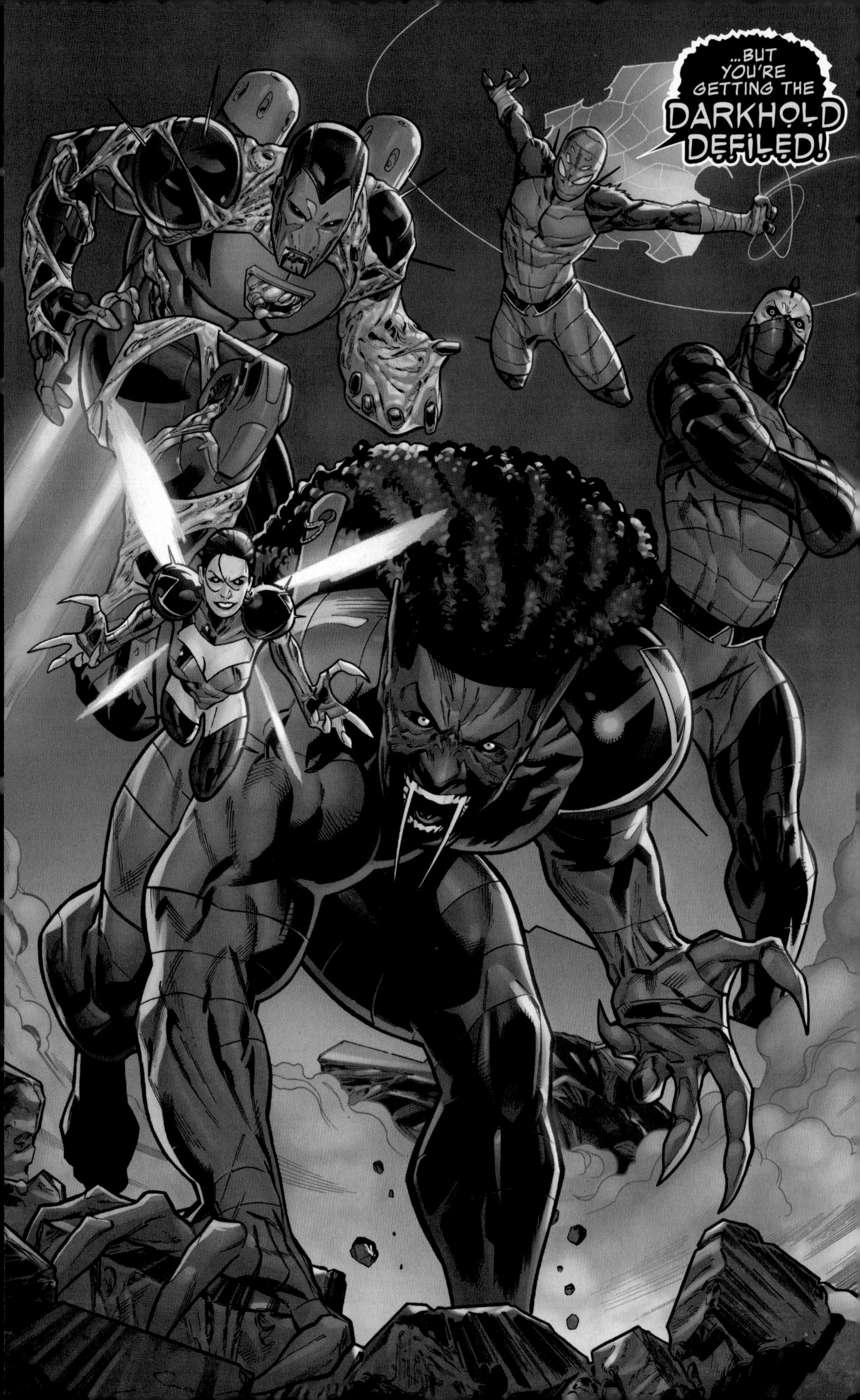
...BUT YOU'RE GETTING THE DARKHOLD DEFILED!

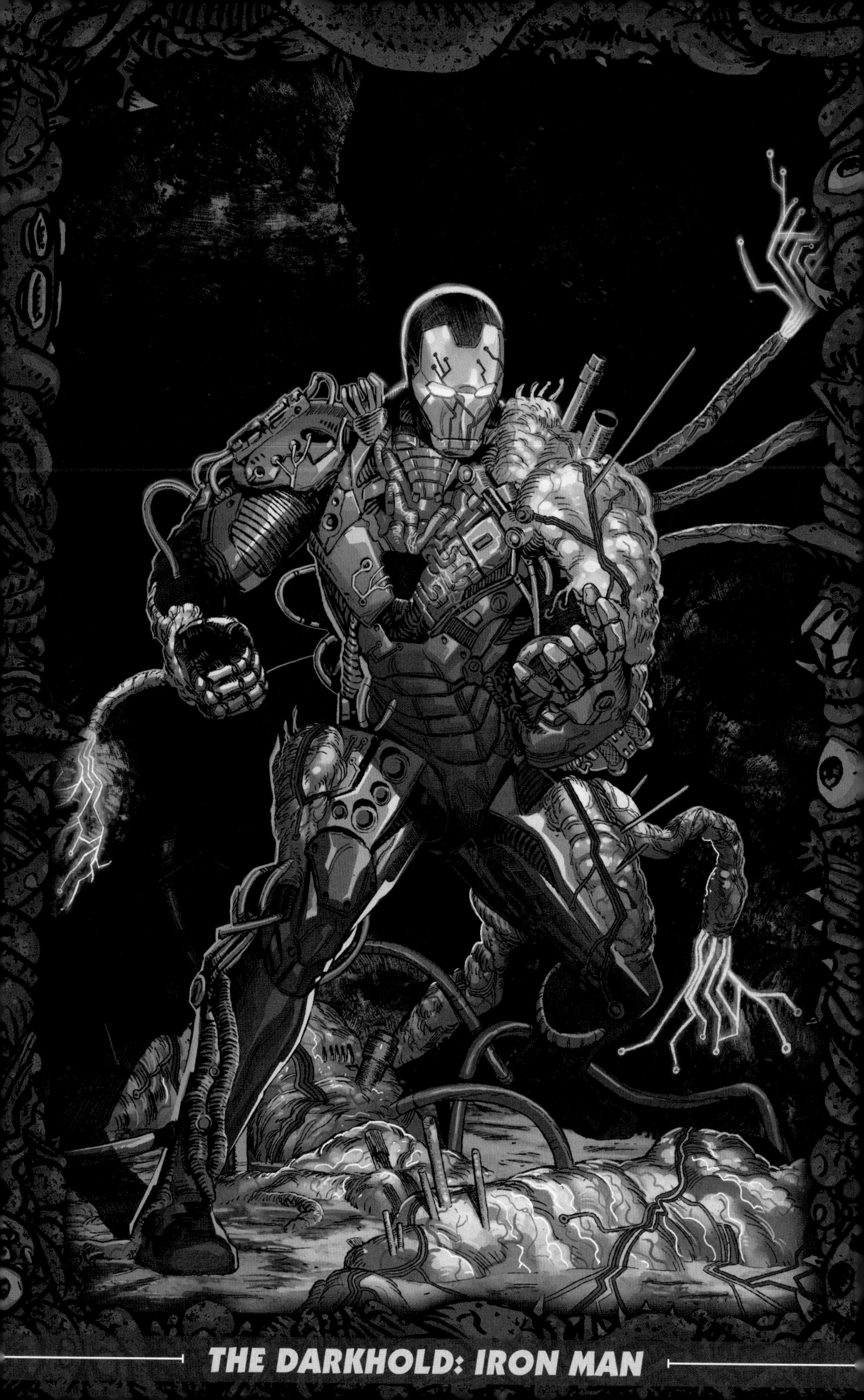

THE DARKHOLD: IRON MAN

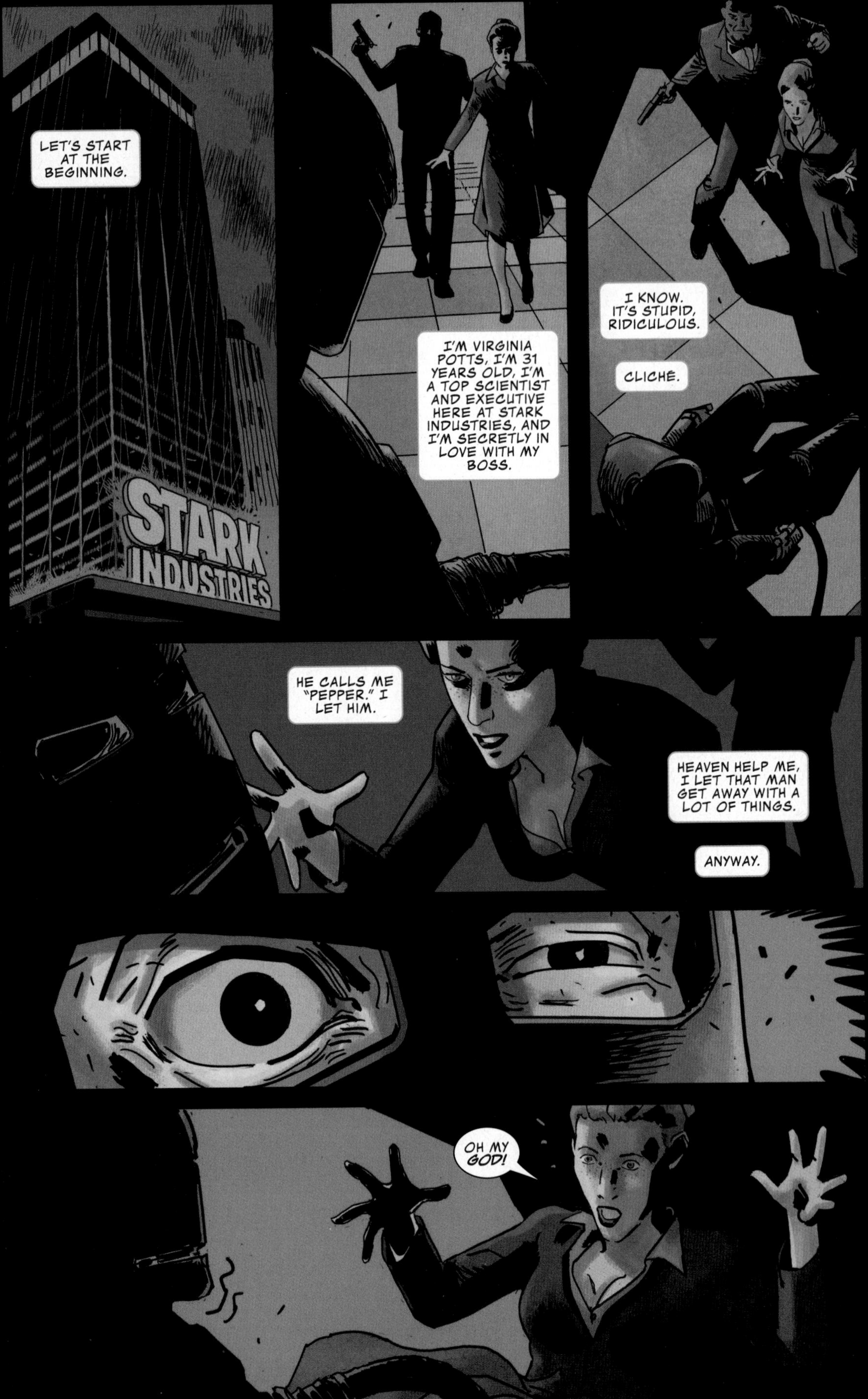

LET'S START AT THE BEGINNING.
STARK INDUSTRIES
I'M VIRGINIA POTTS, I'M 31 YEARS OLD, I'M A TOP SCIENTIST AND EXECUTIVE HERE AT STARK INDUSTRIES, AND I'M SECRETLY IN LOVE WITH MY BOSS.
I KNOW. IT'S STUPID, RIDICULOUS.
CLICHE.
HE CALLS ME "PEPPER." I LET HIM.
HEAVEN HELP ME, I LET THAT MAN GET AWAY WITH A LOT OF THINGS.
ANYWAY.
OH MY GOD!

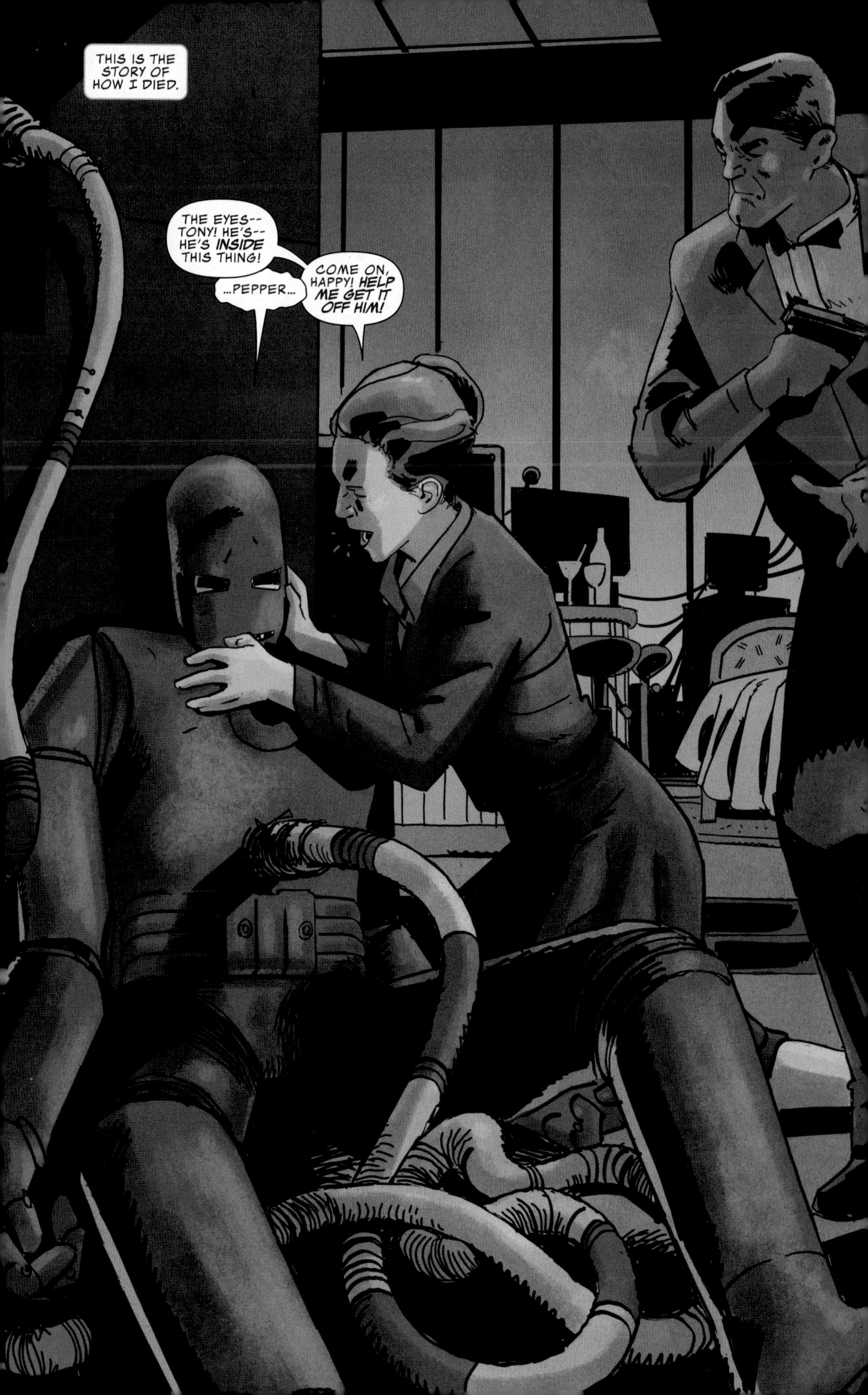
THIS IS THE STORY OF HOW I DIED.
THE EYES-- TONY! HE'S-- HE'S INSIDE THIS THING!
...PEPPER...
COME ON, HAPPY! HELP ME GET IT OFF HIM!

CHAPTER ONE

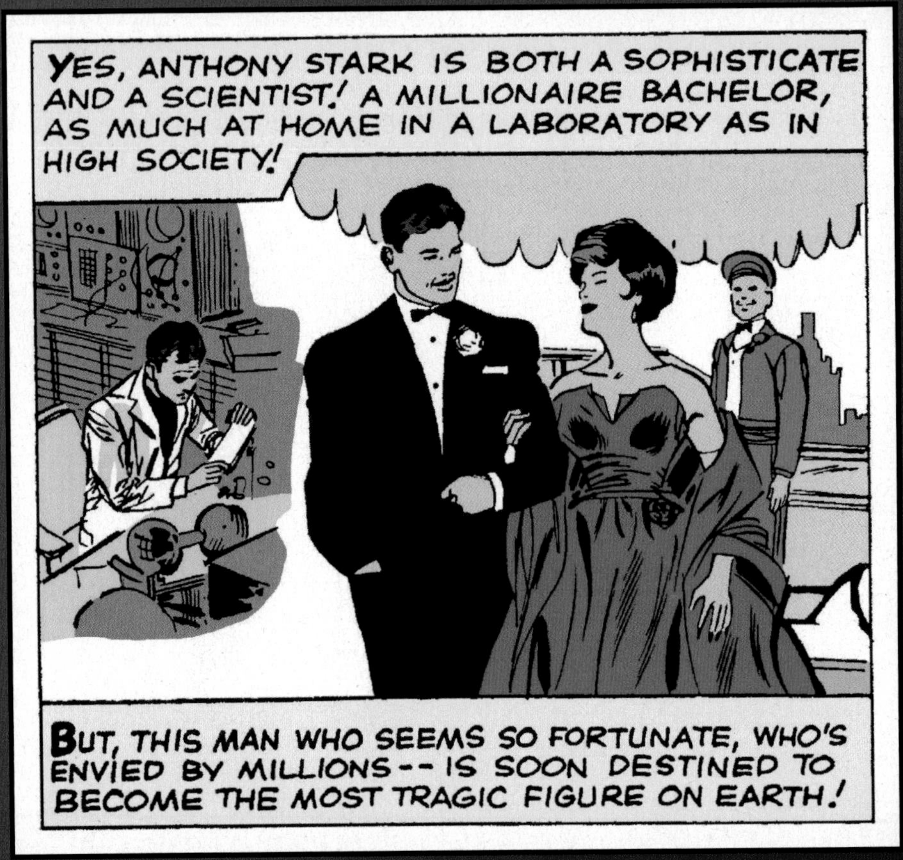
YES, ANTHONY STARK IS BOTH A SOPHISTICATE AND A SCIENTIST! A MILLIONAIRE BACHELOR, AS MUCH AT HOME IN A LABORATORY AS IN HIGH SOCIETY!
BUT, THIS MAN WHO SEEMS SO FORTUNATE, WHO'S ENVIED BY MILLIONS -- IS SOON DESTINED TO BECOME THE MOST TRAGIC FIGURE ON EARTH!

THE MOST TRAGIC FIGURE ON EARTH

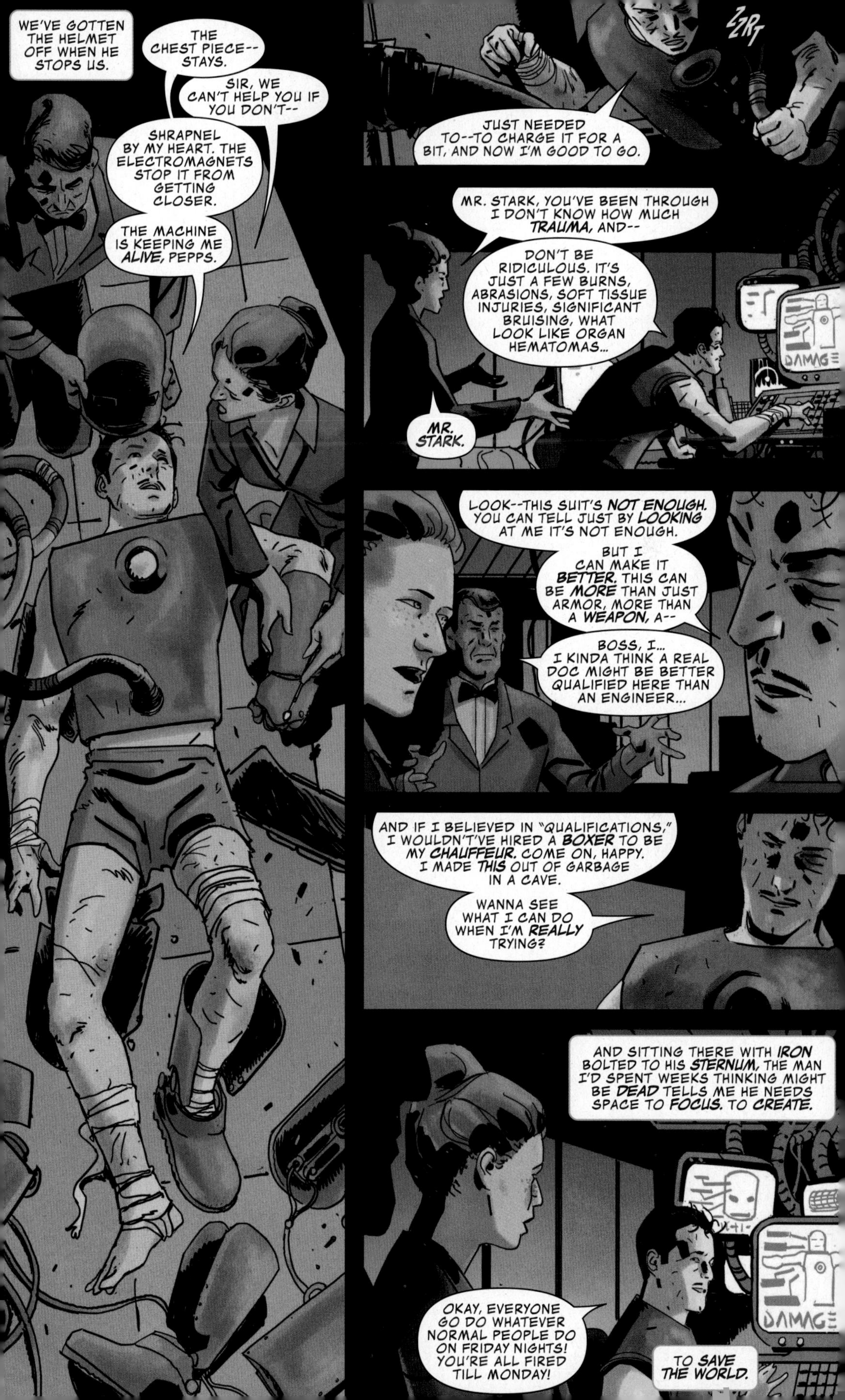
WE'VE GOTTEN THE HELMET OFF WHEN HE STOPS US.
THE CHEST PIECE--STAYS.
SIR, WE CAN'T HELP YOU IF YOU DON'T--
SHRAPNEL BY MY HEART. THE ELECTROMAGNETS STOP IT FROM GETTING CLOSER.
THE MACHINE IS KEEPING ME ALIVE, PEPPS.
ZZRT
JUST NEEDED TO--TO CHARGE IT FOR A BIT, AND NOW I'M GOOD TO GO.
MR. STARK, YOU'VE BEEN THROUGH I DON'T KNOW HOW MUCH TRAUMA, AND--
DON'T BE RIDICULOUS. IT'S JUST A FEW BURNS, ABRASIONS, SOFT TISSUE INJURIES, SIGNIFICANT BRUISING, WHAT LOOK LIKE ORGAN HEMATOMAS...
DAMAGE
MR. STARK.
LOOK--THIS SUIT'S NOT ENOUGH. YOU CAN TELL JUST BY LOOKING AT ME IT'S NOT ENOUGH.
BUT I CAN MAKE IT BETTER. THIS CAN BE MORE THAN JUST ARMOR, MORE THAN A WEAPON, A--
BOSS, I... I KINDA THINK A REAL DOC MIGHT BE BETTER QUALIFIED HERE THAN AN ENGINEER...
AND IF I BELIEVED IN "QUALIFICATIONS," I WOULDN'T'VE HIRED A BOXER TO BE MY CHAUFFEUR. COME ON, HAPPY. I MADE THIS OUT OF GARBAGE IN A CAVE.
WANNA SEE WHAT I CAN DO WHEN I'M REALLY TRYING?
AND SITTING THERE WITH IRON BOLTED TO HIS STERNUM, THE MAN I'D SPENT WEEKS THINKING MIGHT BE DEAD TELLS ME HE NEEDS SPACE TO FOCUS. TO CREATE.
OKAY, EVERYONE GO DO WHATEVER NORMAL PEOPLE DO ON FRIDAY NIGHTS! YOU'RE ALL FIRED TILL MONDAY!
DAMAGE
TO SAVE THE WORLD.

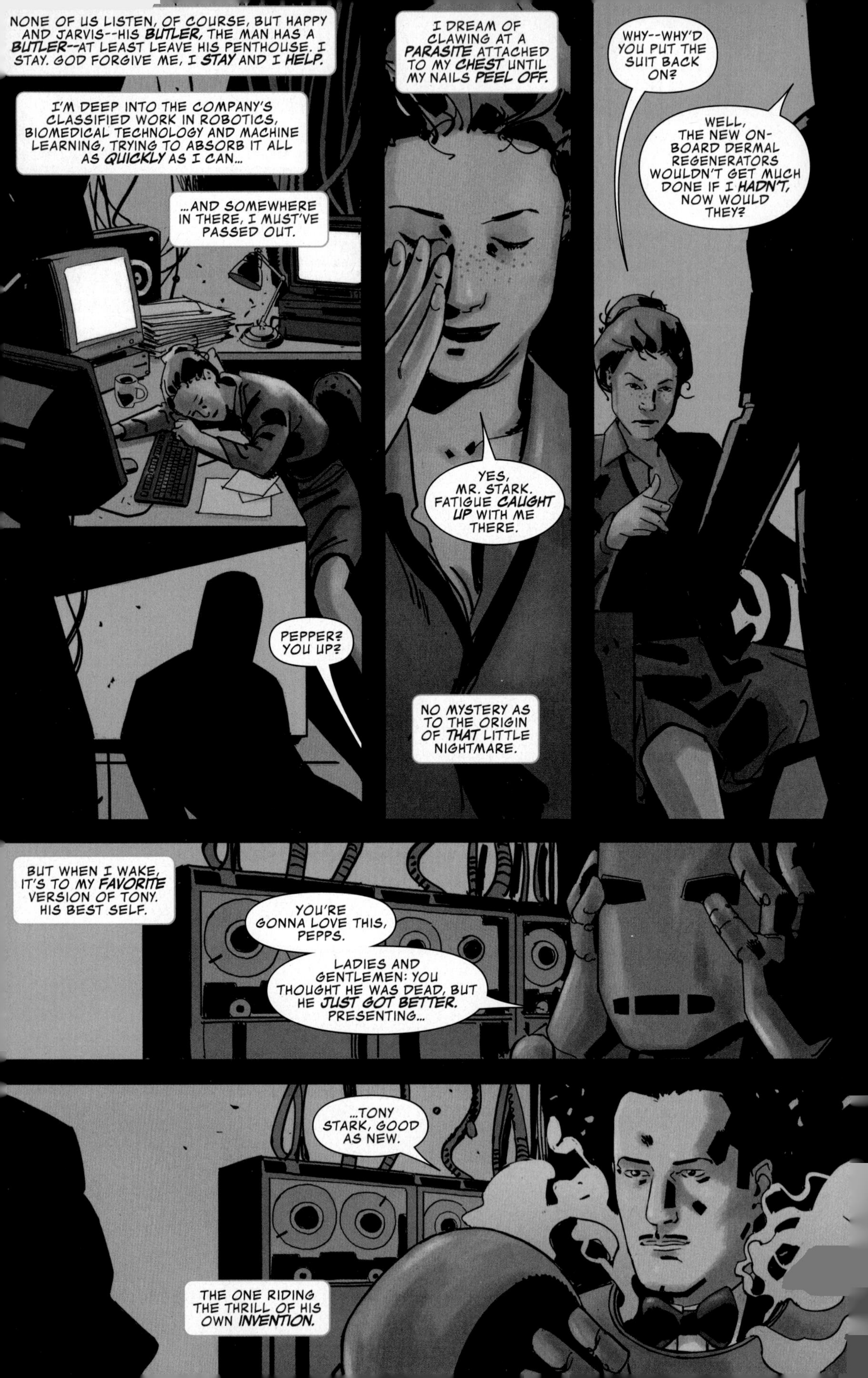
NONE OF US LISTEN, OF COURSE, BUT HAPPY AND JARVIS--HIS BUTLER, THE MAN HAS A BUTLER--AT LEAST LEAVE HIS PENTHOUSE. I STAY. GOD FORGIVE ME, I STAY AND I HELP.
I'M DEEP INTO THE COMPANY'S CLASSIFIED WORK IN ROBOTICS, BIOMEDICAL TECHNOLOGY AND MACHINE LEARNING, TRYING TO ABSORB IT ALL AS QUICKLY AS I CAN...
...AND SOMEWHERE IN THERE, I MUST'VE PASSED OUT.
PEPPER? YOU UP?
I DREAM OF CLAWING AT A PARASITE ATTACHED TO MY CHEST UNTIL MY NAILS PEEL OFF.
YES, MR. STARK. FATIGUE CAUGHT UP WITH ME THERE.
NO MYSTERY AS TO THE ORIGIN OF THAT LITTLE NIGHTMARE.
WHY--WHY'D YOU PUT THE SUIT BACK ON?
WELL, THE NEW ON-BOARD DERMAL REGENERATORS WOULDN'T GET MUCH DONE IF I HADN'T, NOW WOULD THEY?
BUT WHEN I WAKE, IT'S TO MY FAVORITE VERSION OF TONY. HIS BEST SELF.
YOU'RE GONNA LOVE THIS, PEPPS.
LADIES AND GENTLEMEN: YOU THOUGHT HE WAS DEAD, BUT HE JUST GOT BETTER. PRESENTING...
...TONY STARK, GOOD AS NEW.
THE ONE RIDING THE THRILL OF HIS OWN INVENTION.

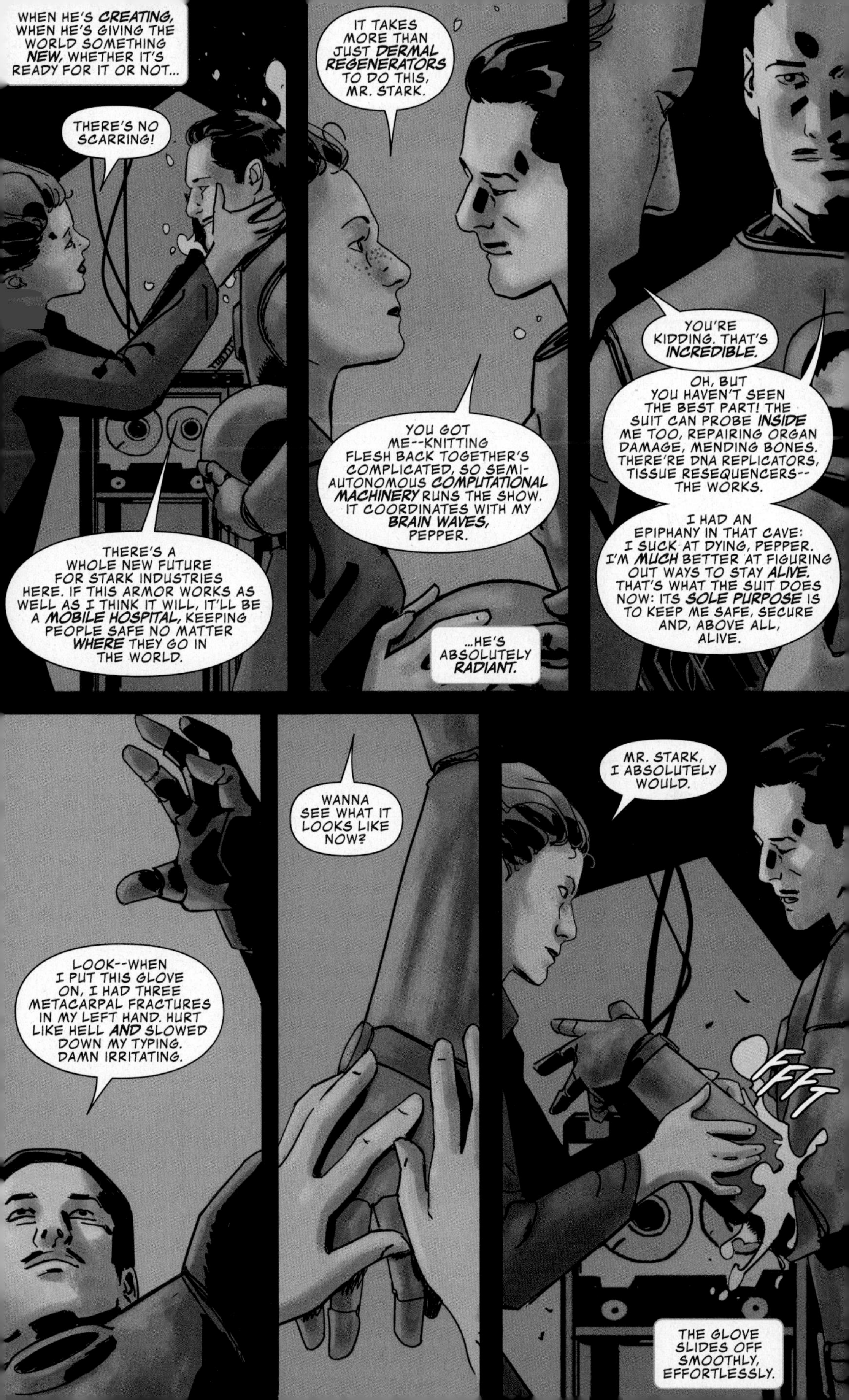
WHEN HE'S CREATING, WHEN HE'S GIVING THE WORLD SOMETHING NEW, WHETHER IT'S READY FOR IT OR NOT...
THERE'S NO SCARRING!
THERE'S A WHOLE NEW FUTURE FOR STARK INDUSTRIES HERE. IF THIS ARMOR WORKS AS WELL AS I THINK IT WILL, IT'LL BE A MOBILE HOSPITAL, KEEPING PEOPLE SAFE NO MATTER WHERE THEY GO IN THE WORLD.
IT TAKES MORE THAN JUST DERMAL REGENERATORS TO DO THIS, MR. STARK.
YOU GOT ME--KNITTING FLESH BACK TOGETHER'S COMPLICATED, SO SEMI-AUTONOMOUS COMPUTATIONAL MACHINERY RUNS THE SHOW. IT COORDINATES WITH MY BRAIN WAVES, PEPPER.
...HE'S ABSOLUTELY RADIANT.
YOU'RE KIDDING. THAT'S INCREDIBLE.
OH, BUT YOU HAVEN'T SEEN THE BEST PART! THE SUIT CAN PROBE INSIDE ME TOO, REPAIRING ORGAN DAMAGE, MENDING BONES. THERE'RE DNA REPLICATORS, TISSUE RESEQUENCERS-- THE WORKS.
I HAD AN EPIPHANY IN THAT CAVE: I SUCK AT DYING, PEPPER. I'M MUCH BETTER AT FIGURING OUT WAYS TO STAY ALIVE. THAT'S WHAT THE SUIT DOES NOW: ITS SOLE PURPOSE IS TO KEEP ME SAFE, SECURE AND, ABOVE ALL, ALIVE.
LOOK--WHEN I PUT THIS GLOVE ON, I HAD THREE METACARPAL FRACTURES IN MY LEFT HAND. HURT LIKE HELL AND SLOWED DOWN MY TYPING. DAMN IRRITATING.
WANNA SEE WHAT IT LOOKS LIKE NOW?
MR. STARK, I ABSOLUTELY WOULD.
FFFT
THE GLOVE SLIDES OFF SMOOTHLY, EFFORTLESSLY.

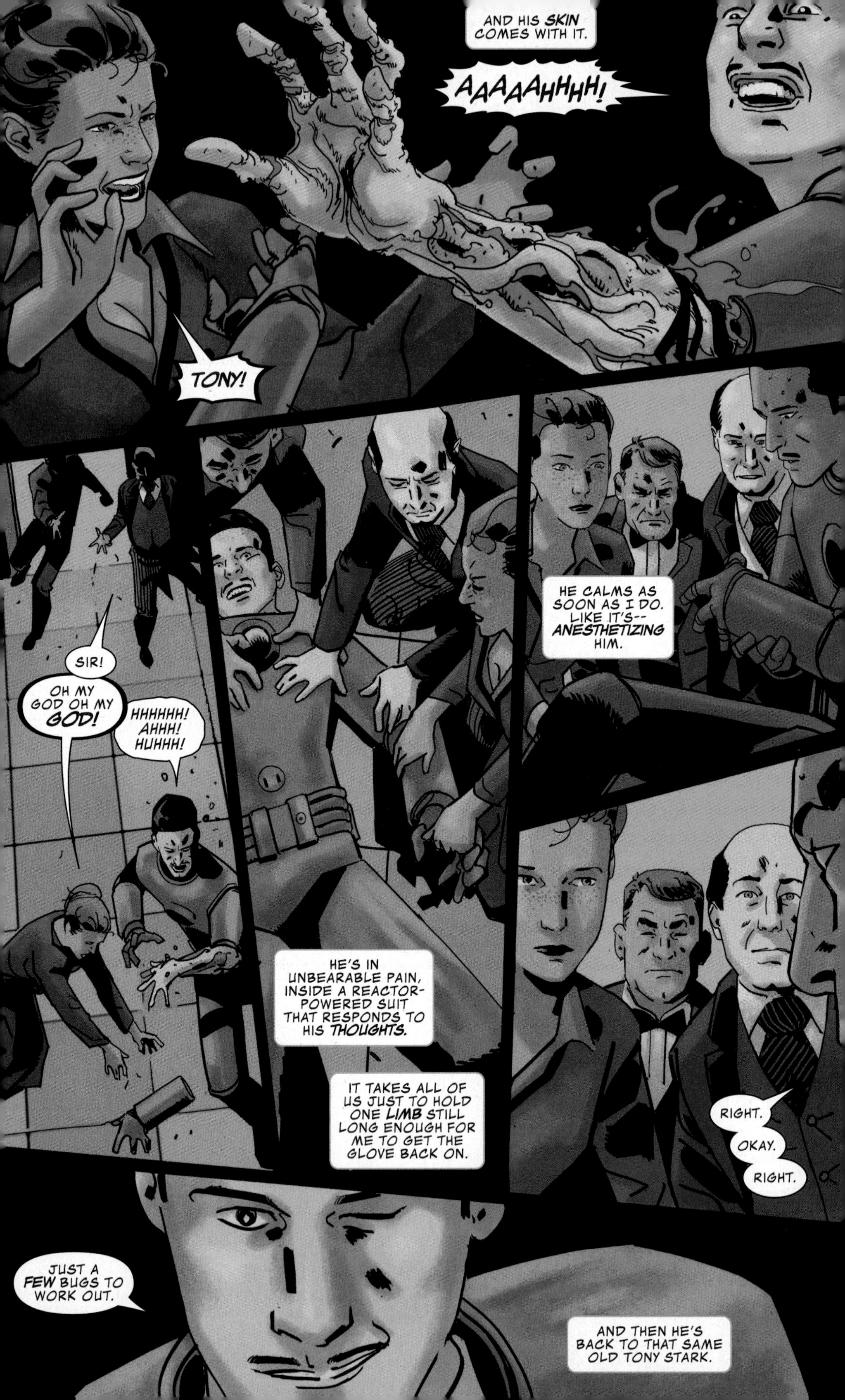

AND HIS SKIN COMES WITH IT.
AAAAAHHHH!
TONY!
SIR!
OH MY GOD OH MY GOD!
HHHHHH! AHHH! HUHHH!
HE'S IN UNBEARABLE PAIN, INSIDE A REACTOR-POWERED SUIT THAT RESPONDS TO HIS THOUGHTS.
IT TAKES ALL OF US JUST TO HOLD ONE LIMB STILL LONG ENOUGH FOR ME TO GET THE GLOVE BACK ON.
HE CALMS AS SOON AS I DO. LIKE IT'S-- ANESTHETIZING HIM.
RIGHT.
OKAY.
RIGHT.
JUST A FEW BUGS TO WORK OUT.
AND THEN HE'S BACK TO THAT SAME OLD TONY STARK.

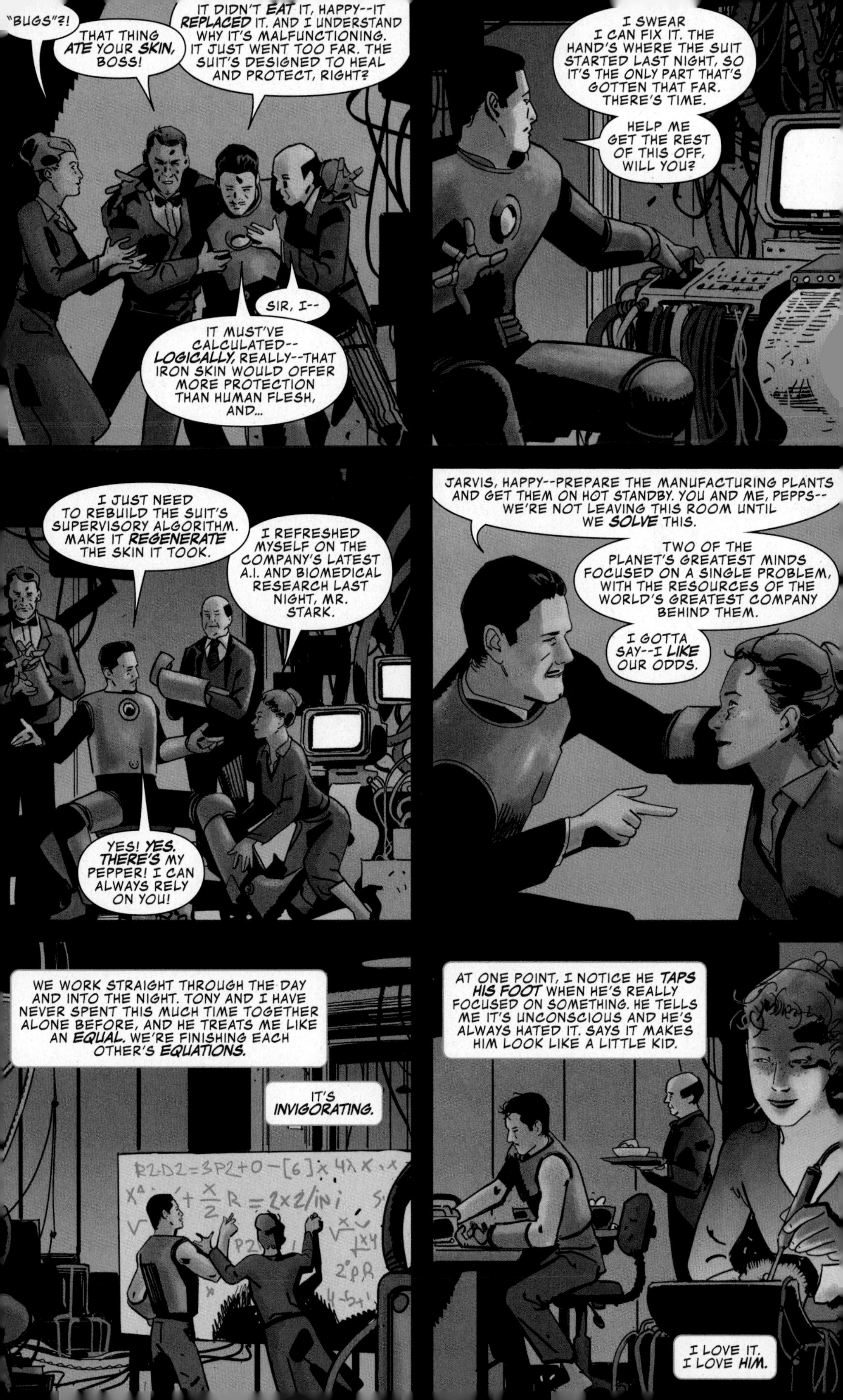
"BUGS"?!
THAT THING ATE YOUR SKIN, BOSS!
IT DIDN'T EAT IT, HAPPY--IT REPLACED IT. AND I UNDERSTAND WHY IT'S MALFUNCTIONING. IT JUST WENT TOO FAR. THE SUIT'S DESIGNED TO HEAL AND PROTECT, RIGHT?
SIR, I--
IT MUST'VE CALCULATED--LOGICALLY, REALLY--THAT IRON SKIN WOULD OFFER MORE PROTECTION THAN HUMAN FLESH, AND...
I SWEAR I CAN FIX IT. THE HAND'S WHERE THE SUIT STARTED LAST NIGHT, SO IT'S THE ONLY PART THAT'S GOTTEN THAT FAR. THERE'S TIME.
HELP ME GET THE REST OF THIS OFF, WILL YOU?
I JUST NEED TO REBUILD THE SUIT'S SUPERVISORY ALGORITHM. MAKE IT REGENERATE THE SKIN IT TOOK.
I REFRESHED MYSELF ON THE COMPANY'S LATEST A.I. AND BIOMEDICAL RESEARCH LAST NIGHT, MR. STARK.
YES! YES. THERE'S MY PEPPER! I CAN ALWAYS RELY ON YOU!
JARVIS, HAPPY--PREPARE THE MANUFACTURING PLANTS AND GET THEM ON HOT STANDBY. YOU AND ME, PEPPS--WE'RE NOT LEAVING THIS ROOM UNTIL WE SOLVE THIS.
TWO OF THE PLANET'S GREATEST MINDS FOCUSED ON A SINGLE PROBLEM, WITH THE RESOURCES OF THE WORLD'S GREATEST COMPANY BEHIND THEM.
I GOTTA SAY--I LIKE OUR ODDS.
WE WORK STRAIGHT THROUGH THE DAY AND INTO THE NIGHT. TONY AND I HAVE NEVER SPENT THIS MUCH TIME TOGETHER ALONE BEFORE, AND HE TREATS ME LIKE AN EQUAL. WE'RE FINISHING EACH OTHER'S EQUATIONS.
IT'S INVIGORATING.
AT ONE POINT, I NOTICE HE TAPS HIS FOOT WHEN HE'S REALLY FOCUSED ON SOMETHING. HE TELLS ME IT'S UNCONSCIOUS AND HE'S ALWAYS HATED IT. SAYS IT MAKES HIM LOOK LIKE A LITTLE KID.
I LOVE IT. I LOVE HIM.

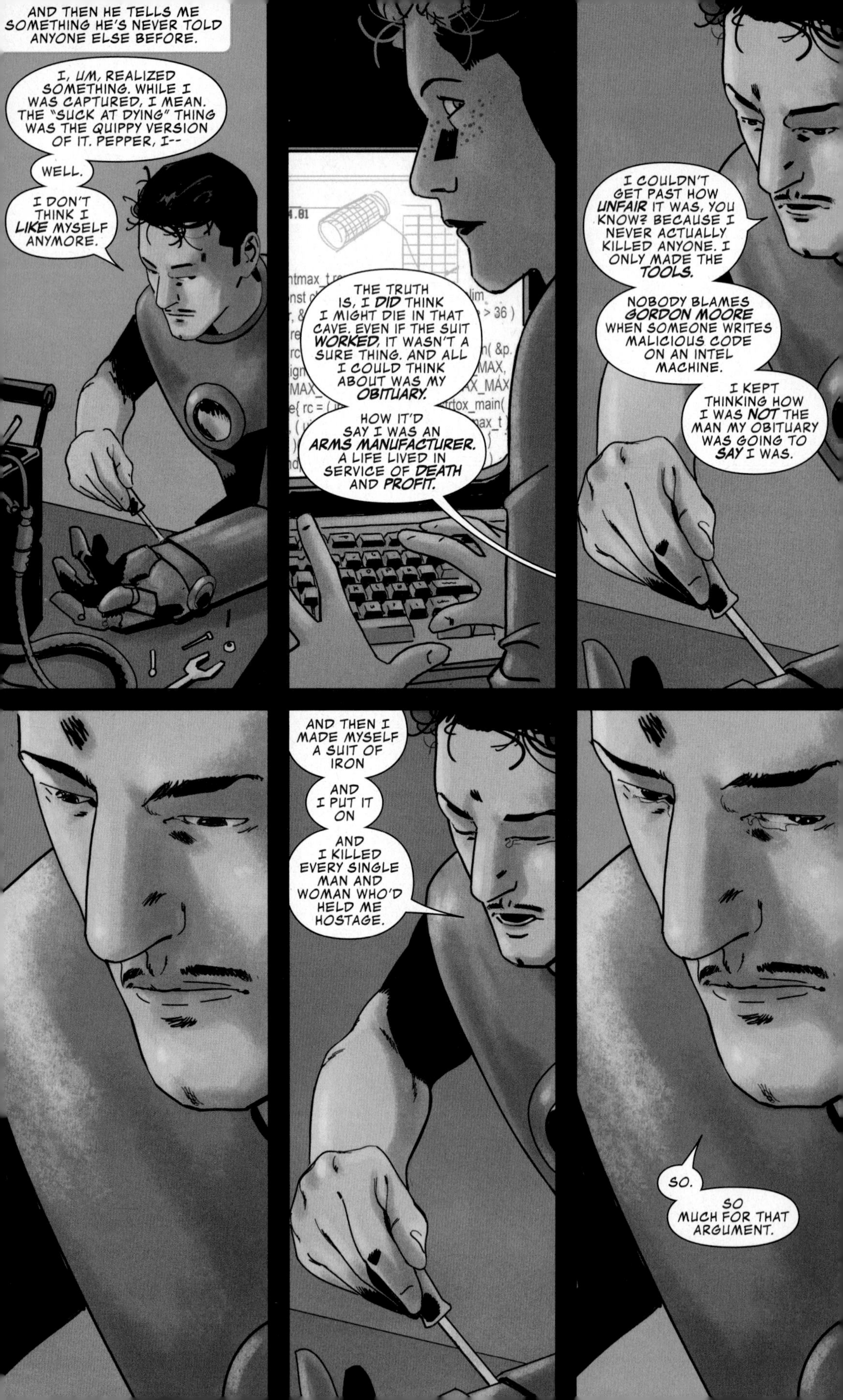
AND THEN HE TELLS ME SOMETHING HE'S NEVER TOLD ANYONE ELSE BEFORE.
I, UM, REALIZED SOMETHING. WHILE I WAS CAPTURED, I MEAN. THE "SUCK AT DYING" THING WAS THE QUIPPY VERSION OF IT. PEPPER, I--
WELL.
I DON'T THINK I LIKE MYSELF ANYMORE.
THE TRUTH IS, I DID THINK I MIGHT DIE IN THAT CAVE. EVEN IF THE SUIT WORKED, IT WASN'T A SURE THING. AND ALL I COULD THINK ABOUT WAS MY OBITUARY.
HOW IT'D SAY I WAS AN ARMS MANUFACTURER. A LIFE LIVED IN SERVICE OF DEATH AND PROFIT.
I COULDN'T GET PAST HOW UNFAIR IT WAS, YOU KNOW? BECAUSE I NEVER ACTUALLY KILLED ANYONE. I ONLY MADE THE TOOLS.
NOBODY BLAMES GORDON MOORE WHEN SOMEONE WRITES MALICIOUS CODE ON AN INTEL MACHINE.
I KEPT THINKING HOW I WAS NOT THE MAN MY OBITUARY WAS GOING TO SAY I WAS.
AND THEN I MADE MYSELF A SUIT OF IRON
AND I PUT IT ON
AND I KILLED EVERY SINGLE MAN AND WOMAN WHO'D HELD ME HOSTAGE.
SO.
SO MUCH FOR THAT ARGUMENT.

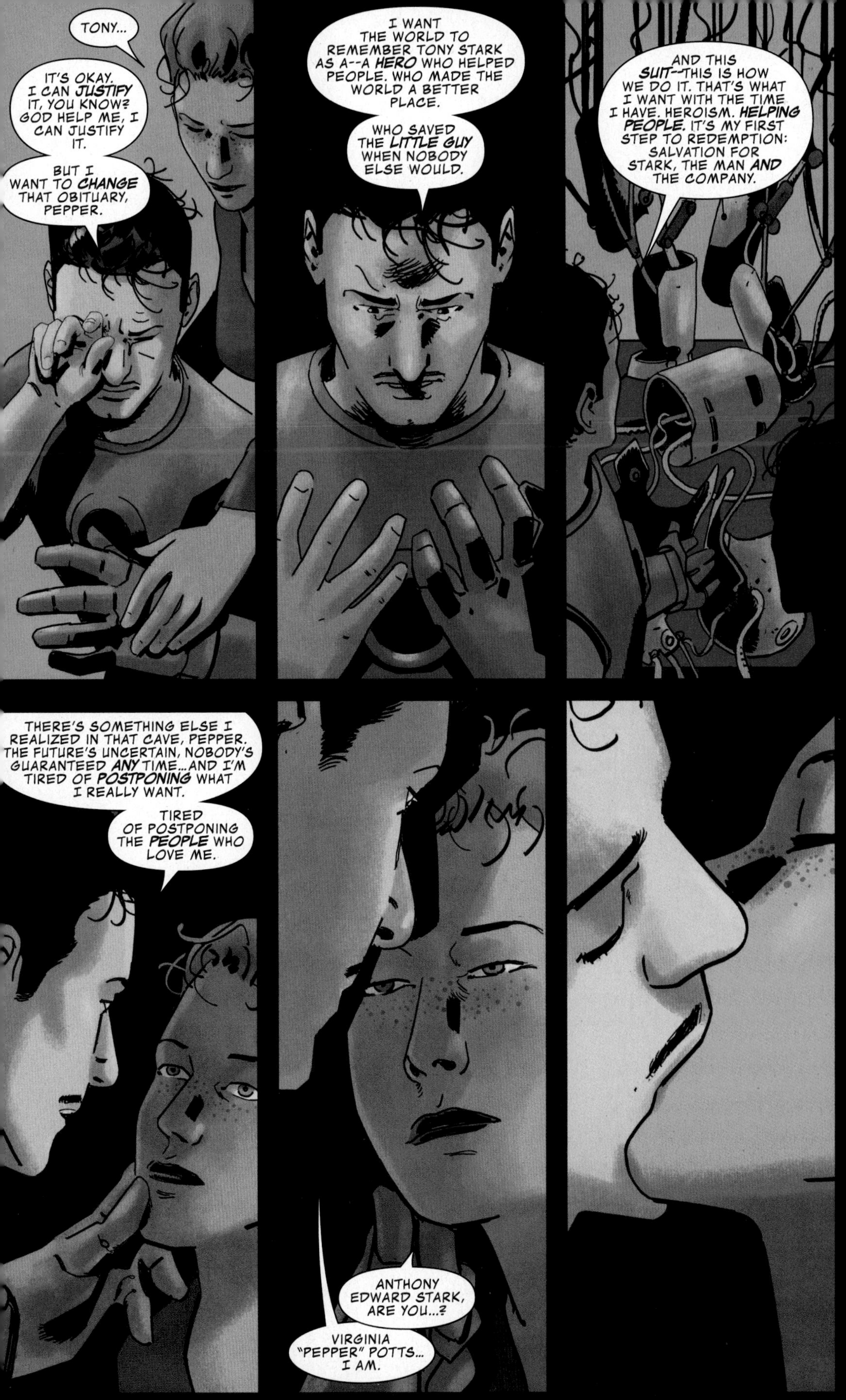
TONY...
IT'S OKAY. I CAN JUSTIFY IT, YOU KNOW? GOD HELP ME, I CAN JUSTIFY IT.
BUT I WANT TO CHANGE THAT OBITUARY, PEPPER.
I WANT THE WORLD TO REMEMBER TONY STARK AS A--A HERO WHO HELPED PEOPLE. WHO MADE THE WORLD A BETTER PLACE.
WHO SAVED THE LITTLE GUY WHEN NOBODY ELSE WOULD.
AND THIS SUIT--THIS IS HOW WE DO IT. THAT'S WHAT I WANT WITH THE TIME I HAVE. HEROISM. HELPING PEOPLE. IT'S MY FIRST STEP TO REDEMPTION: SALVATION FOR STARK, THE MAN AND THE COMPANY.
THERE'S SOMETHING ELSE I REALIZED IN THAT CAVE, PEPPER. THE FUTURE'S UNCERTAIN, NOBODY'S GUARANTEED ANY TIME...AND I'M TIRED OF POSTPONING WHAT I REALLY WANT.
TIRED OF POSTPONING THE PEOPLE WHO LOVE ME.
ANTHONY EDWARD STARK, ARE YOU...?
VIRGINIA "PEPPER" POTTS... I AM.

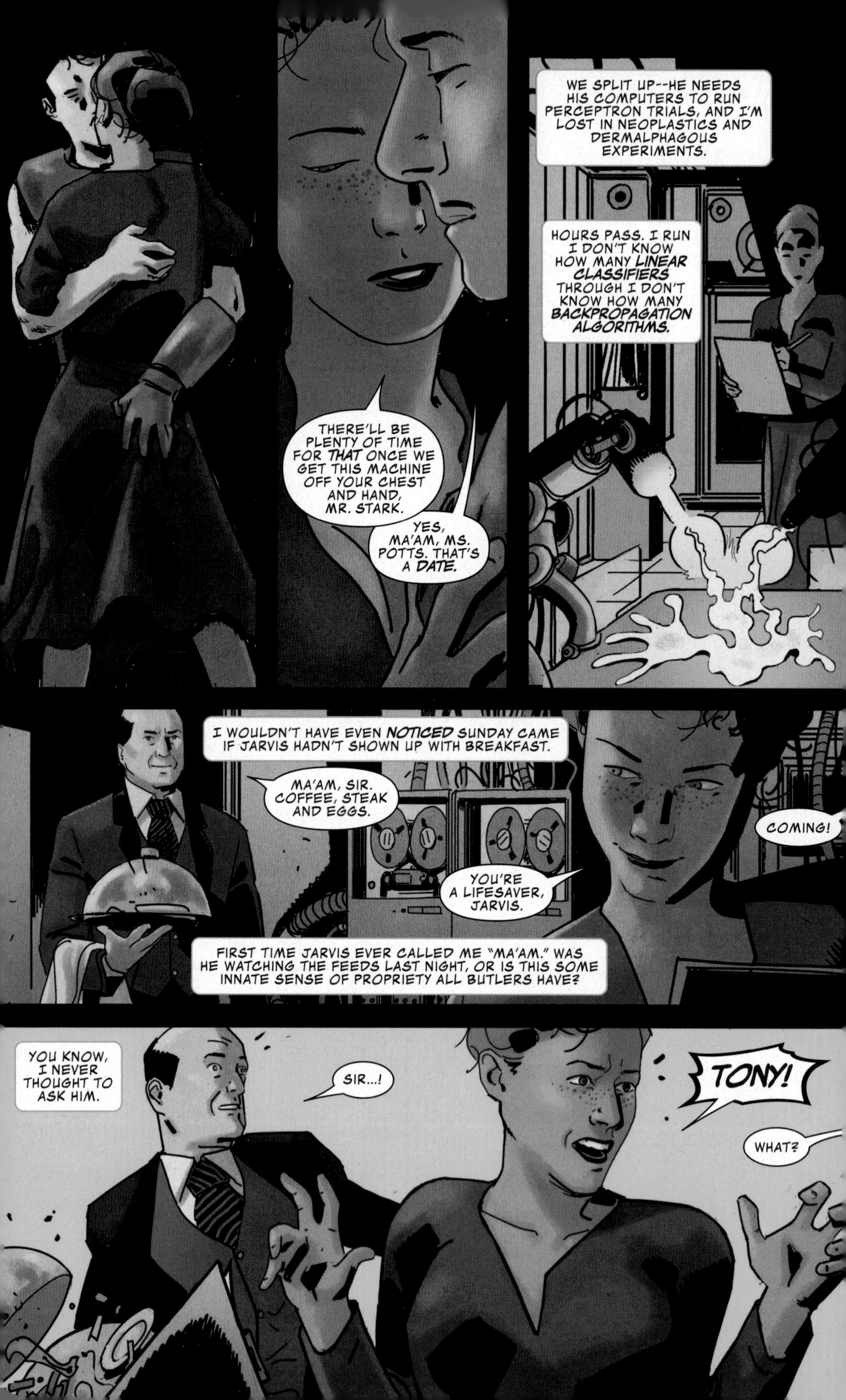
THERE'LL BE PLENTY OF TIME FOR THAT ONCE WE GET THIS MACHINE OFF YOUR CHEST AND HAND, MR. STARK.
YES, MA'AM, MS. POTTS. THAT'S A DATE.
WE SPLIT UP--HE NEEDS HIS COMPUTERS TO RUN PERCEPTRON TRIALS, AND I'M LOST IN NEOPLASTICS AND DERMALPHAGOUS EXPERIMENTS.
HOURS PASS. I RUN I DON'T KNOW HOW MANY LINEAR CLASSIFIERS THROUGH I DON'T KNOW HOW MANY BACKPROPAGATION ALGORITHMS.
I WOULDN'T HAVE EVEN NOTICED SUNDAY CAME IF JARVIS HADN'T SHOWN UP WITH BREAKFAST.
MA'AM, SIR. COFFEE, STEAK AND EGGS.
COMING!
YOU'RE A LIFESAVER, JARVIS.
FIRST TIME JARVIS EVER CALLED ME "MA'AM." WAS HE WATCHING THE FEEDS LAST NIGHT, OR IS THIS SOME INNATE SENSE OF PROPRIETY ALL BUTLERS HAVE?
YOU KNOW, I NEVER THOUGHT TO ASK HIM.
SIR...!
TONY!
WHAT?

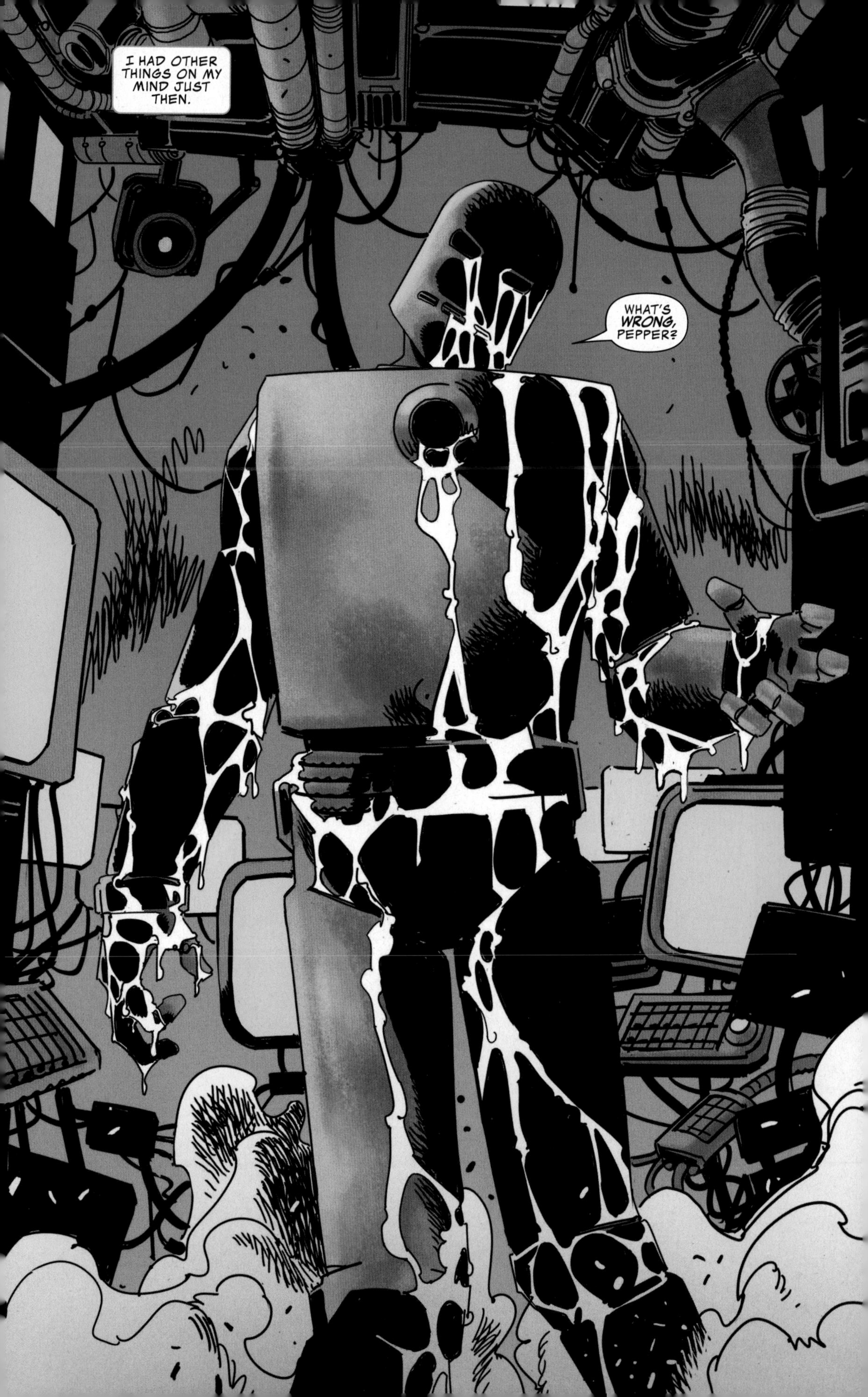
I HAD OTHER THINGS ON MY MIND JUST THEN.
WHAT'S WRONG, PEPPER?

CHAPTER TWO

THEY'RE COMING! THIS IS MY GREATEST TEST! CAN THE THING I HAVE CREATED SURVIVE? THE THING WHICH IS LESS THAN HUMAN...YET, FAR MORE THAN MERELY HUMAN! THIS THING WHICH IS NOW-- ANTHONY STARK!!
WHAM
MY BRAIN STILL THINKS! MY HEART STILL BEATS! BUT, IN ORDER TO REMAIN ALIVE, I MUST SPEND THE REST OF MY LIFE IN THIS IRON PRISON!!

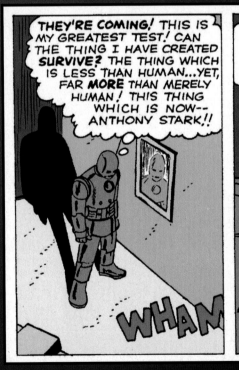

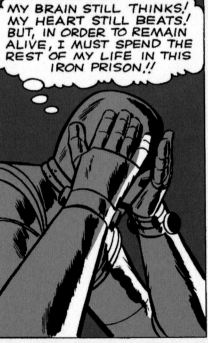

MY HEART STILL BEATS

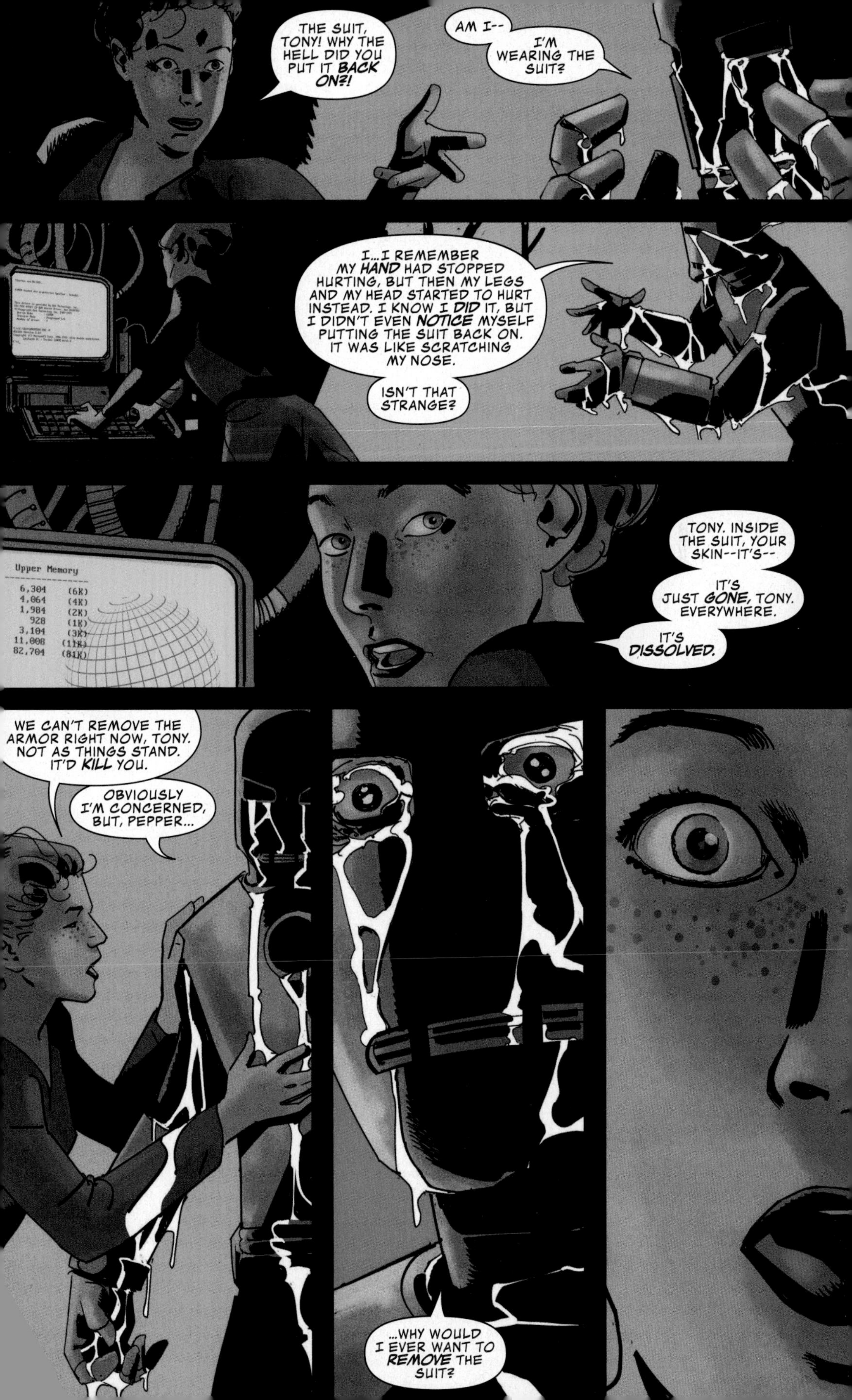

THE SUIT, TONY! WHY THE HELL DID YOU PUT IT BACK ON?!
AM I--
I'M WEARING THE SUIT?
I...I REMEMBER MY HAND HAD STOPPED HURTING, BUT THEN MY LEGS AND MY HEAD STARTED TO HURT INSTEAD. I KNOW I DID IT, BUT I DIDN'T EVEN NOTICE MYSELF PUTTING THE SUIT BACK ON. IT WAS LIKE SCRATCHING MY NOSE.
ISN'T THAT STRANGE?
Upper Memory
6,304 (6K)
4,064 (4K)
1,984 (2K)
928 (1K)
3,104 (3K)
11,008 (11K)
82,704 (81K)
TONY. INSIDE THE SUIT, YOUR SKIN--IT'S--
IT'S JUST GONE, TONY. EVERYWHERE.
IT'S DISSOLVED.
WE CAN'T REMOVE THE ARMOR RIGHT NOW, TONY. NOT AS THINGS STAND. IT'D KILL YOU.
OBVIOUSLY I'M CONCERNED, BUT, PEPPER...
...WHY WOULD I EVER WANT TO REMOVE THE SUIT?

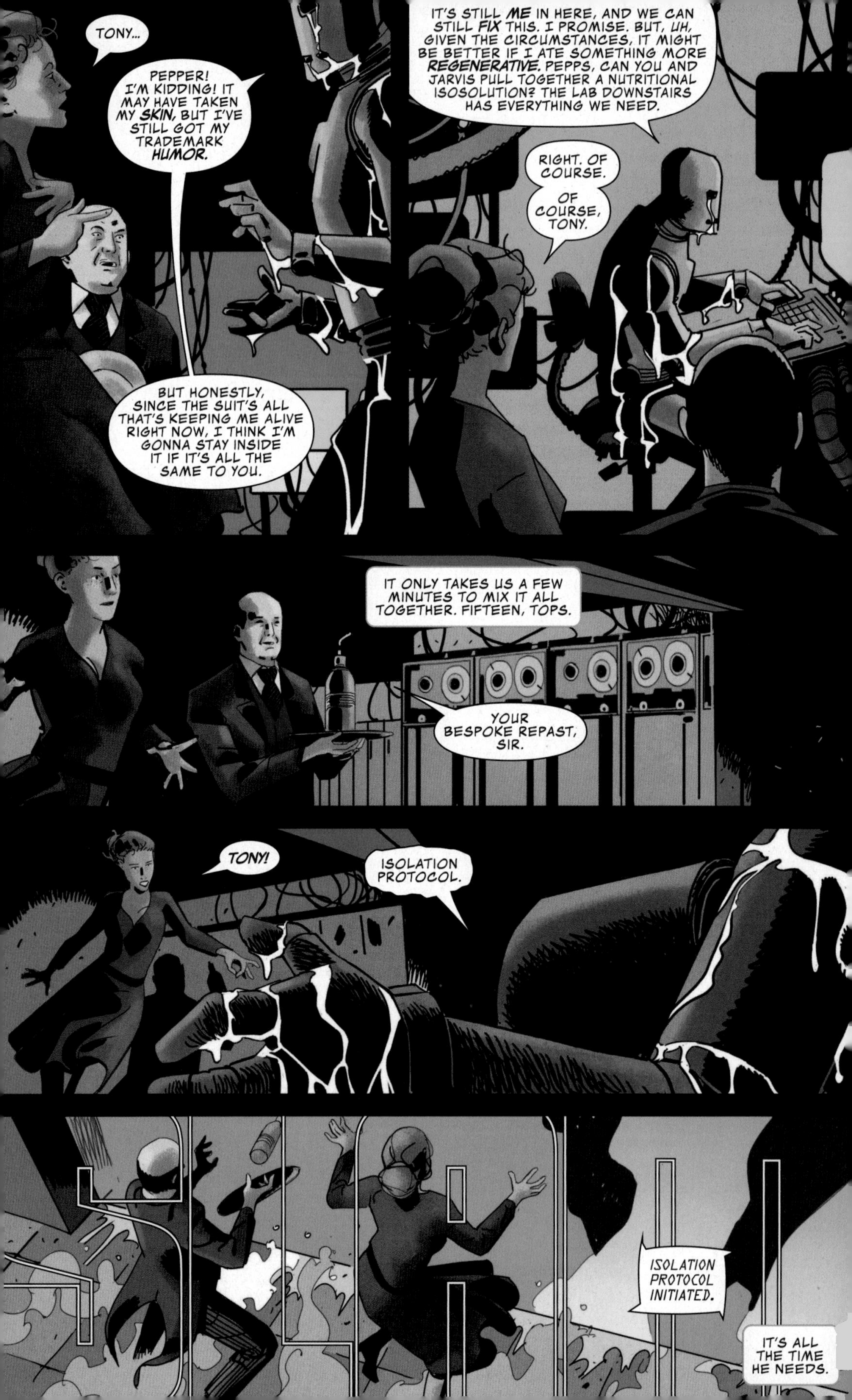
TONY...
PEPPER! I'M KIDDING! IT MAY HAVE TAKEN MY SKIN, BUT I'VE STILL GOT MY TRADEMARK HUMOR.
BUT HONESTLY, SINCE THE SUIT'S ALL THAT'S KEEPING ME ALIVE RIGHT NOW, I THINK I'M GONNA STAY INSIDE IT IF IT'S ALL THE SAME TO YOU.
IT'S STILL ME IN HERE, AND WE CAN STILL FIX THIS. I PROMISE. BUT, UH, GIVEN THE CIRCUMSTANCES, IT MIGHT BE BETTER IF I ATE SOMETHING MORE REGENERATIVE. PEPPS, CAN YOU AND JARVIS PULL TOGETHER A NUTRITIONAL ISOSOLUTION? THE LAB DOWNSTAIRS HAS EVERYTHING WE NEED.
RIGHT. OF COURSE.
OF COURSE, TONY.
IT ONLY TAKES US A FEW MINUTES TO MIX IT ALL TOGETHER. FIFTEEN, TOPS.
YOUR BESPOKE REPAST, SIR.
TONY!
ISOLATION PROTOCOL.
ISOLATION PROTOCOL INITIATED.
IT'S ALL THE TIME HE NEEDS.

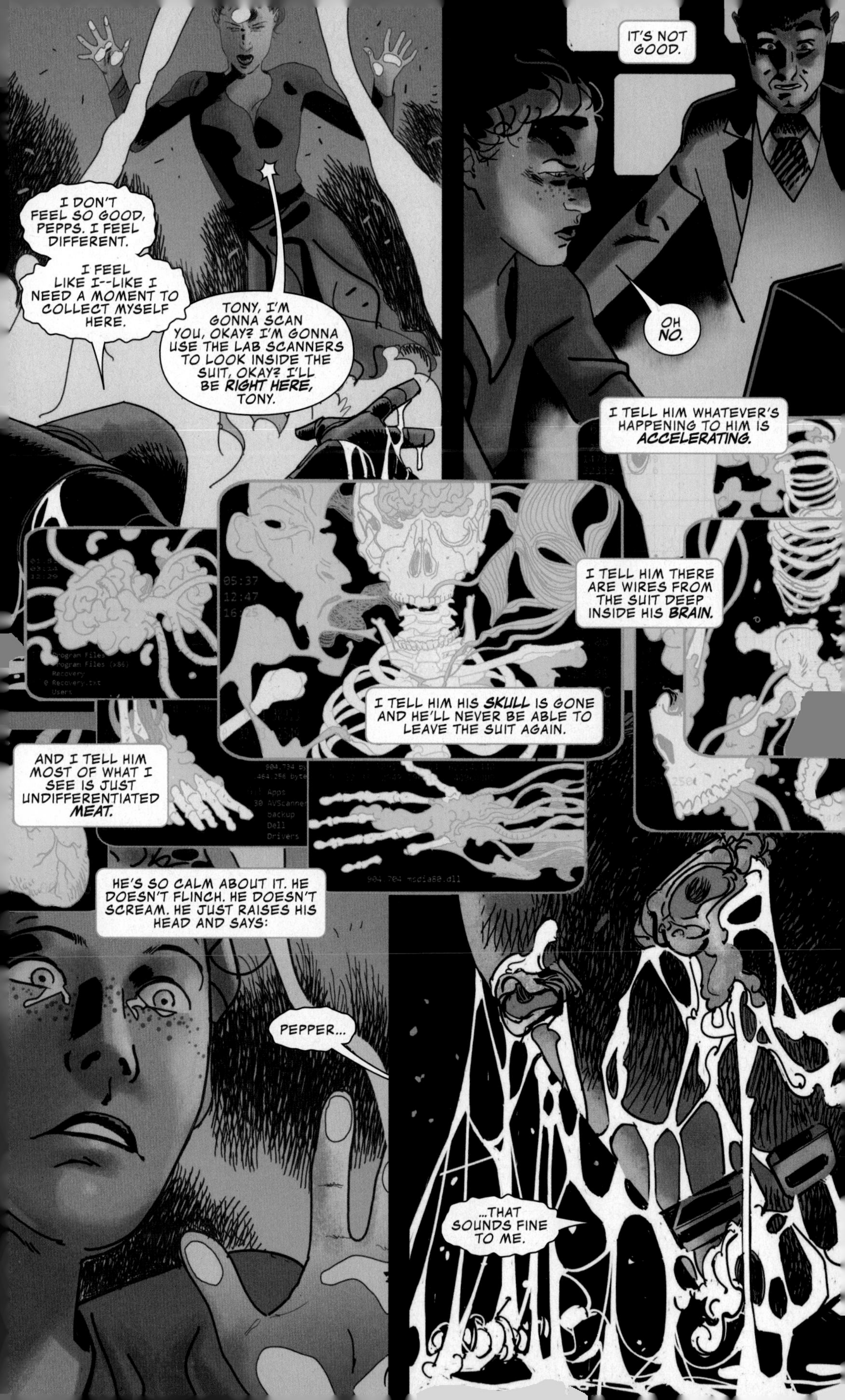
I DON'T FEEL SO GOOD, PEPPS. I FEEL DIFFERENT.
I FEEL LIKE I--LIKE I NEED A MOMENT TO COLLECT MYSELF HERE.
TONY, I'M GONNA SCAN YOU, OKAY? I'M GONNA USE THE LAB SCANNERS TO LOOK INSIDE THE SUIT, OKAY? I'LL BE RIGHT HERE, TONY.
IT'S NOT GOOD.
OH NO.
I TELL HIM WHATEVER'S HAPPENING TO HIM IS ACCELERATING.
I TELL HIM THERE ARE WIRES FROM THE SUIT DEEP INSIDE HIS BRAIN.
I TELL HIM HIS SKULL IS GONE AND HE'LL NEVER BE ABLE TO LEAVE THE SUIT AGAIN.
AND I TELL HIM MOST OF WHAT I SEE IS JUST UNDIFFERENTIATED MEAT.
HE'S SO CALM ABOUT IT. HE DOESN'T FLINCH. HE DOESN'T SCREAM. HE JUST RAISES HIS HEAD AND SAYS:
PEPPER...
...THAT SOUNDS FINE TO ME.

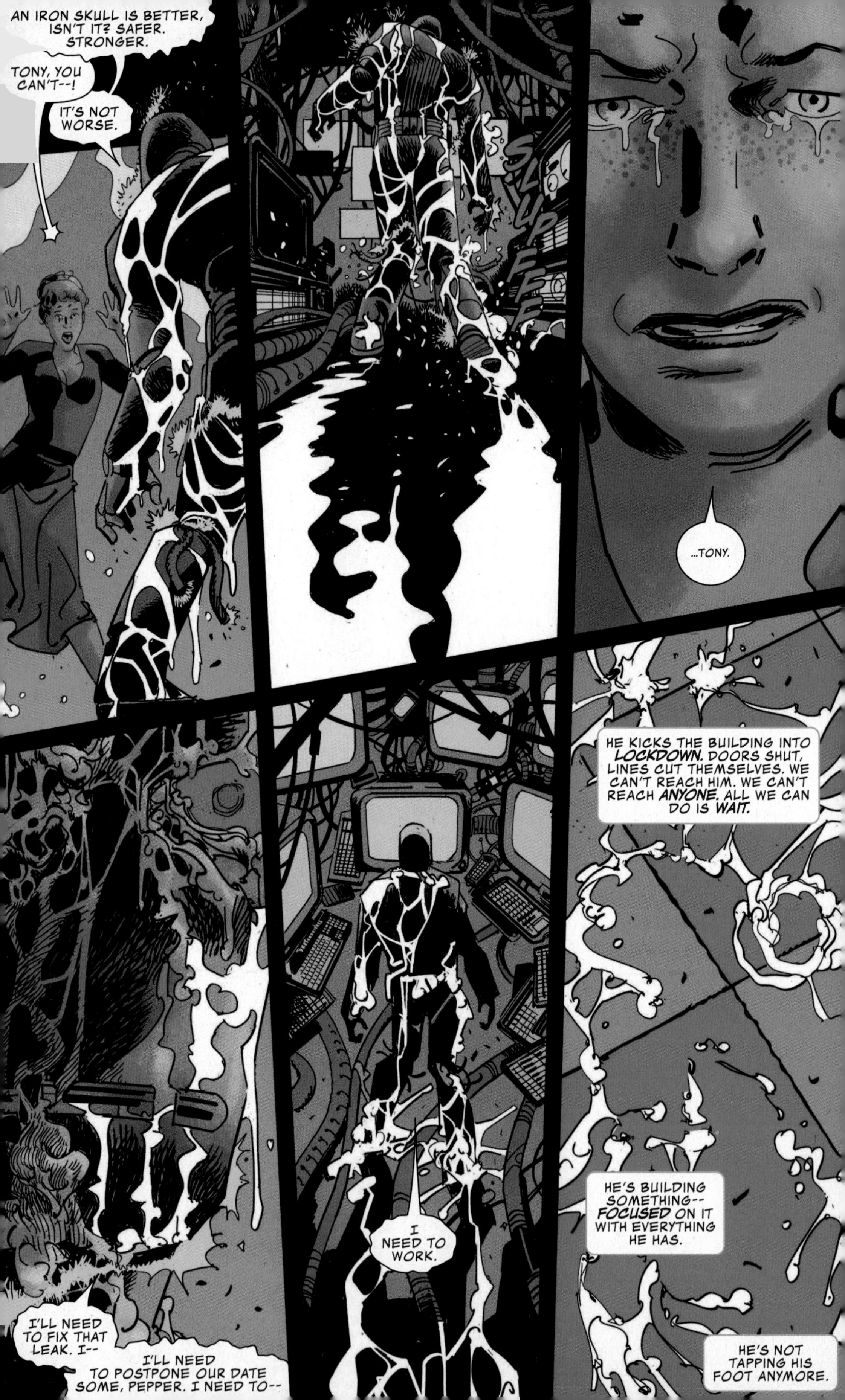
AN IRON SKULL IS BETTER, ISN'T IT? SAFER. STRONGER.
TONY, YOU CAN'T--!
IT'S NOT WORSE.
SLUPEEEE
...TONY.
I'LL NEED TO FIX THAT LEAK. I--
I'LL NEED TO POSTPONE OUR DATE SOME, PEPPER. I NEED TO--
I NEED TO WORK.
HE KICKS THE BUILDING INTO LOCKDOWN. DOORS SHUT, LINES CUT THEMSELVES. WE CAN'T REACH HIM. WE CAN'T REACH ANYONE. ALL WE CAN DO IS WAIT.
HE'S BUILDING SOMETHING-- FOCUSED ON IT WITH EVERYTHING HE HAS.
HE'S NOT TAPPING HIS FOOT ANYMORE.

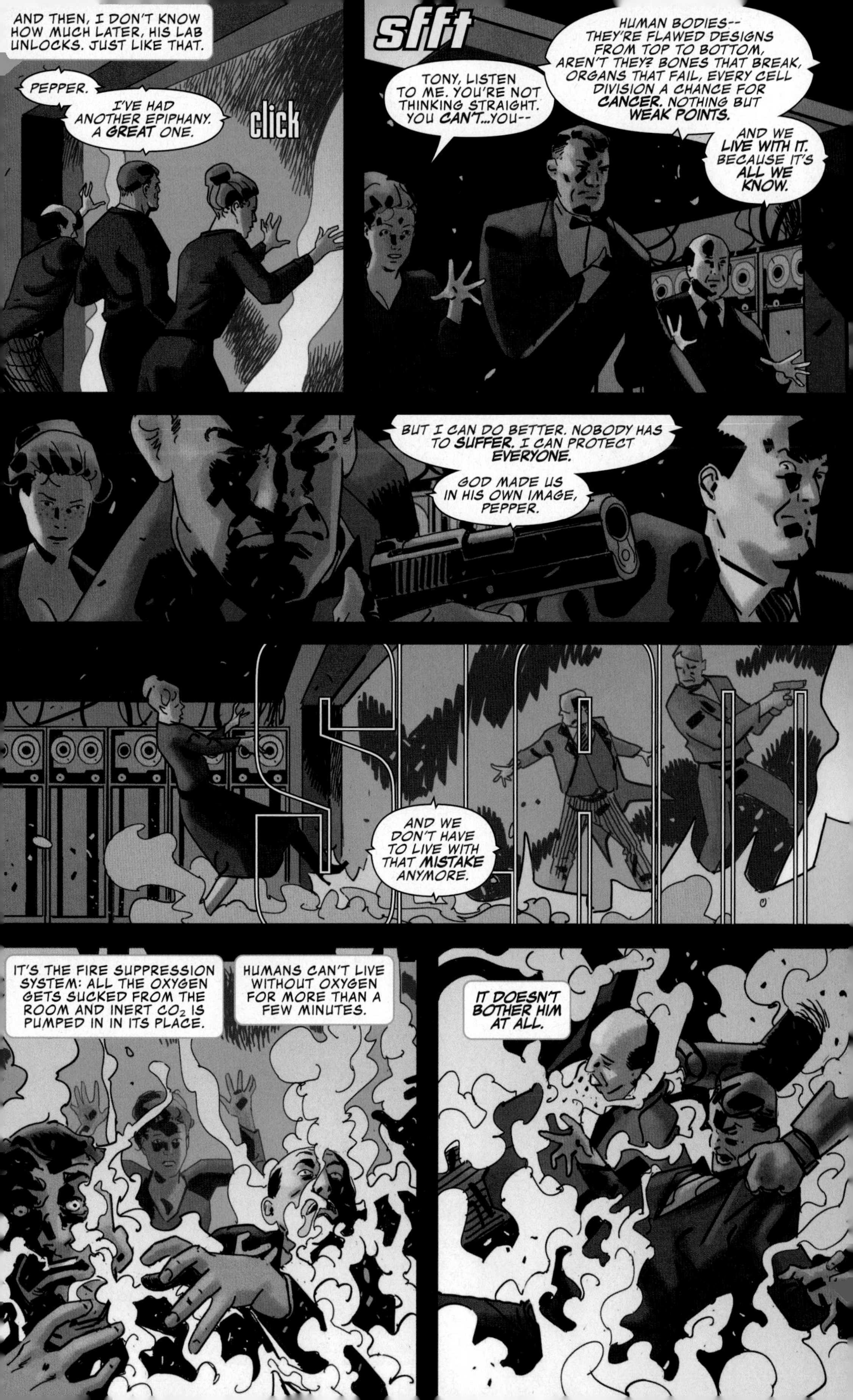

AND THEN, I DON'T KNOW HOW MUCH LATER, HIS LAB UNLOCKS. JUST LIKE THAT.
PEPPER.
I'VE HAD ANOTHER EPIPHANY. A GREAT ONE.
click
sfft
TONY, LISTEN TO ME. YOU'RE NOT THINKING STRAIGHT. YOU CAN'T...YOU--
HUMAN BODIES-- THEY'RE FLAWED DESIGNS FROM TOP TO BOTTOM, AREN'T THEY? BONES THAT BREAK, ORGANS THAT FAIL, EVERY CELL DIVISION A CHANCE FOR CANCER. NOTHING BUT WEAK POINTS.
AND WE LIVE WITH IT. BECAUSE IT'S ALL WE KNOW.
BUT I CAN DO BETTER. NOBODY HAS TO SUFFER. I CAN PROTECT EVERYONE.
GOD MADE US IN HIS OWN IMAGE, PEPPER.
AND WE DON'T HAVE TO LIVE WITH THAT MISTAKE ANYMORE.
IT'S THE FIRE SUPPRESSION SYSTEM: ALL THE OXYGEN GETS SUCKED FROM THE ROOM AND INERT CO_2 IS PUMPED IN IN ITS PLACE.
HUMANS CAN'T LIVE WITHOUT OXYGEN FOR MORE THAN A FEW MINUTES.
IT DOESN'T BOTHER HIM AT ALL.

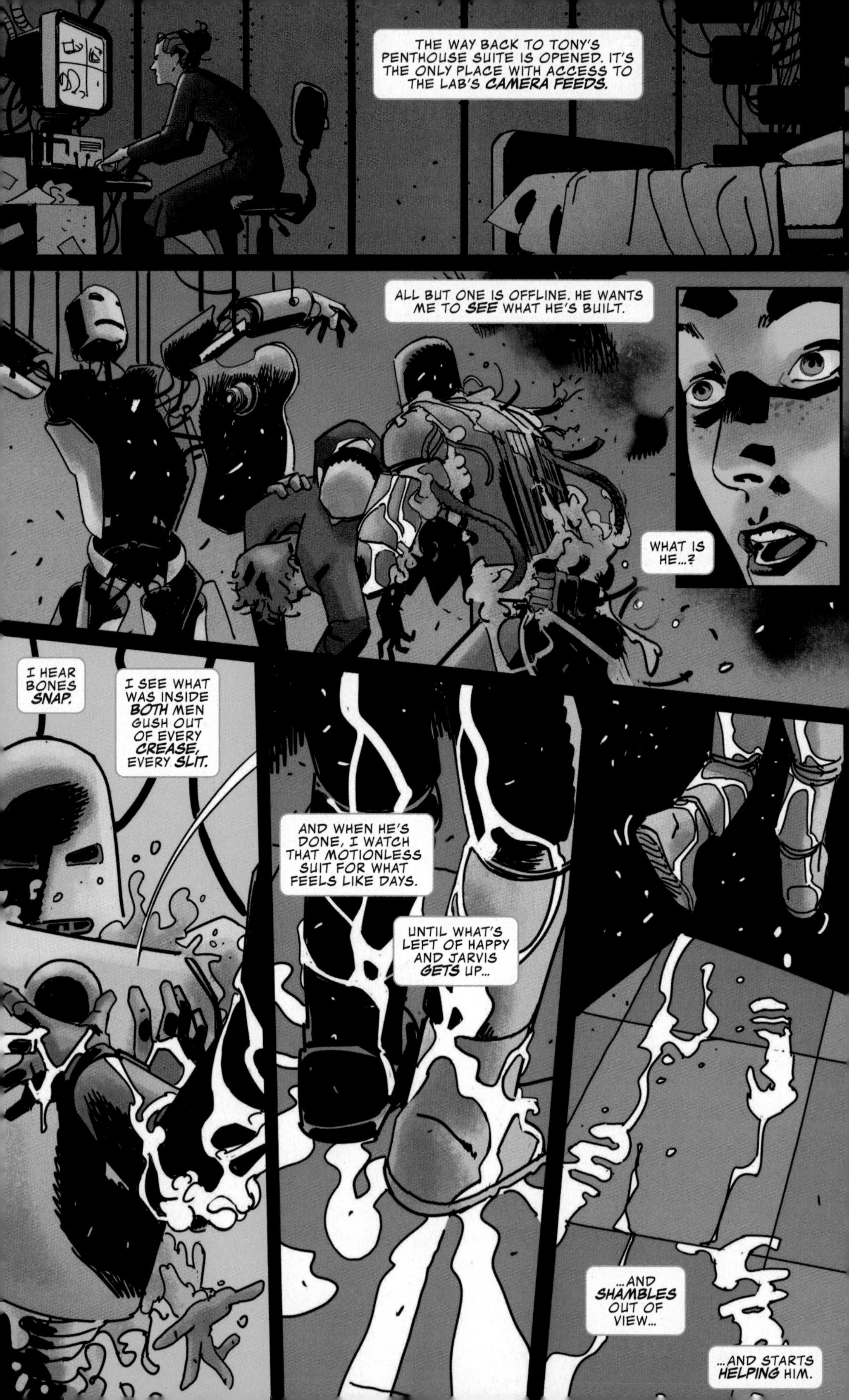
THE WAY BACK TO TONY'S PENTHOUSE SUITE IS OPENED. IT'S THE ONLY PLACE WITH ACCESS TO THE LAB'S CAMERA FEEDS.
ALL BUT ONE IS OFFLINE. HE WANTS ME TO SEE WHAT HE'S BUILT.
WHAT IS HE...?
I HEAR BONES SNAP.
I SEE WHAT WAS INSIDE BOTH MEN GUSH OUT OF EVERY CREASE, EVERY SLIT.
AND WHEN HE'S DONE, I WATCH THAT MOTIONLESS SUIT FOR WHAT FEELS LIKE DAYS.
UNTIL WHAT'S LEFT OF HAPPY AND JARVIS GETS UP...
...AND SHAMBLES OUT OF VIEW...
...AND STARTS HELPING HIM.

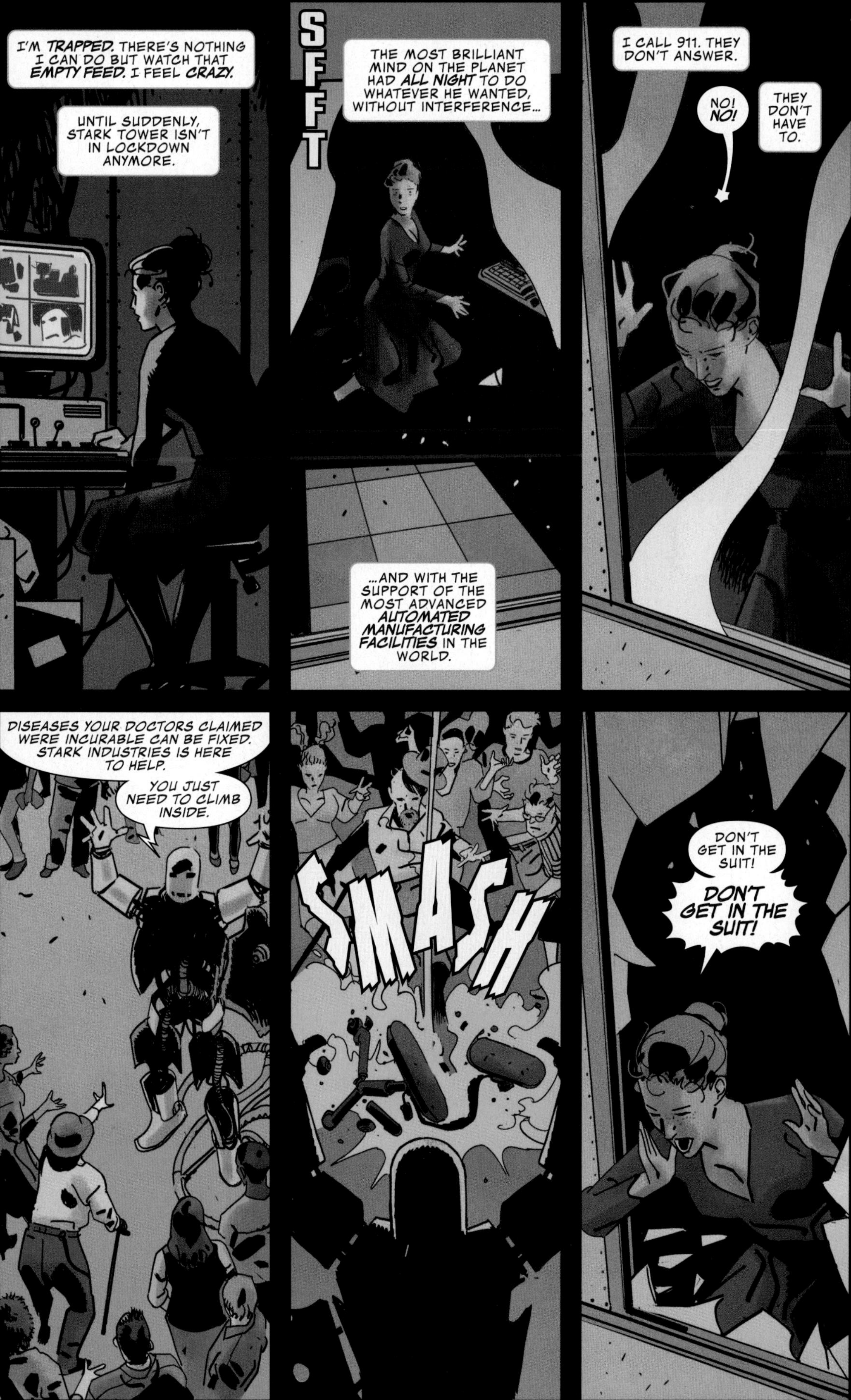
I'M TRAPPED. THERE'S NOTHING I CAN DO BUT WATCH THAT EMPTY FEED. I FEEL CRAZY.
UNTIL SUDDENLY, STARK TOWER ISN'T IN LOCKDOWN ANYMORE.
SFFT
THE MOST BRILLIANT MIND ON THE PLANET HAD ALL NIGHT TO DO WHATEVER HE WANTED, WITHOUT INTERFERENCE...
...AND WITH THE SUPPORT OF THE MOST ADVANCED AUTOMATED MANUFACTURING FACILITIES IN THE WORLD.
I CALL 911. THEY DON'T ANSWER.
NO! NO!
THEY DON'T HAVE TO.
DISEASES YOUR DOCTORS CLAIMED WERE INCURABLE CAN BE FIXED. STARK INDUSTRIES IS HERE TO HELP.
YOU JUST NEED TO CLIMB INSIDE.
SMASH
DON'T GET IN THE SUIT!
DON'T GET IN THE SUIT!

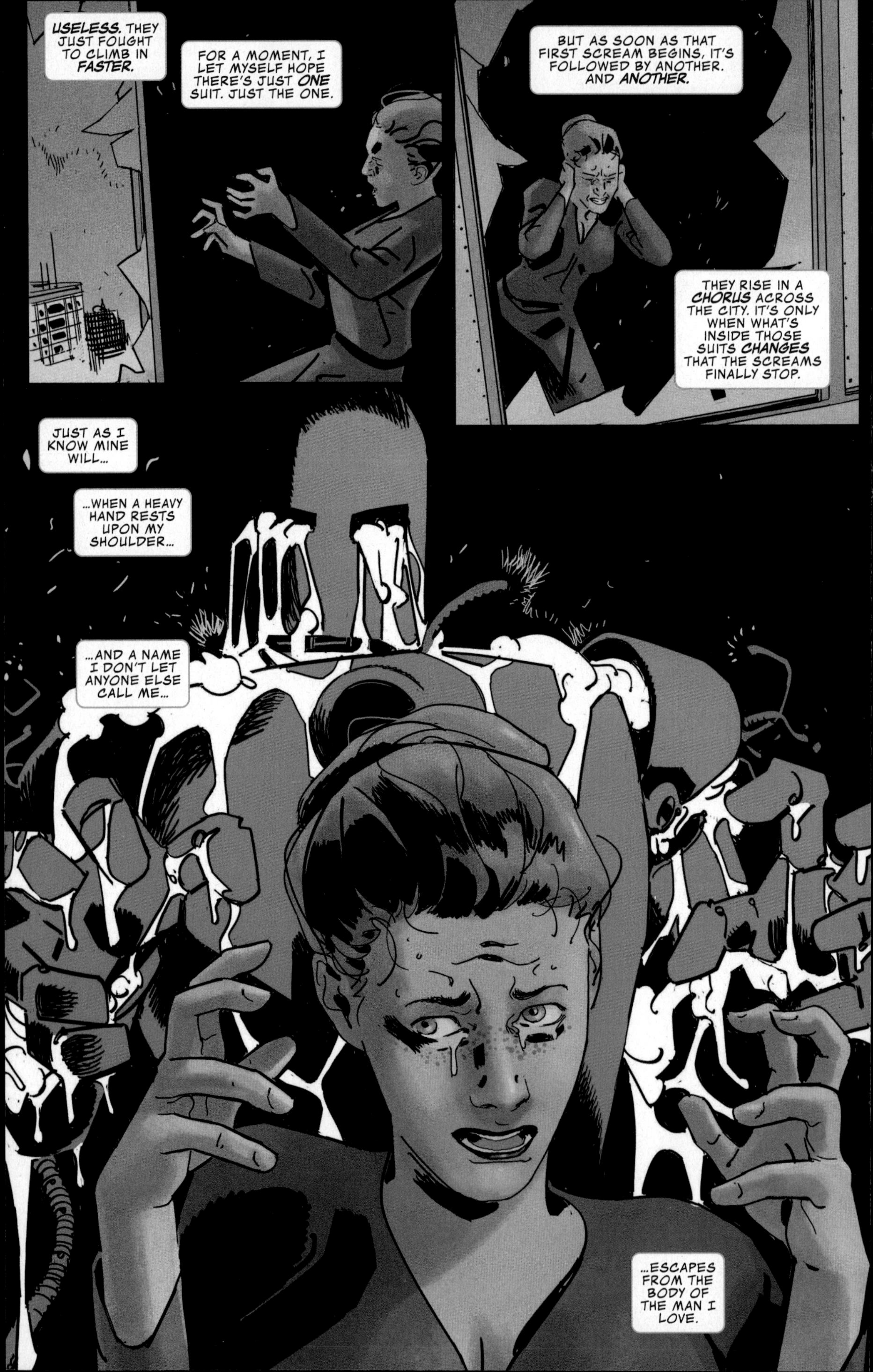
USELESS. THEY JUST FOUGHT TO CLIMB IN FASTER.
FOR A MOMENT, I LET MYSELF HOPE THERE'S JUST ONE SUIT. JUST THE ONE.
BUT AS SOON AS THAT FIRST SCREAM BEGINS, IT'S FOLLOWED BY ANOTHER. AND ANOTHER.
THEY RISE IN A CHORUS ACROSS THE CITY. IT'S ONLY WHEN WHAT'S INSIDE THOSE SUITS CHANGES THAT THE SCREAMS FINALLY STOP.
JUST AS I KNOW MINE WILL...
...WHEN A HEAVY HAND RESTS UPON MY SHOULDER...
...AND A NAME I DON'T LET ANYONE ELSE CALL ME...
...ESCAPES FROM THE BODY OF THE MAN I LOVE.

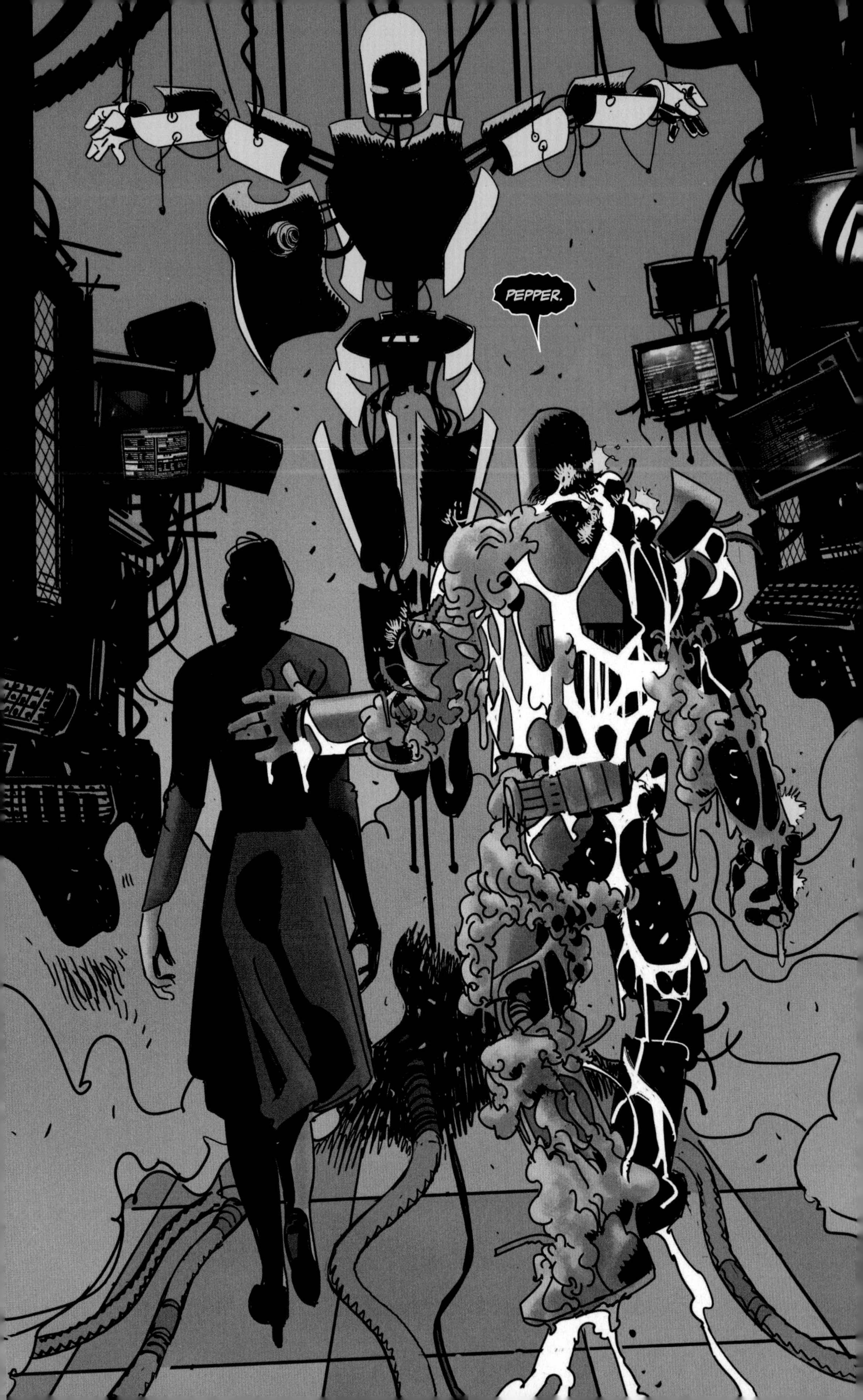
PEPPER.

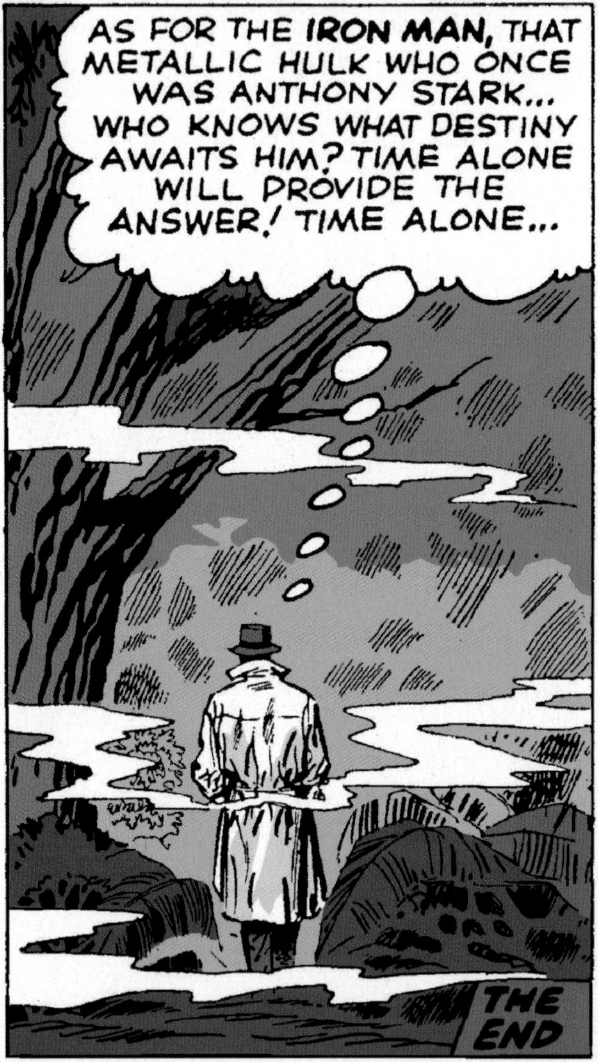
AS FOR THE **IRON MAN,** THAT METALLIC HULK WHO ONCE WAS ANTHONY STARK... WHO KNOWS WHAT DESTINY AWAITS HIM? TIME ALONE WILL PROVIDE THE ANSWER! TIME ALONE...
THE END

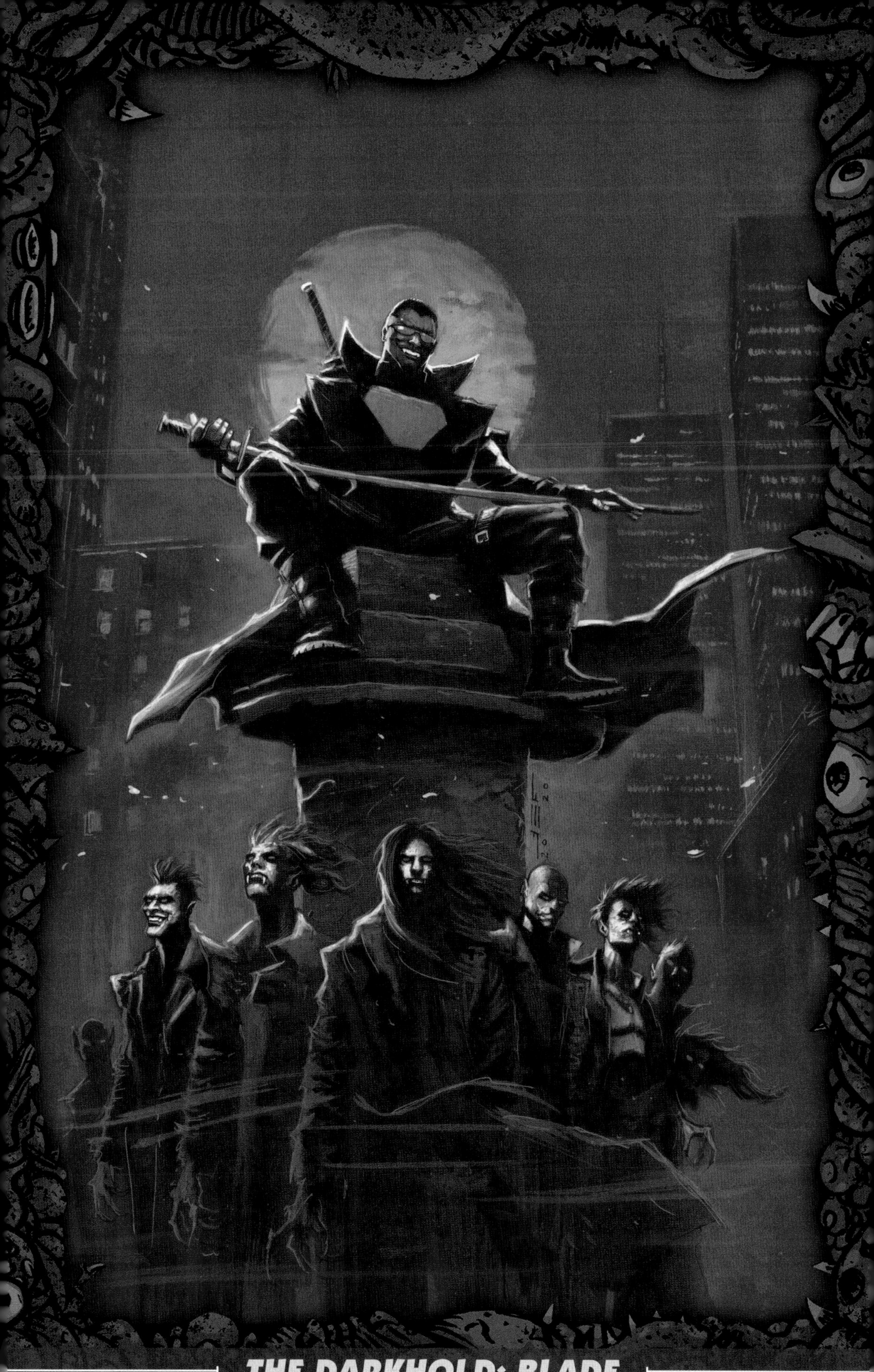

THE DARKHOLD: BLADE

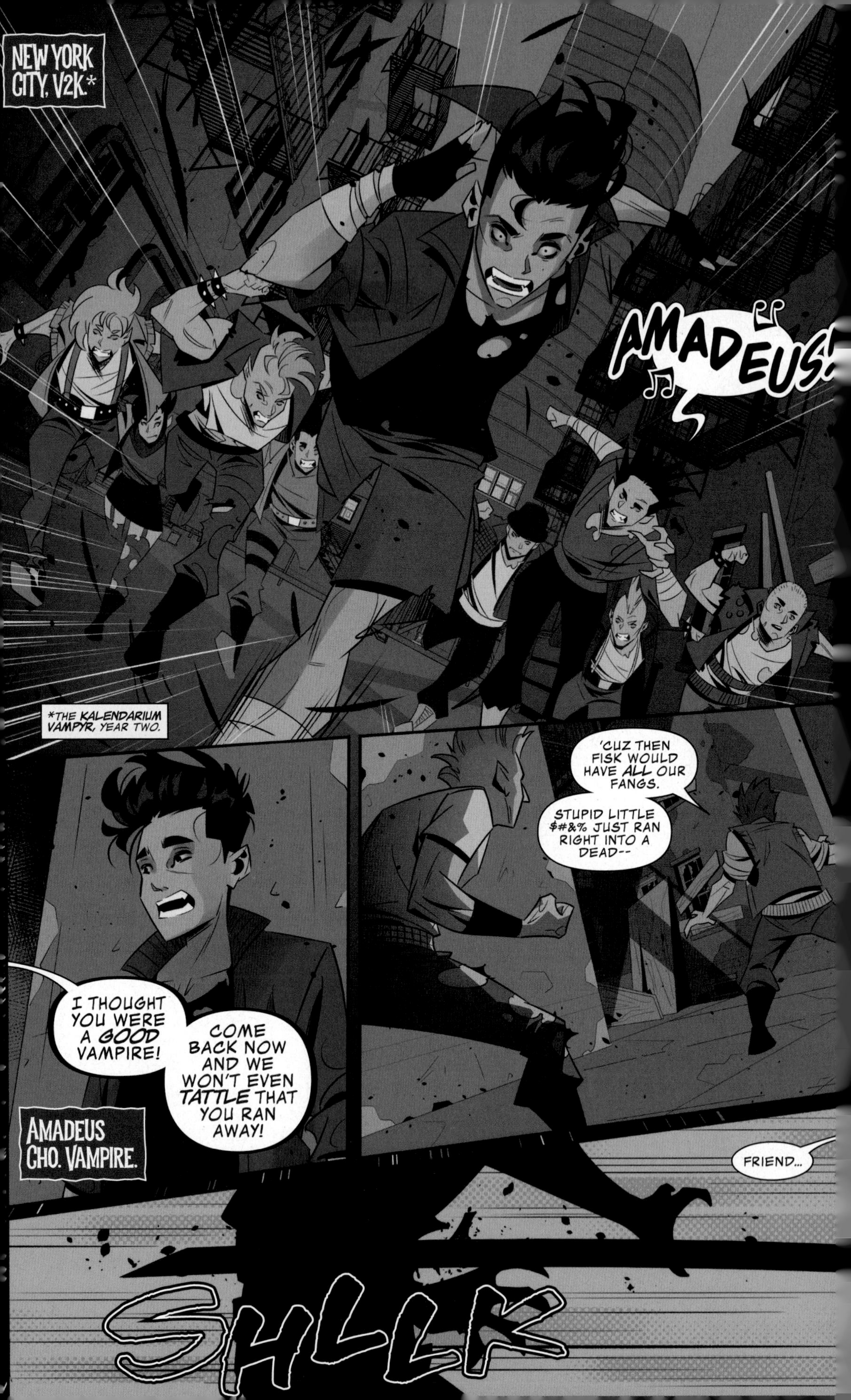

NEW YORK CITY, V2K.*
AMADEUS!
*THE KALENDARIUM VAMPYR, YEAR TWO.
I THOUGHT YOU WERE A GOOD VAMPIRE!
COME BACK NOW AND WE WON'T EVEN TATTLE THAT YOU RAN AWAY!
AMADEUS CHO. VAMPIRE.
'CUZ THEN FISK WOULD HAVE ALL OUR FANGS.
STUPID LITTLE $#&% JUST RAN RIGHT INTO A DEAD--
FRIEND...
SHLLK

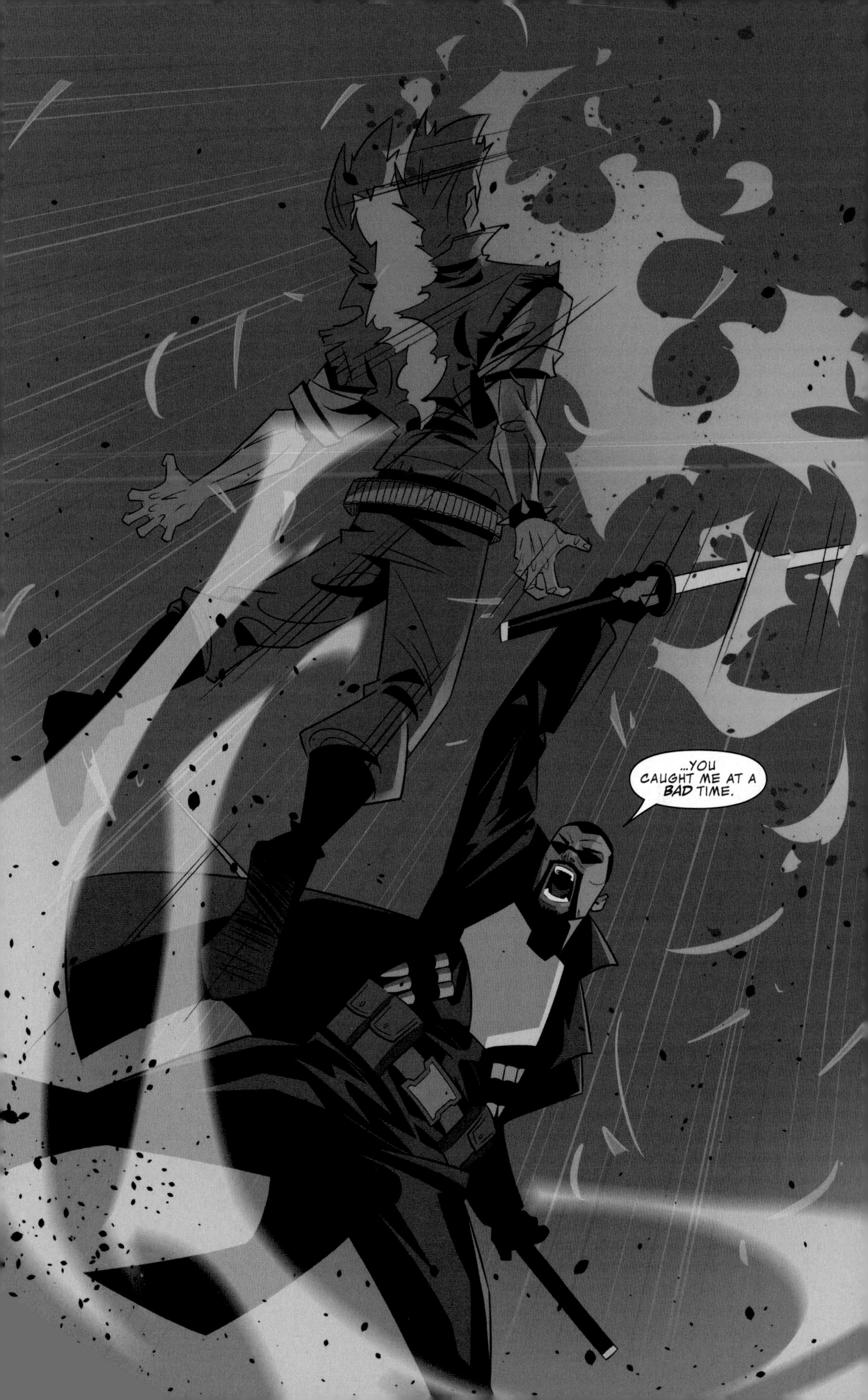
...YOU CAUGHT ME AT A BAD TIME.

Two years ago, vampire terrorist Deacon Frost offered himself as host to the ancient Blood Demon **La Magra** -- annihilating himself and unleashing **the V-Wave.**

Billions of humans instantly became vampires. The millions turned under daylight **burned.**

Superhumans were transformed -- becoming either human or vampire, by random chance or unholy design.

The **A.I.s** went blank. The **Gods** of men were banished. No more mutants. Or Inhumans. Or Eternals. There are now only two races on this earth: The fanged and the food.

And there's only one man who can walk in both worlds…and save what's left of ours. Put your last drop of hope in…

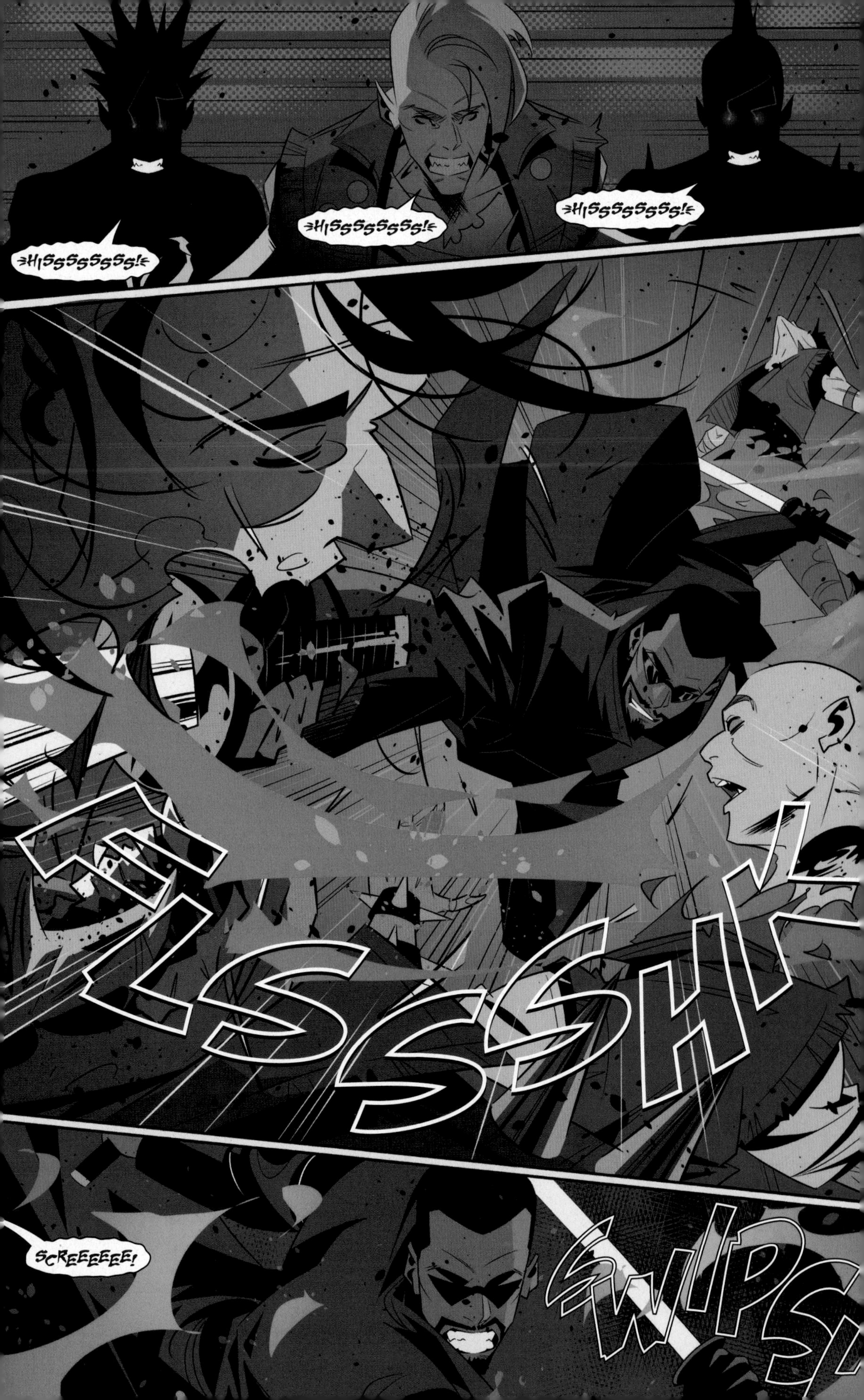
HISSSSSSS!
HISSSSSSS!
HISSSSSSS!
FLSSSHK
SCREEEEEE!
SWIPSL

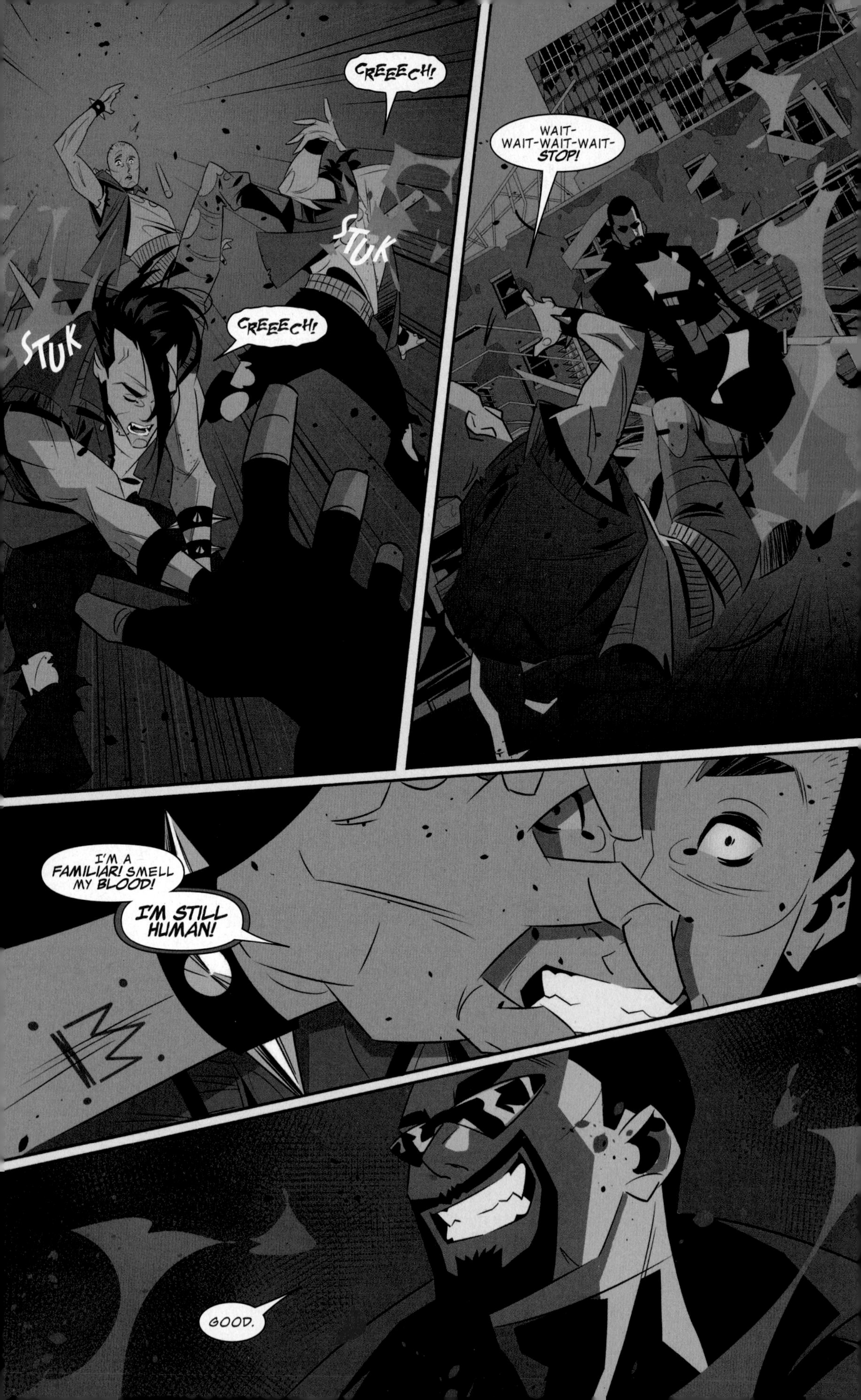
CREEECH!
STUK
STUK
CREEECH!
WAIT-
WAIT-WAIT-WAIT-
STOP!
I'M A
FAMILIAR! SMELL
MY BLOOD!
I'M STILL
HUMAN!
GOOD.

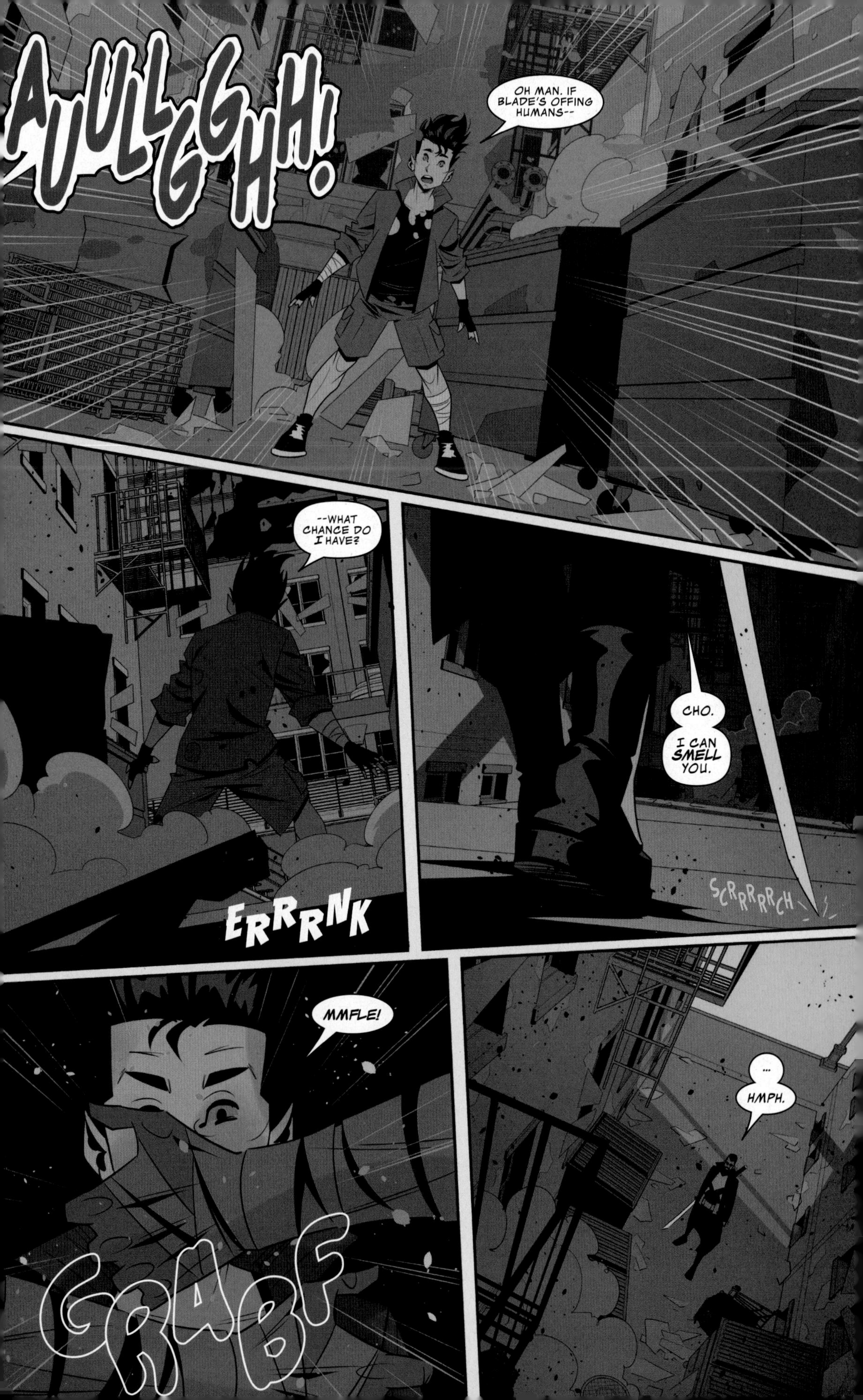
AUULLGGHH!
OH MAN. IF BLADE'S OFFING HUMANS--
--WHAT CHANCE DO I HAVE?
ERRRNK
CHO.
I CAN SMELL YOU.
SCRRRRRCH
MMFLE!
GRABF
...
HMPH.

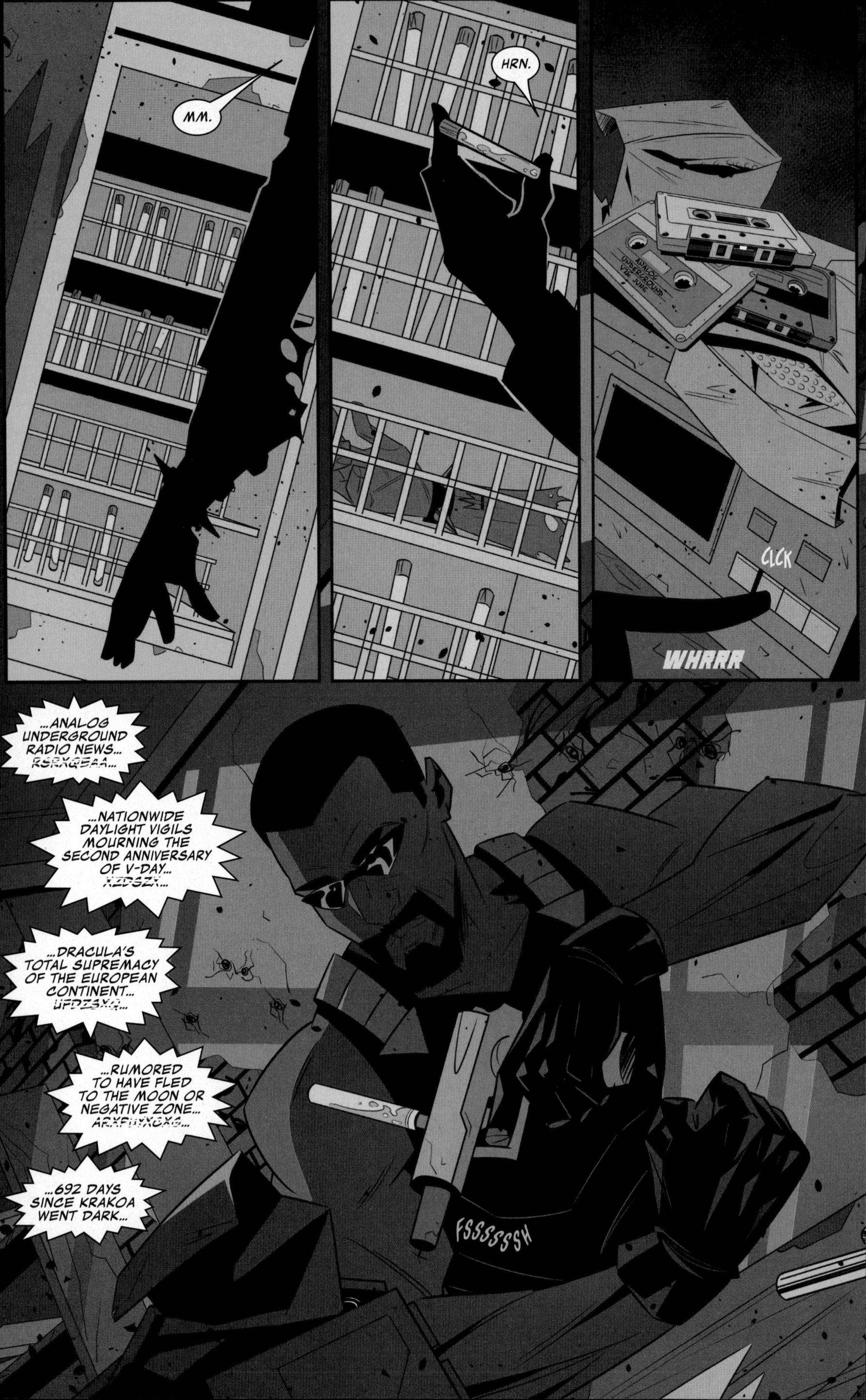
MM.
HRN.
ANALOG
UNDERGROUND
CLCK
WHRRR
...ANALOG UNDERGROUND RADIO NEWS... RSRXQSAA...
...NATIONWIDE DAYLIGHT VIGILS MOURNING THE SECOND ANNIVERSARY OF V-DAY... XZDSZX...
...DRACULA'S TOTAL SUPREMACY OF THE EUROPEAN CONTINENT...
...RUMORED TO HAVE FLED TO THE MOON OR NEGATIVE ZONE...
...692 DAYS SINCE KRAKOA WENT DARK...
FSSSSSSH

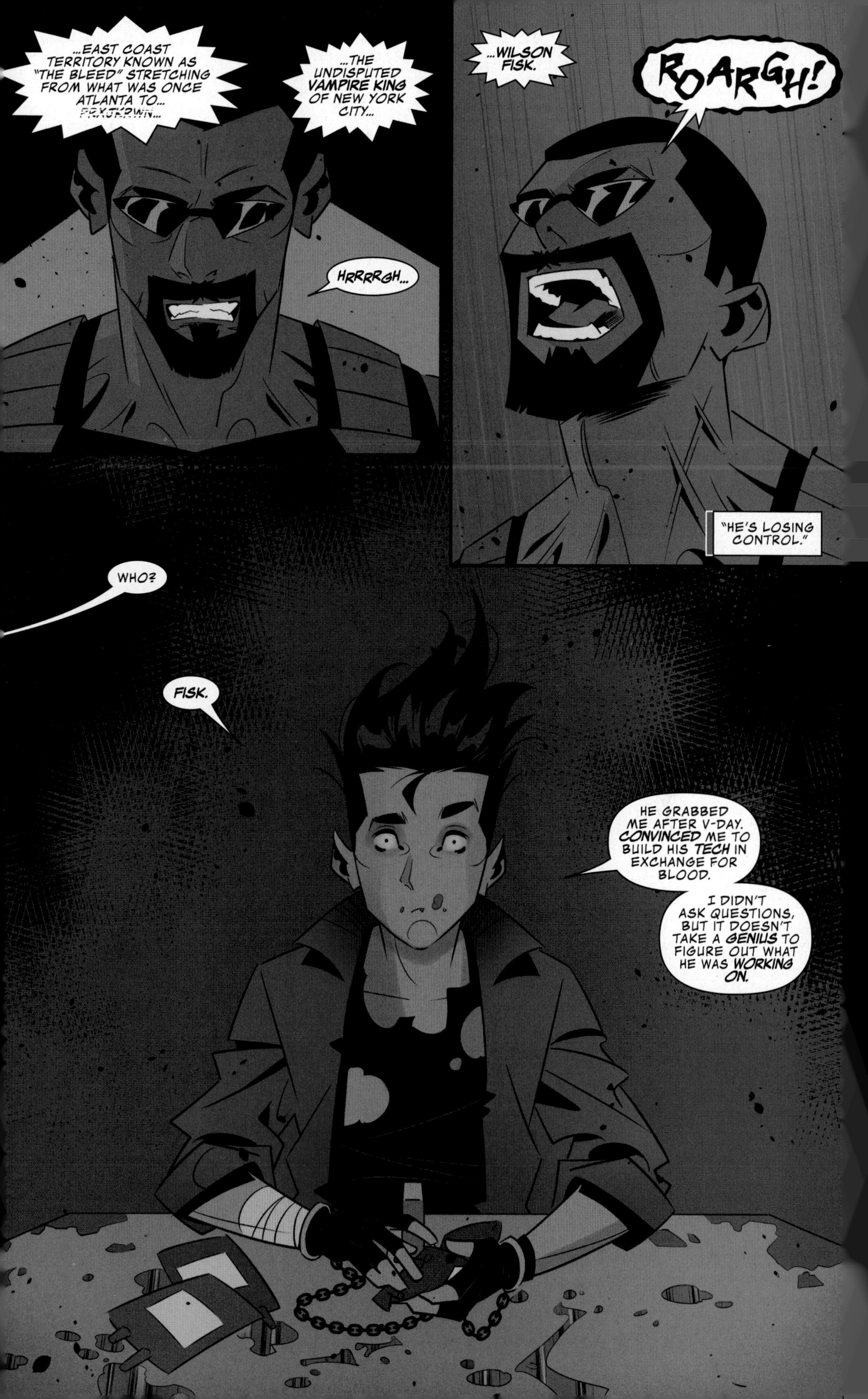
...EAST COAST TERRITORY KNOWN AS "THE BLEED" STRETCHING FROM WHAT WAS ONCE ATLANTA TO... PRXJKRWN...
...THE UNDISPUTED VAMPIRE KING OF NEW YORK CITY...
HRRRRGH...
...WILSON FISK.
ROARGH!
"HE'S LOSING CONTROL."
WHO?
FISK.
HE GRABBED ME AFTER V-DAY. CONVINCED ME TO BUILD HIS TECH IN EXCHANGE FOR BLOOD.
I DIDN'T ASK QUESTIONS, BUT IT DOESN'T TAKE A GENIUS TO FIGURE OUT WHAT HE WAS WORKING ON.

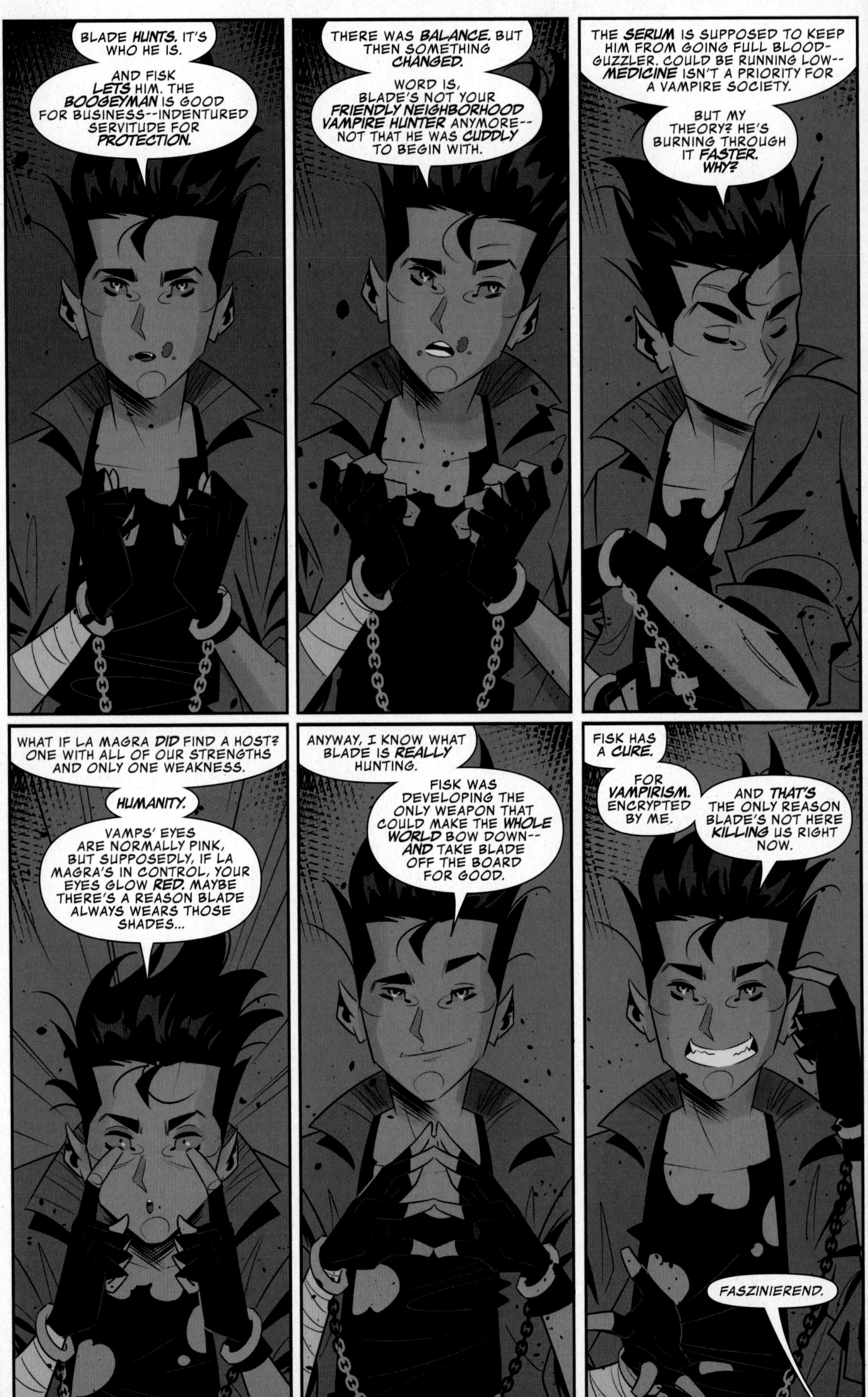
BLADE HUNTS. IT'S WHO HE IS.
AND FISK LETS HIM. THE BOOGEYMAN IS GOOD FOR BUSINESS--INDENTURED SERVITUDE FOR PROTECTION.
THERE WAS BALANCE. BUT THEN SOMETHING CHANGED.
WORD IS, BLADE'S NOT YOUR FRIENDLY NEIGHBORHOOD VAMPIRE HUNTER ANYMORE--NOT THAT HE WAS CUDDLY TO BEGIN WITH.
THE SERUM IS SUPPOSED TO KEEP HIM FROM GOING FULL BLOOD-GUZZLER. COULD BE RUNNING LOW--MEDICINE ISN'T A PRIORITY FOR A VAMPIRE SOCIETY.
BUT MY THEORY? HE'S BURNING THROUGH IT FASTER. WHY?
WHAT IF LA MAGRA DID FIND A HOST? ONE WITH ALL OF OUR STRENGTHS AND ONLY ONE WEAKNESS.
HUMANITY.
VAMPS' EYES ARE NORMALLY PINK, BUT SUPPOSEDLY, IF LA MAGRA'S IN CONTROL, YOUR EYES GLOW RED. MAYBE THERE'S A REASON BLADE ALWAYS WEARS THOSE SHADES...
ANYWAY, I KNOW WHAT BLADE IS REALLY HUNTING.
FISK WAS DEVELOPING THE ONLY WEAPON THAT COULD MAKE THE WHOLE WORLD BOW DOWN--AND TAKE BLADE OFF THE BOARD FOR GOOD.
FISK HAS A CURE.
FOR VAMPIRISM. ENCRYPTED BY ME.
AND THAT'S THE ONLY REASON BLADE'S NOT HERE KILLING US RIGHT NOW.
FASZINIEREND.

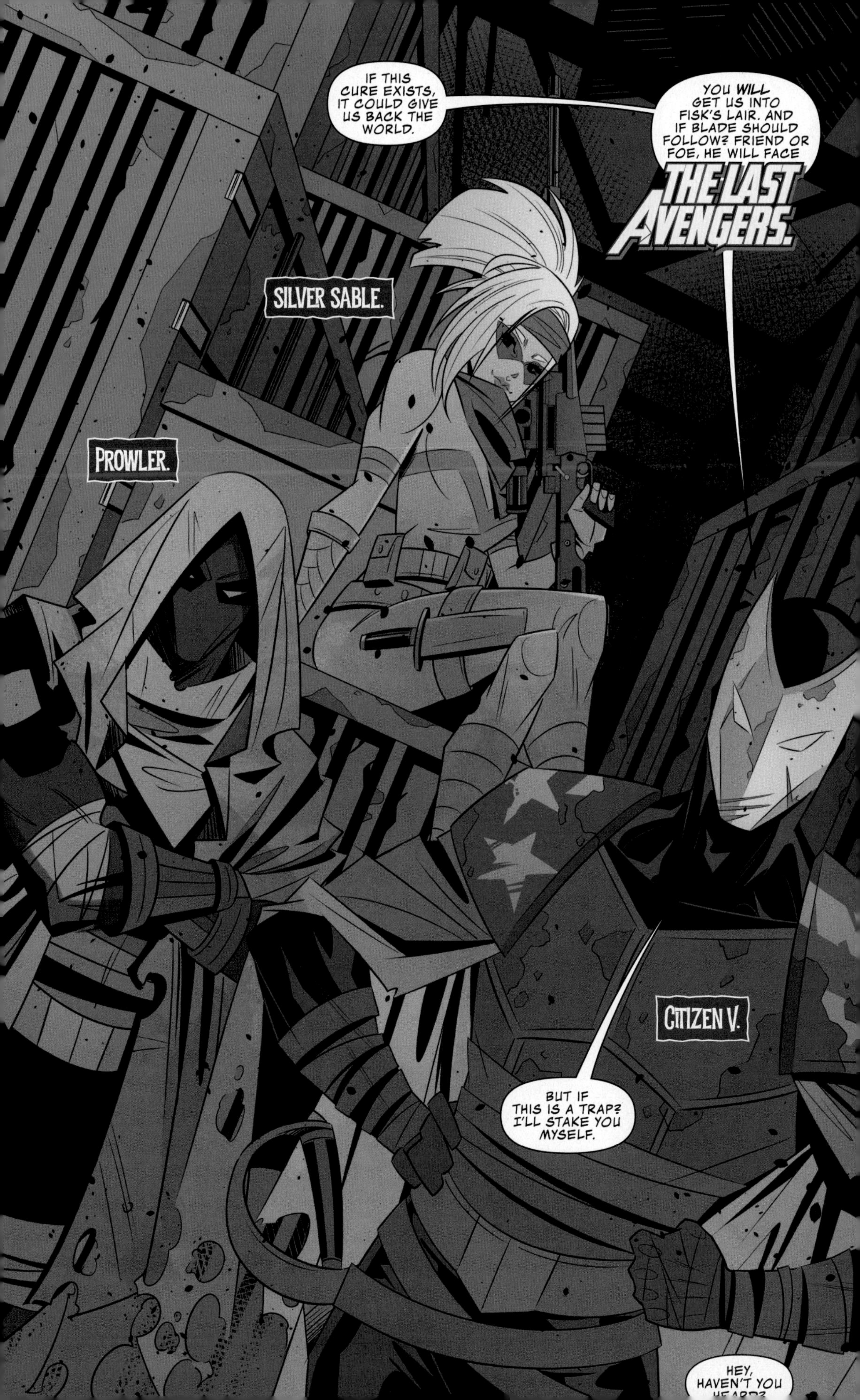
IF THIS CURE EXISTS, IT COULD GIVE US BACK THE WORLD.
YOU WILL GET US INTO FISK'S LAIR. AND IF BLADE SHOULD FOLLOW? FRIEND OR FOE, HE WILL FACE
THE LAST AVENGERS.
SILVER SABLE.
PROWLER.
CITIZEN V.
BUT IF THIS IS A TRAP? I'LL STAKE YOU MYSELF.
HEY, HAVEN'T YOU

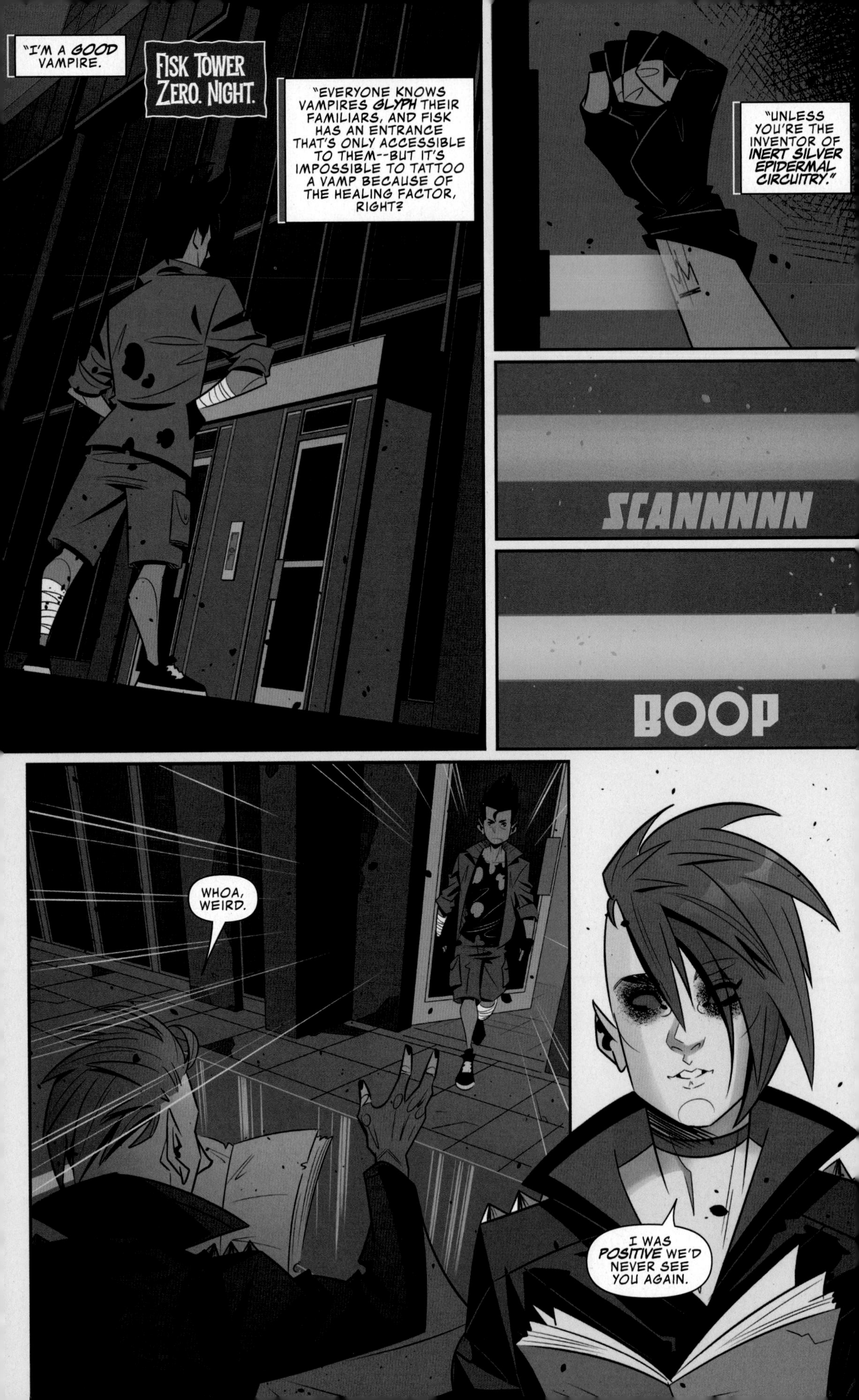
"I'M A GOOD VAMPIRE.
FISK TOWER ZERO. NIGHT.
"EVERYONE KNOWS VAMPIRES GLYPH THEIR FAMILIARS, AND FISK HAS AN ENTRANCE THAT'S ONLY ACCESSIBLE TO THEM--BUT IT'S IMPOSSIBLE TO TATTOO A VAMP BECAUSE OF THE HEALING FACTOR, RIGHT?
"UNLESS YOU'RE THE INVENTOR OF INERT SILVER EPIDERMAL CIRCUITRY."
SCANNNNN
BOOP
WHOA, WEIRD.
I WAS POSITIVE WE'D NEVER SEE YOU AGAIN.

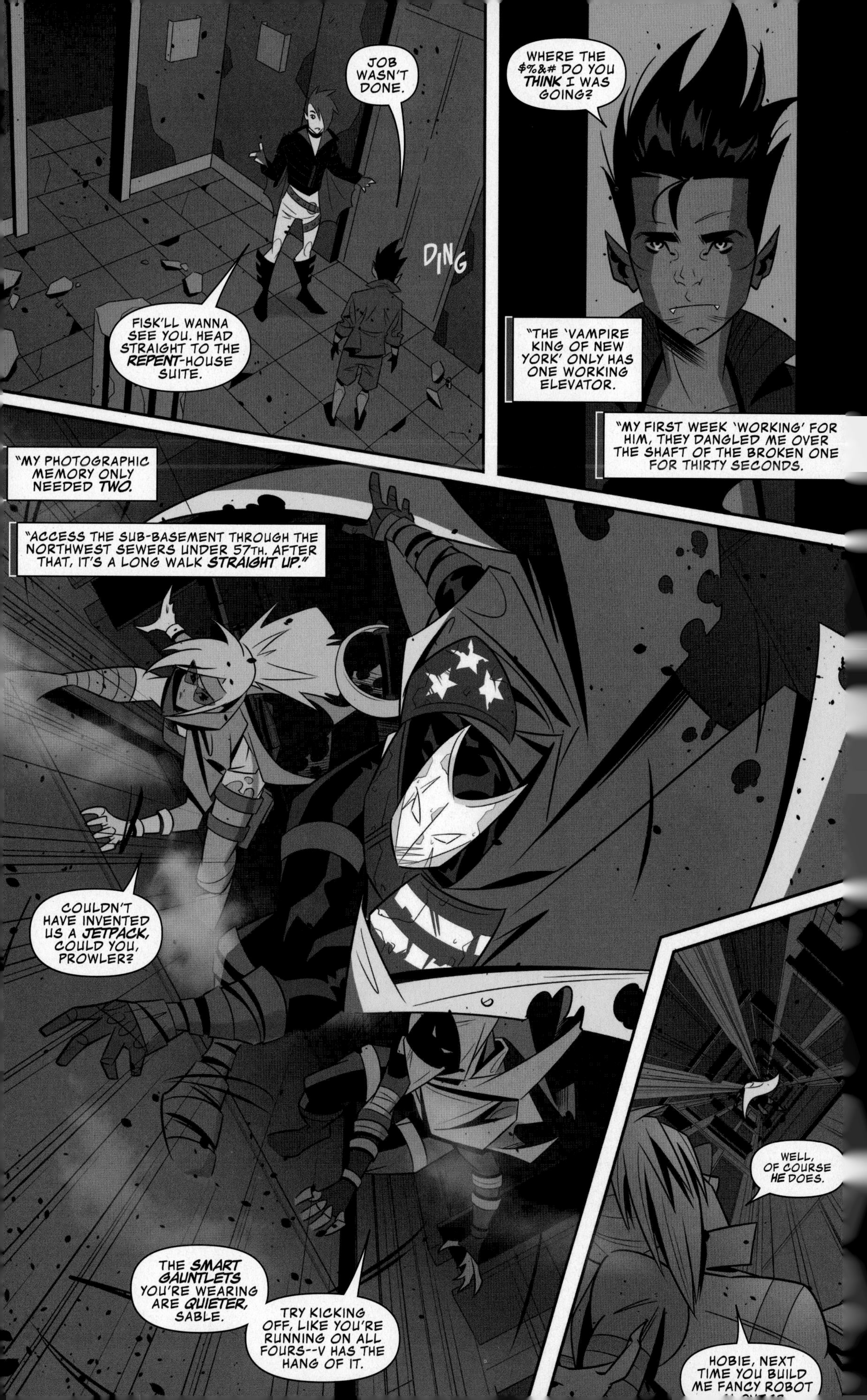

JOB WASN'T DONE.
FISK'LL WANNA SEE YOU. HEAD STRAIGHT TO THE REPENT-HOUSE SUITE.
DING
WHERE THE $%&# DO YOU THINK I WAS GOING?
"THE 'VAMPIRE KING OF NEW YORK' ONLY HAS ONE WORKING ELEVATOR.
"MY FIRST WEEK 'WORKING' FOR HIM, THEY DANGLED ME OVER THE SHAFT OF THE BROKEN ONE FOR THIRTY SECONDS.
"MY PHOTOGRAPHIC MEMORY ONLY NEEDED TWO.
"ACCESS THE SUB-BASEMENT THROUGH THE NORTHWEST SEWERS UNDER 57TH. AFTER THAT, IT'S A LONG WALK STRAIGHT UP."
COULDN'T HAVE INVENTED US A JETPACK, COULD YOU, PROWLER?
THE SMART GAUNTLETS YOU'RE WEARING ARE QUIETER, SABLE.
TRY KICKING OFF, LIKE YOU'RE RUNNING ON ALL FOURS--V HAS THE HANG OF IT.
WELL, OF COURSE HE DOES.
HOBIE, NEXT TIME YOU BUILD ME FANCY ROBOT

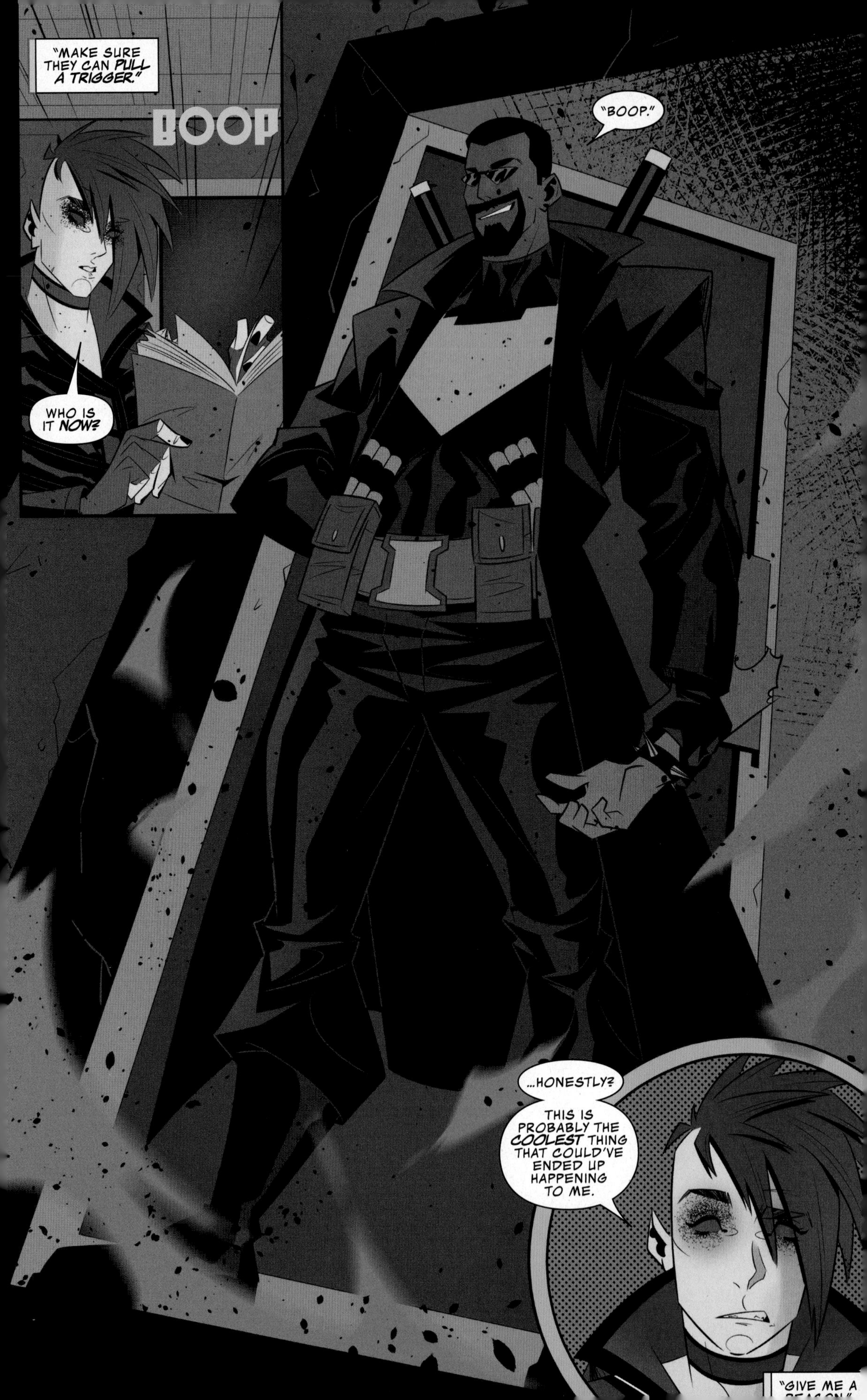
"MAKE SURE THEY CAN PULL A TRIGGER."
BOOP
WHO IS IT NOW?
"BOOP."
...HONESTLY?
THIS IS PROBABLY THE COOLEST THING THAT COULD'VE ENDED UP HAPPENING TO ME.
"GIVE ME A

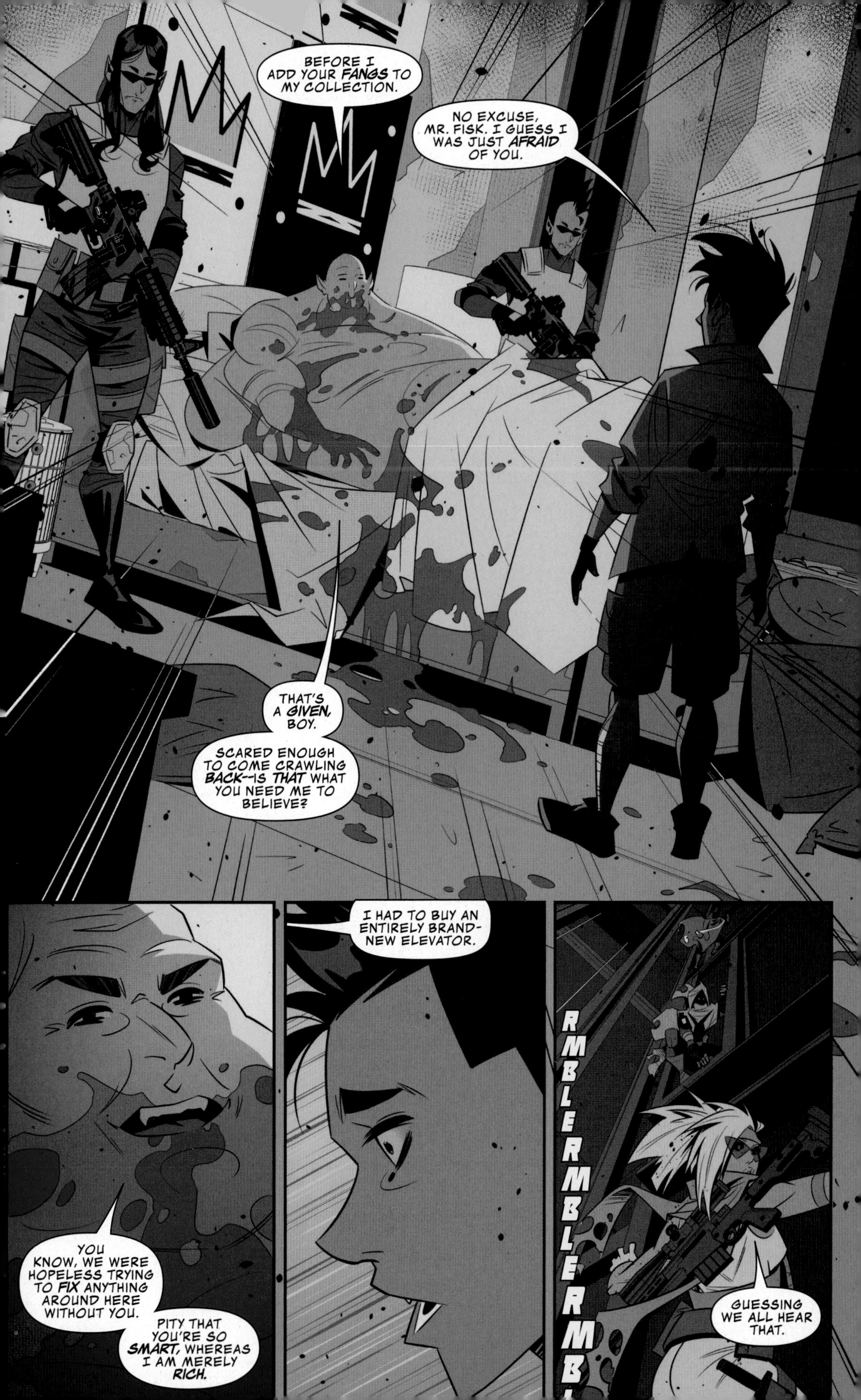
BEFORE I ADD YOUR FANGS TO MY COLLECTION.
NO EXCUSE, MR. FISK. I GUESS I WAS JUST AFRAID OF YOU.
THAT'S A GIVEN, BOY.
SCARED ENOUGH TO COME CRAWLING BACK--IS THAT WHAT YOU NEED ME TO BELIEVE?
YOU KNOW, WE WERE HOPELESS TRYING TO FIX ANYTHING AROUND HERE WITHOUT YOU.
PITY THAT YOU'RE SO SMART, WHEREAS I AM MERELY RICH.
I HAD TO BUY AN ENTIRELY BRAND-NEW ELEVATOR.
RMBLERMBLERMBL
GUESSING WE ALL HEAR THAT.

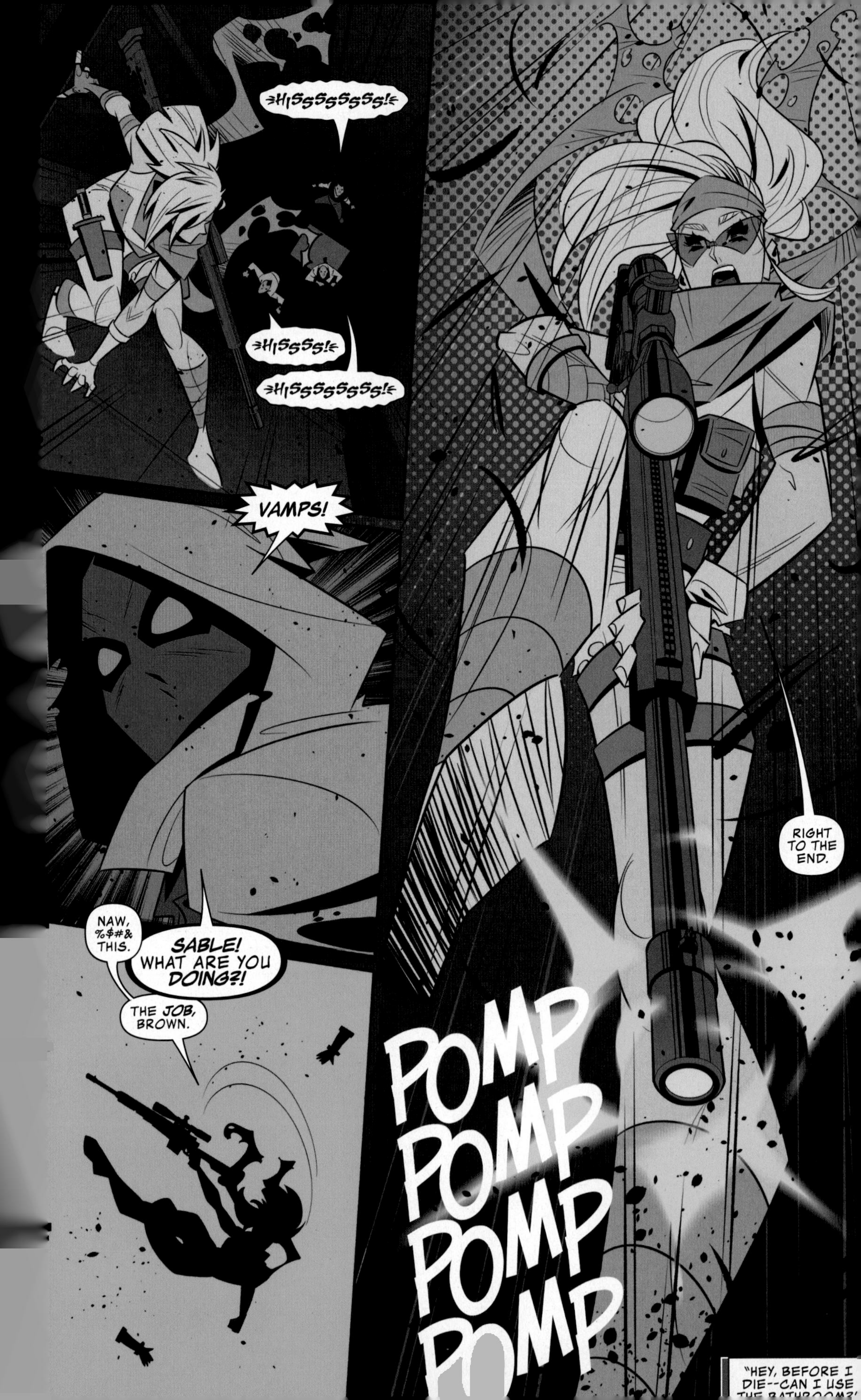

HISSSSSSSS!
HISSSS!
HISSSSSSSS!
VAMPS!
SABLE! WHAT ARE YOU DOING?!
NAW, %$#& THIS.
THE JOB, BROWN.
RIGHT TO THE END.
POMP POMP POMP POMP POMP
"HEY, BEFORE I DIE--CAN I USE

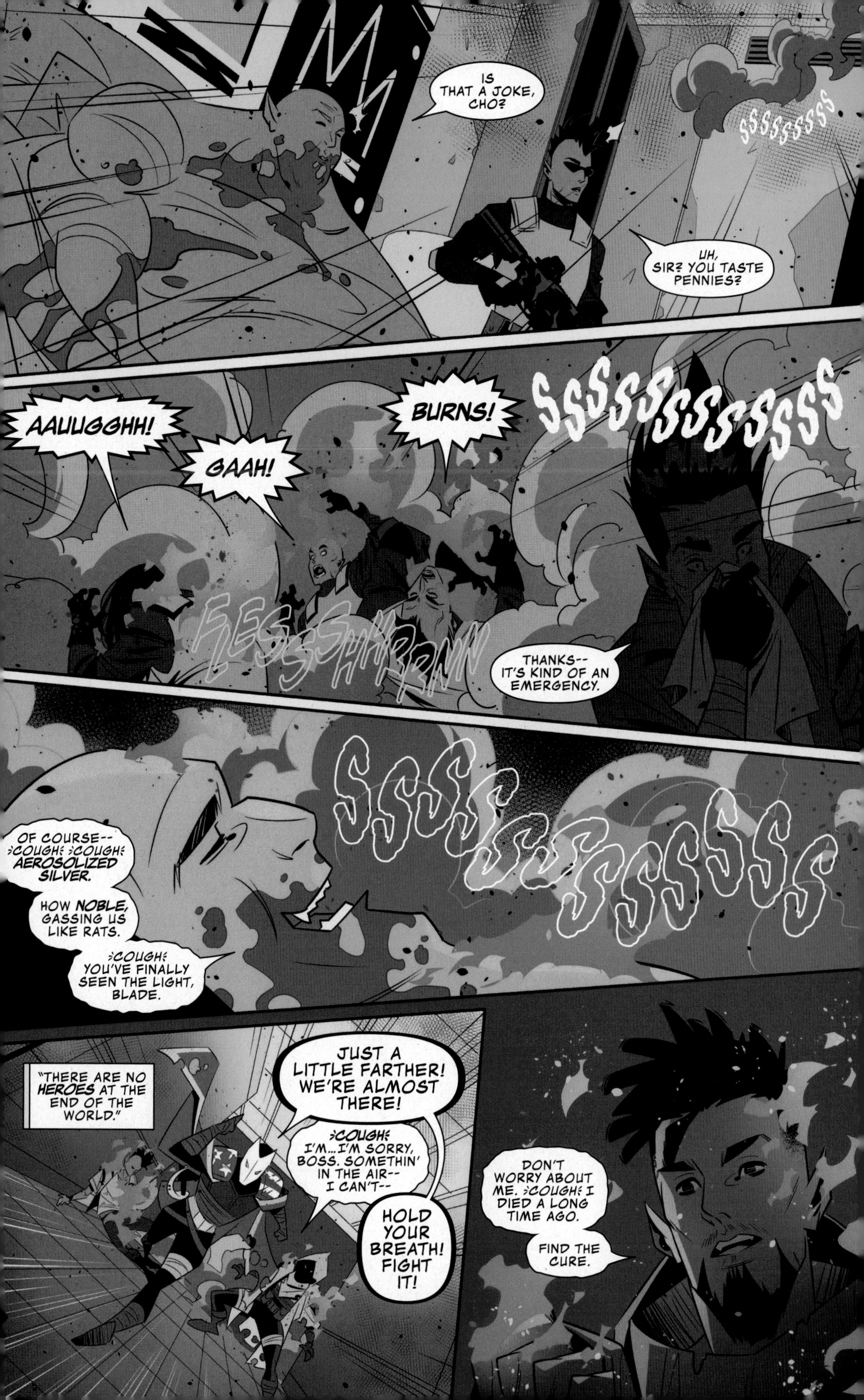

IS THAT A JOKE, CHO?
SSSSSSSS
UH, SIR? YOU TASTE PENNIES?
AAUUGGHH!
GAAH!
BURNS!
SSSSSSSSSSSSS
THANKS-- IT'S KIND OF AN EMERGENCY.
OF COURSE-- ›COUGH‹ ›COUGH‹ AEROSOLIZED SILVER.
HOW NOBLE, GASSING US LIKE RATS.
›COUGH‹ YOU'VE FINALLY SEEN THE LIGHT, BLADE.
"THERE ARE NO HEROES AT THE END OF THE WORLD."
JUST A LITTLE FARTHER! WE'RE ALMOST THERE!
›COUGH‹ I'M...I'M SORRY, BOSS. SOMETHIN' IN THE AIR-- I CAN'T--
HOLD YOUR BREATH! FIGHT IT!
DON'T WORRY ABOUT ME. ›COUGH‹ I DIED A LONG TIME AGO.
FIND THE CURE.

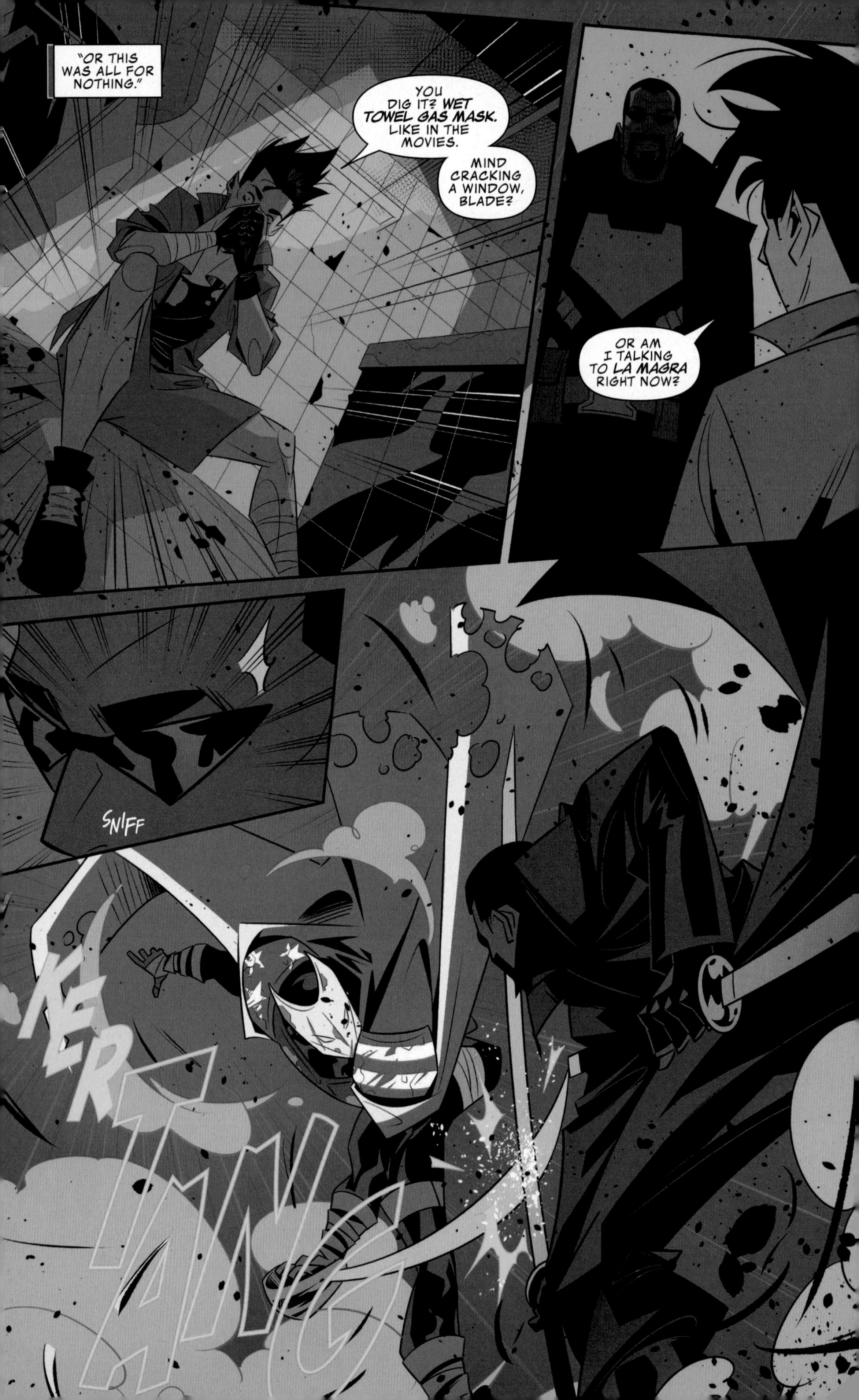
"OR THIS WAS ALL FOR NOTHING."
YOU DIG IT? WET TOWEL GAS MASK. LIKE IN THE MOVIES.
MIND CRACKING A WINDOW, BLADE?
OR AM I TALKING TO LA MAGRA RIGHT NOW?
SNIFF
KERTANG

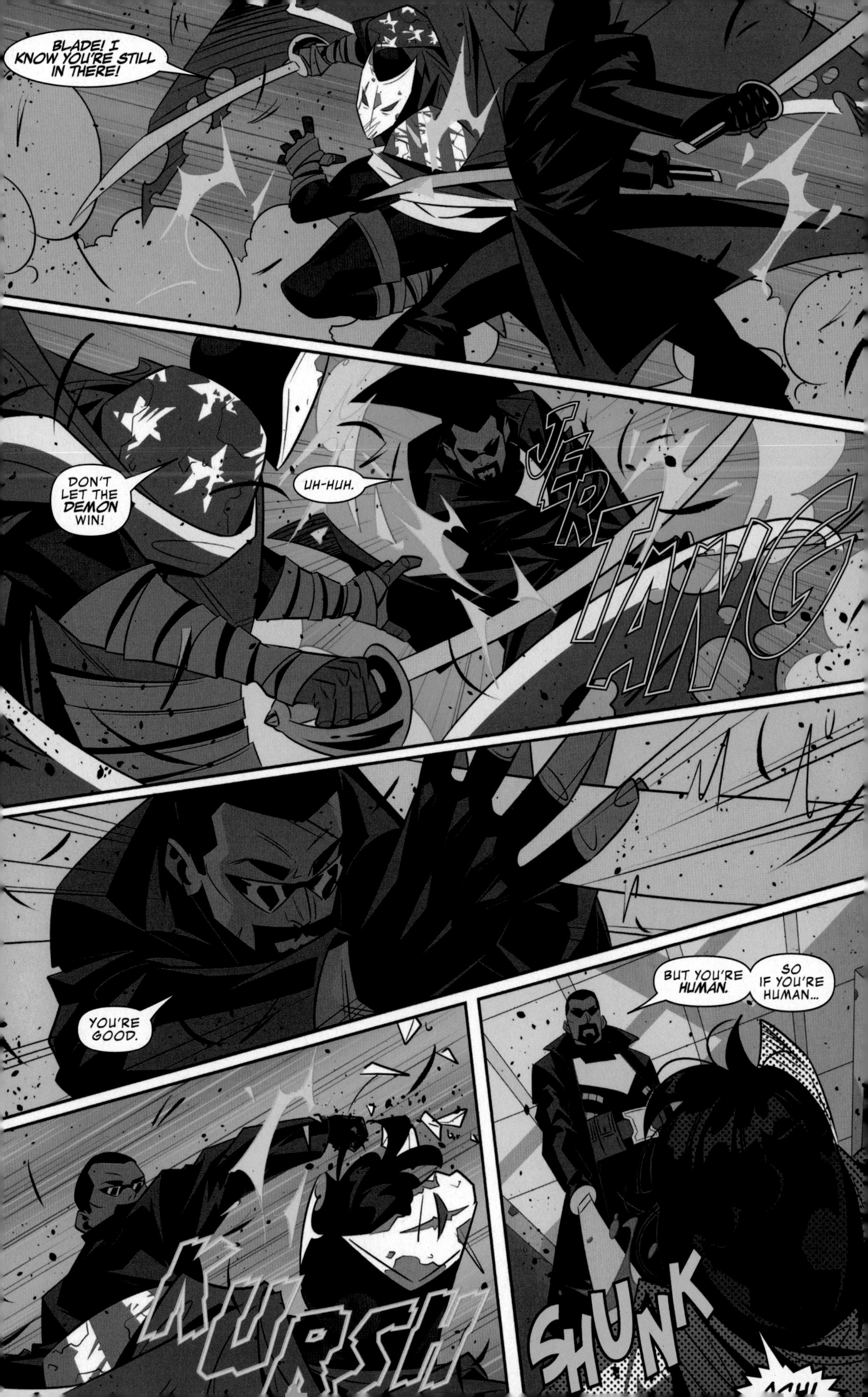
BLADE! I KNOW YOU'RE STILL IN THERE!
DON'T LET THE DEMON WIN!
UH-HUH.
JERTANG
YOU'RE GOOD.
BUT YOU'RE HUMAN.
SO IF YOU'RE HUMAN...
SHUNK

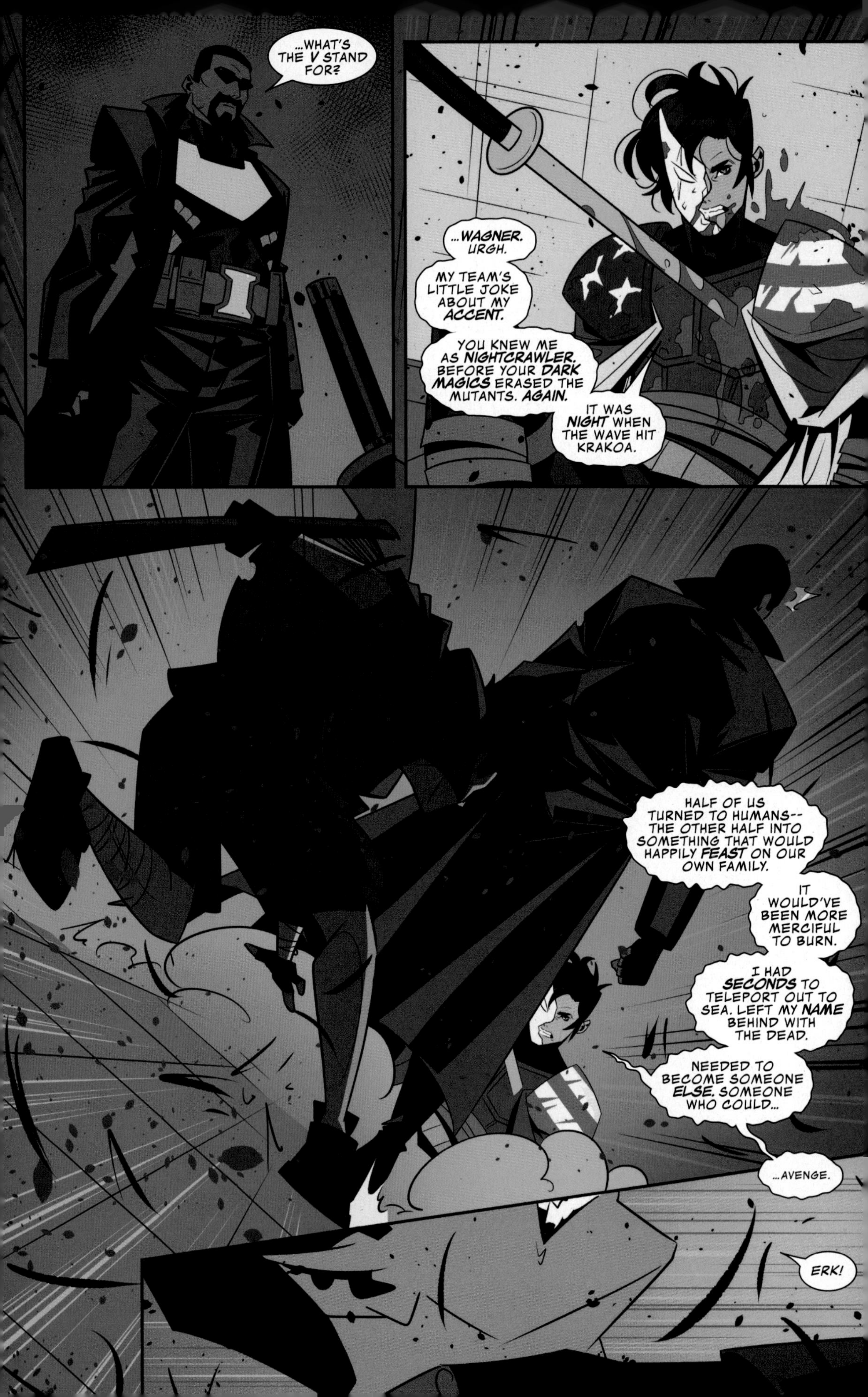
...WHAT'S THE V STAND FOR?
...WAGNER. URGH.
MY TEAM'S LITTLE JOKE ABOUT MY ACCENT.
YOU KNEW ME AS NIGHTCRAWLER. BEFORE YOUR DARK MAGICS ERASED THE MUTANTS. AGAIN.
IT WAS NIGHT WHEN THE WAVE HIT KRAKOA.
HALF OF US TURNED TO HUMANS-- THE OTHER HALF INTO SOMETHING THAT WOULD HAPPILY FEAST ON OUR OWN FAMILY.
IT WOULD'VE BEEN MORE MERCIFUL TO BURN.
I HAD SECONDS TO TELEPORT OUT TO SEA. LEFT MY NAME BEHIND WITH THE DEAD.
NEEDED TO BECOME SOMEONE ELSE. SOMEONE WHO COULD...
...AVENGE.
ERK!

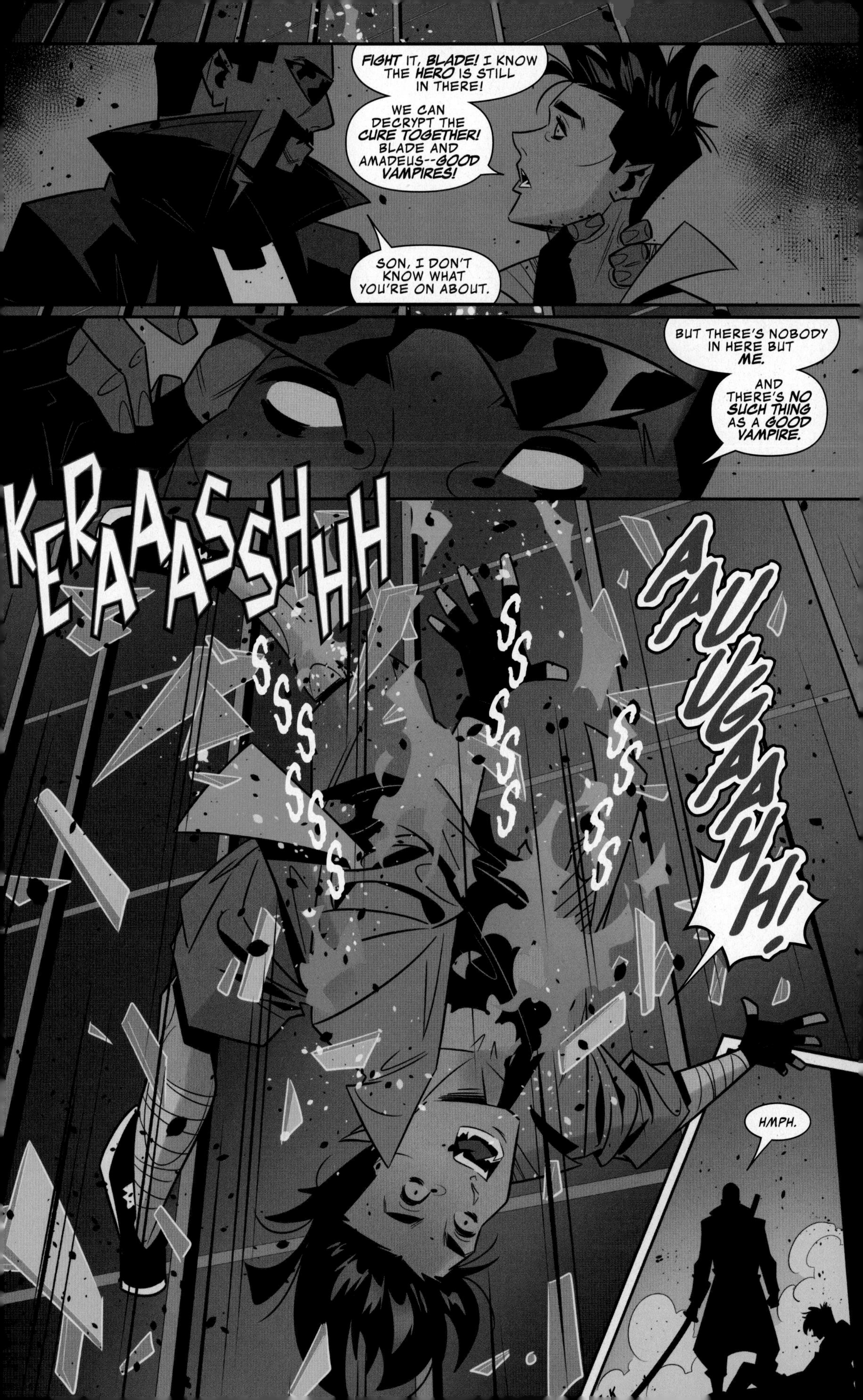
FIGHT IT, BLADE! I KNOW THE HERO IS STILL IN THERE!
WE CAN DECRYPT THE CURE TOGETHER! BLADE AND AMADEUS--GOOD VAMPIRES!
SON, I DON'T KNOW WHAT YOU'RE ON ABOUT.
BUT THERE'S NOBODY IN HERE BUT ME.
AND THERE'S NO SUCH THING AS A GOOD VAMPIRE.
KERAAASSHHH
SSSSSS
SSSS
SSSSS
AAUUGAAHH!
HMPH.

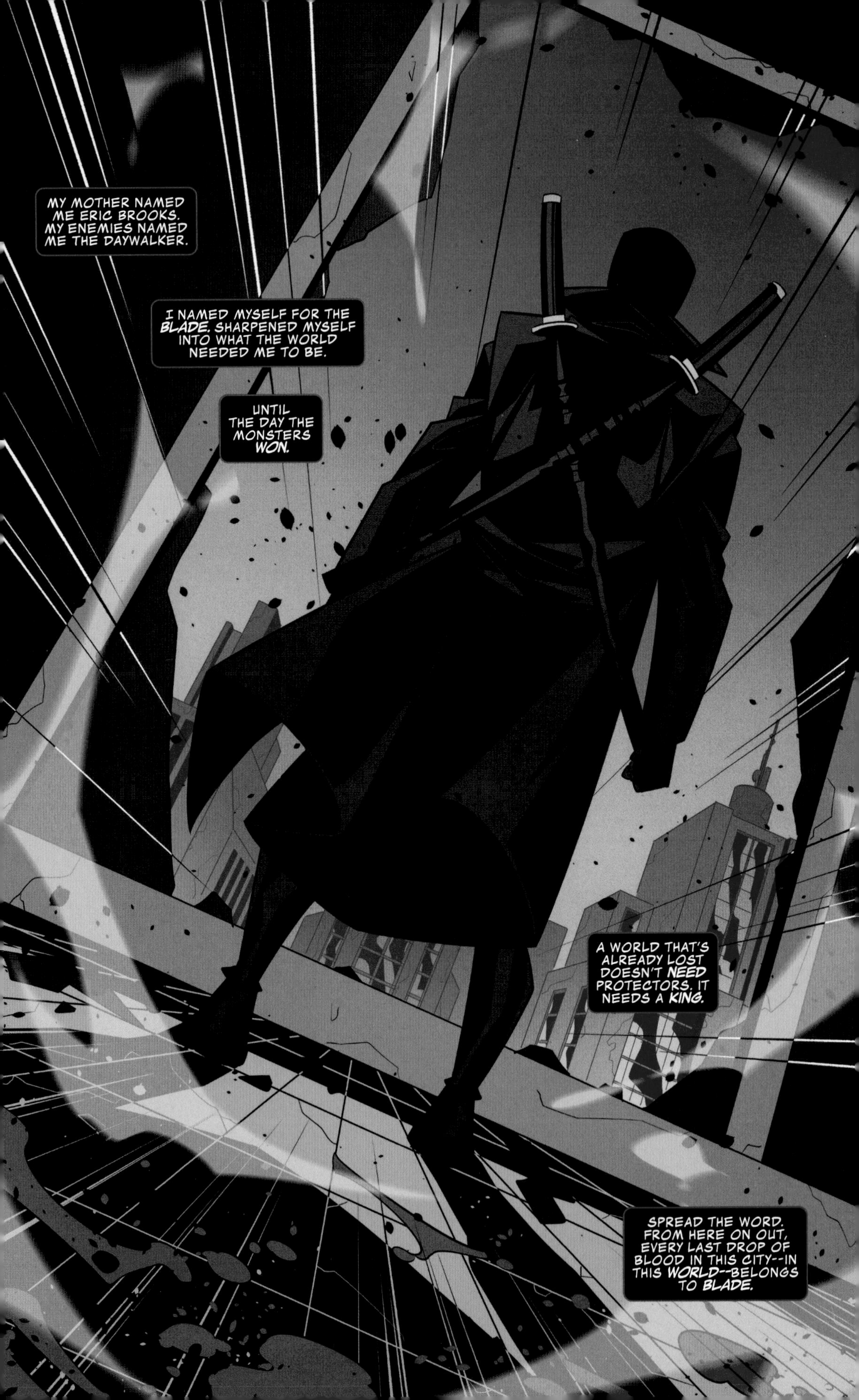

MY MOTHER NAMED ME ERIC BROOKS. MY ENEMIES NAMED ME THE DAYWALKER.
I NAMED MYSELF FOR THE *BLADE.* SHARPENED MYSELF INTO WHAT THE WORLD NEEDED ME TO BE.
UNTIL THE DAY THE MONSTERS *WON.*
A WORLD THAT'S ALREADY LOST DOESN'T **NEED** PROTECTORS. IT NEEDS A **KING.**
SPREAD THE WORD. FROM HERE ON OUT, EVERY LAST DROP OF BLOOD IN THIS CITY--IN THIS *WORLD*--BELONGS TO *BLADE.*

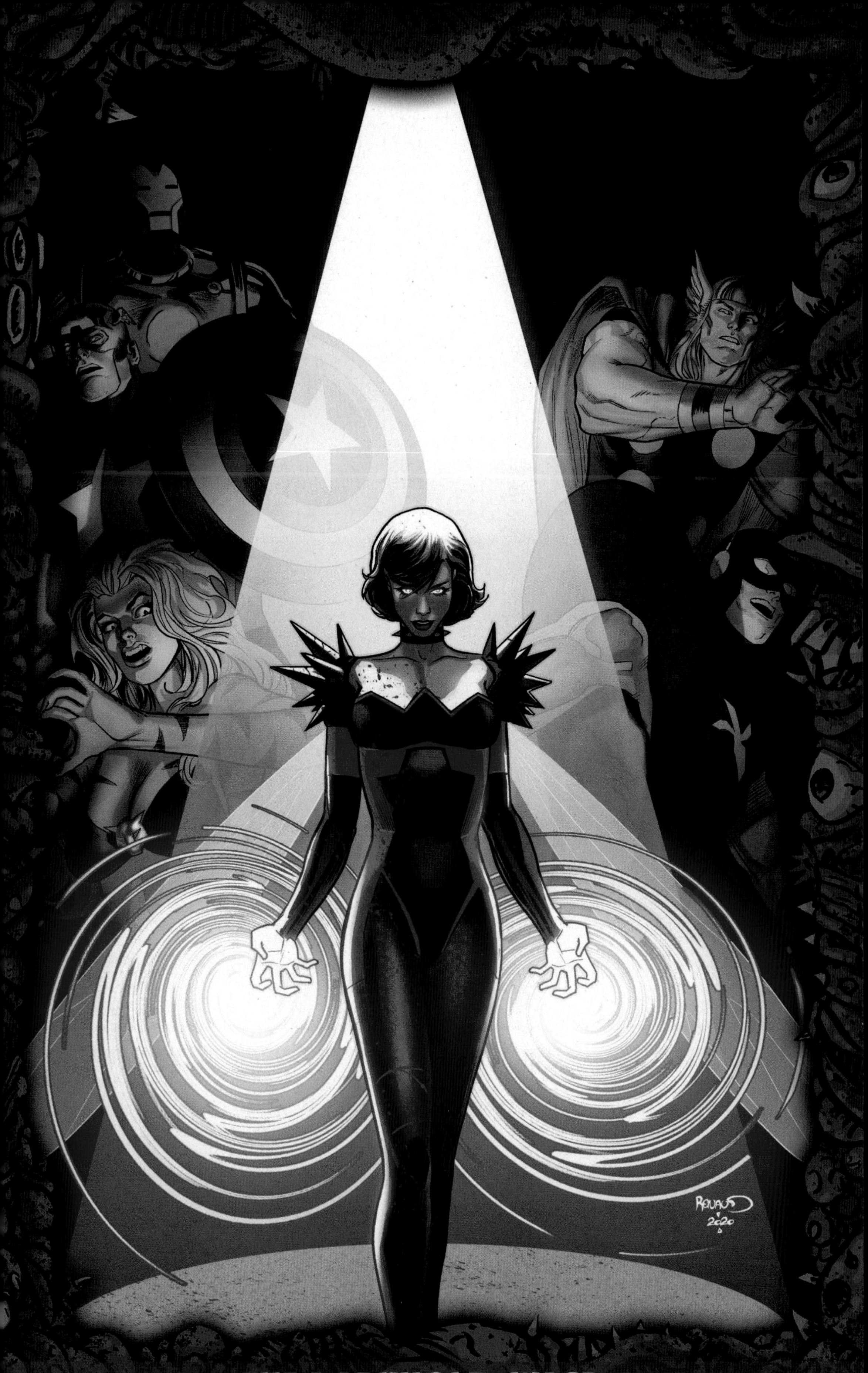

RENAUD
2020

THE DARKHOLD: WASP

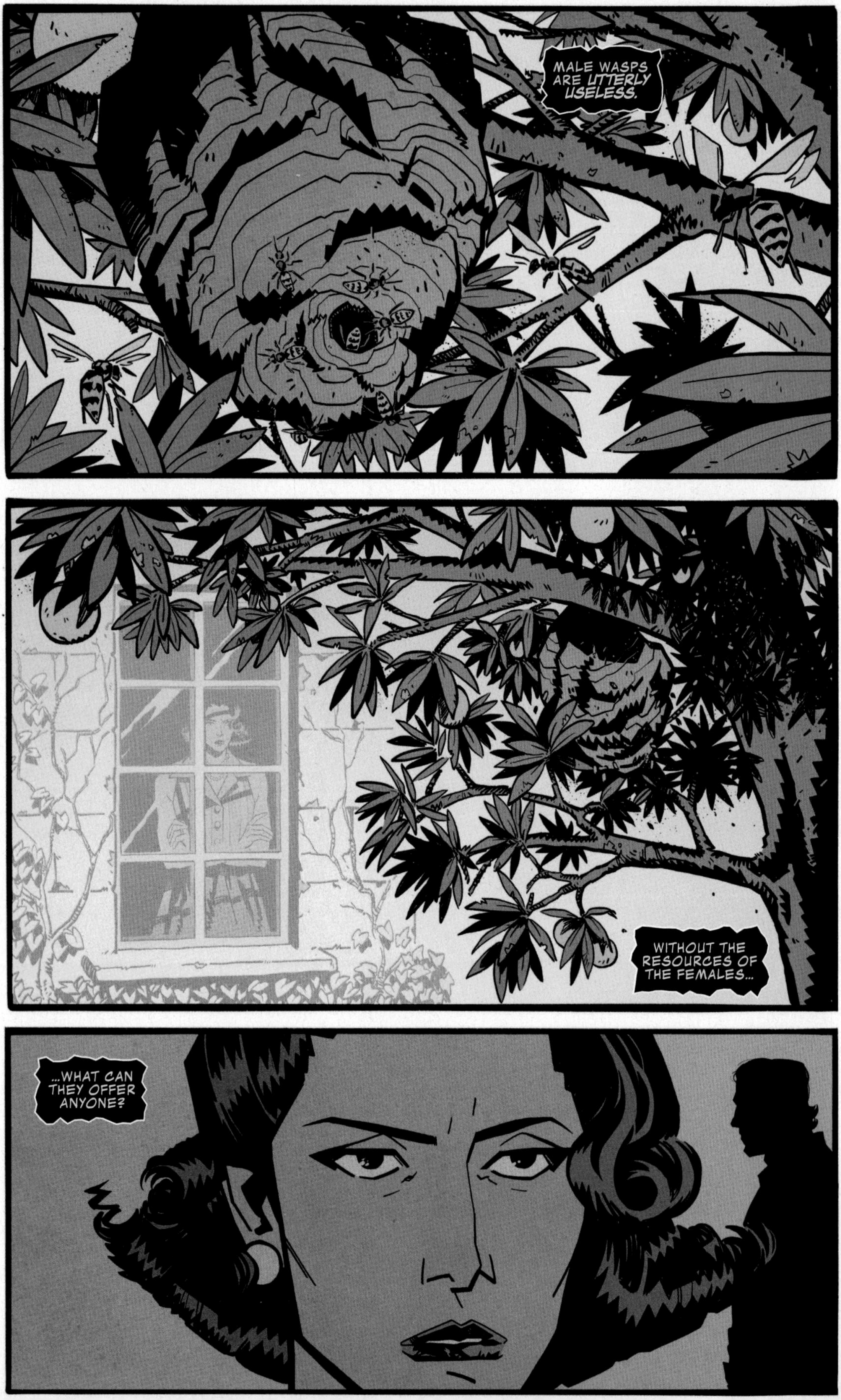
MALE WASPS ARE UTTERLY USELESS.
WITHOUT THE RESOURCES OF THE FEMALES...
...WHAT CAN THEY OFFER ANYONE?

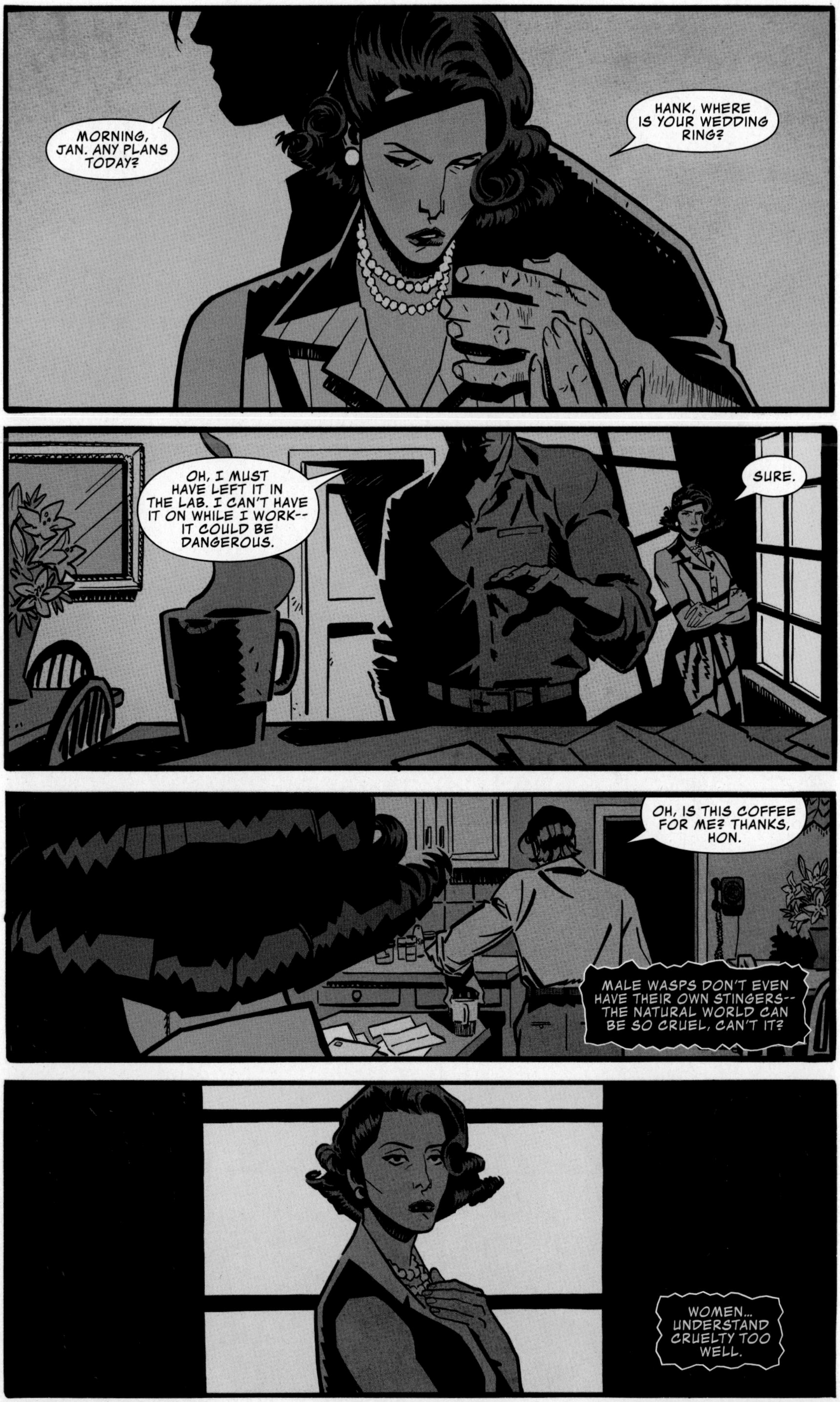
MORNING, JAN. ANY PLANS TODAY?
HANK, WHERE IS YOUR WEDDING RING?
OH, I MUST HAVE LEFT IT IN THE LAB. I CAN'T HAVE IT ON WHILE I WORK-- IT COULD BE DANGEROUS.
SURE.
OH, IS THIS COFFEE FOR ME? THANKS, HON.
MALE WASPS DON'T EVEN HAVE THEIR OWN STINGERS-- THE NATURAL WORLD CAN BE SO CRUEL, CAN'T IT?
WOMEN... UNDERSTAND CRUELTY TOO WELL.

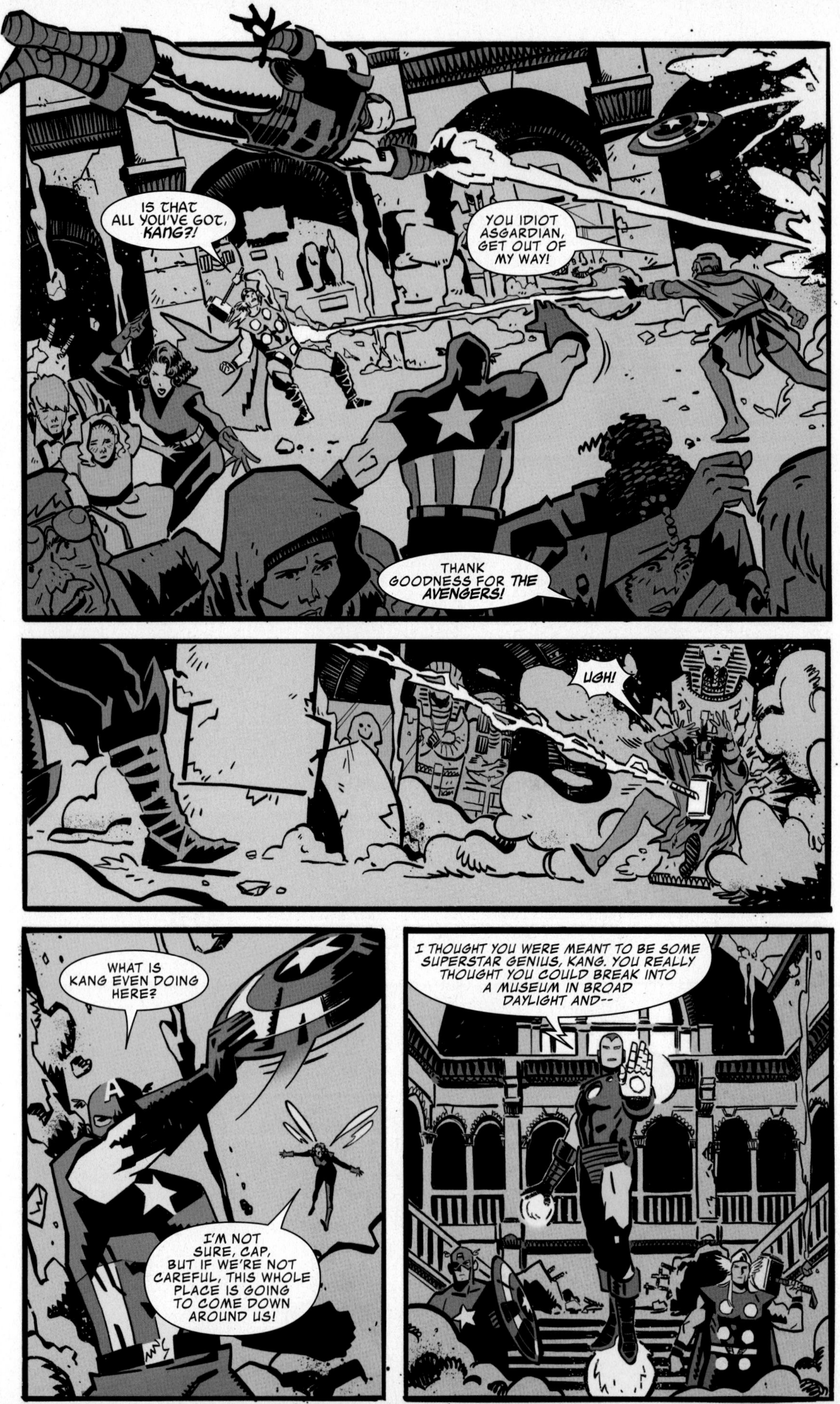
IS THAT ALL YOU'VE GOT, KANG?!
YOU IDIOT ASGARDIAN, GET OUT OF MY WAY!
THANK GOODNESS FOR THE AVENGERS!
UGH!
WHAT IS KANG EVEN DOING HERE?
I'M NOT SURE, CAP, BUT IF WE'RE NOT CAREFUL, THIS WHOLE PLACE IS GOING TO COME DOWN AROUND US!
I THOUGHT YOU WERE MEANT TO BE SOME SUPERSTAR GENIUS, KANG. YOU REALLY THOUGHT YOU COULD BREAK INTO A MUSEUM IN BROAD DAYLIGHT AND--

WHAT? MY SUIT--

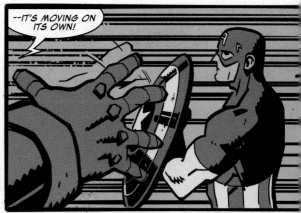

--IT'S MOVING ON ITS OWN!

NO!

ARGH!

UNH!

HOW ARE YOU--?! STOP!

KRAK

I ALWAYS *LOVE* PLAYING WITH IRON MAN'S LITTLE TOYS. HE FORGETS I CAN CONTROL EVEN *HIS* GREATEST INVENTIONS.

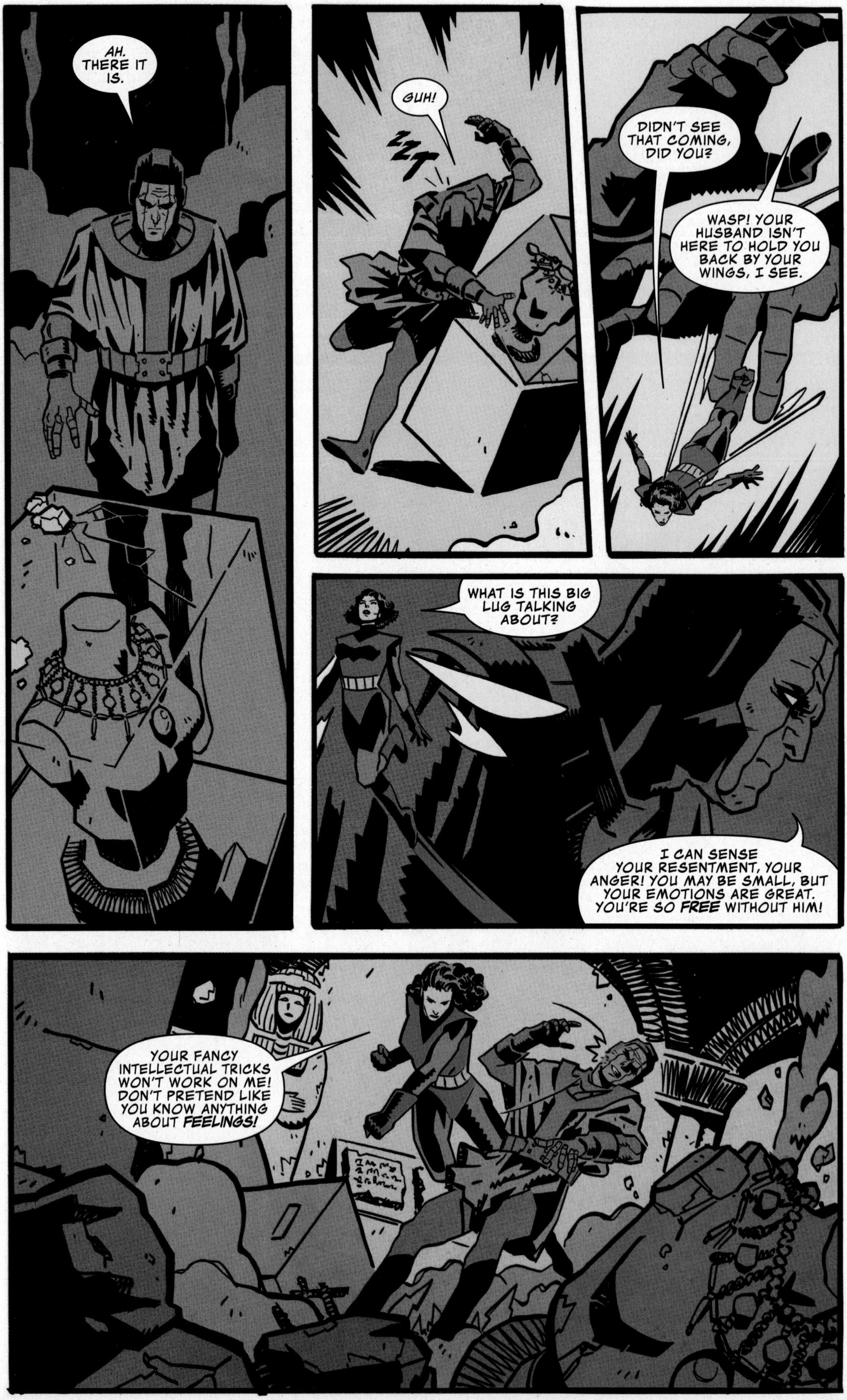
AH. THERE IT IS.
GUH!
ZZZT
DIDN'T SEE THAT COMING, DID YOU?
WASP! YOUR HUSBAND ISN'T HERE TO HOLD YOU BACK BY YOUR WINGS, I SEE.
WHAT IS THIS BIG LUG TALKING ABOUT?
I CAN SENSE YOUR RESENTMENT, YOUR ANGER! YOU MAY BE SMALL, BUT YOUR EMOTIONS ARE GREAT. YOU'RE SO **FREE** WITHOUT HIM!
YOUR FANCY INTELLECTUAL TRICKS WON'T WORK ON ME! DON'T PRETEND LIKE YOU KNOW ANYTHING ABOUT **FEELINGS!**

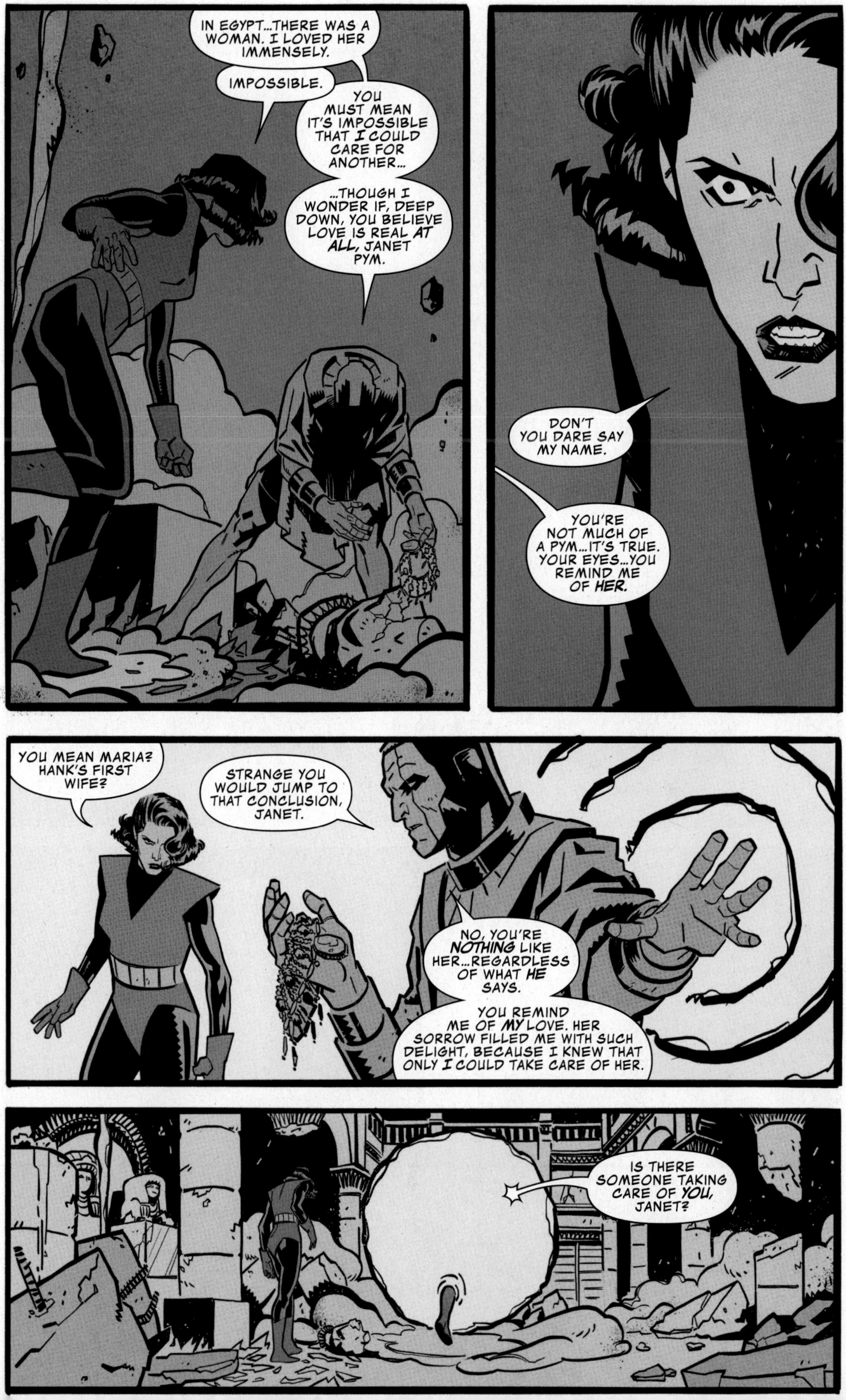
IN EGYPT...THERE WAS A WOMAN. I LOVED HER IMMENSELY.
IMPOSSIBLE.
YOU MUST MEAN IT'S IMPOSSIBLE THAT I COULD CARE FOR ANOTHER...
...THOUGH I WONDER IF, DEEP DOWN, YOU BELIEVE LOVE IS REAL AT ALL, JANET PYM.
DON'T YOU DARE SAY MY NAME.
YOU'RE NOT MUCH OF A PYM...IT'S TRUE. YOUR EYES...YOU REMIND ME OF HER.
YOU MEAN MARIA? HANK'S FIRST WIFE?
STRANGE YOU WOULD JUMP TO THAT CONCLUSION, JANET.
NO, YOU'RE NOTHING LIKE HER...REGARDLESS OF WHAT HE SAYS.
YOU REMIND ME OF MY LOVE. HER SORROW FILLED ME WITH SUCH DELIGHT, BECAUSE I KNEW THAT ONLY I COULD TAKE CARE OF HER.
IS THERE SOMEONE TAKING CARE OF YOU, JANET?

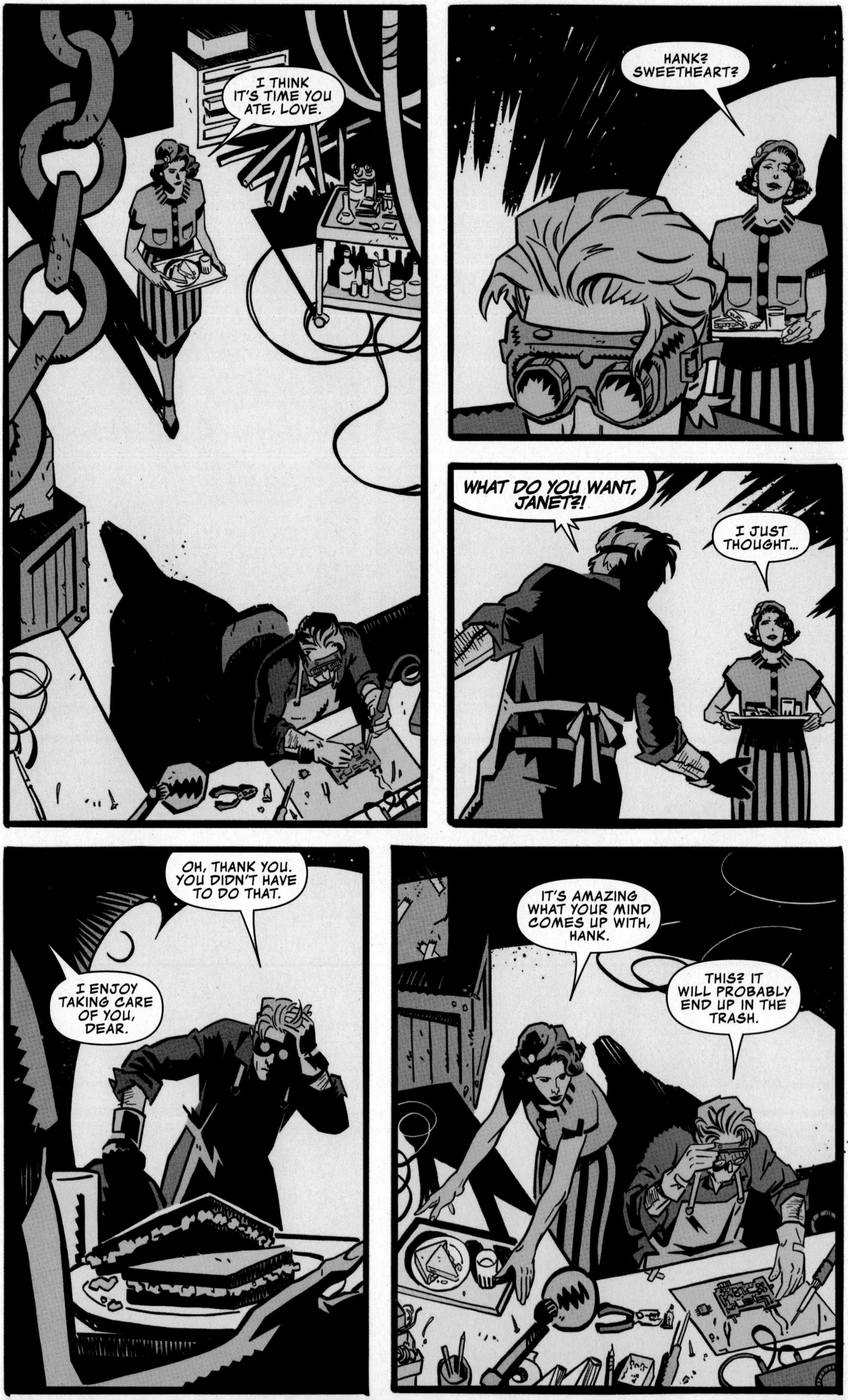
I THINK IT'S TIME YOU ATE, LOVE.
HANK? SWEETHEART?
WHAT DO YOU WANT, JANET?!
I JUST THOUGHT...
OH, THANK YOU. YOU DIDN'T HAVE TO DO THAT.
I ENJOY TAKING CARE OF YOU, DEAR.
IT'S AMAZING WHAT YOUR MIND COMES UP WITH, HANK.
THIS? IT WILL PROBABLY END UP IN THE TRASH.

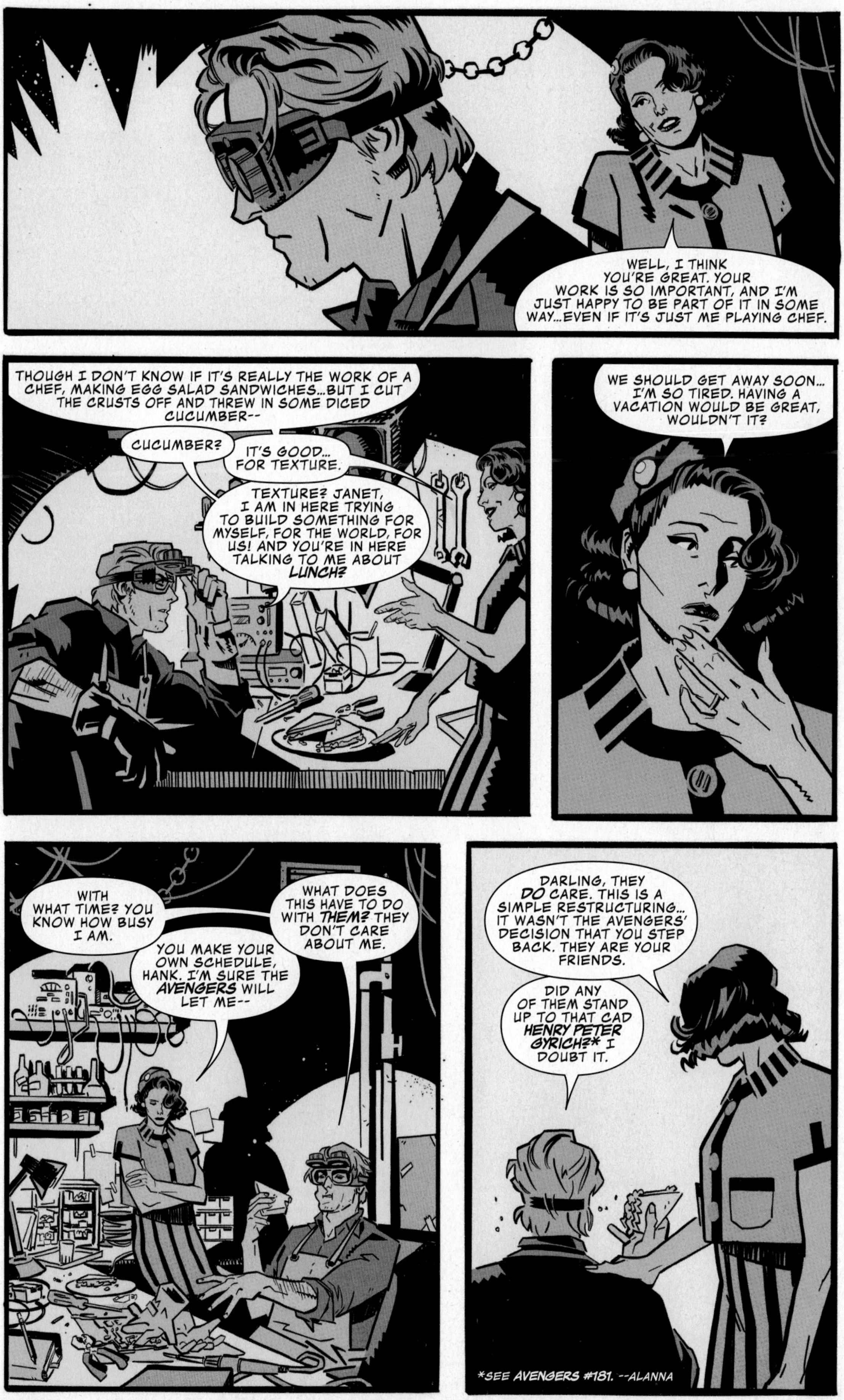
WELL, I THINK YOU'RE GREAT. YOUR WORK IS SO IMPORTANT, AND I'M JUST HAPPY TO BE PART OF IT IN SOME WAY...EVEN IF IT'S JUST ME PLAYING CHEF.
THOUGH I DON'T KNOW IF IT'S REALLY THE WORK OF A CHEF, MAKING EGG SALAD SANDWICHES...BUT I CUT THE CRUSTS OFF AND THREW IN SOME DICED CUCUMBER--
CUCUMBER?
IT'S GOOD... FOR TEXTURE.
TEXTURE? JANET, I AM IN HERE TRYING TO BUILD SOMETHING FOR MYSELF, FOR THE WORLD, FOR US! AND YOU'RE IN HERE TALKING TO ME ABOUT LUNCH?
WE SHOULD GET AWAY SOON... I'M SO TIRED. HAVING A VACATION WOULD BE GREAT, WOULDN'T IT?
WITH WHAT TIME? YOU KNOW HOW BUSY I AM.
YOU MAKE YOUR OWN SCHEDULE, HANK. I'M SURE THE AVENGERS WILL LET ME--
WHAT DOES THIS HAVE TO DO WITH THEM? THEY DON'T CARE ABOUT ME.
DARLING, THEY DO CARE. THIS IS A SIMPLE RESTRUCTURING... IT WASN'T THE AVENGERS' DECISION THAT YOU STEP BACK. THEY ARE YOUR FRIENDS.
DID ANY OF THEM STAND UP TO THAT CAD HENRY PETER GYRICH?* I DOUBT IT.
*SEE AVENGERS #181. --ALANNA

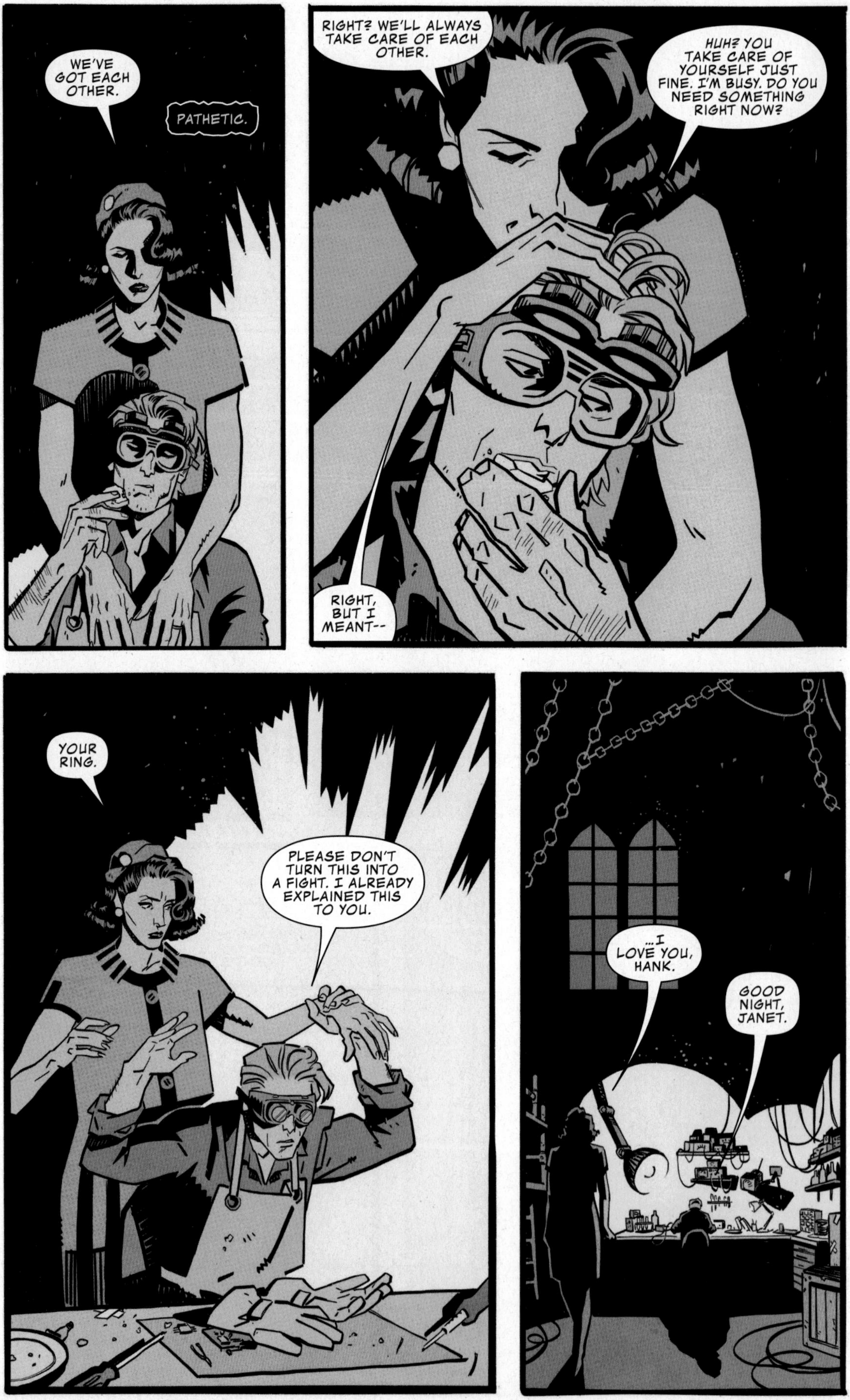
WE'VE GOT EACH OTHER.
PATHETIC.
RIGHT? WE'LL ALWAYS TAKE CARE OF EACH OTHER.
HUH? YOU TAKE CARE OF YOURSELF JUST FINE. I'M BUSY. DO YOU NEED SOMETHING RIGHT NOW?
RIGHT, BUT I MEANT--
YOUR RING.
PLEASE DON'T TURN THIS INTO A FIGHT. I ALREADY EXPLAINED THIS TO YOU.
...I LOVE YOU, HANK.
GOOD NIGHT, JANET.

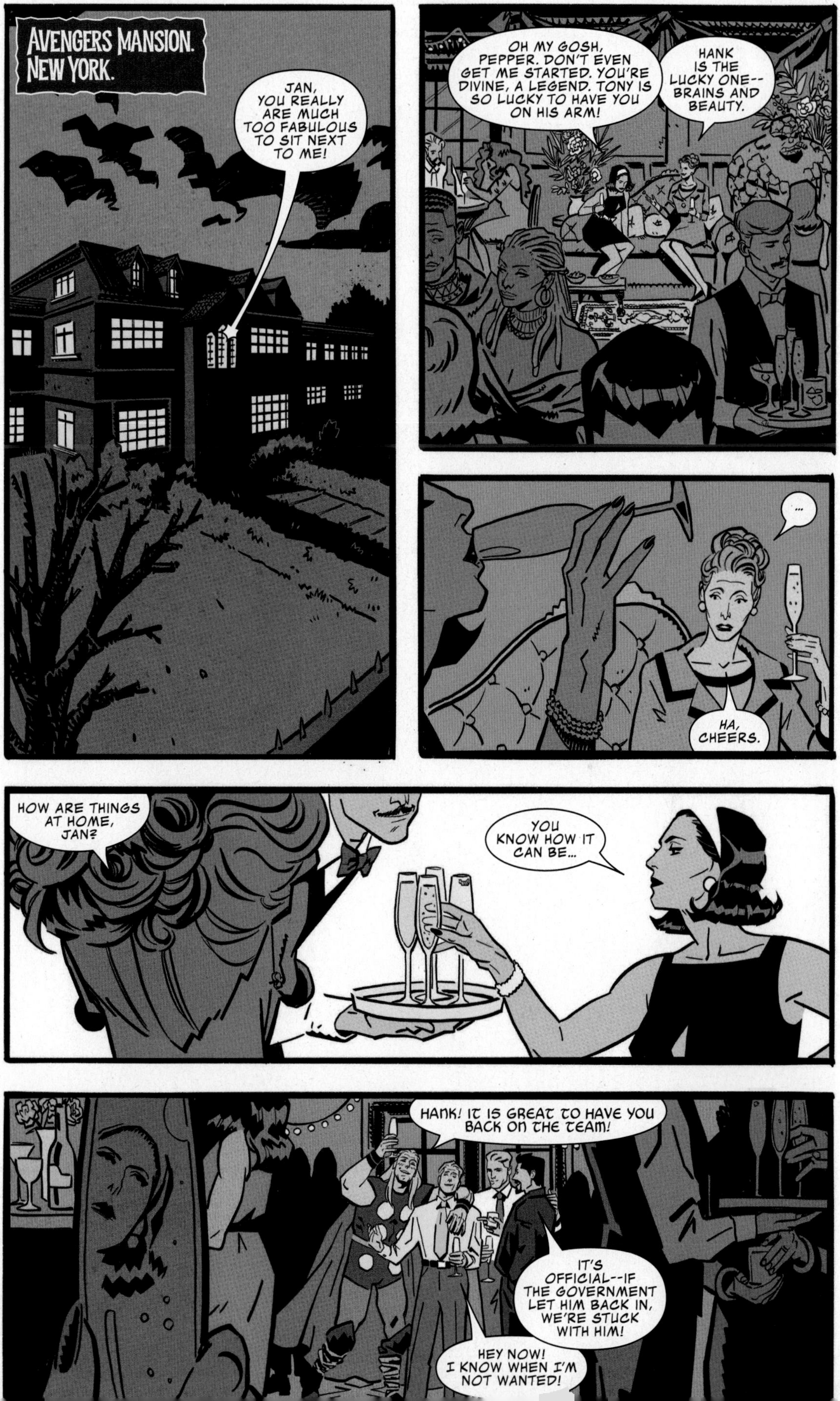
AVENGERS MANSION. NEW YORK.
JAN, YOU REALLY ARE MUCH TOO FABULOUS TO SIT NEXT TO ME!
OH MY GOSH, PEPPER. DON'T EVEN GET ME STARTED. YOU'RE DIVINE, A LEGEND. TONY IS SO LUCKY TO HAVE YOU ON HIS ARM!
HANK IS THE LUCKY ONE--BRAINS AND BEAUTY.
...
HA, CHEERS.
HOW ARE THINGS AT HOME, JAN?
YOU KNOW HOW IT CAN BE...
HANK! IT IS GREAT TO HAVE YOU BACK ON THE TEAM!
IT'S OFFICIAL--IF THE GOVERNMENT LET HIM BACK IN, WE'RE STUCK WITH HIM!
HEY NOW! I KNOW WHEN I'M NOT WANTED!

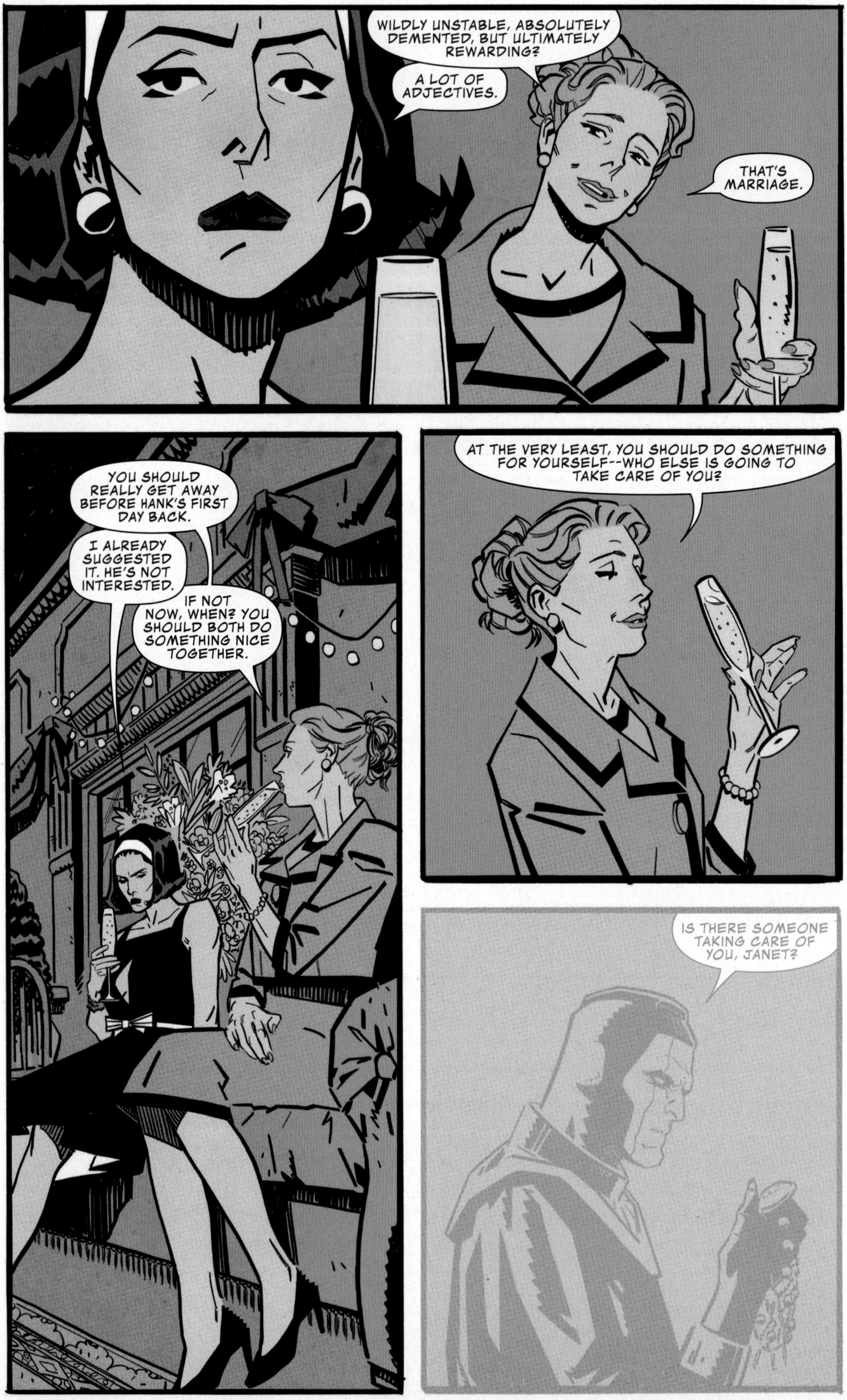
WILDLY UNSTABLE, ABSOLUTELY DEMENTED, BUT ULTIMATELY REWARDING?
A LOT OF ADJECTIVES.
THAT'S MARRIAGE.
YOU SHOULD REALLY GET AWAY BEFORE HANK'S FIRST DAY BACK.
I ALREADY SUGGESTED IT. HE'S NOT INTERESTED.
IF NOT NOW, WHEN? YOU SHOULD BOTH DO SOMETHING NICE TOGETHER.
AT THE VERY LEAST, YOU SHOULD DO SOMETHING FOR YOURSELF--WHO ELSE IS GOING TO TAKE CARE OF YOU?
IS THERE SOMEONE TAKING CARE OF YOU, JANET?

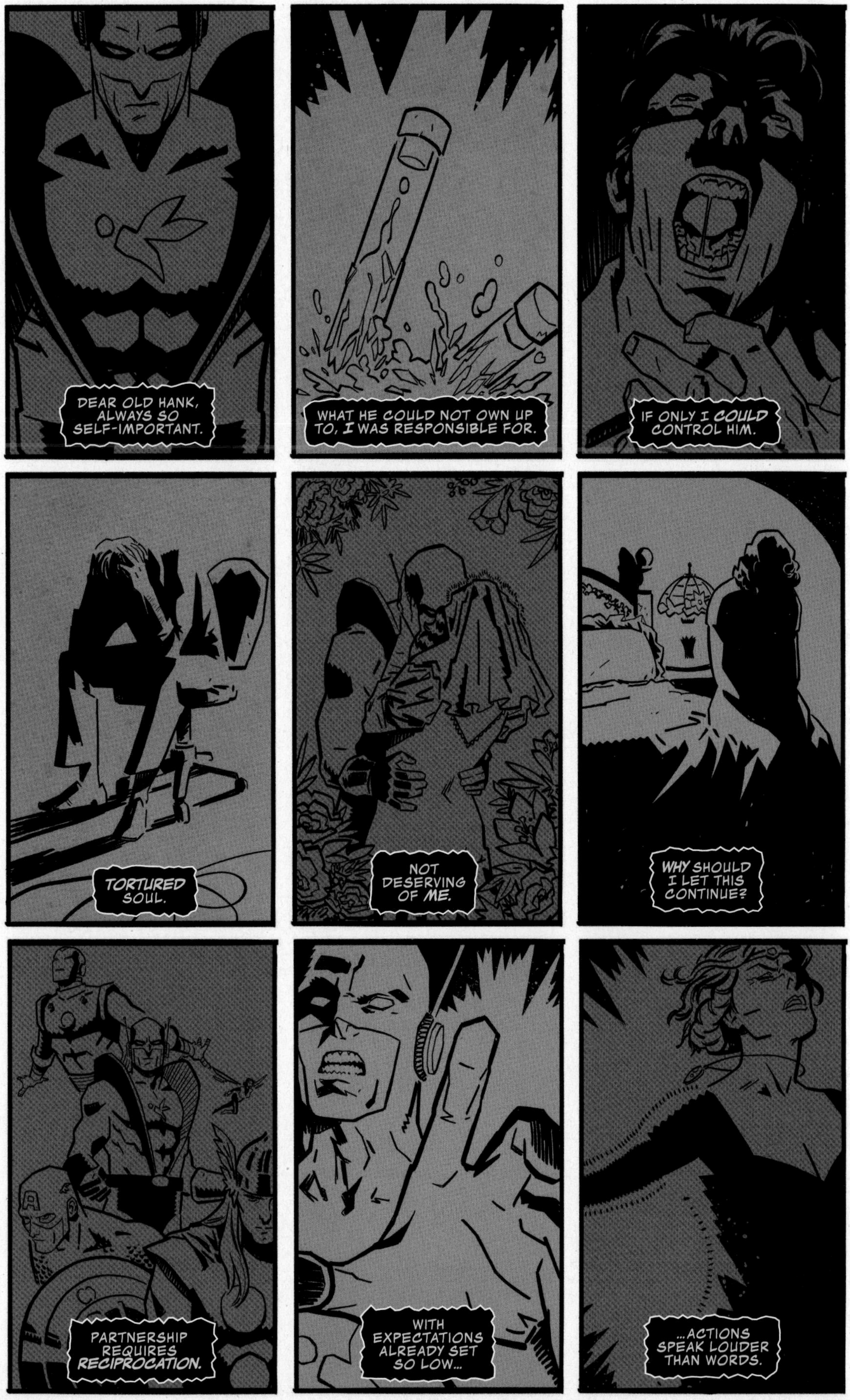
DEAR OLD HANK, ALWAYS SO SELF-IMPORTANT.
WHAT HE COULD NOT OWN UP TO, I WAS RESPONSIBLE FOR.
IF ONLY I COULD CONTROL HIM.
TORTURED SOUL.
NOT DESERVING OF ME.
WHY SHOULD I LET THIS CONTINUE?
PARTNERSHIP REQUIRES RECIPROCATION.
WITH EXPECTATIONS ALREADY SET SO LOW...
...ACTIONS SPEAK LOUDER THAN WORDS.

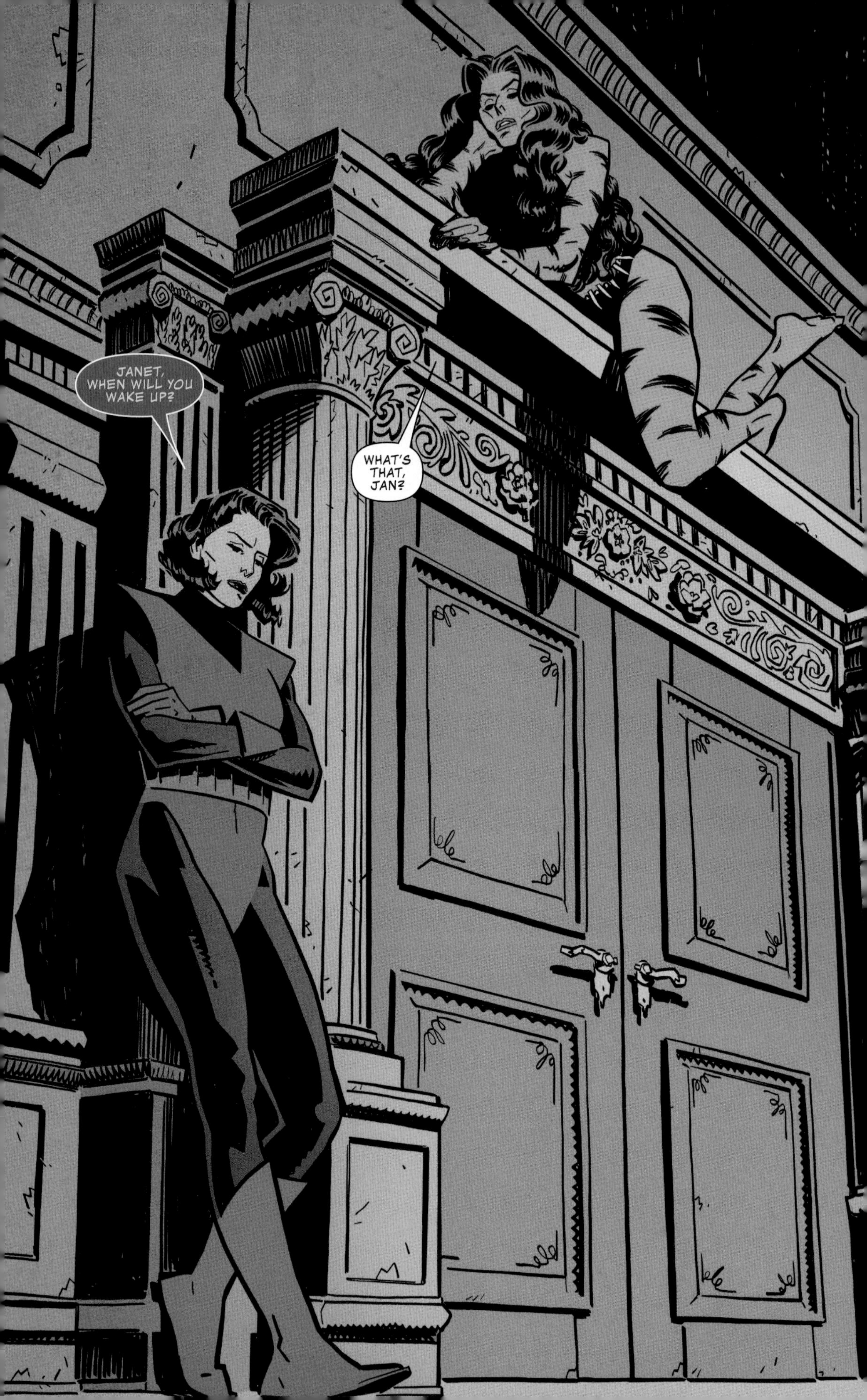
JANET, WHEN WILL YOU WAKE UP?
WHAT'S THAT, JAN?

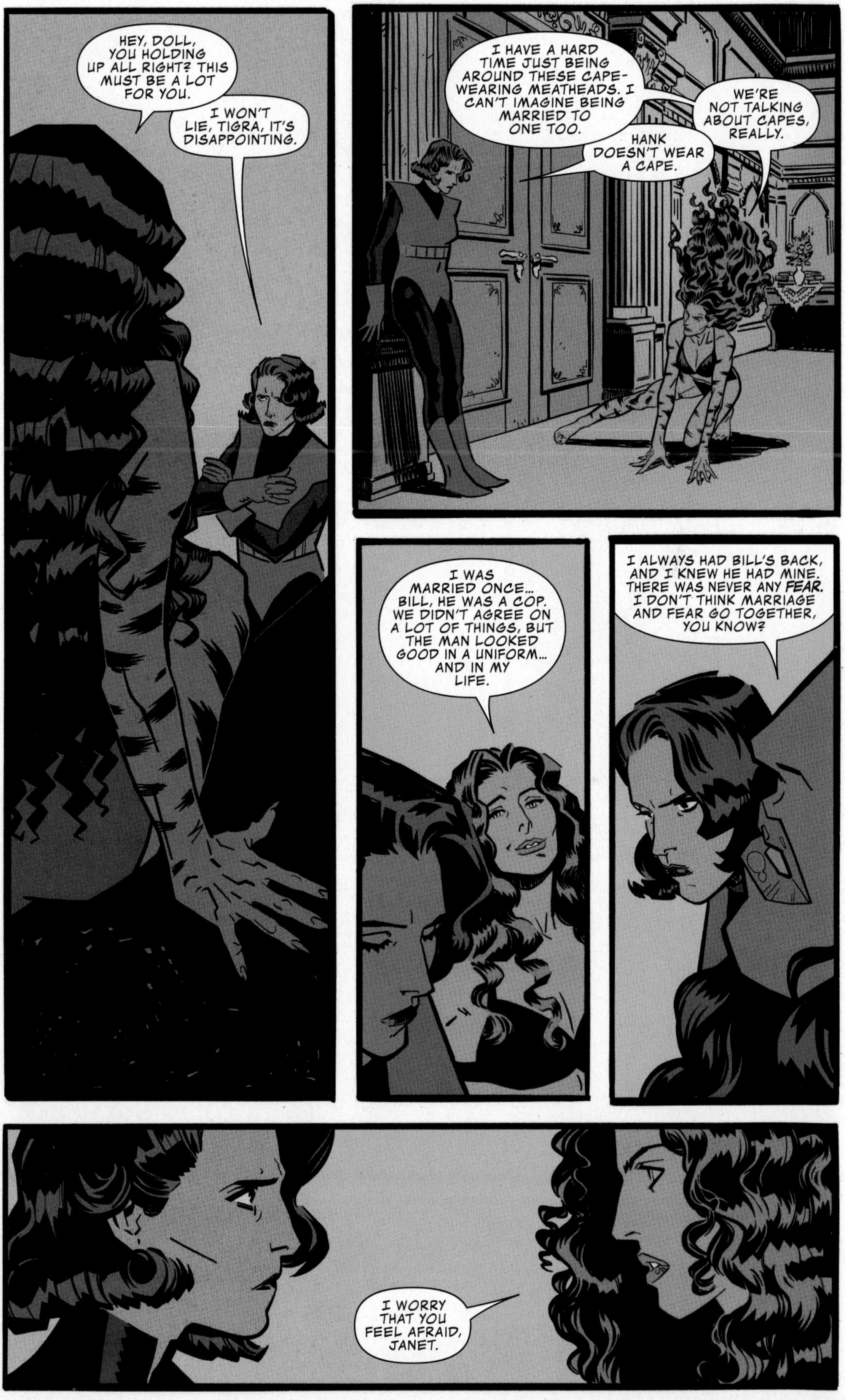
HEY, DOLL, YOU HOLDING UP ALL RIGHT? THIS MUST BE A LOT FOR YOU.
I WON'T LIE, TIGRA, IT'S DISAPPOINTING.
I HAVE A HARD TIME JUST BEING AROUND THESE CAPE-WEARING MEATHEADS. I CAN'T IMAGINE BEING MARRIED TO ONE TOO.
HANK DOESN'T WEAR A CAPE.
WE'RE NOT TALKING ABOUT CAPES, REALLY.
I WAS MARRIED ONCE... BILL, HE WAS A COP. WE DIDN'T AGREE ON A LOT OF THINGS, BUT THE MAN LOOKED GOOD IN A UNIFORM... AND IN MY LIFE.
I ALWAYS HAD BILL'S BACK, AND I KNEW HE HAD MINE. THERE WAS NEVER ANY FEAR. I DON'T THINK MARRIAGE AND FEAR GO TOGETHER, YOU KNOW?
I WORRY THAT YOU FEEL AFRAID, JANET.

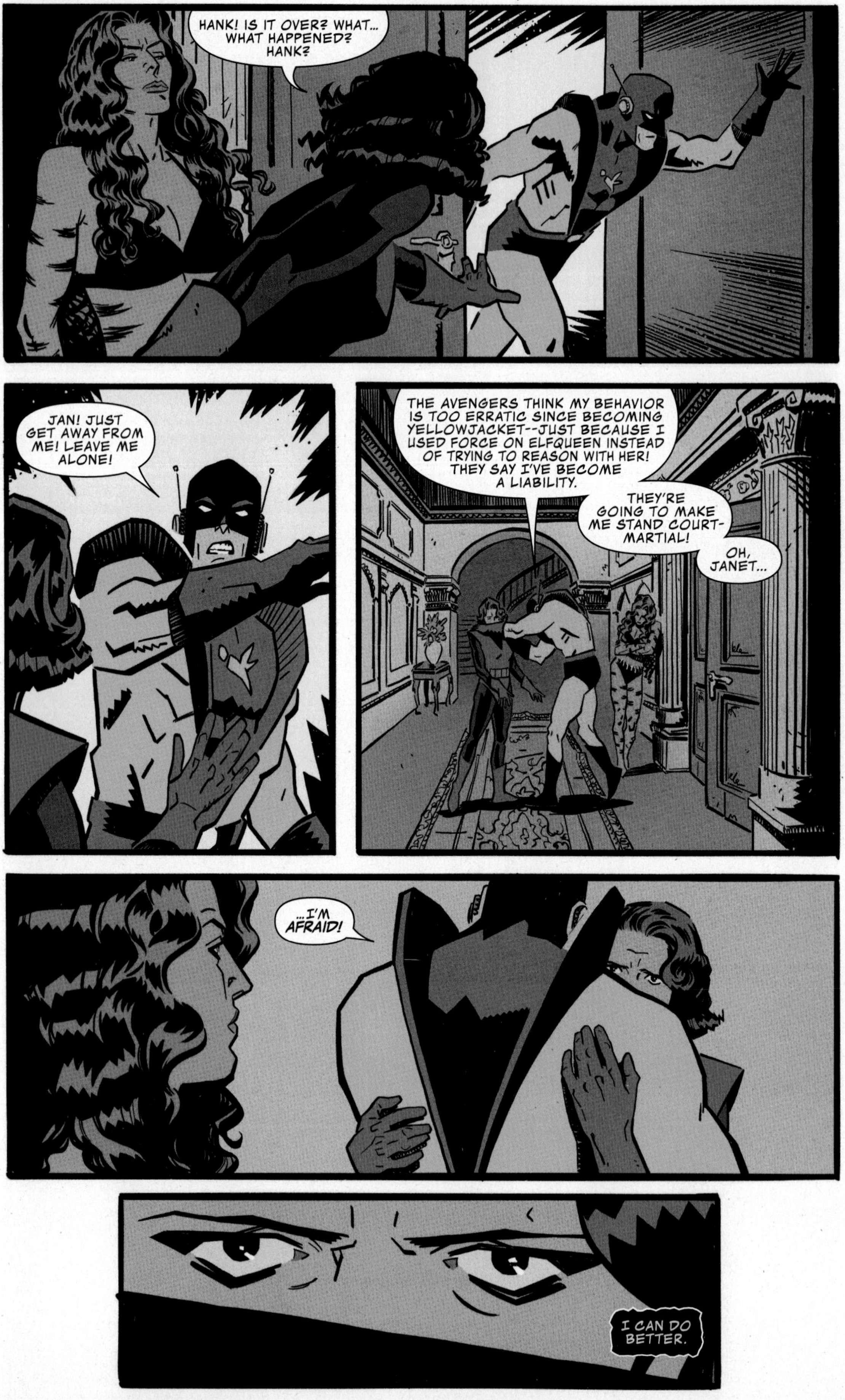
HANK! IS IT OVER? WHAT... WHAT HAPPENED? HANK?
JAN! JUST GET AWAY FROM ME! LEAVE ME ALONE!
THE AVENGERS THINK MY BEHAVIOR IS TOO ERRATIC SINCE BECOMING YELLOWJACKET--JUST BECAUSE I USED FORCE ON ELFQUEEN INSTEAD OF TRYING TO REASON WITH HER! THEY SAY I'VE BECOME A LIABILITY.
THEY'RE GOING TO MAKE ME STAND COURT-MARTIAL!
OH, JANET...
...I'M AFRAID!
I CAN DO BETTER.

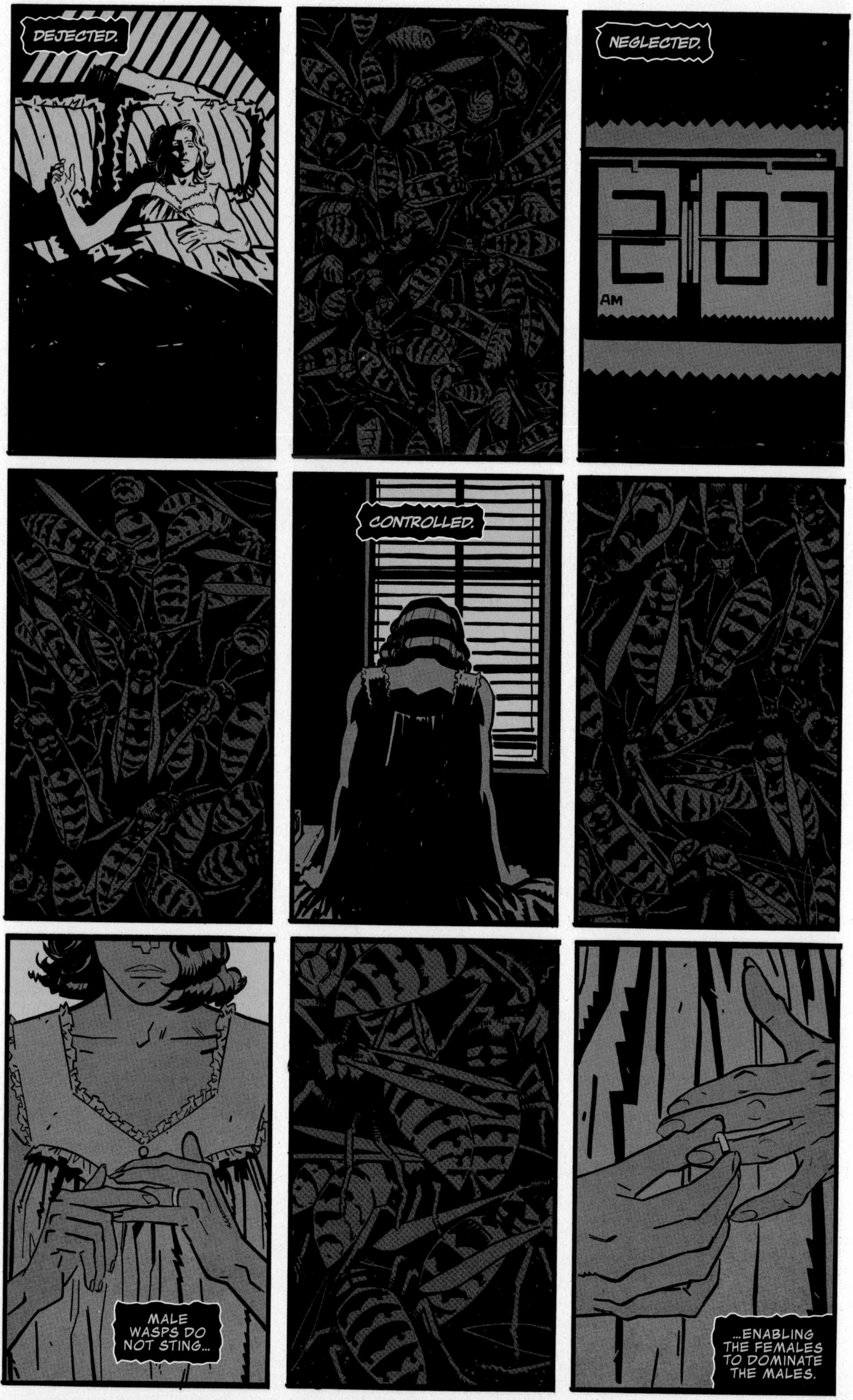
DEJECTED.
NEGLECTED.
2:07
AM
CONTROLLED.
MALE WASPS DO NOT STING...
...ENABLING THE FEMALES TO DOMINATE THE MALES.

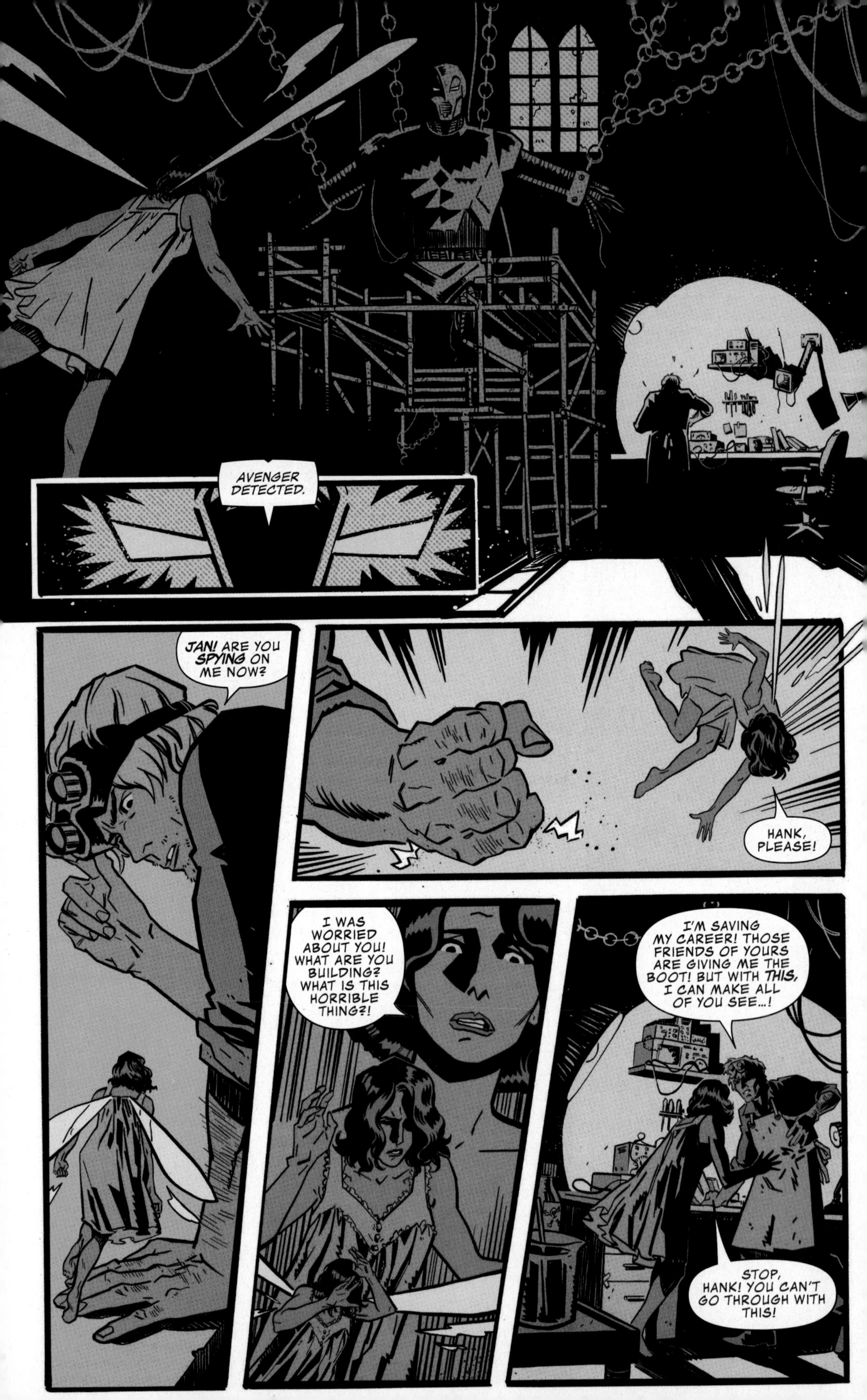
AVENGER DETECTED.
JAN! ARE YOU SPYING ON ME NOW?
HANK, PLEASE!
I WAS WORRIED ABOUT YOU! WHAT ARE YOU BUILDING? WHAT IS THIS HORRIBLE THING?!
I'M SAVING MY CAREER! THOSE FRIENDS OF YOURS ARE GIVING ME THE BOOT! BUT WITH THIS, I CAN MAKE ALL OF YOU SEE...!
STOP, HANK! YOU CAN'T GO THROUGH WITH THIS!

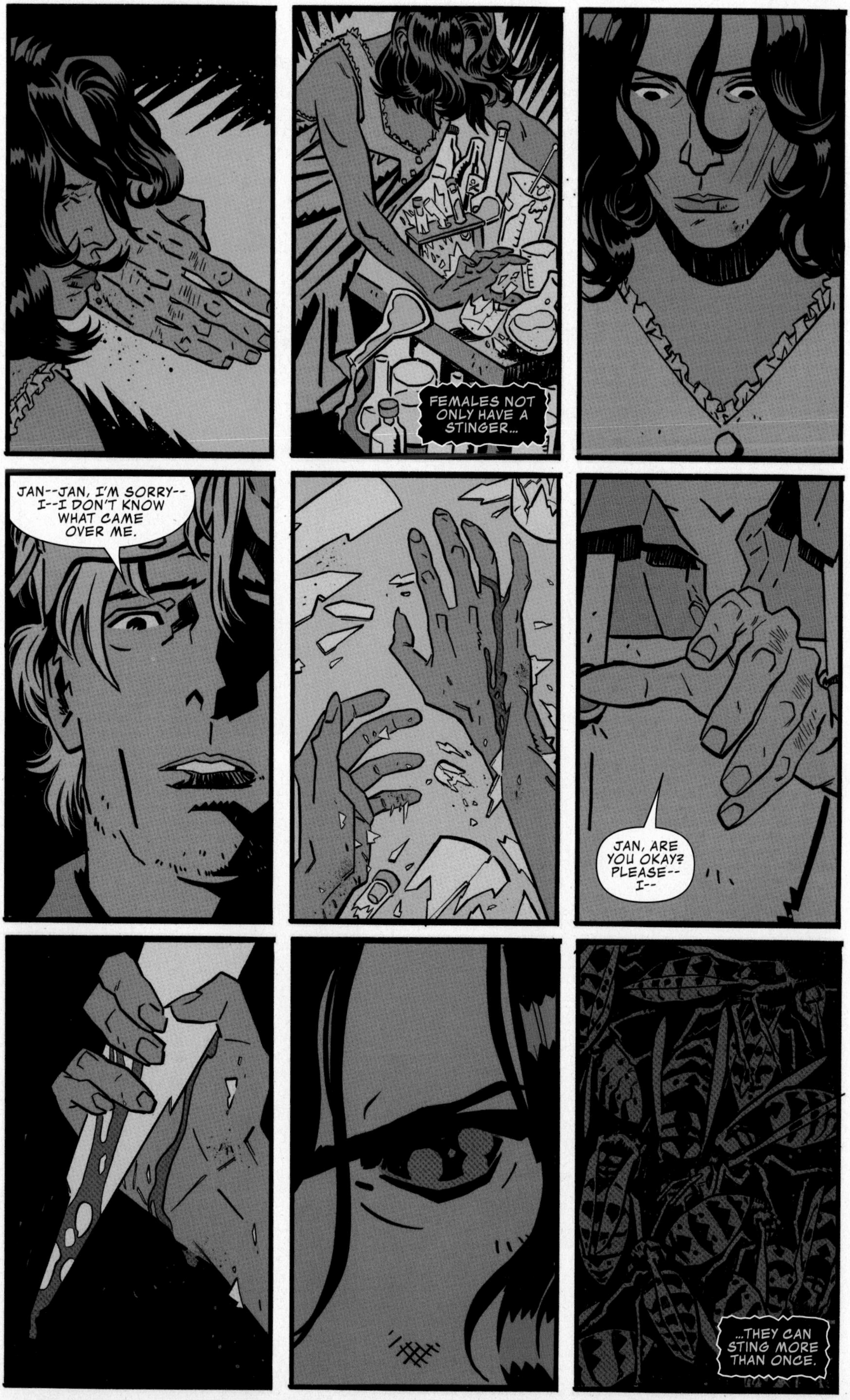
FEMALES NOT ONLY HAVE A STINGER...
JAN--JAN, I'M SORRY-- I--I DON'T KNOW WHAT CAME OVER ME.
JAN, ARE YOU OKAY? PLEASE-- I--
...THEY CAN STING MORE THAN ONCE.

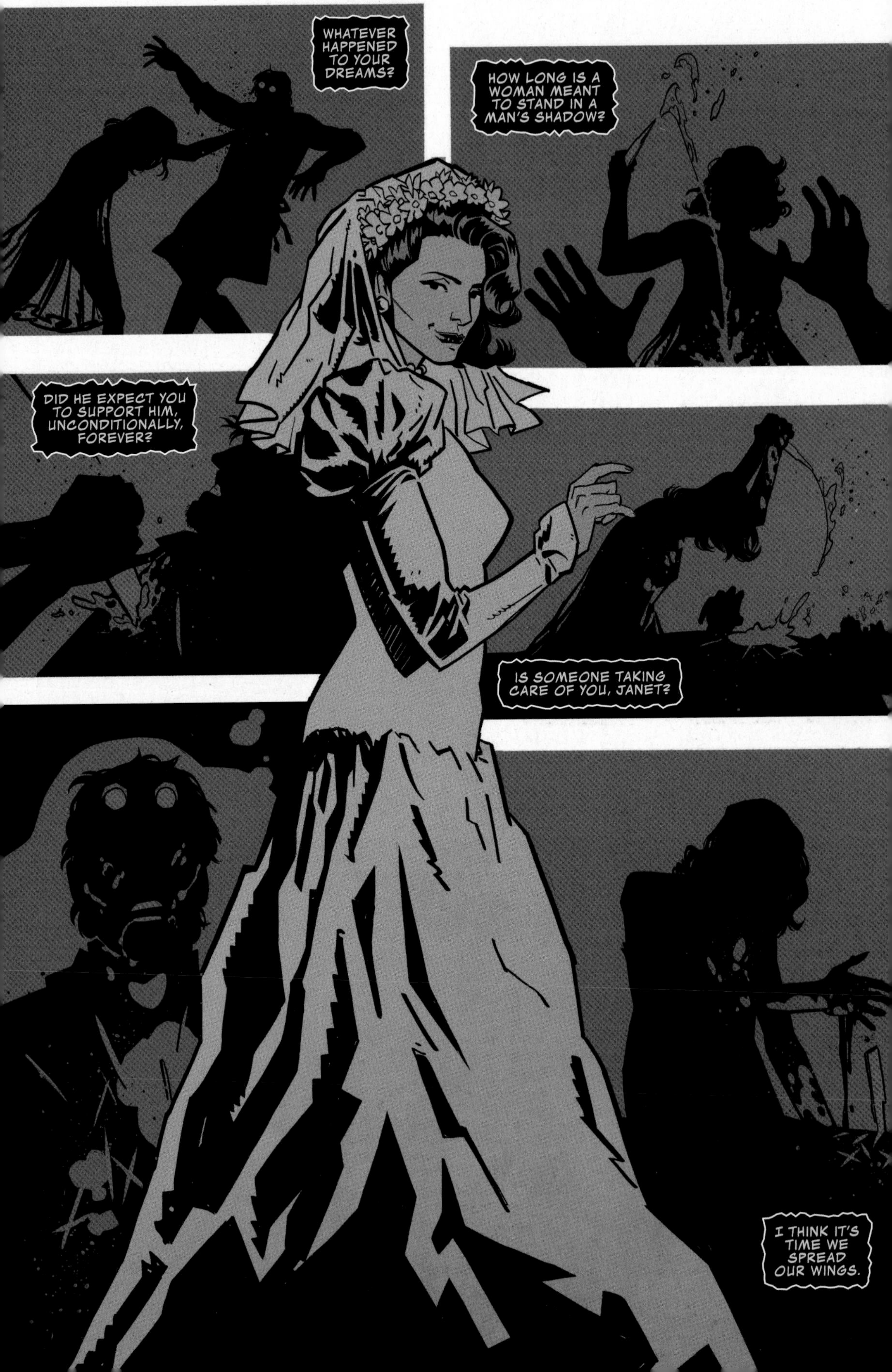
WHATEVER HAPPENED TO YOUR DREAMS?
HOW LONG IS A WOMAN MEANT TO STAND IN A MAN'S SHADOW?
DID HE EXPECT YOU TO SUPPORT HIM, UNCONDITIONALLY, FOREVER?
IS SOMEONE TAKING CARE OF YOU, JANET?
I THINK IT'S TIME WE SPREAD OUR WINGS.

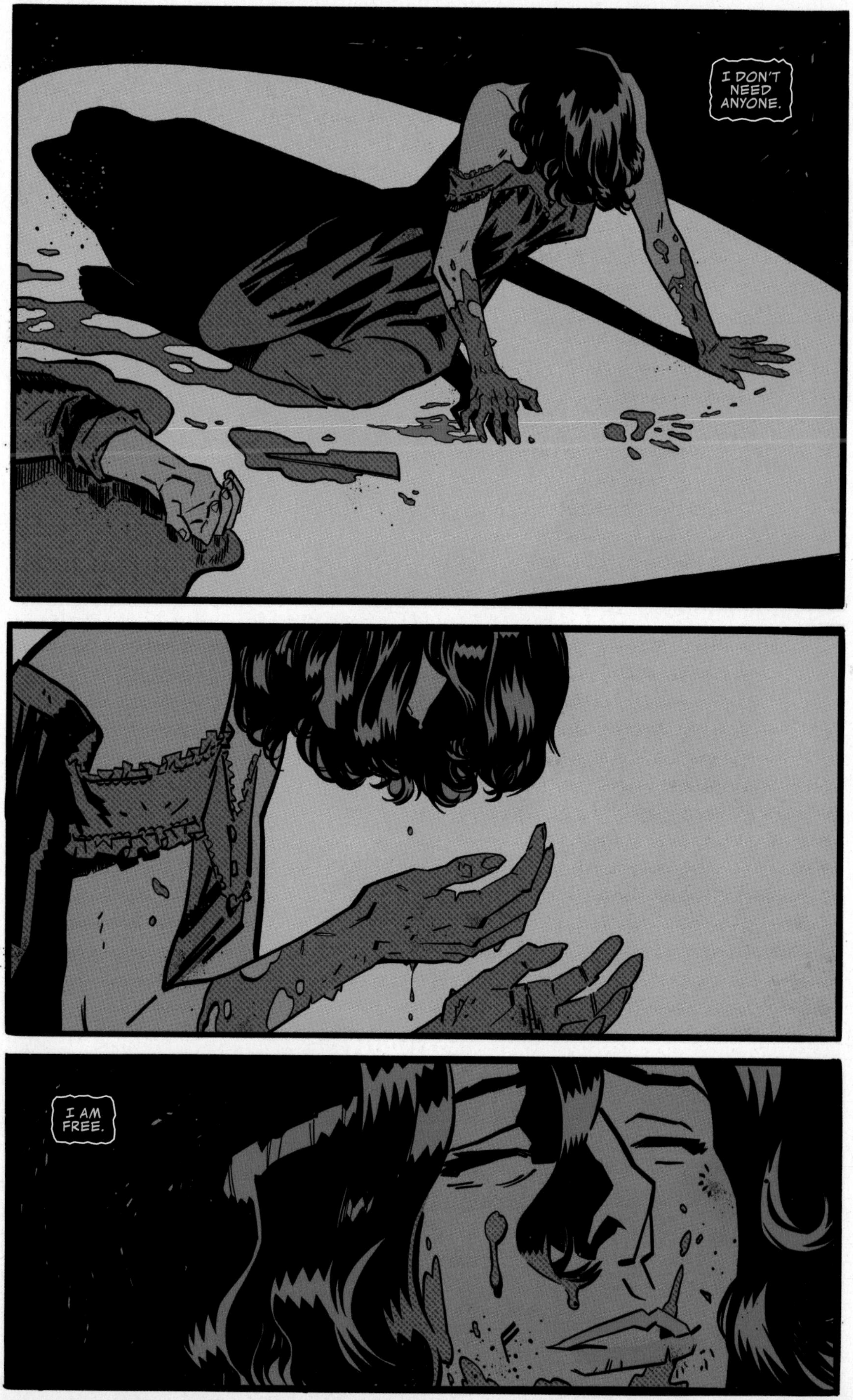
I DON'T NEED ANYONE.
I AM FREE.

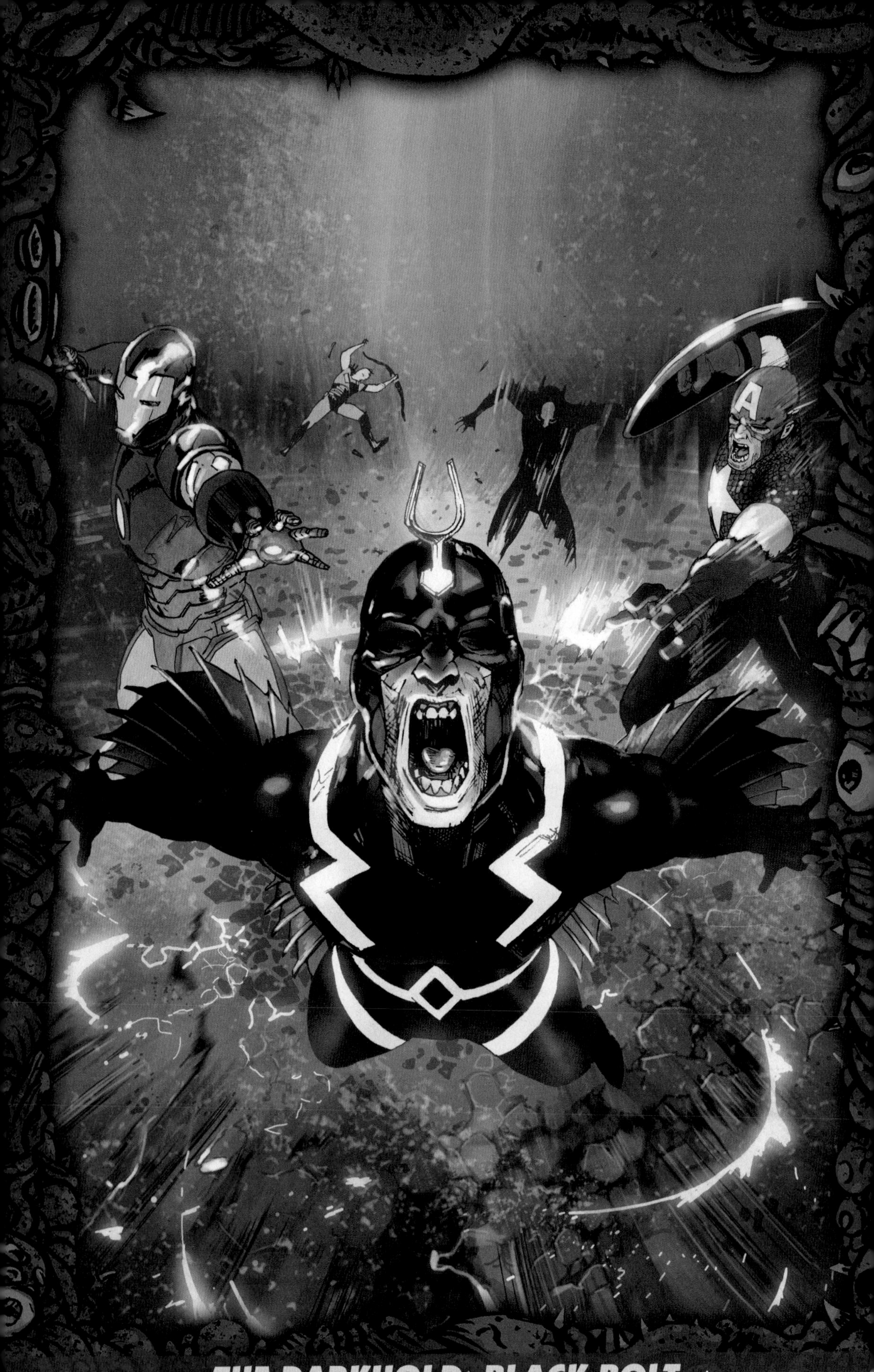

THE DARKHOLD: BLACK BOLT

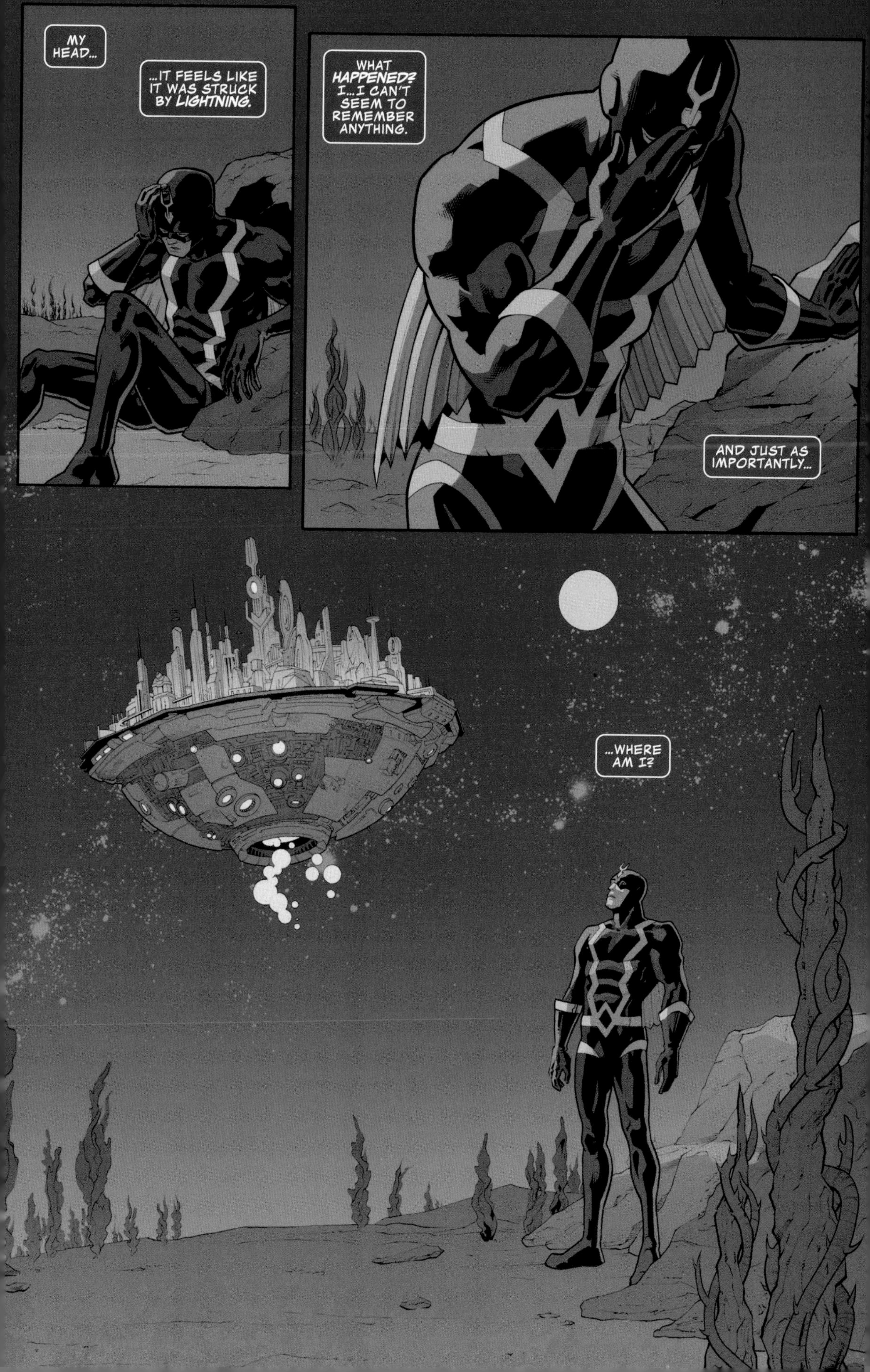
MY HEAD...
...IT FEELS LIKE IT WAS STRUCK BY LIGHTNING.
WHAT HAPPENED? I...I CAN'T SEEM TO REMEMBER ANYTHING.
AND JUST AS IMPORTANTLY...
...WHERE AM I?

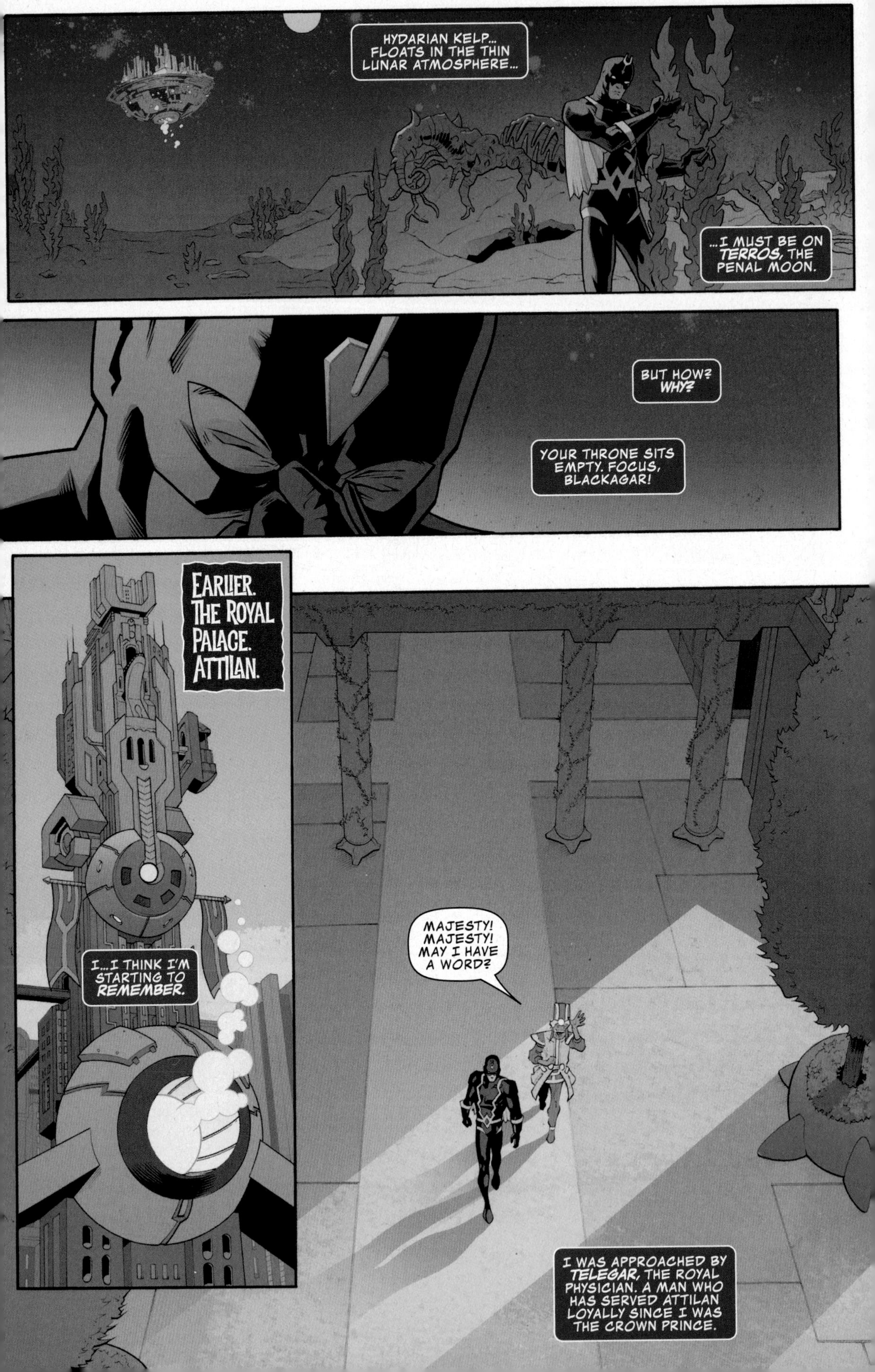
HYDARIAN KELP... FLOATS IN THE THIN LUNAR ATMOSPHERE...
...I MUST BE ON TERROS, THE PENAL MOON.
BUT HOW? WHY?
YOUR THRONE SITS EMPTY. FOCUS, BLACKAGAR!
EARLIER. THE ROYAL PALACE. ATTILAN.
I...I THINK I'M STARTING TO REMEMBER.
MAJESTY! MAJESTY! MAY I HAVE A WORD?
I WAS APPROACHED BY TELEGAR, THE ROYAL PHYSICIAN. A MAN WHO HAS SERVED ATTILAN LOYALLY SINCE I WAS THE CROWN PRINCE.

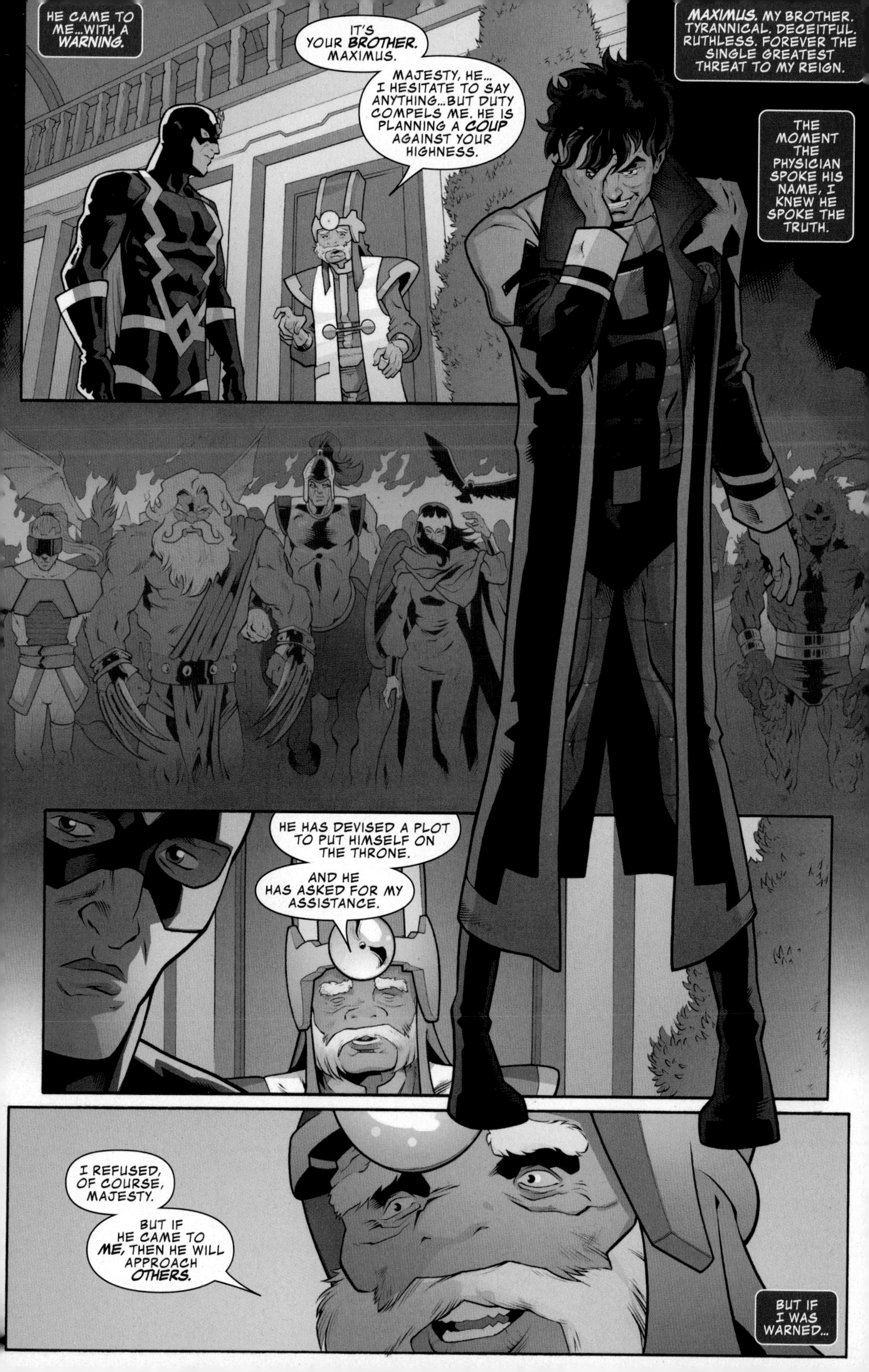
HE CAME TO ME...WITH A WARNING.
IT'S YOUR BROTHER. MAXIMUS.
MAJESTY, HE... I HESITATE TO SAY ANYTHING...BUT DUTY COMPELS ME. HE IS PLANNING A COUP AGAINST YOUR HIGHNESS.
MAXIMUS. MY BROTHER. TYRANNICAL. DECEITFUL. RUTHLESS. FOREVER THE SINGLE GREATEST THREAT TO MY REIGN.
THE MOMENT THE PHYSICIAN SPOKE HIS NAME, I KNEW HE SPOKE THE TRUTH.
HE HAS DEVISED A PLOT TO PUT HIMSELF ON THE THRONE.
AND HE HAS ASKED FOR MY ASSISTANCE.
I REFUSED, OF COURSE, MAJESTY.
BUT IF HE CAME TO ME, THEN HE WILL APPROACH OTHERS.
BUT IF I WAS WARNED...

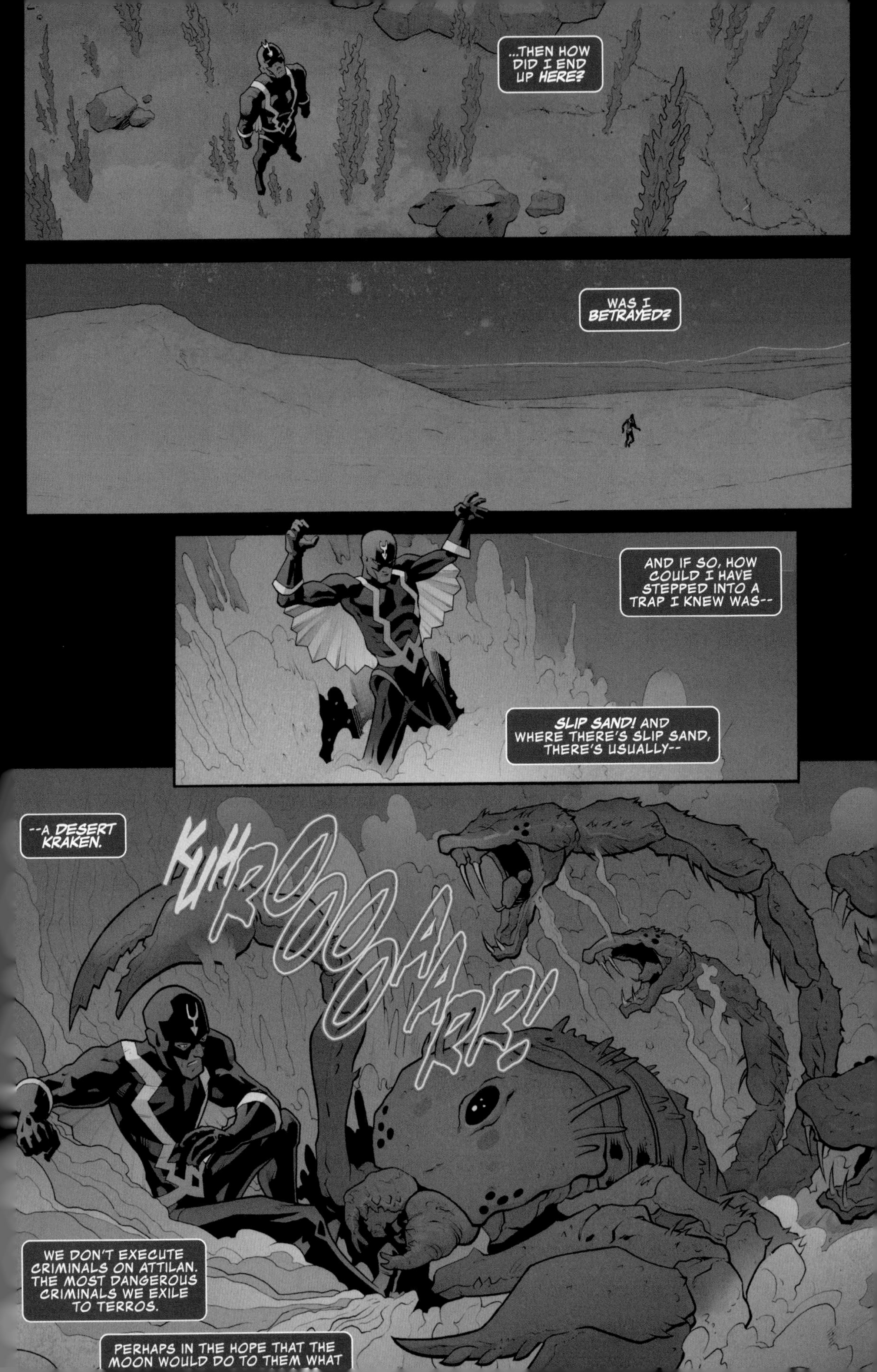
...THEN HOW DID I END UP HERE?
WAS I BETRAYED?
AND IF SO, HOW COULD I HAVE STEPPED INTO A TRAP I KNEW WAS--
SLIP SAND! AND WHERE THERE'S SLIP SAND, THERE'S USUALLY--
--A DESERT KRAKEN.
KUHROOOOAARR!
WE DON'T EXECUTE CRIMINALS ON ATTILAN. THE MOST DANGEROUS CRIMINALS WE EXILE TO TERROS.
PERHAPS IN THE HOPE THAT THE MOON WOULD DO TO THEM WHAT

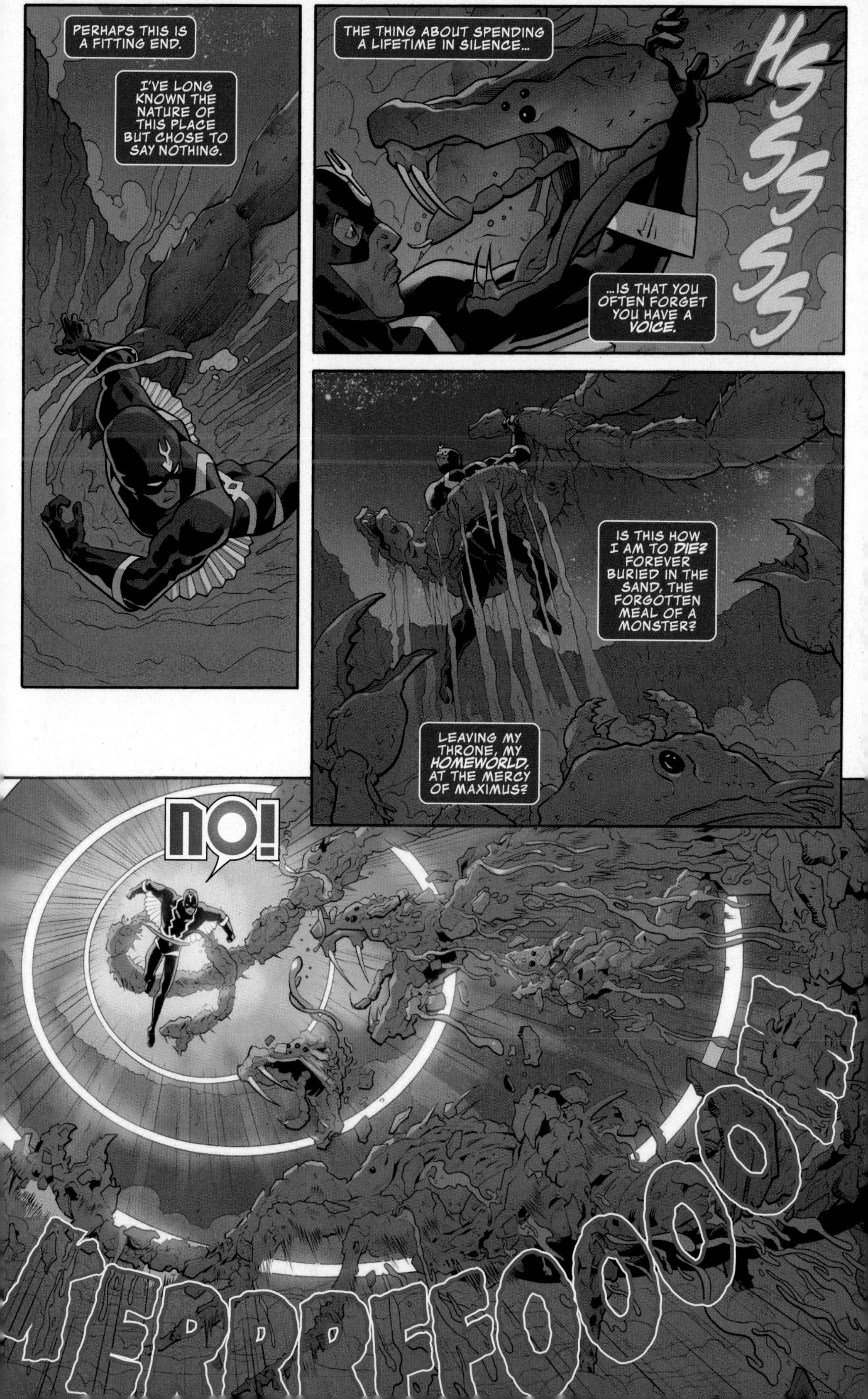
PERHAPS THIS IS A FITTING END.
I'VE LONG KNOWN THE NATURE OF THIS PLACE BUT CHOSE TO SAY NOTHING.
THE THING ABOUT SPENDING A LIFETIME IN SILENCE...
HSSSSS
...IS THAT YOU OFTEN FORGET YOU HAVE A *VOICE*.
IS THIS HOW I AM TO *DIE?* FOREVER BURIED IN THE SAND, THE FORGOTTEN MEAL OF A MONSTER?
LEAVING MY THRONE, MY *HOMEWORLD,* AT THE MERCY OF MAXIMUS?
NO!

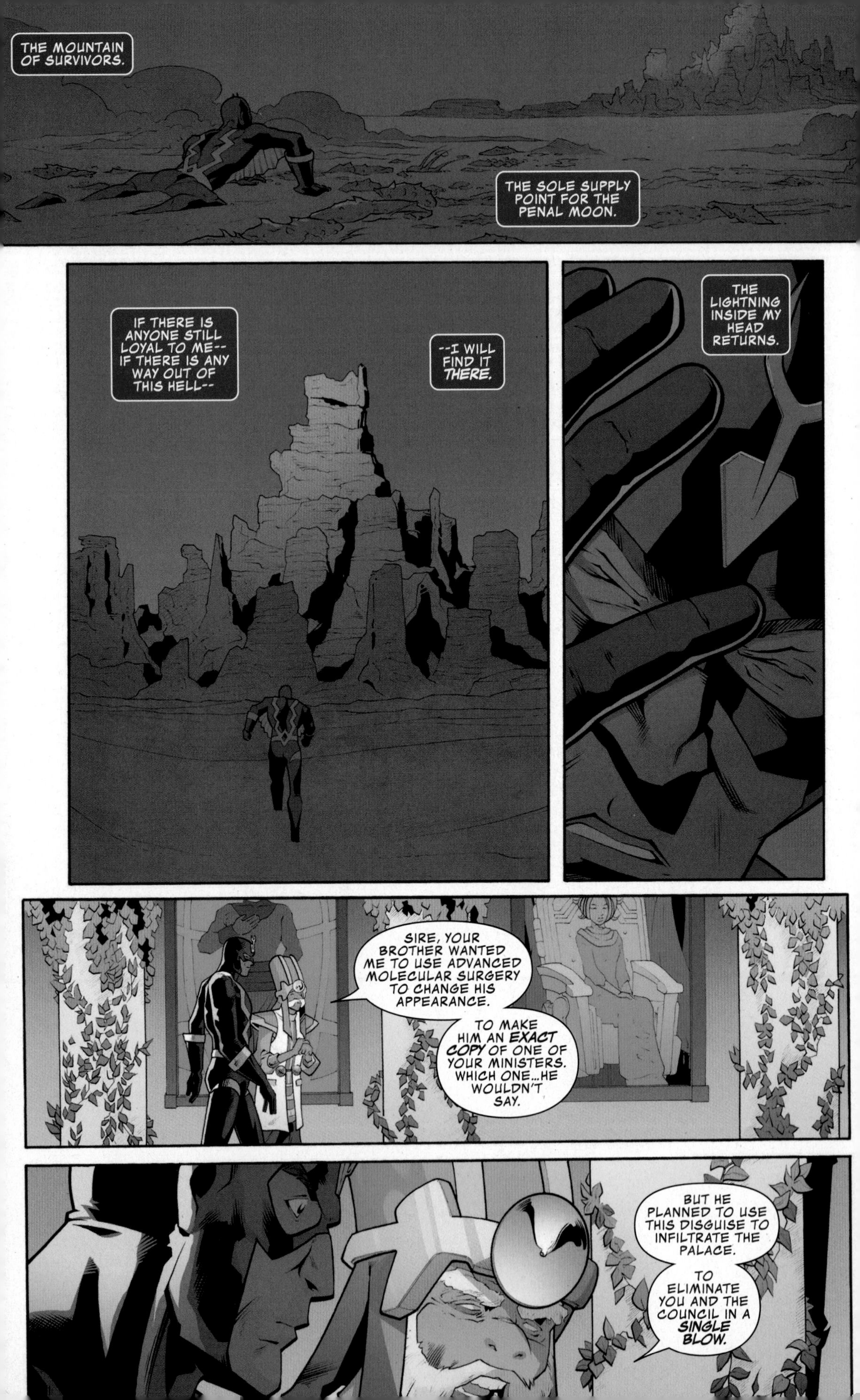
THE MOUNTAIN OF SURVIVORS.
THE SOLE SUPPLY POINT FOR THE PENAL MOON.
IF THERE IS ANYONE STILL LOYAL TO ME-- IF THERE IS ANY WAY OUT OF THIS HELL--
--I WILL FIND IT THERE.
THE LIGHTNING INSIDE MY HEAD RETURNS.
SIRE, YOUR BROTHER WANTED ME TO USE ADVANCED MOLECULAR SURGERY TO CHANGE HIS APPEARANCE.
TO MAKE HIM AN EXACT COPY OF ONE OF YOUR MINISTERS. WHICH ONE...HE WOULDN'T SAY.
BUT HE PLANNED TO USE THIS DISGUISE TO INFILTRATE THE PALACE.
TO ELIMINATE YOU AND THE COUNCIL IN A SINGLE BLOW.

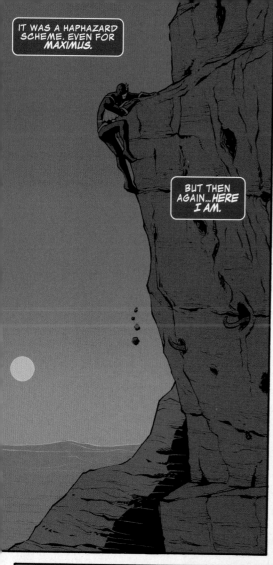

IT WAS A HAPHAZARD SCHEME. EVEN FOR *MAXIMUS.*

BUT THEN AGAIN... *HERE I AM.*

WHETHER IT IS BECAUSE OF THE THIN ATMOSPHERE OF THIS MOON OR WHAT MAXIMUS HAS DONE TO ME--I HAVE LOST THE POWER OF FLIGHT.

BUT IF I AM TO GET OFF THIS HATEFUL MOON... IF I AM TO *SURVIVE...* I NEED TO GET TO THE TOP.

THE *MOUNTAIN OF SURVIVORS.* APTLY NAMED...

...FOR THE MOST PART.

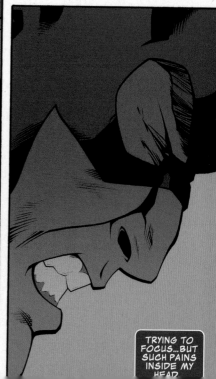

TRYING TO FOCUS... BUT SUCH PAINS INSIDE MY HEAD...

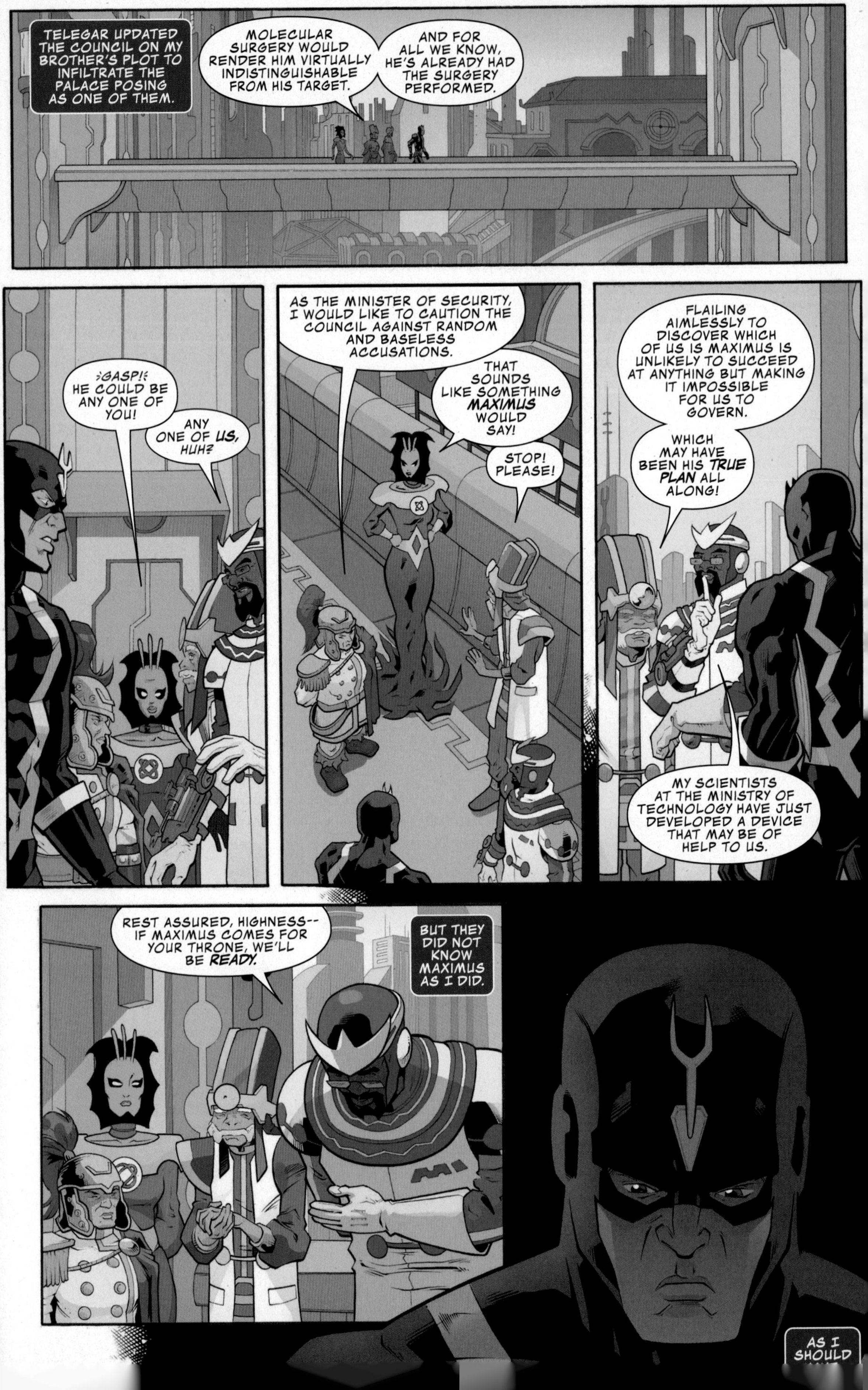

TELEGAR UPDATED THE COUNCIL ON MY BROTHER'S PLOT TO INFILTRATE THE PALACE POSING AS ONE OF THEM.
MOLECULAR SURGERY WOULD RENDER HIM VIRTUALLY INDISTINGUISHABLE FROM HIS TARGET.
AND FOR ALL WE KNOW, HE'S ALREADY HAD THE SURGERY PERFORMED.
GASP! HE COULD BE ANY ONE OF YOU!
ANY ONE OF US, HUH?
AS THE MINISTER OF SECURITY, I WOULD LIKE TO CAUTION THE COUNCIL AGAINST RANDOM AND BASELESS ACCUSATIONS.
THAT SOUNDS LIKE SOMETHING MAXIMUS WOULD SAY!
STOP! PLEASE!
FLAILING AIMLESSLY TO DISCOVER WHICH OF US IS MAXIMUS IS UNLIKELY TO SUCCEED AT ANYTHING BUT MAKING IT IMPOSSIBLE FOR US TO GOVERN.
WHICH MAY HAVE BEEN HIS TRUE PLAN ALL ALONG!
MY SCIENTISTS AT THE MINISTRY OF TECHNOLOGY HAVE JUST DEVELOPED A DEVICE THAT MAY BE OF HELP TO US.
REST ASSURED, HIGHNESS-- IF MAXIMUS COMES FOR YOUR THRONE, WE'LL BE READY.
BUT THEY DID NOT KNOW MAXIMUS AS I DID.
AS I SHOULD

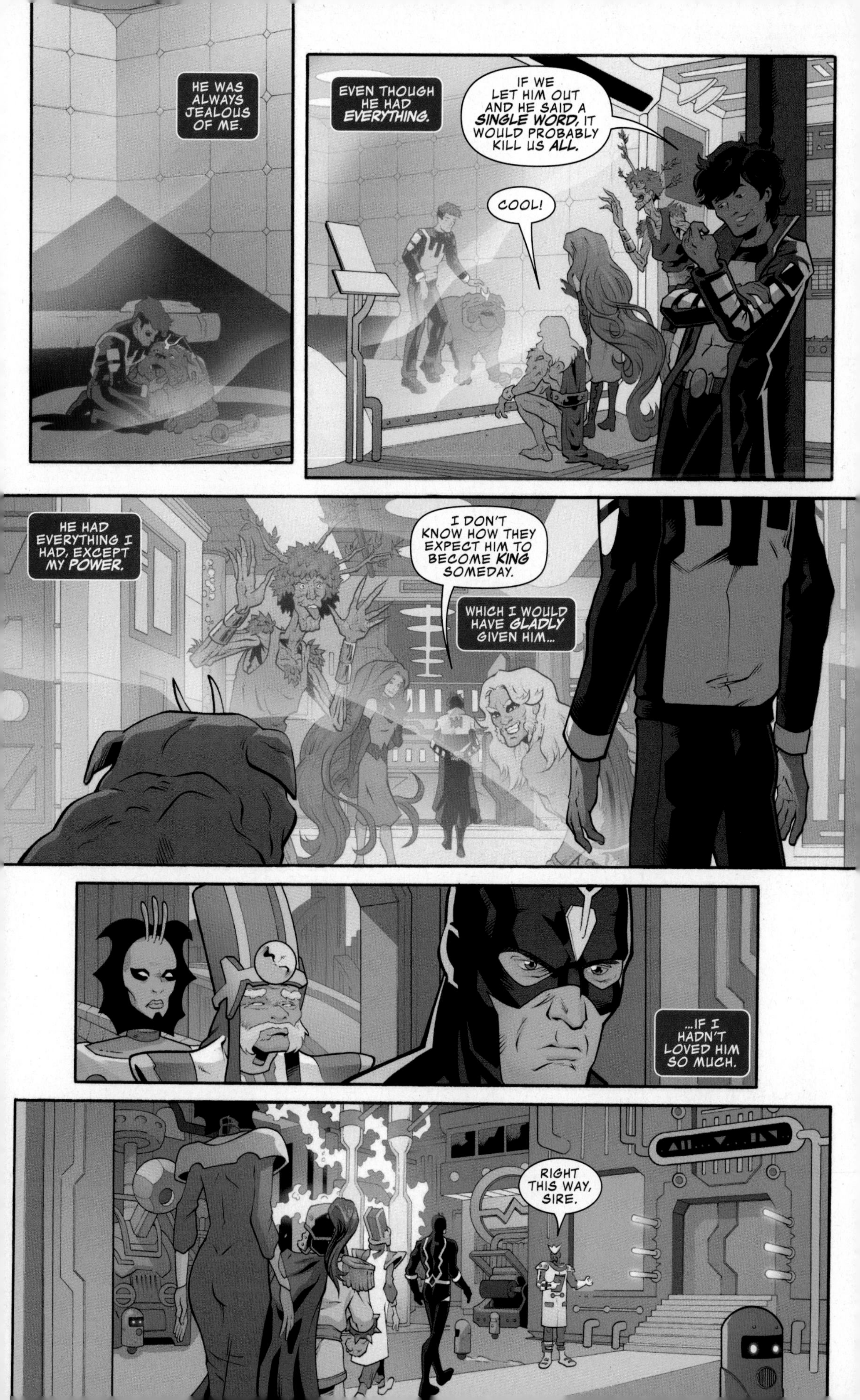
HE WAS ALWAYS JEALOUS OF ME.
EVEN THOUGH HE HAD EVERYTHING.
IF WE LET HIM OUT AND HE SAID A SINGLE WORD, IT WOULD PROBABLY KILL US ALL.
COOL!
HE HAD EVERYTHING I HAD, EXCEPT MY POWER.
I DON'T KNOW HOW THEY EXPECT HIM TO BECOME KING SOMEDAY.
WHICH I WOULD HAVE GLADLY GIVEN HIM...
...IF I HADN'T LOVED HIM SO MUCH.
RIGHT THIS WAY, SIRE.

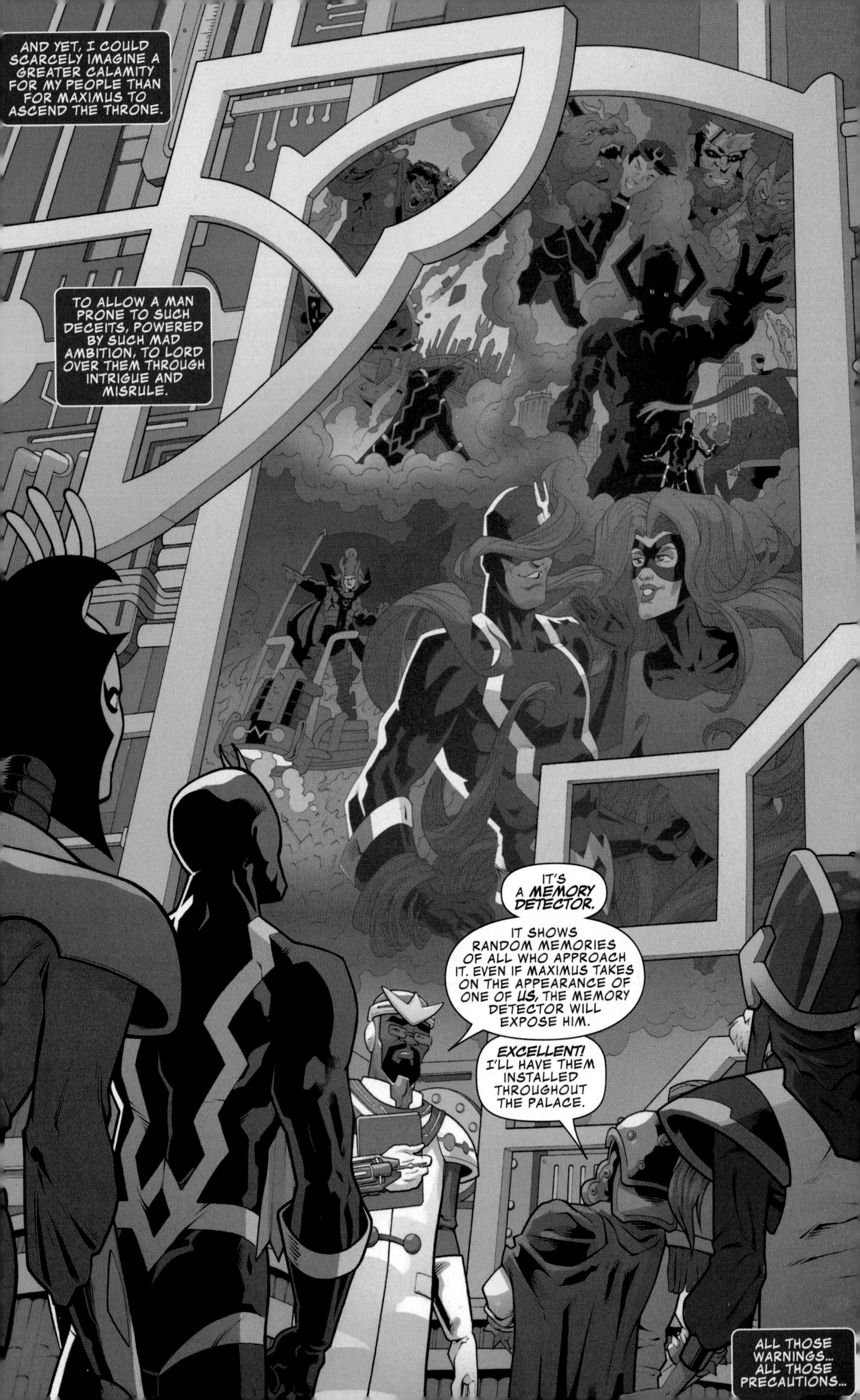
AND YET, I COULD SCARCELY IMAGINE A GREATER CALAMITY FOR MY PEOPLE THAN FOR MAXIMUS TO ASCEND THE THRONE.
TO ALLOW A MAN PRONE TO SUCH DECEITS, POWERED BY SUCH MAD AMBITION, TO LORD OVER THEM THROUGH INTRIGUE AND MISRULE.
IT'S A *MEMORY DETECTOR.*
IT SHOWS RANDOM MEMORIES OF ALL WHO APPROACH IT. EVEN IF MAXIMUS TAKES ON THE APPEARANCE OF ONE OF *US*, THE MEMORY DETECTOR WILL EXPOSE HIM.
EXCELLENT! I'LL HAVE THEM INSTALLED THROUGHOUT THE PALACE.
ALL THOSE WARNINGS... ALL THOSE PRECAUTIONS...

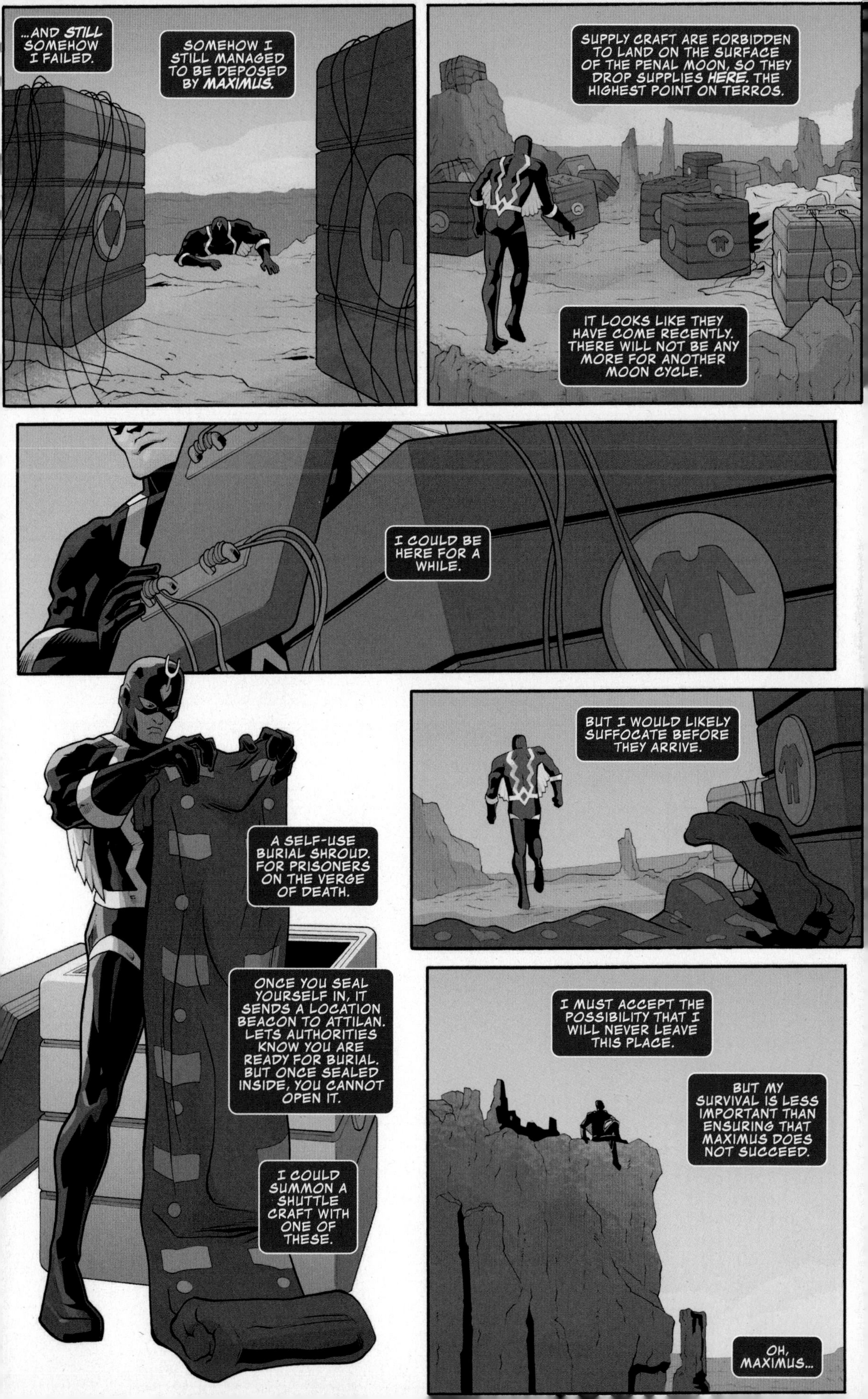
...AND STILL SOMEHOW I FAILED.
SOMEHOW I STILL MANAGED TO BE DEPOSED BY MAXIMUS.
SUPPLY CRAFT ARE FORBIDDEN TO LAND ON THE SURFACE OF THE PENAL MOON, SO THEY DROP SUPPLIES HERE. THE HIGHEST POINT ON TERROS.
IT LOOKS LIKE THEY HAVE COME RECENTLY. THERE WILL NOT BE ANY MORE FOR ANOTHER MOON CYCLE.
I COULD BE HERE FOR A WHILE.
A SELF-USE BURIAL SHROUD. FOR PRISONERS ON THE VERGE OF DEATH.
ONCE YOU SEAL YOURSELF IN, IT SENDS A LOCATION BEACON TO ATTILAN. LETS AUTHORITIES KNOW YOU ARE READY FOR BURIAL. BUT ONCE SEALED INSIDE, YOU CANNOT OPEN IT.
I COULD SUMMON A SHUTTLE CRAFT WITH ONE OF THESE.
BUT I WOULD LIKELY SUFFOCATE BEFORE THEY ARRIVE.
I MUST ACCEPT THE POSSIBILITY THAT I WILL NEVER LEAVE THIS PLACE.
BUT MY SURVIVAL IS LESS IMPORTANT THAN ENSURING THAT MAXIMUS DOES NOT SUCCEED.
OH, MAXIMUS...

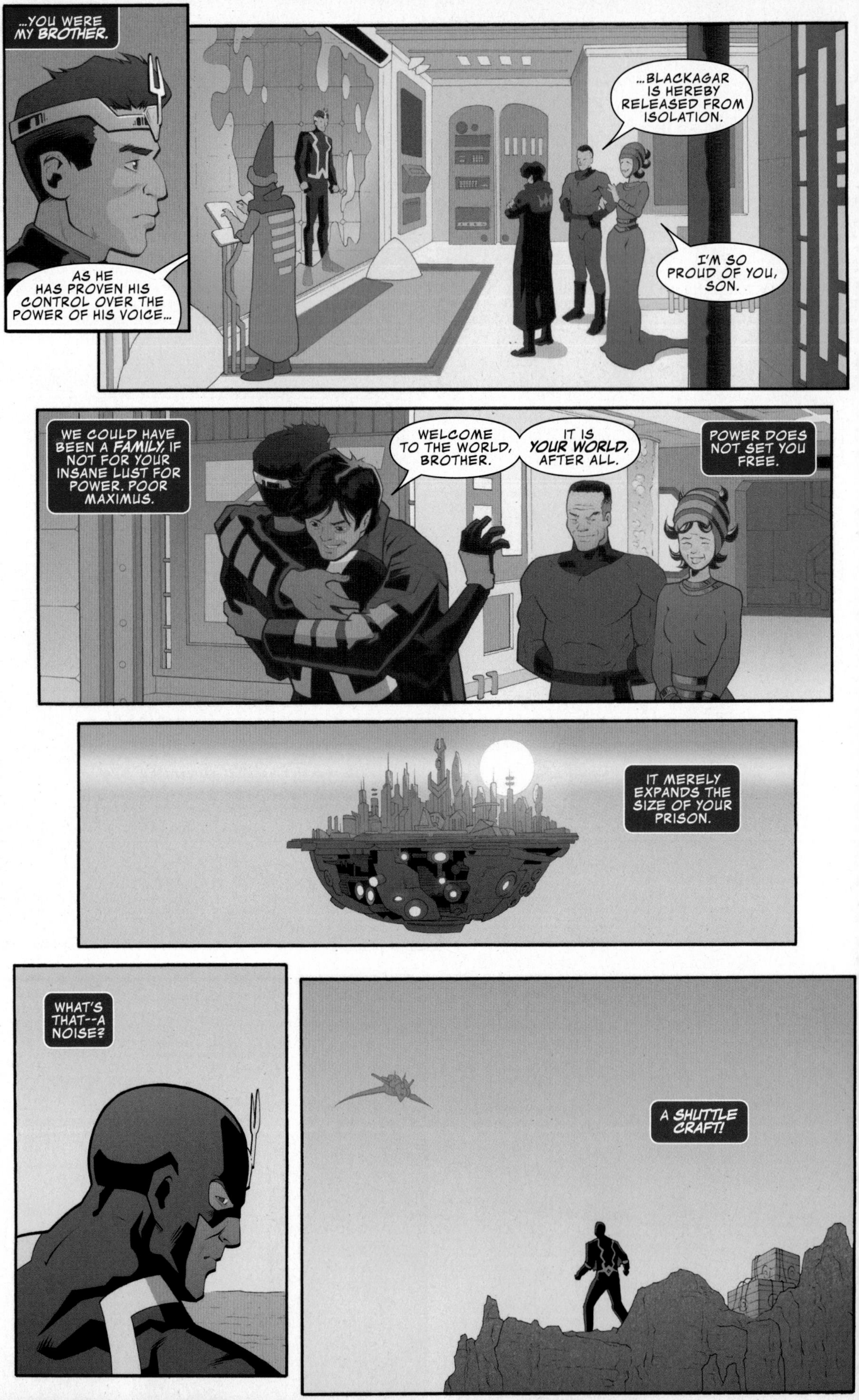
...YOU WERE MY BROTHER.
...BLACKAGAR IS HEREBY RELEASED FROM ISOLATION.
AS HE HAS PROVEN HIS CONTROL OVER THE POWER OF HIS VOICE...
I'M SO PROUD OF YOU, SON.
WE COULD HAVE BEEN A FAMILY, IF NOT FOR YOUR INSANE LUST FOR POWER. POOR MAXIMUS.
WELCOME TO THE WORLD, BROTHER.
IT IS YOUR WORLD, AFTER ALL.
POWER DOES NOT SET YOU FREE.
IT MERELY EXPANDS THE SIZE OF YOUR PRISON.
WHAT'S THAT--A NOISE?
A SHUTTLE CRAFT!

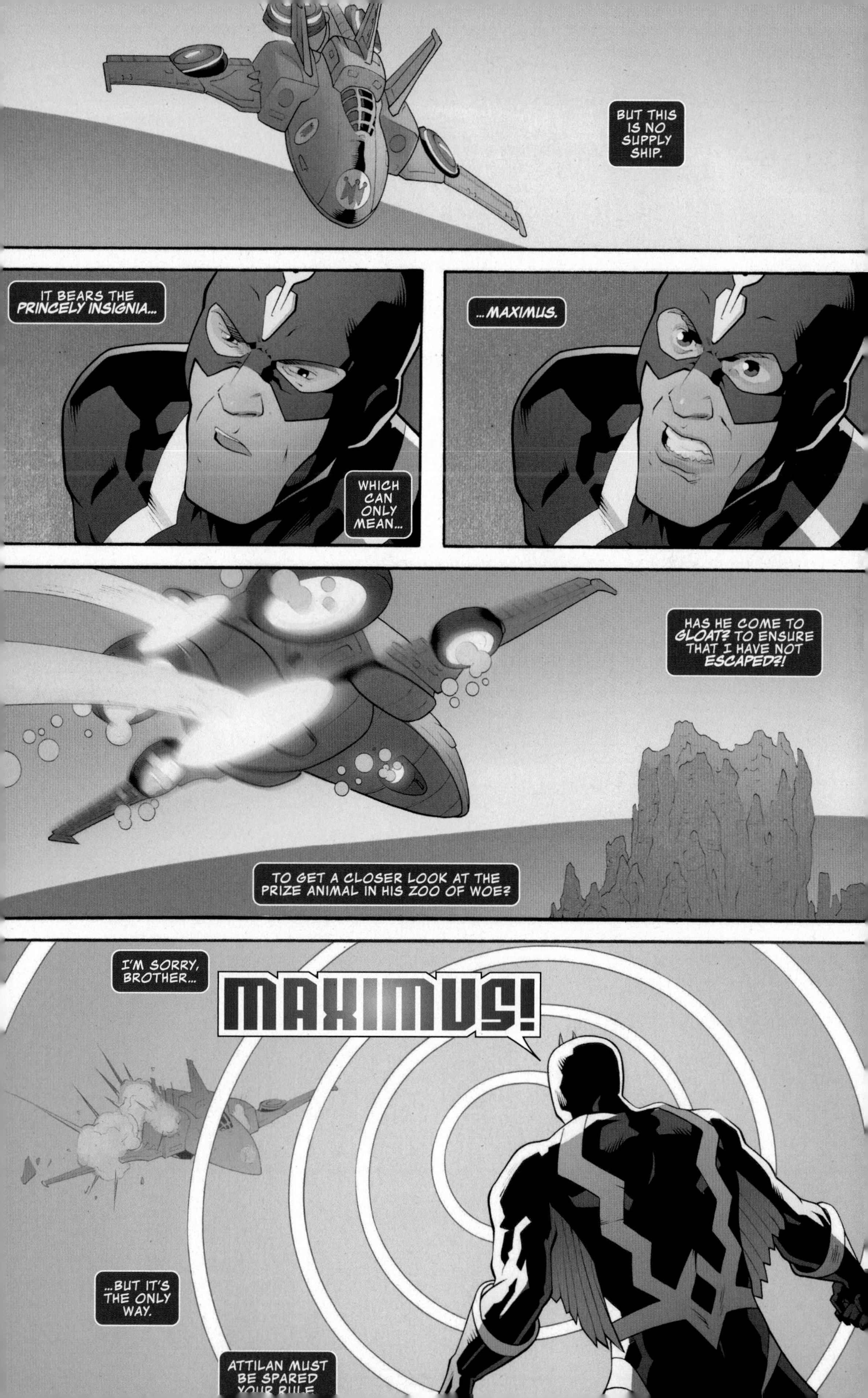

BUT THIS IS NO SUPPLY SHIP.
IT BEARS THE PRINCELY INSIGNIA...
WHICH CAN ONLY MEAN...
...MAXIMUS.
HAS HE COME TO GLOAT? TO ENSURE THAT I HAVE NOT ESCAPED?!
TO GET A CLOSER LOOK AT THE PRIZE ANIMAL IN HIS ZOO OF WOE?
I'M SORRY, BROTHER...
MAXIMUS!
...BUT IT'S THE ONLY WAY.
ATTILAN MUST BE SPARED

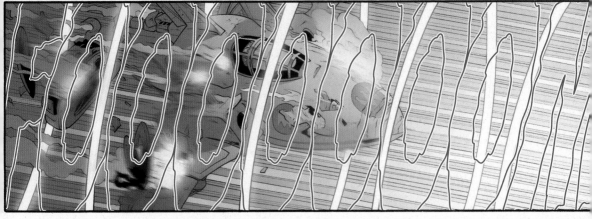

KA_A*THUUD*

HAVE I **DONE IT?**
HAVE I **SAVED**
ATTILAN?

COULD
SAVING IT
REALLY HAVE
BEEN THAT
EASY?

COULD
ANYTHING?

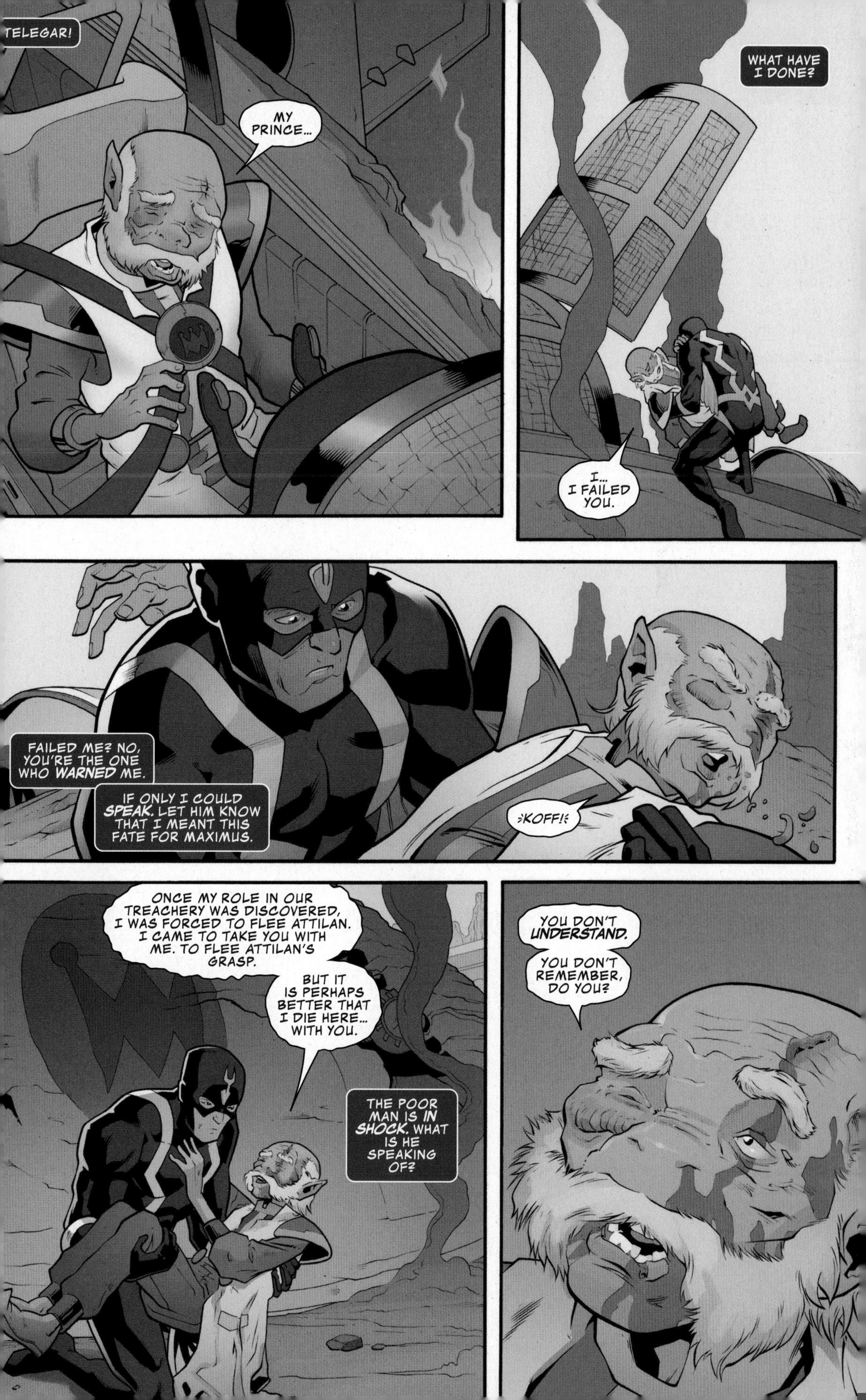
TELEGAR!
MY PRINCE...
WHAT HAVE I DONE?
I... I FAILED YOU.
FAILED ME? NO, YOU'RE THE ONE WHO WARNED ME.
IF ONLY I COULD SPEAK. LET HIM KNOW THAT I MEANT THIS FATE FOR MAXIMUS.
KOFF!
ONCE MY ROLE IN OUR TREACHERY WAS DISCOVERED, I WAS FORCED TO FLEE ATTILAN. I CAME TO TAKE YOU WITH ME. TO FLEE ATTILAN'S GRASP.
BUT IT IS PERHAPS BETTER THAT I DIE HERE... WITH YOU.
THE POOR MAN IS IN SHOCK. WHAT IS HE SPEAKING OF?
YOU DON'T UNDERSTAND.
YOU DON'T REMEMBER, DO YOU?

YOU'RE NOT BLACKAGAR BOLTAGON, MY PRINCE.

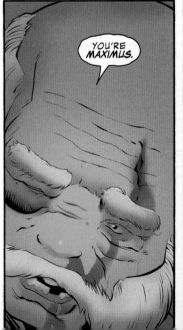

YOU'RE MAXIMUS.

HOW IS THIS POSSIBLE?

IS HE MAD?!

AM I?

WE PLANNED THIS COUP FOR YEARS, MY PRINCE.

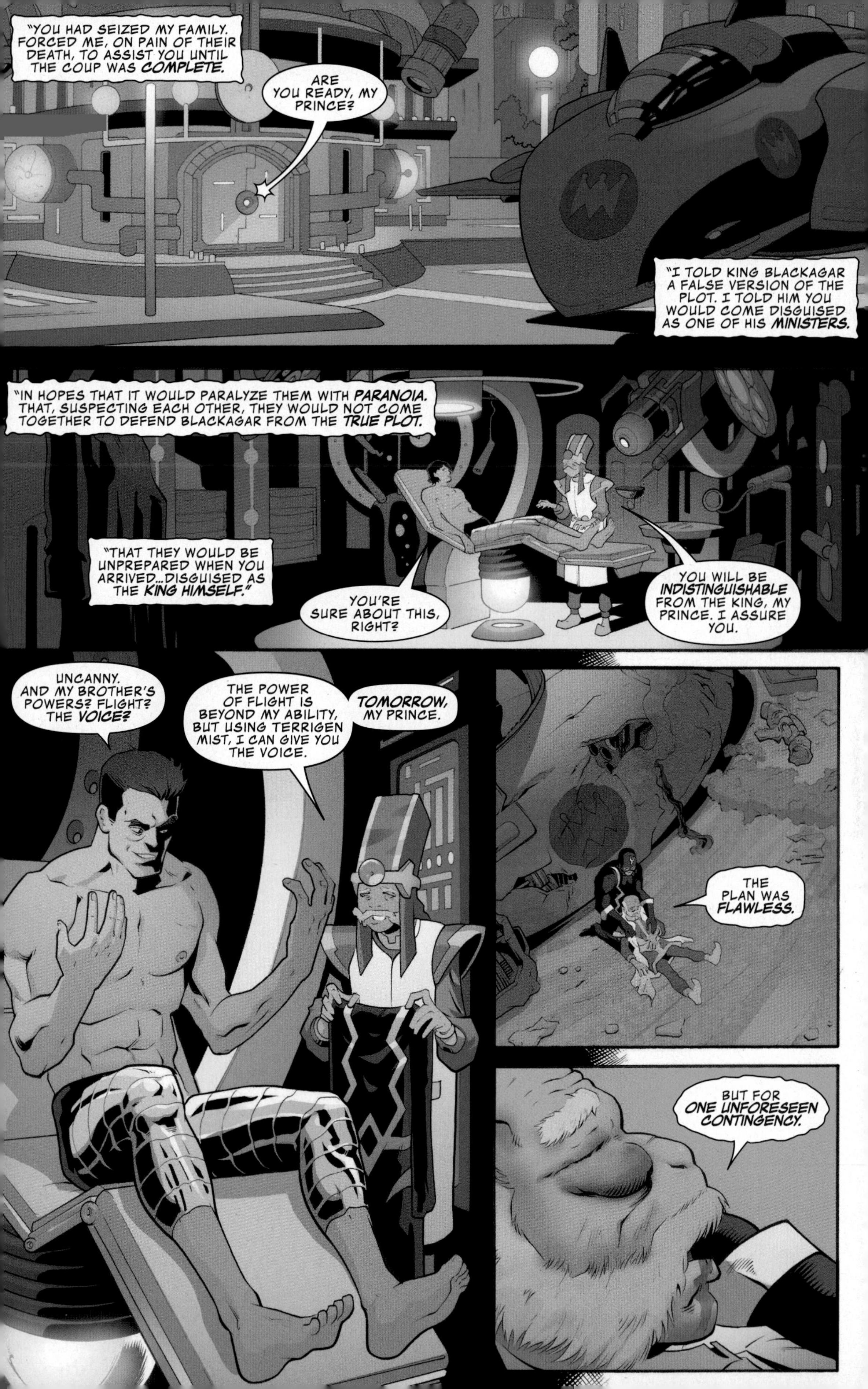
"YOU HAD SEIZED MY FAMILY. FORCED ME, ON PAIN OF THEIR DEATH, TO ASSIST YOU UNTIL THE COUP WAS *COMPLETE*.
ARE YOU READY, MY PRINCE?
"I TOLD KING BLACKAGAR A FALSE VERSION OF THE PLOT. I TOLD HIM YOU WOULD COME DISGUISED AS ONE OF HIS *MINISTERS*.
"IN HOPES THAT IT WOULD PARALYZE THEM WITH *PARANOIA*. THAT, SUSPECTING EACH OTHER, THEY WOULD NOT COME TOGETHER TO DEFEND BLACKAGAR FROM THE *TRUE PLOT*.
"THAT THEY WOULD BE UNPREPARED WHEN YOU ARRIVED...DISGUISED AS THE *KING HIMSELF*."
YOU'RE SURE ABOUT THIS, RIGHT?
YOU WILL BE *INDISTINGUISHABLE* FROM THE KING, MY PRINCE. I ASSURE YOU.
UNCANNY. AND MY BROTHER'S POWERS? FLIGHT? THE *VOICE*?
THE POWER OF FLIGHT IS BEYOND MY ABILITY, BUT USING TERRIGEN MIST, I CAN GIVE YOU THE VOICE.
TOMORROW, MY PRINCE.
THE PLAN WAS *FLAWLESS*.
BUT FOR *ONE UNFORESEEN CONTINGENCY*.

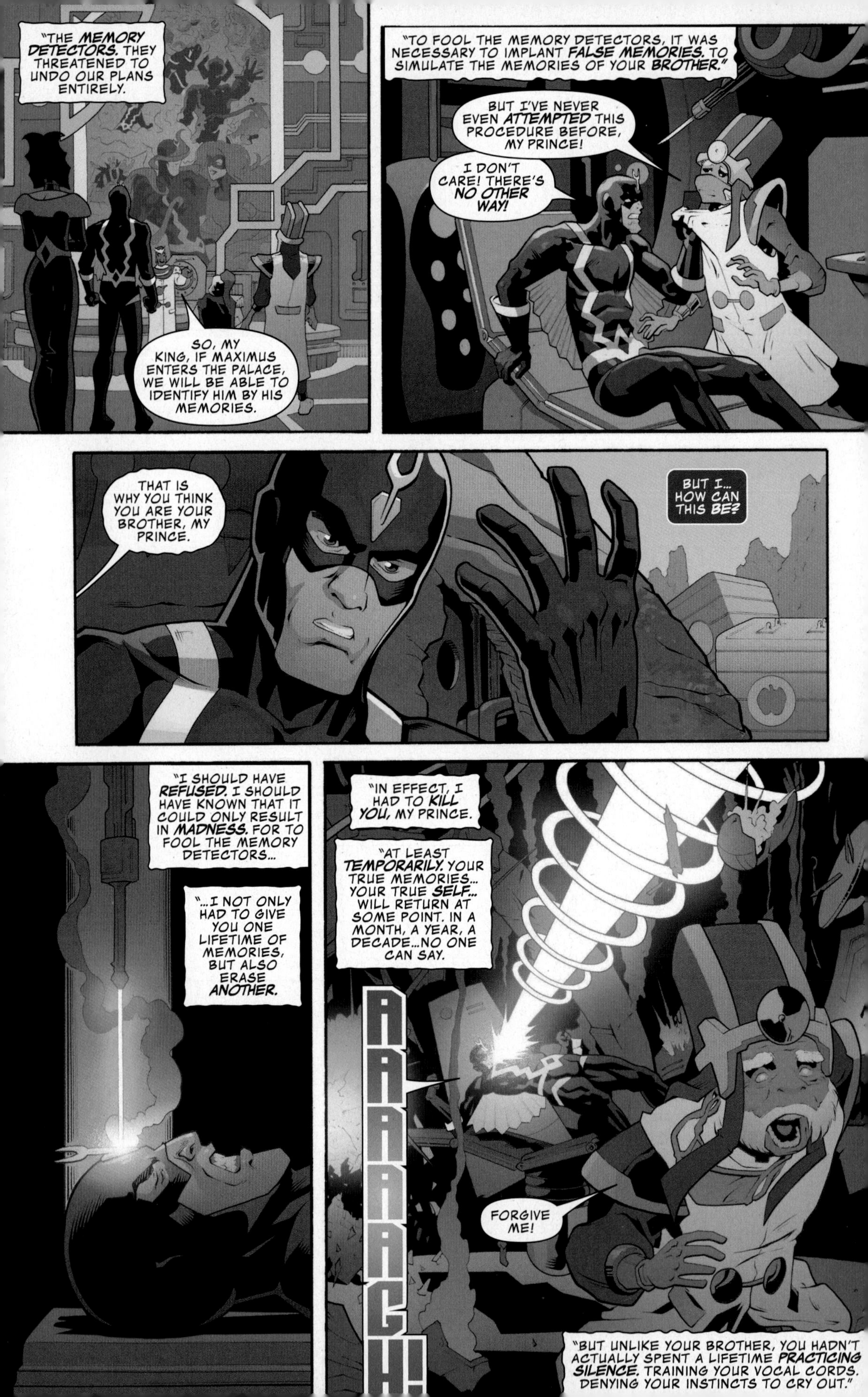
"THE MEMORY DETECTORS. THEY THREATENED TO UNDO OUR PLANS ENTIRELY.
SO, MY KING, IF MAXIMUS ENTERS THE PALACE, WE WILL BE ABLE TO IDENTIFY HIM BY HIS MEMORIES.
"TO FOOL THE MEMORY DETECTORS, IT WAS NECESSARY TO IMPLANT FALSE MEMORIES, TO SIMULATE THE MEMORIES OF YOUR BROTHER."
BUT I'VE NEVER EVEN ATTEMPTED THIS PROCEDURE BEFORE, MY PRINCE!
I DON'T CARE! THERE'S NO OTHER WAY!
THAT IS WHY YOU THINK YOU ARE YOUR BROTHER, MY PRINCE.
BUT I... HOW CAN THIS BE?
"I SHOULD HAVE REFUSED. I SHOULD HAVE KNOWN THAT IT COULD ONLY RESULT IN MADNESS. FOR TO FOOL THE MEMORY DETECTORS...
"...I NOT ONLY HAD TO GIVE YOU ONE LIFETIME OF MEMORIES, BUT ALSO ERASE ANOTHER.
"IN EFFECT, I HAD TO KILL YOU, MY PRINCE.
"AT LEAST TEMPORARILY. YOUR TRUE MEMORIES... YOUR TRUE SELF... WILL RETURN AT SOME POINT. IN A MONTH, A YEAR, A DECADE...NO ONE CAN SAY.
AAAAAAGH!
FORGIVE ME!
"BUT UNLIKE YOUR BROTHER, YOU HADN'T ACTUALLY SPENT A LIFETIME PRACTICING SILENCE. TRAINING YOUR VOCAL CORDS. DENYING YOUR INSTINCTS TO CRY OUT."

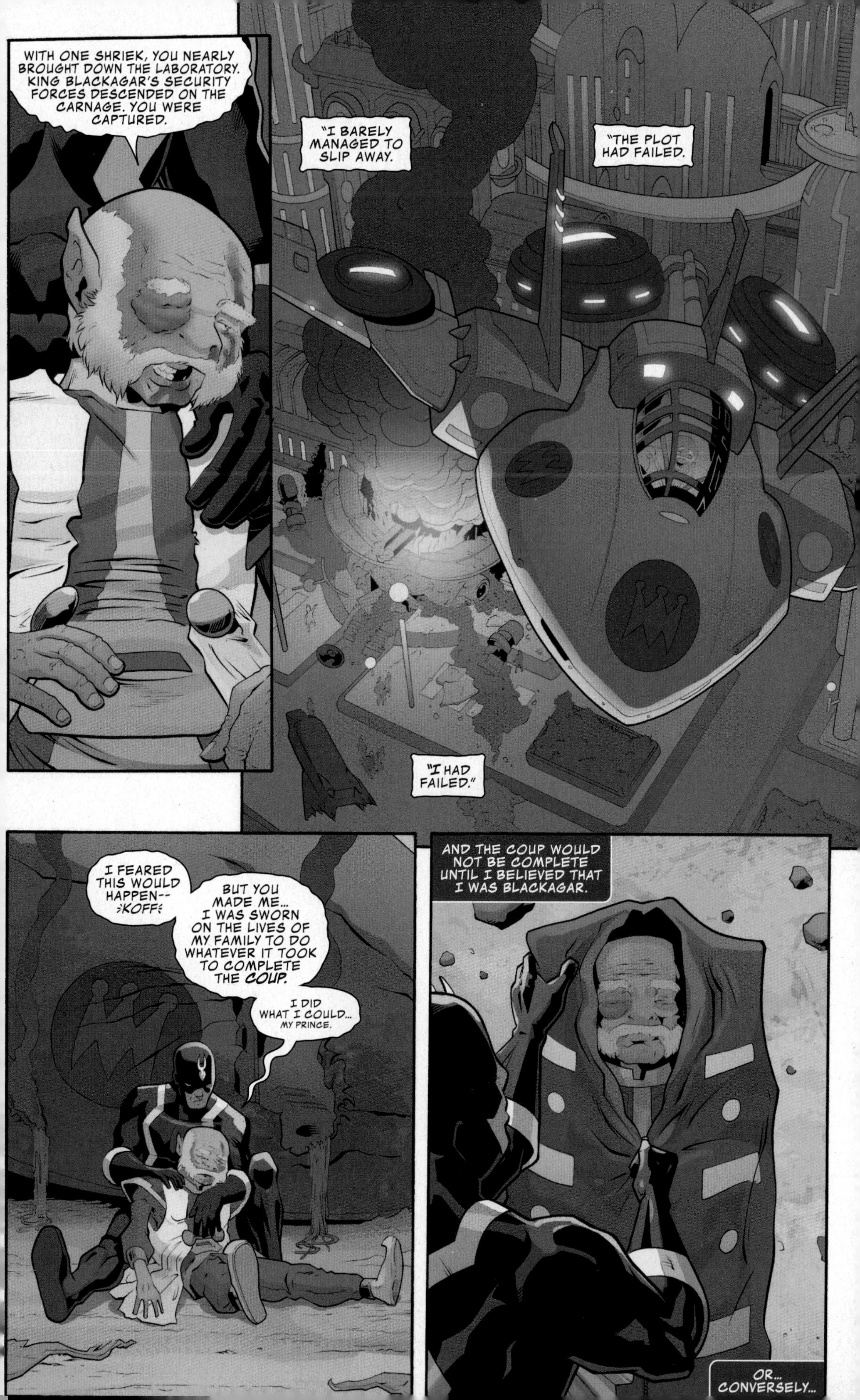

WITH ONE SHRIEK, YOU NEARLY BROUGHT DOWN THE LABORATORY. KING BLACKAGAR'S SECURITY FORCES DESCENDED ON THE CARNAGE. YOU WERE CAPTURED.
"I BARELY MANAGED TO SLIP AWAY.
"THE PLOT HAD FAILED.
"I HAD FAILED."
I FEARED THIS WOULD HAPPEN-- KOFF
BUT YOU MADE ME... I WAS SWORN ON THE LIVES OF MY FAMILY TO DO WHATEVER IT TOOK TO COMPLETE THE COUP.
I DID WHAT I COULD... MY PRINCE.
AND THE COUP WOULD NOT BE COMPLETE UNTIL I BELIEVED THAT I WAS BLACKAGAR.
OR... CONVERSELY...

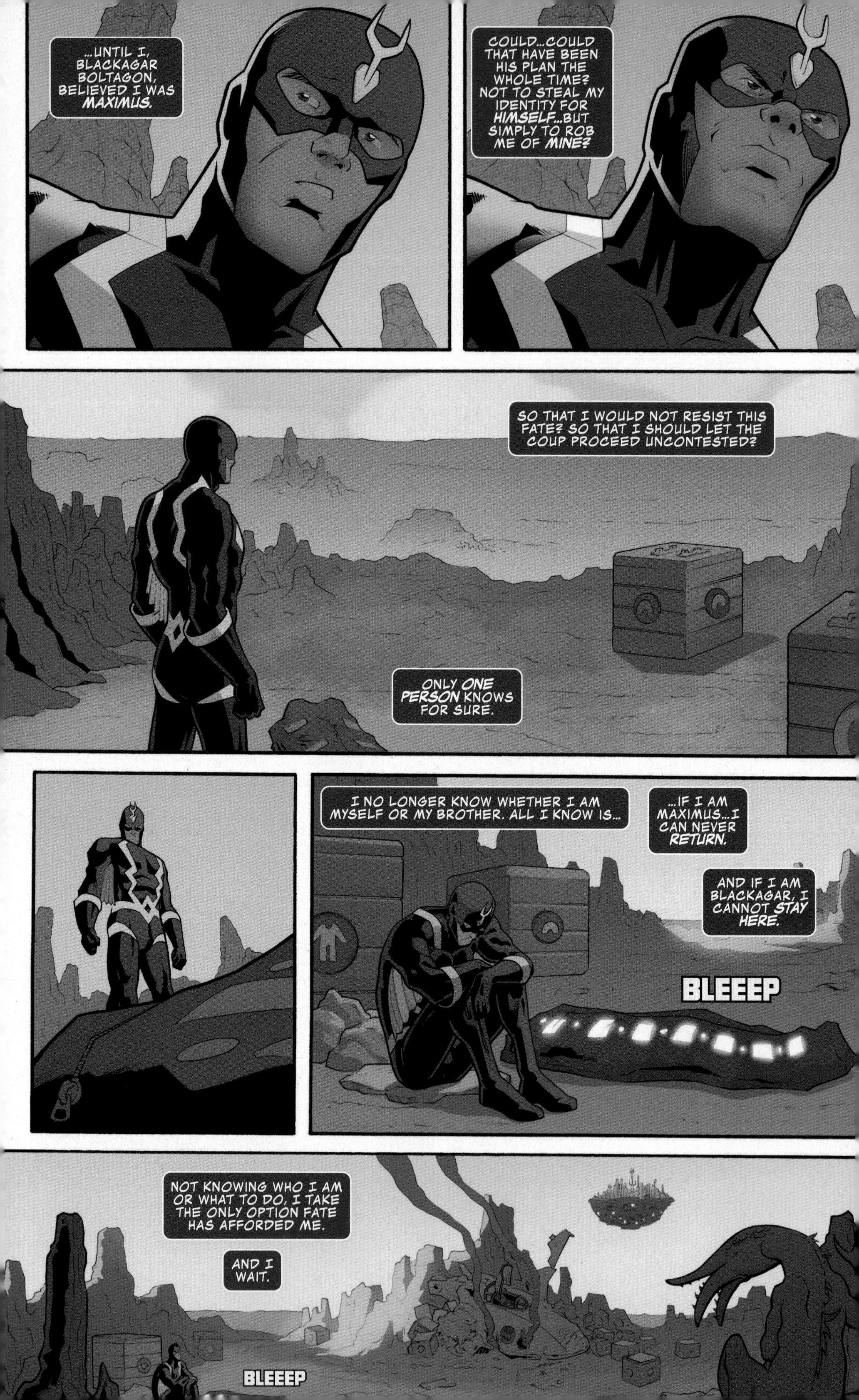
...UNTIL I, BLACKAGAR BOLTAGON, BELIEVED I WAS MAXIMUS.
COULD...COULD THAT HAVE BEEN HIS PLAN THE WHOLE TIME? NOT TO STEAL MY IDENTITY FOR HIMSELF...BUT SIMPLY TO ROB ME OF MINE?
SO THAT I WOULD NOT RESIST THIS FATE? SO THAT I SHOULD LET THE COUP PROCEED UNCONTESTED?
ONLY ONE PERSON KNOWS FOR SURE.
I NO LONGER KNOW WHETHER I AM MYSELF OR MY BROTHER. ALL I KNOW IS...
...IF I AM MAXIMUS...I CAN NEVER RETURN.
AND IF I AM BLACKAGAR, I CANNOT STAY HERE.
BLEEEP
NOT KNOWING WHO I AM OR WHAT TO DO, I TAKE THE ONLY OPTION FATE HAS AFFORDED ME.
AND I WAIT.
BLEEEP

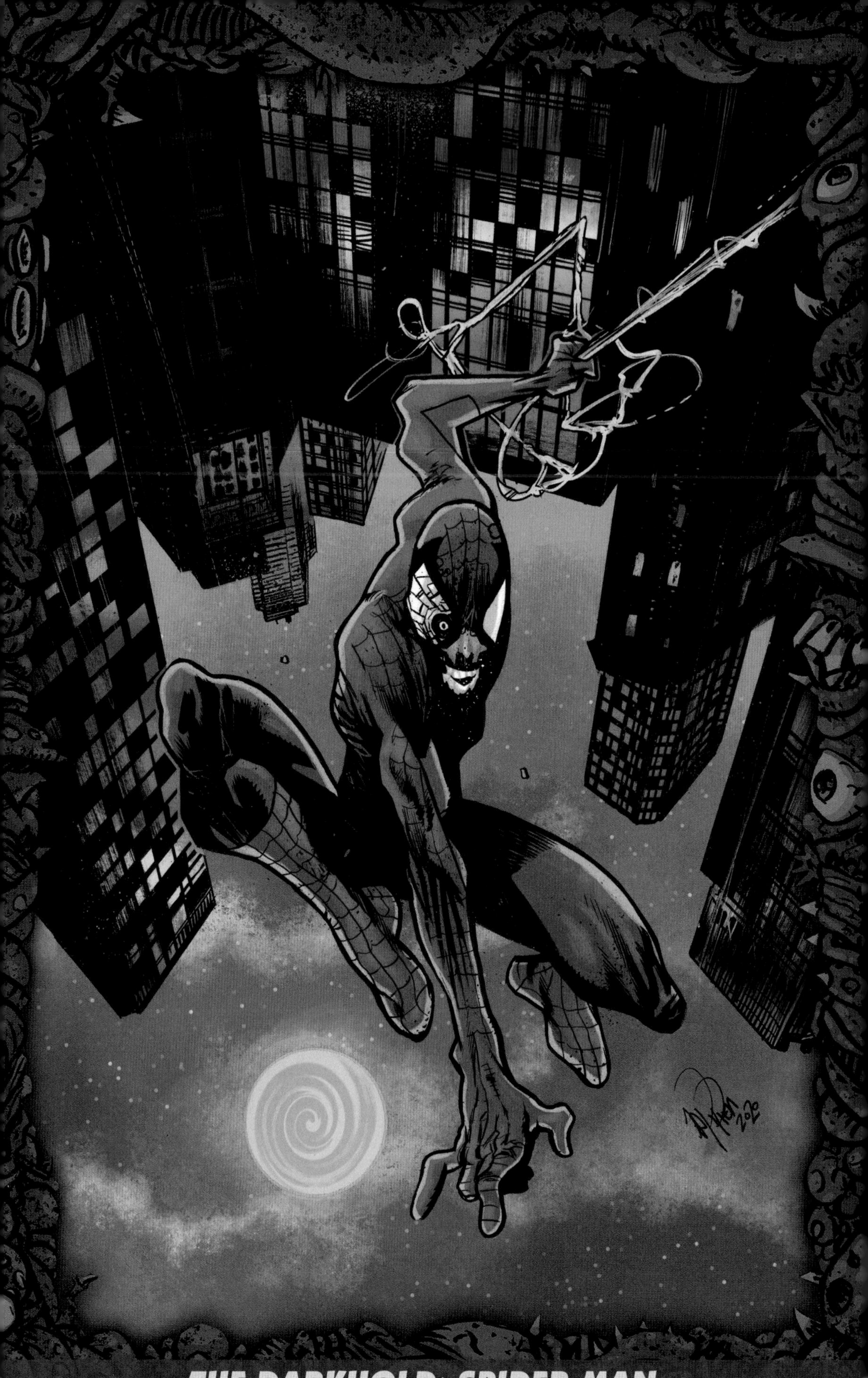

THE DARKHOLD: SPIDER-MAN

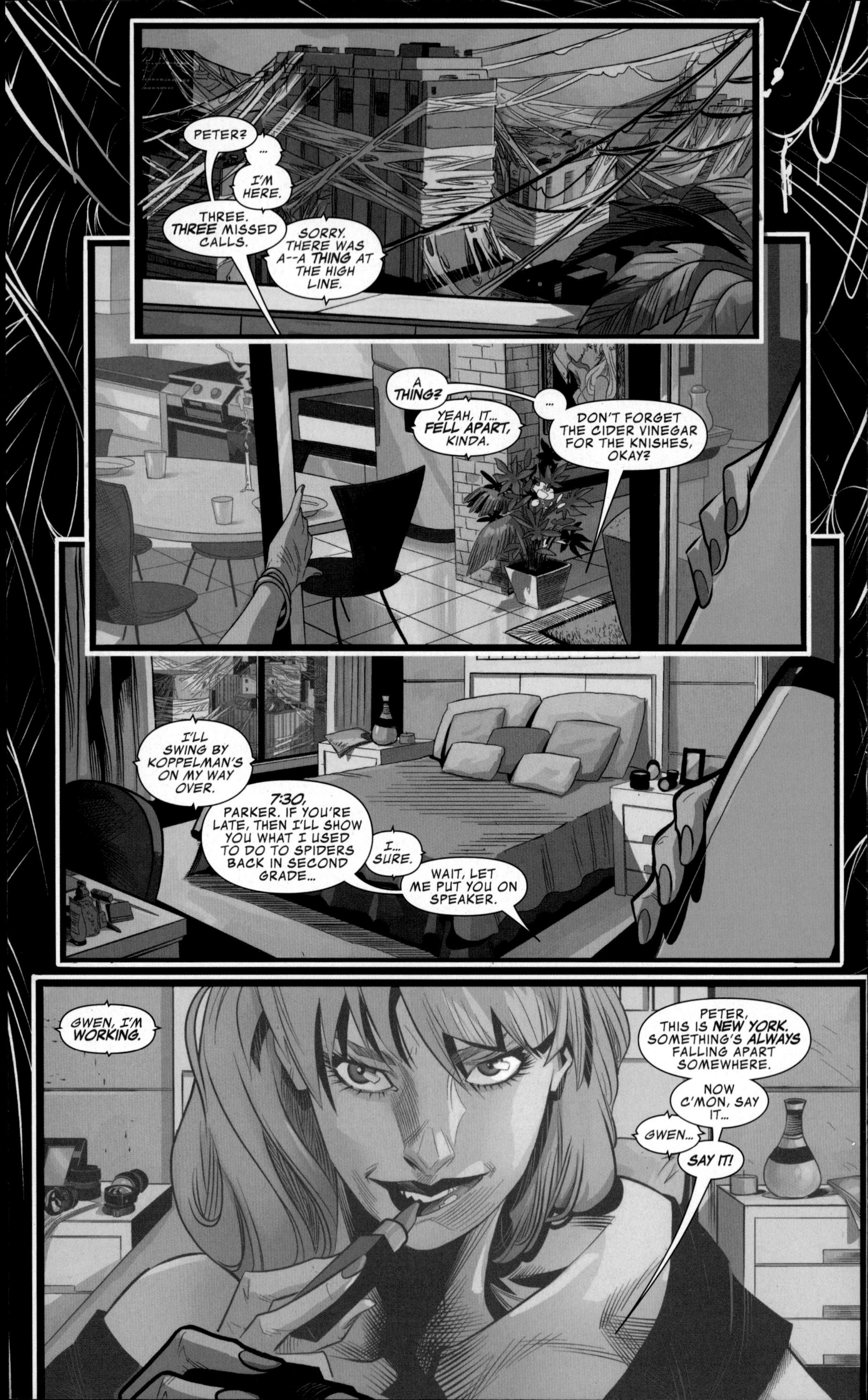
PETER?
...
I'M HERE.
THREE. THREE MISSED CALLS.
SORRY. THERE WAS A--A THING AT THE HIGH LINE.
A THING?
YEAH, IT... FELL APART, KINDA.
...
DON'T FORGET THE CIDER VINEGAR FOR THE KNISHES, OKAY?
I'LL SWING BY KOPPELMAN'S ON MY WAY OVER.
7:30, PARKER. IF YOU'RE LATE, THEN I'LL SHOW YOU WHAT I USED TO DO TO SPIDERS BACK IN SECOND GRADE...
I... SURE.
WAIT, LET ME PUT YOU ON SPEAKER.
GWEN, I'M WORKING.
PETER, THIS IS NEW YORK. SOMETHING'S ALWAYS FALLING APART SOMEWHERE.
NOW C'MON, SAY IT...
GWEN...
SAY IT!

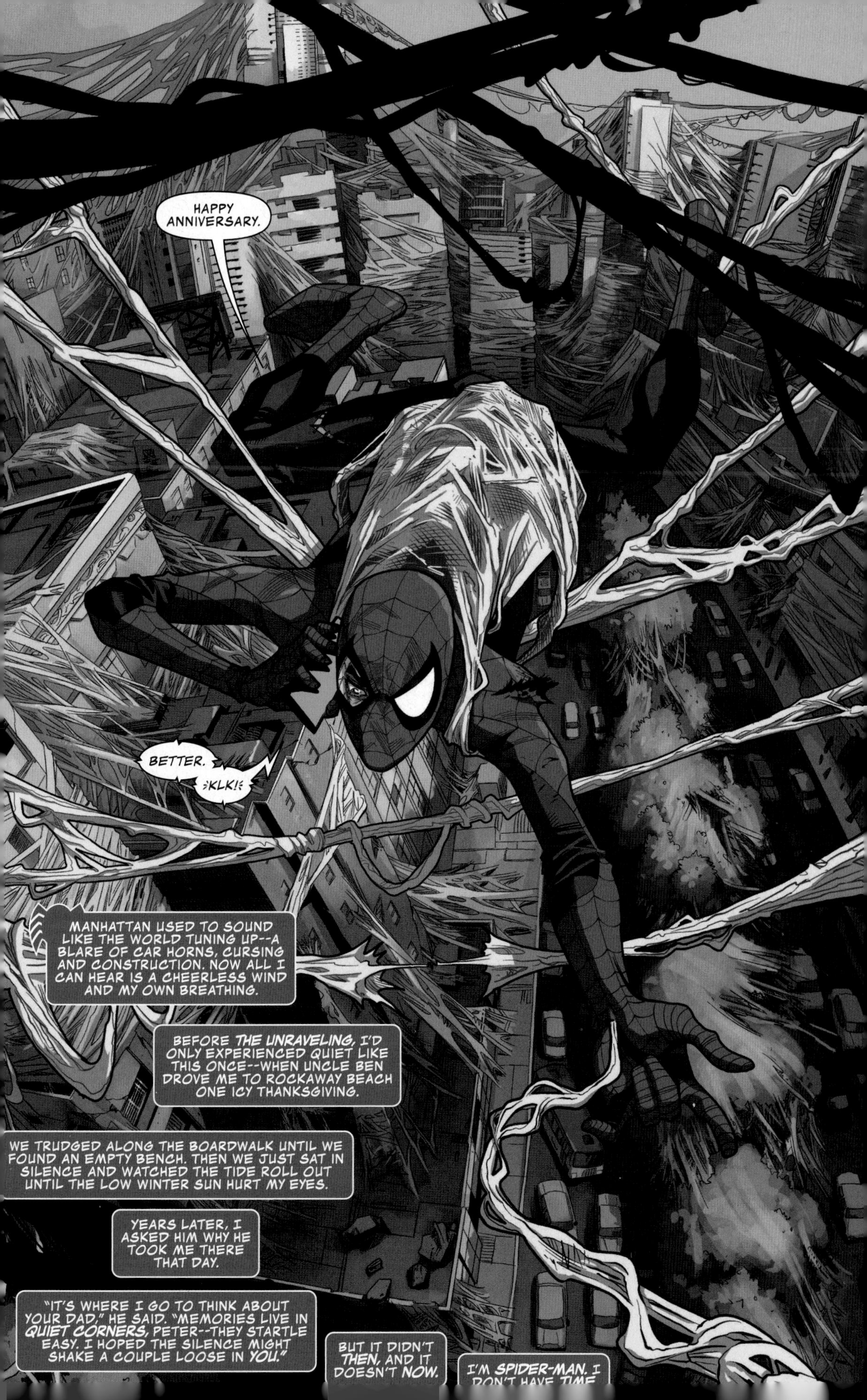

HAPPY ANNIVERSARY.
BETTER.
KLK!
MANHATTAN USED TO SOUND LIKE THE WORLD TUNING UP--A BLARE OF CAR HORNS, CURSING AND CONSTRUCTION. NOW ALL I CAN HEAR IS A CHEERLESS WIND AND MY OWN BREATHING.
BEFORE *THE UNRAVELING,* I'D ONLY EXPERIENCED QUIET LIKE THIS ONCE--WHEN UNCLE BEN DROVE ME TO ROCKAWAY BEACH ONE ICY THANKSGIVING.
WE TRUDGED ALONG THE BOARDWALK UNTIL WE FOUND AN EMPTY BENCH. THEN WE JUST SAT IN SILENCE AND WATCHED THE TIDE ROLL OUT UNTIL THE LOW WINTER SUN HURT MY EYES.
YEARS LATER, I ASKED HIM WHY HE TOOK ME THERE THAT DAY.
"IT'S WHERE I GO TO THINK ABOUT YOUR DAD," HE SAID. "MEMORIES LIVE IN *QUIET CORNERS,* PETER--THEY STARTLE EASY. I HOPED THE SILENCE MIGHT SHAKE A COUPLE LOOSE IN *YOU.*"
BUT IT DIDN'T *THEN,* AND IT DOESN'T *NOW.*
I'M *SPIDER-MAN.* I DON'T HAVE *TIME*

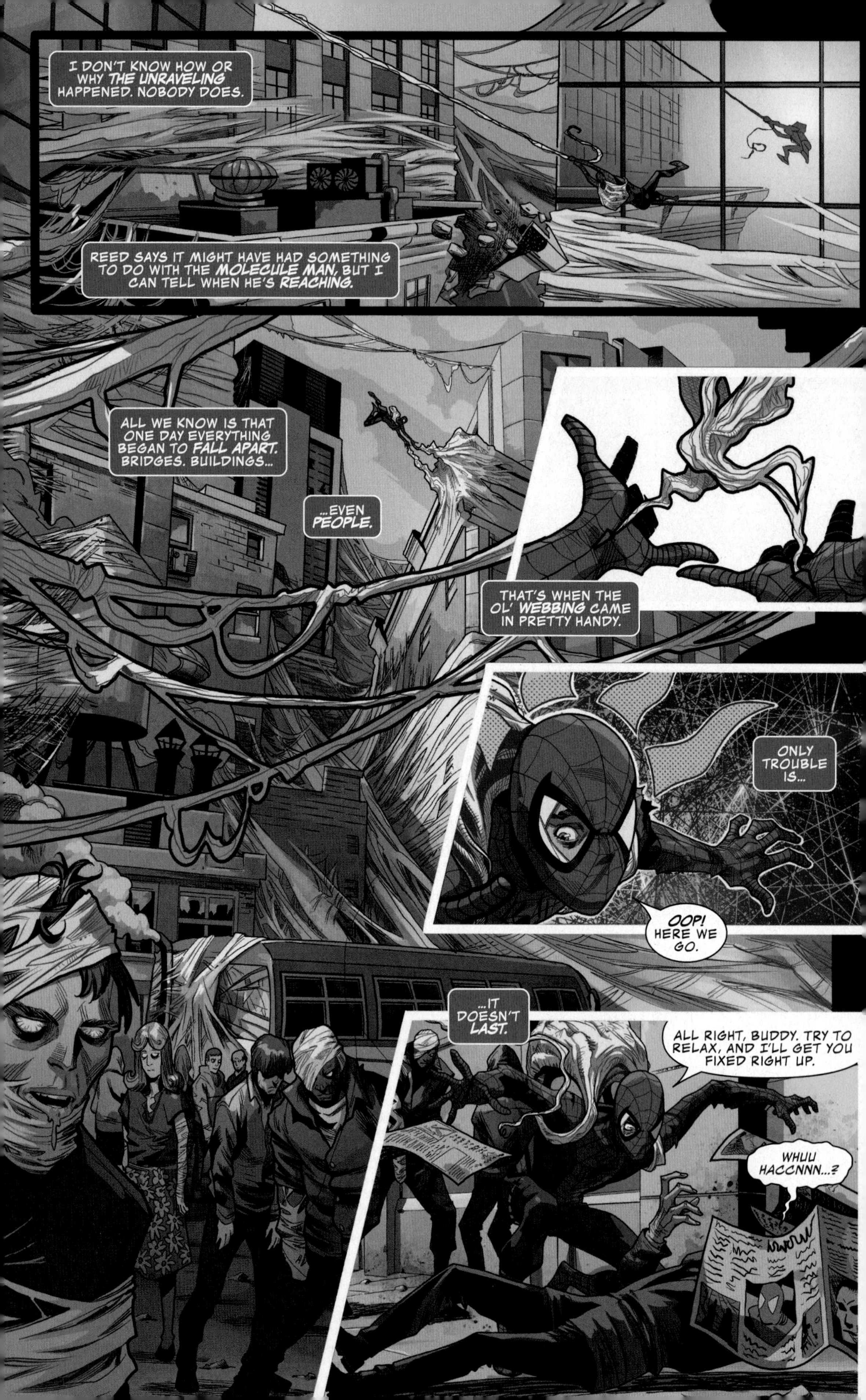
I DON'T KNOW HOW OR WHY THE UNRAVELING HAPPENED. NOBODY DOES.
REED SAYS IT MIGHT HAVE HAD SOMETHING TO DO WITH THE MOLECULE MAN, BUT I CAN TELL WHEN HE'S REACHING.
ALL WE KNOW IS THAT ONE DAY EVERYTHING BEGAN TO FALL APART. BRIDGES. BUILDINGS...
...EVEN PEOPLE.
THAT'S WHEN THE OL' WEBBING CAME IN PRETTY HANDY.
ONLY TROUBLE IS...
OOP! HERE WE GO.
...IT DOESN'T LAST.
ALL RIGHT, BUDDY. TRY TO RELAX, AND I'LL GET YOU FIXED RIGHT UP.
WHUU HACCNNN...?

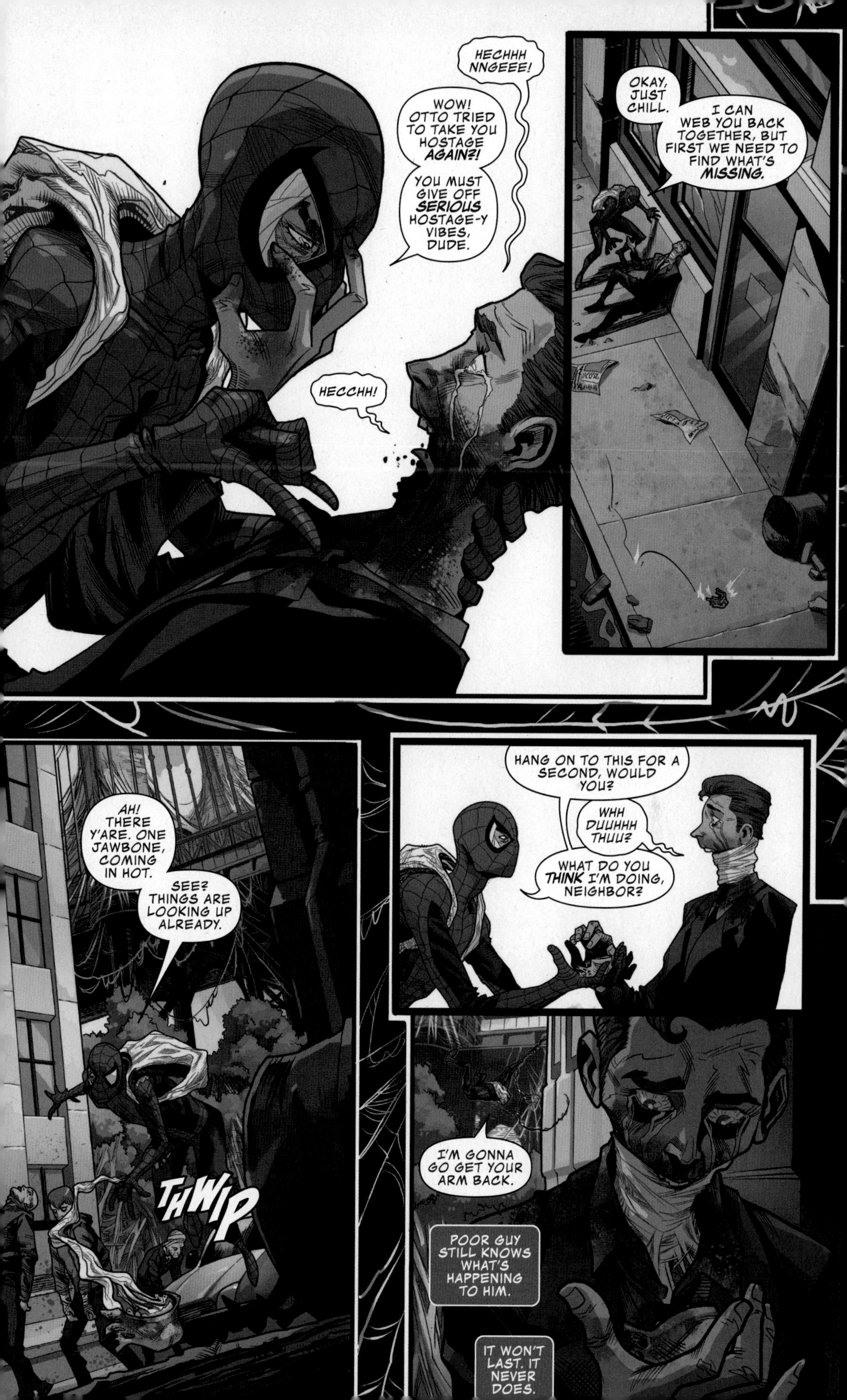
HECHHH NNGEEE!
WOW! OTTO TRIED TO TAKE YOU HOSTAGE AGAIN?!
YOU MUST GIVE OFF SERIOUS HOSTAGE-Y VIBES, DUDE.
HECCHH!
OKAY, JUST CHILL.
I CAN WEB YOU BACK TOGETHER, BUT FIRST WE NEED TO FIND WHAT'S MISSING.
AH! THERE Y'ARE. ONE JAWBONE, COMING IN HOT.
SEE? THINGS ARE LOOKING UP ALREADY.
THWIP
HANG ON TO THIS FOR A SECOND, WOULD YOU?
WHH DUUHHH THUU?
WHAT DO YOU THINK I'M DOING, NEIGHBOR?
I'M GONNA GO GET YOUR ARM BACK.
POOR GUY STILL KNOWS WHAT'S HAPPENING TO HIM.
IT WON'T LAST. IT NEVER DOES.

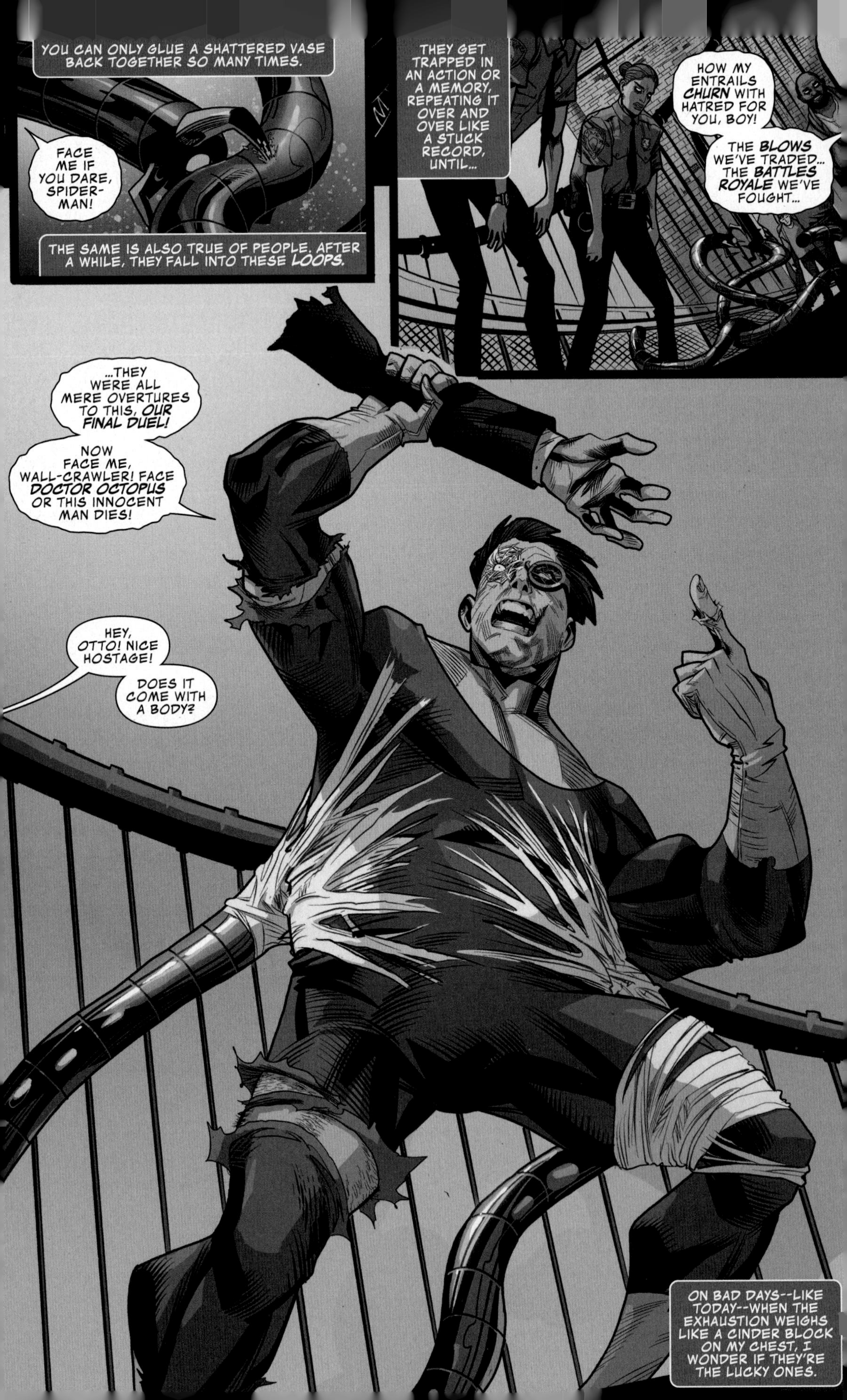
YOU CAN ONLY GLUE A SHATTERED VASE BACK TOGETHER SO MANY TIMES.
FACE ME IF YOU DARE, SPIDER-MAN!
THE SAME IS ALSO TRUE OF PEOPLE. AFTER A WHILE, THEY FALL INTO THESE LOOPS.
THEY GET TRAPPED IN AN ACTION OR A MEMORY, REPEATING IT OVER AND OVER LIKE A STUCK RECORD, UNTIL...
HOW MY ENTRAILS CHURN WITH HATRED FOR YOU, BOY!
THE BLOWS WE'VE TRADED... THE BATTLES ROYALE WE'VE FOUGHT...
...THEY WERE ALL MERE OVERTURES TO THIS, OUR FINAL DUEL!
NOW FACE ME, WALL-CRAWLER! FACE DOCTOR OCTOPUS OR THIS INNOCENT MAN DIES!
HEY, OTTO! NICE HOSTAGE!
DOES IT COME WITH A BODY?
ON BAD DAYS--LIKE TODAY--WHEN THE EXHAUSTION WEIGHS LIKE A CINDER BLOCK ON MY CHEST, I WONDER IF THEY'RE THE LUCKY ONES.

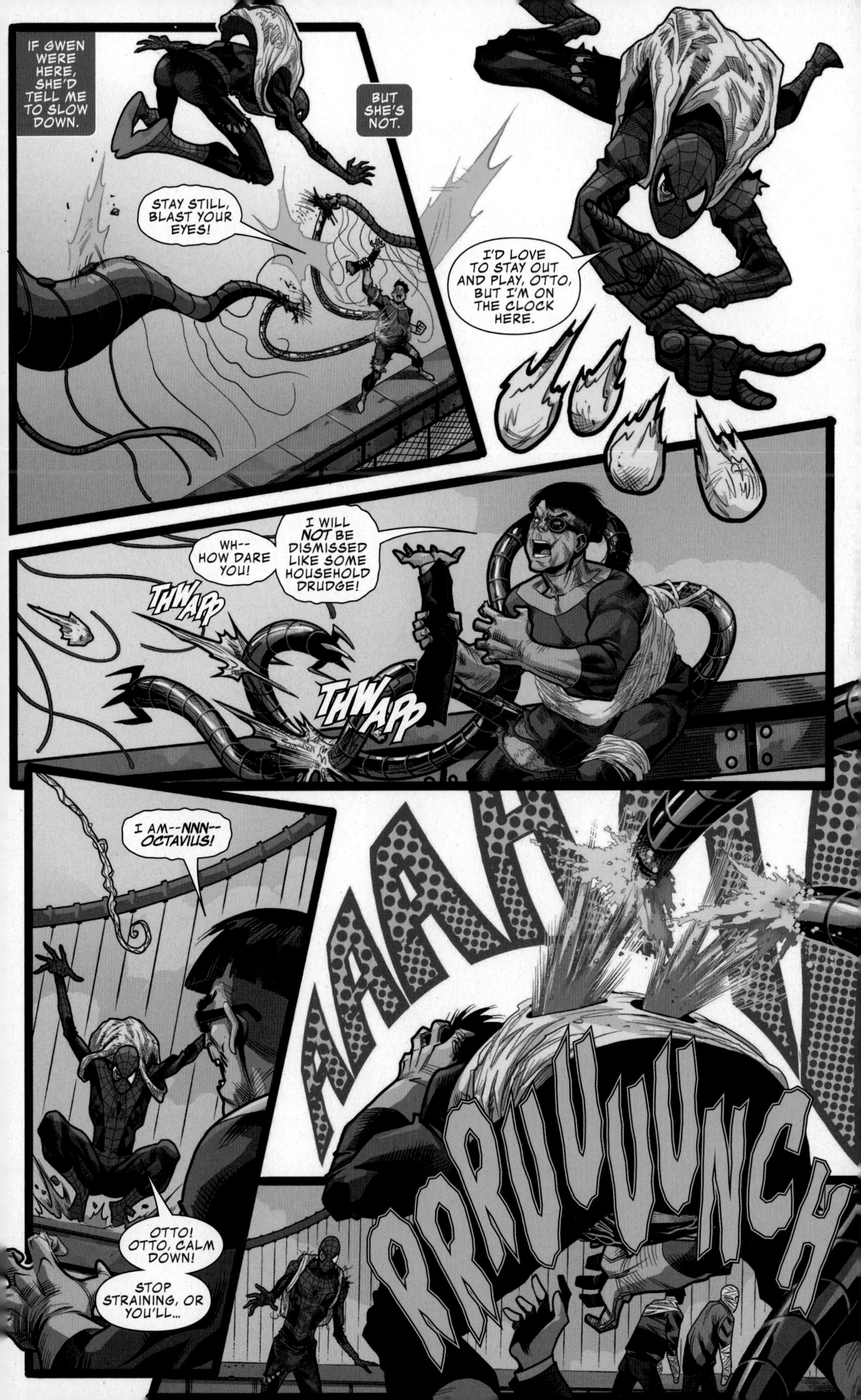
IF GWEN WERE HERE, SHE'D TELL ME TO SLOW DOWN.
BUT SHE'S NOT.
STAY STILL, BLAST YOUR EYES!
I'D LOVE TO STAY OUT AND PLAY, OTTO, BUT I'M ON THE CLOCK HERE.
WH-- HOW DARE YOU!
I WILL NOT BE DISMISSED LIKE SOME HOUSEHOLD DRUDGE!
THWAPP
THWAPP
I AM--NNN-- OCTAVIUS!
AAAH
OTTO! OTTO, CALM DOWN!
STOP STRAINING, OR YOU'LL...
KRRUUUUNCH

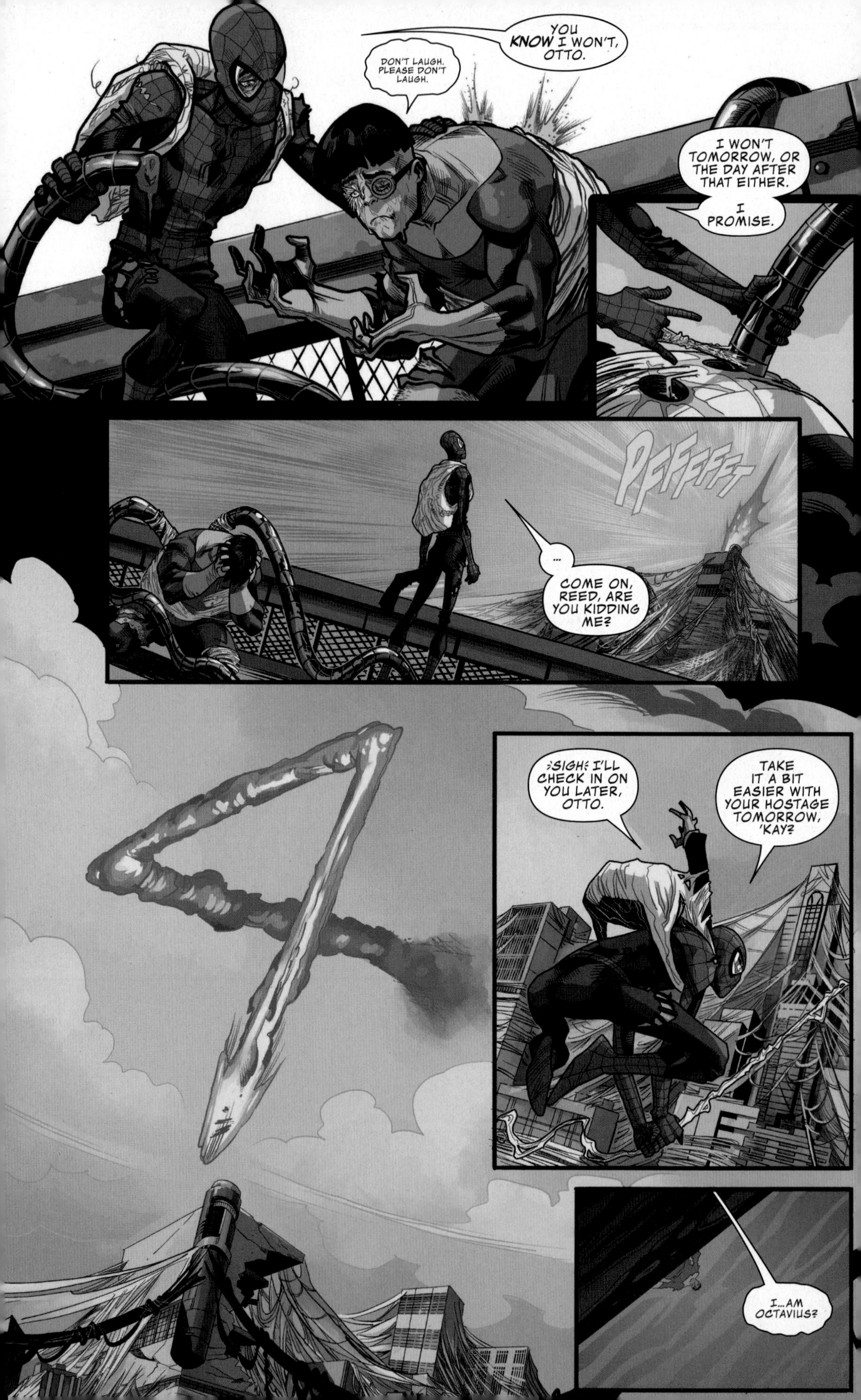
DON'T LAUGH. PLEASE DON'T LAUGH.
YOU KNOW I WON'T, OTTO.
I WON'T TOMORROW, OR THE DAY AFTER THAT EITHER.
I PROMISE.
PFFFFFT
... COME ON, REED, ARE YOU KIDDING ME?
SIGH I'LL CHECK IN ON YOU LATER, OTTO.
TAKE IT A BIT EASIER WITH YOUR HOSTAGE TOMORROW, 'KAY?
I...AM OCTAVIUS?

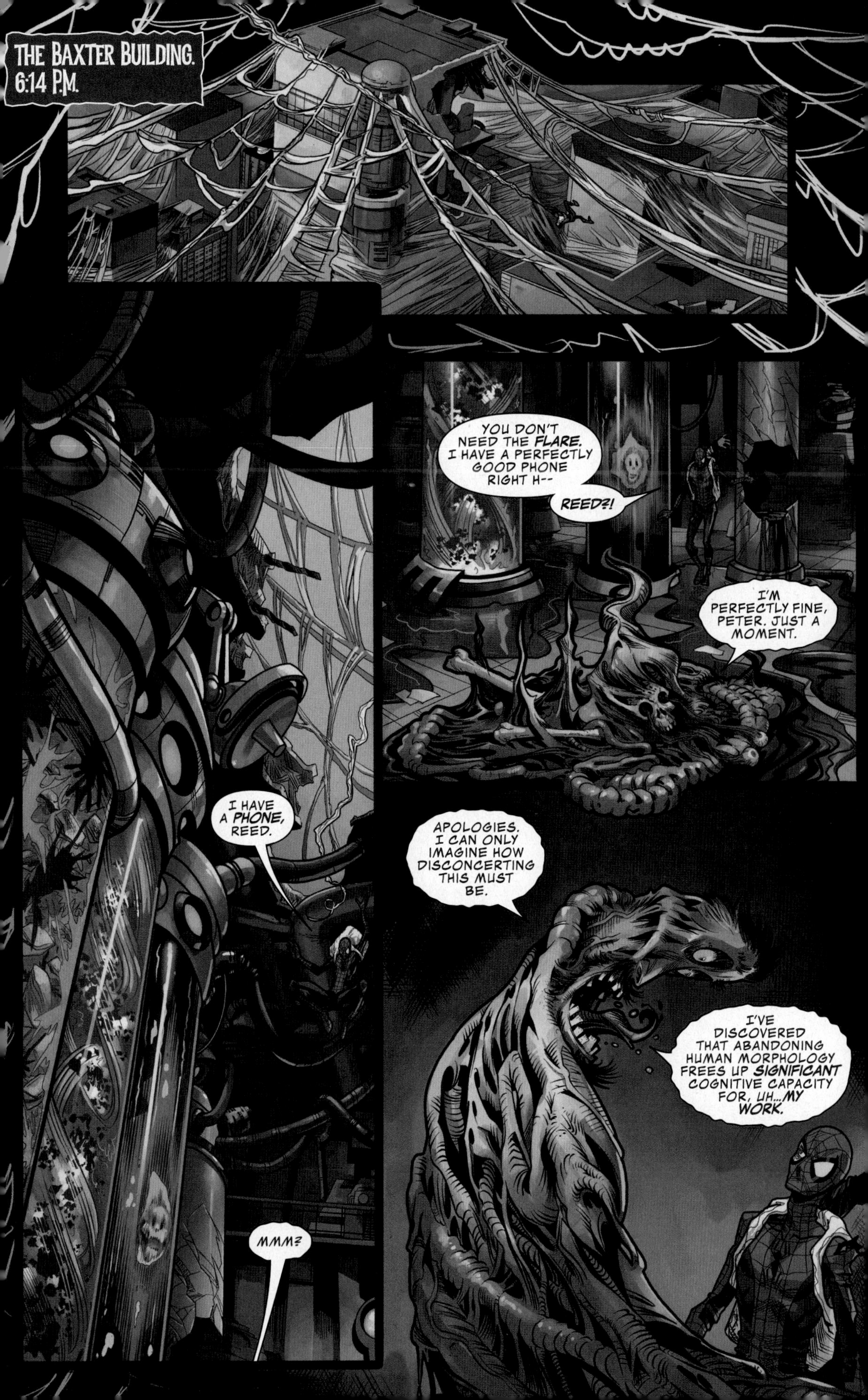
THE BAXTER BUILDING. 6:14 P.M.
YOU DON'T NEED THE FLARE. I HAVE A PERFECTLY GOOD PHONE RIGHT H--
REED?!
I'M PERFECTLY FINE, PETER. JUST A MOMENT.
I HAVE A PHONE, REED.
MMM?
APOLOGIES. I CAN ONLY IMAGINE HOW DISCONCERTING THIS MUST BE.
I'VE DISCOVERED THAT ABANDONING HUMAN MORPHOLOGY FREES UP SIGNIFICANT COGNITIVE CAPACITY FOR, UH... MY WORK.

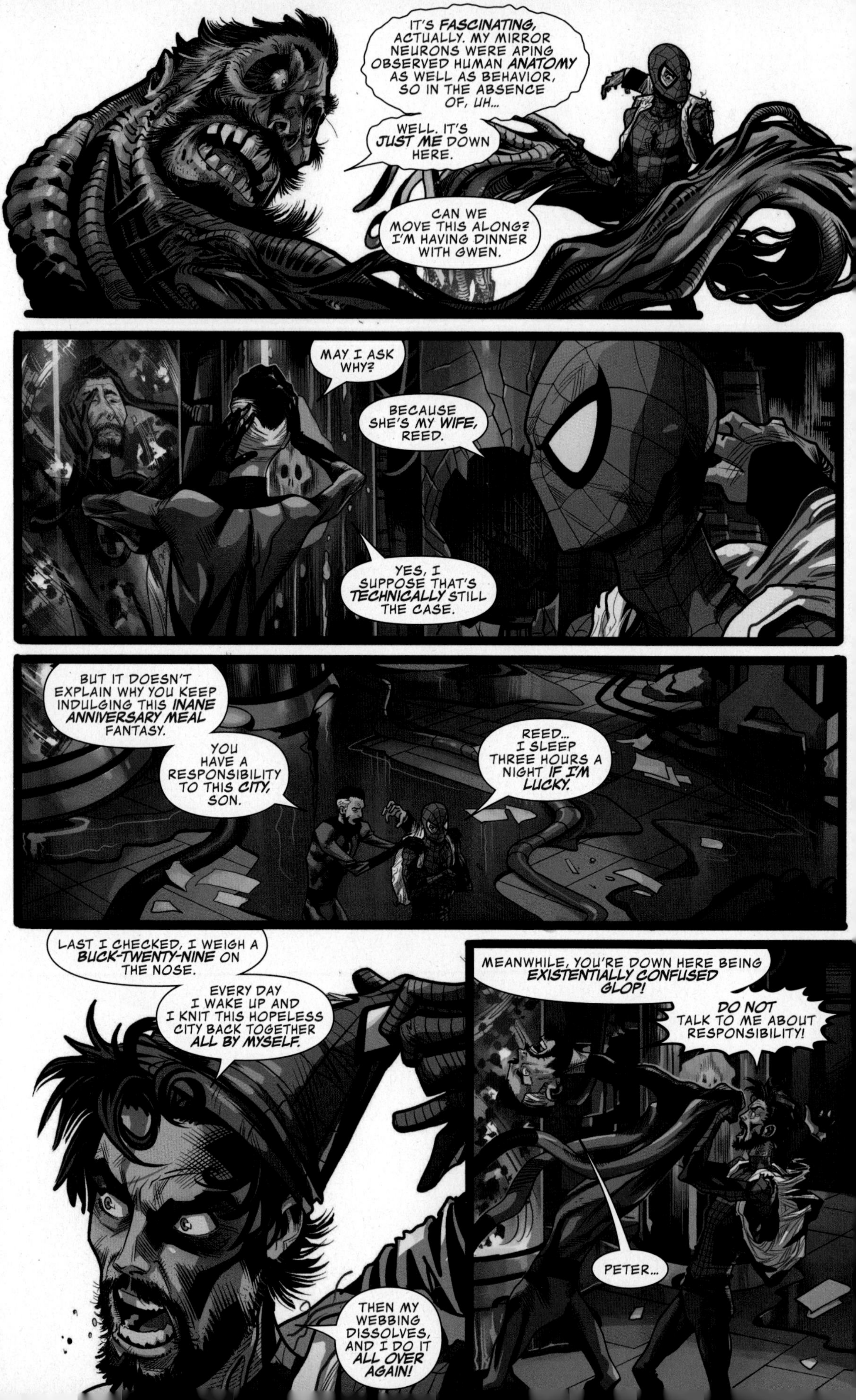
IT'S FASCINATING, ACTUALLY. MY MIRROR NEURONS WERE APING OBSERVED HUMAN ANATOMY AS WELL AS BEHAVIOR, SO IN THE ABSENCE OF, UH...
WELL. IT'S JUST ME DOWN HERE.
CAN WE MOVE THIS ALONG? I'M HAVING DINNER WITH GWEN.
MAY I ASK WHY?
BECAUSE SHE'S MY WIFE, REED.
YES, I SUPPOSE THAT'S TECHNICALLY STILL THE CASE.
BUT IT DOESN'T EXPLAIN WHY YOU KEEP INDULGING THIS INANE ANNIVERSARY MEAL FANTASY.
YOU HAVE A RESPONSIBILITY TO THIS CITY, SON.
REED... I SLEEP THREE HOURS A NIGHT IF I'M LUCKY.
LAST I CHECKED, I WEIGH A BUCK-TWENTY-NINE ON THE NOSE.
EVERY DAY I WAKE UP AND I KNIT THIS HOPELESS CITY BACK TOGETHER ALL BY MYSELF.
THEN MY WEBBING DISSOLVES, AND I DO IT ALL OVER AGAIN!
MEANWHILE, YOU'RE DOWN HERE BEING EXISTENTIALLY CONFUSED GLOP!
DO NOT TALK TO ME ABOUT RESPONSIBILITY!
PETER...

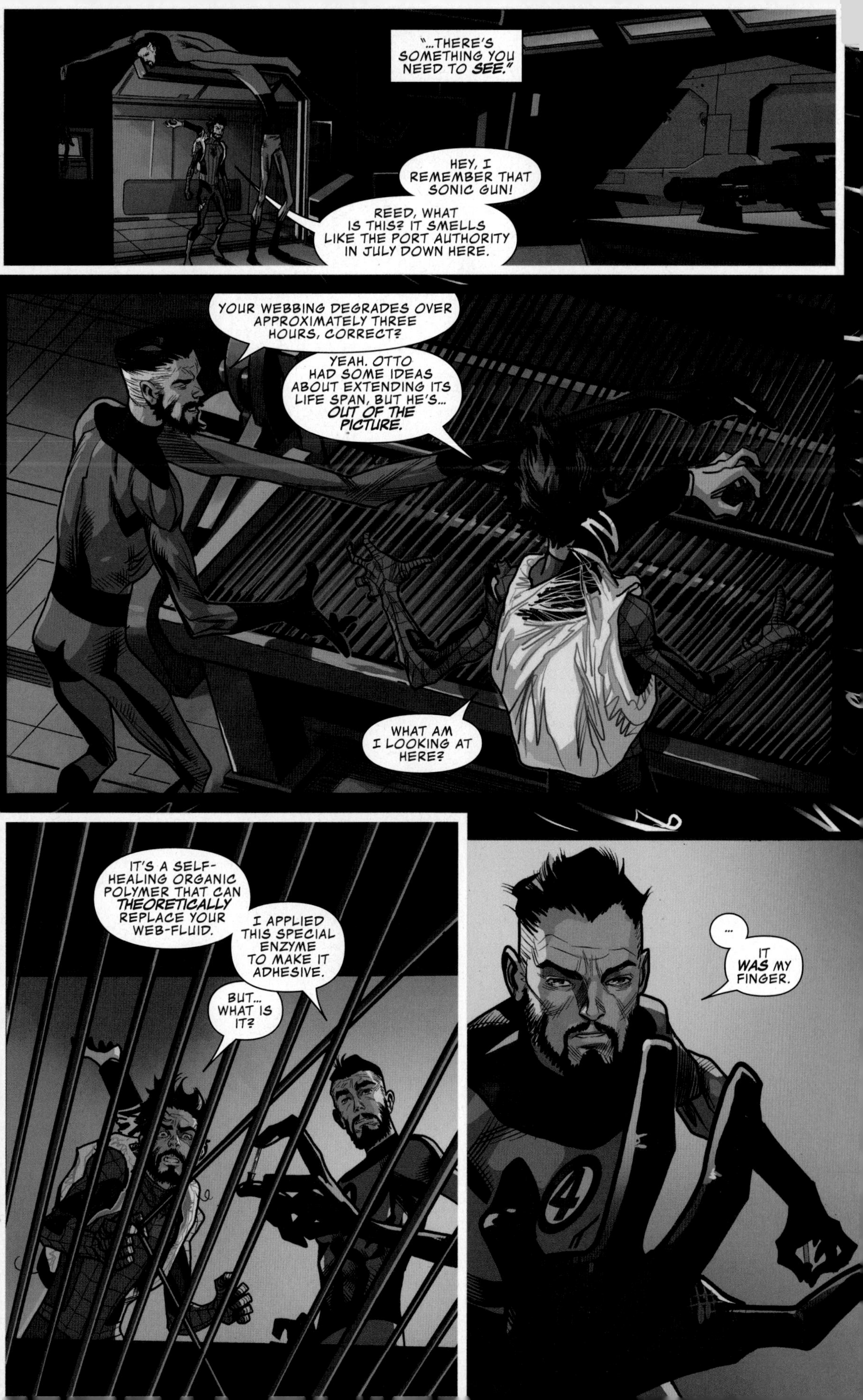
"...THERE'S SOMETHING YOU NEED TO SEE."
HEY, I REMEMBER THAT SONIC GUN!
REED, WHAT IS THIS? IT SMELLS LIKE THE PORT AUTHORITY IN JULY DOWN HERE.
YOUR WEBBING DEGRADES OVER APPROXIMATELY THREE HOURS, CORRECT?
YEAH. OTTO HAD SOME IDEAS ABOUT EXTENDING ITS LIFE SPAN, BUT HE'S... OUT OF THE PICTURE.
WHAT AM I LOOKING AT HERE?
IT'S A SELF-HEALING ORGANIC POLYMER THAT CAN THEORETICALLY REPLACE YOUR WEB-FLUID.
I APPLIED THIS SPECIAL ENZYME TO MAKE IT ADHESIVE.
BUT... WHAT IS IT?
...
IT WAS MY FINGER.

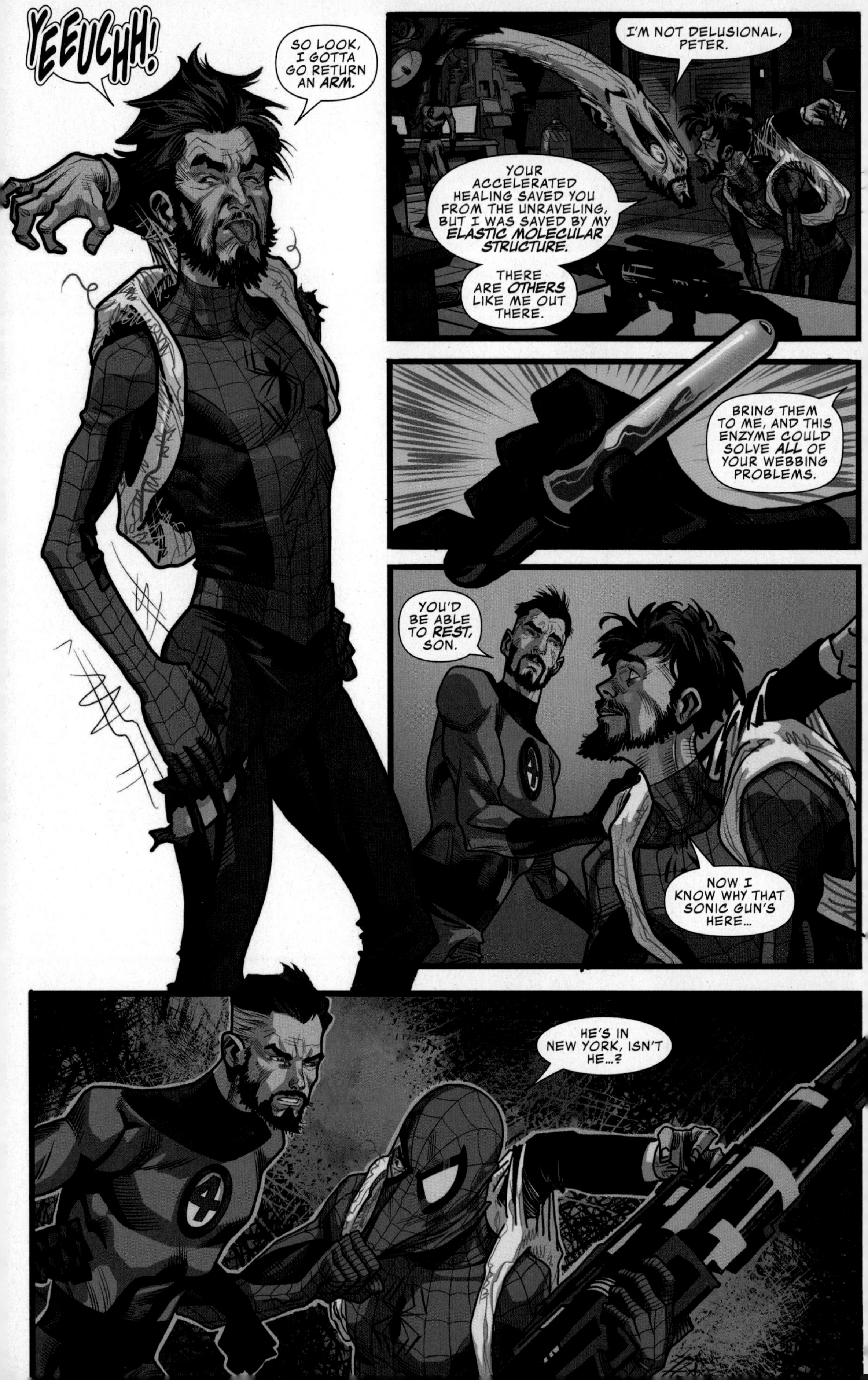
YEEUCHH!
SO LOOK, I GOTTA GO RETURN AN ARM.
I'M NOT DELUSIONAL, PETER.
YOUR ACCELERATED HEALING SAVED YOU FROM THE UNRAVELING, BUT I WAS SAVED BY MY ELASTIC MOLECULAR STRUCTURE.
THERE ARE OTHERS LIKE ME OUT THERE.
BRING THEM TO ME, AND THIS ENZYME COULD SOLVE ALL OF YOUR WEBBING PROBLEMS.
YOU'D BE ABLE TO REST, SON.
NOW I KNOW WHY THAT SONIC GUN'S HERE...
HE'S IN NEW YORK, ISN'T HE...?

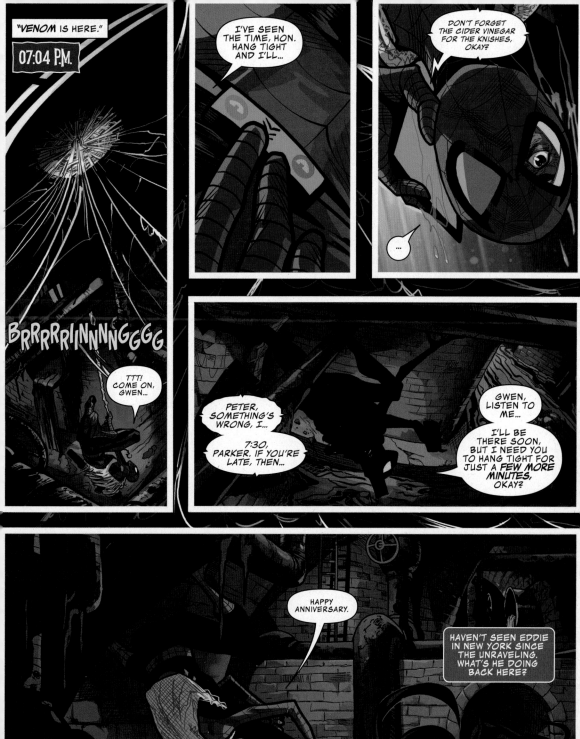

"VENOM IS HERE."

07:04 P.M.

I'VE SEEN THE TIME, HON. HANG TIGHT AND I'LL...

DON'T FORGET THE CIDER VINEGAR FOR THE KNISHES, OKAY?

...

BRRRRRIINNNNGGGG

TTT! COME ON, GWEN...

PETER, SOMETHING'S WRONG, I...

7:30, PARKER. IF YOU'RE LATE, THEN...

GWEN, LISTEN TO ME...

I'LL BE THERE SOON, BUT I NEED YOU TO HANG TIGHT FOR JUST A FEW MORE MINUTES, OKAY?

HAPPY ANNIVERSARY.

HAVEN'T SEEN EDDIE IN NEW YORK SINCE THE UNRAVELING. WHAT'S HE DOING BACK HERE?

NEVER MIND. NEED TO TAKE THE SHOT BEFORE--

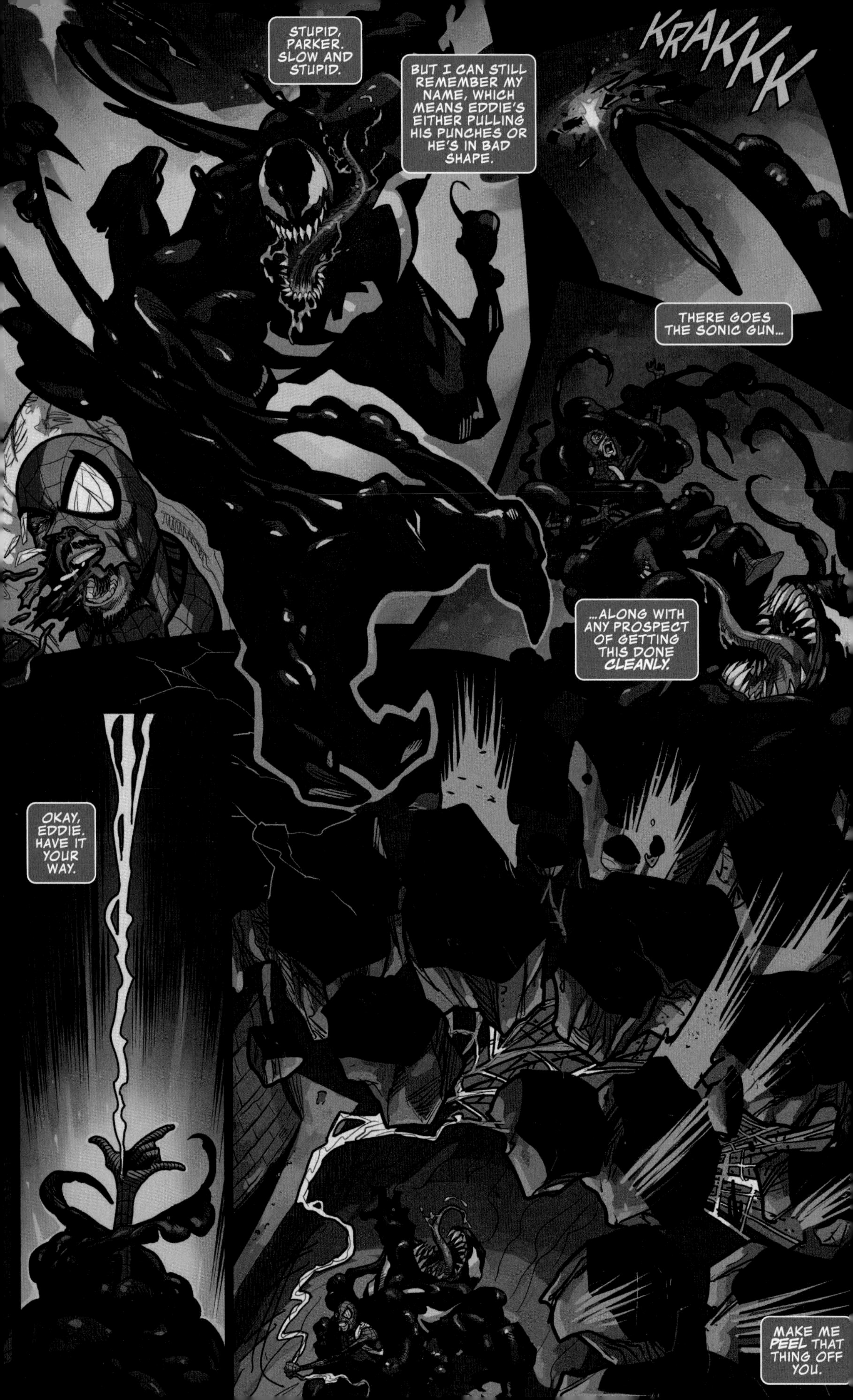
STUPID, PARKER. SLOW AND STUPID.
BUT I CAN STILL REMEMBER MY NAME, WHICH MEANS EDDIE'S EITHER PULLING HIS PUNCHES OR HE'S IN BAD SHAPE.
KRAKKK
THERE GOES THE SONIC GUN...
...ALONG WITH ANY PROSPECT OF GETTING THIS DONE CLEANLY.
OKAY, EDDIE. HAVE IT YOUR WAY.
MAKE ME PEEL THAT THING OFF YOU.

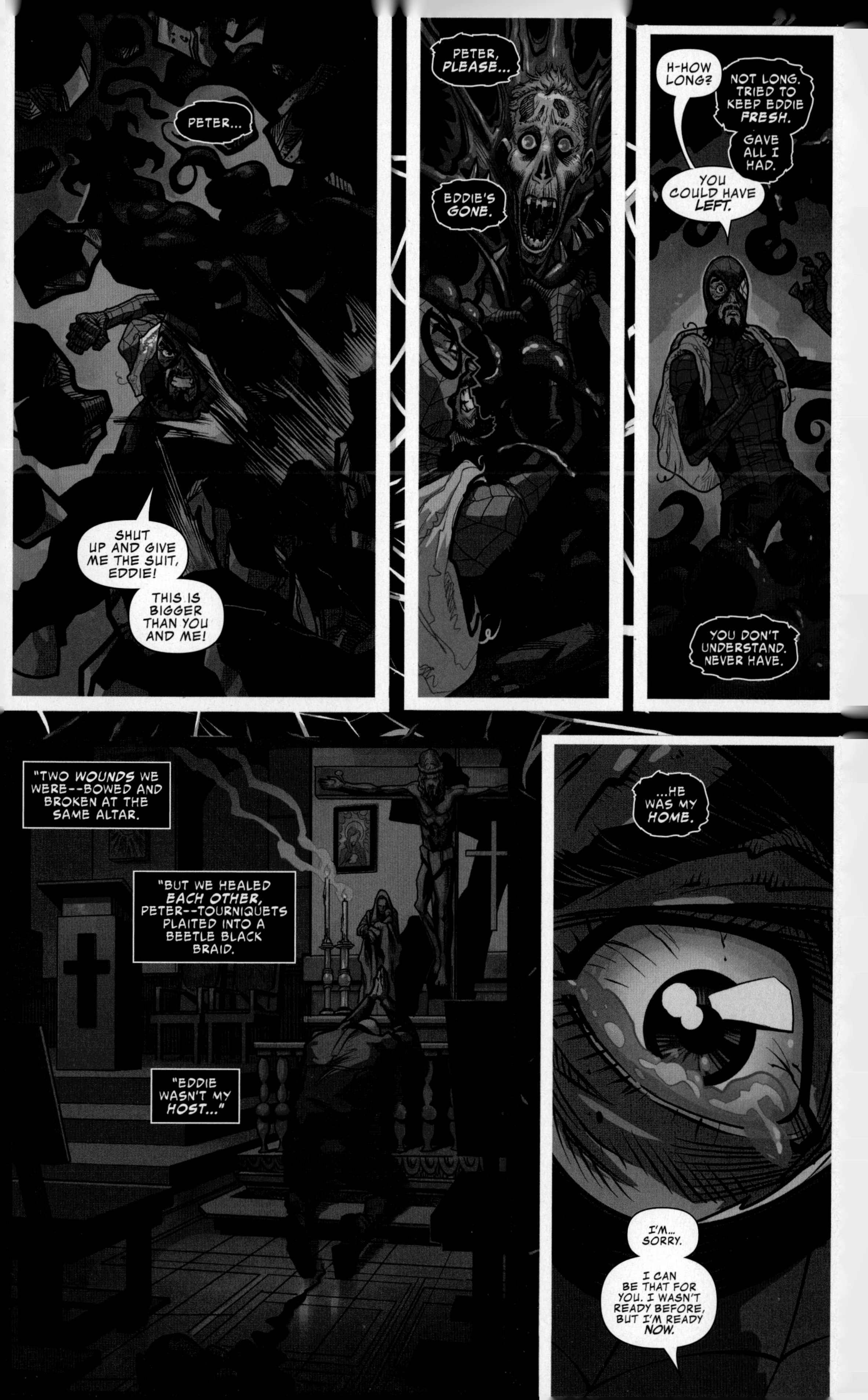
PETER...
SHUT UP AND GIVE ME THE SUIT, EDDIE!
THIS IS BIGGER THAN YOU AND ME!
PETER, PLEASE...
EDDIE'S GONE.
H-HOW LONG?
NOT LONG. TRIED TO KEEP EDDIE FRESH.
GAVE ALL I HAD.
YOU COULD HAVE LEFT.
YOU DON'T UNDERSTAND. NEVER HAVE.
"TWO WOUNDS WE WERE--BOWED AND BROKEN AT THE SAME ALTAR.
"BUT WE HEALED EACH OTHER, PETER--TOURNIQUETS PLAITED INTO A BEETLE BLACK BRAID.
"EDDIE WASN'T MY HOST..."
...HE WAS MY HOME.
I'M... SORRY.
I CAN BE THAT FOR YOU. I WASN'T READY BEFORE, BUT I'M READY NOW.

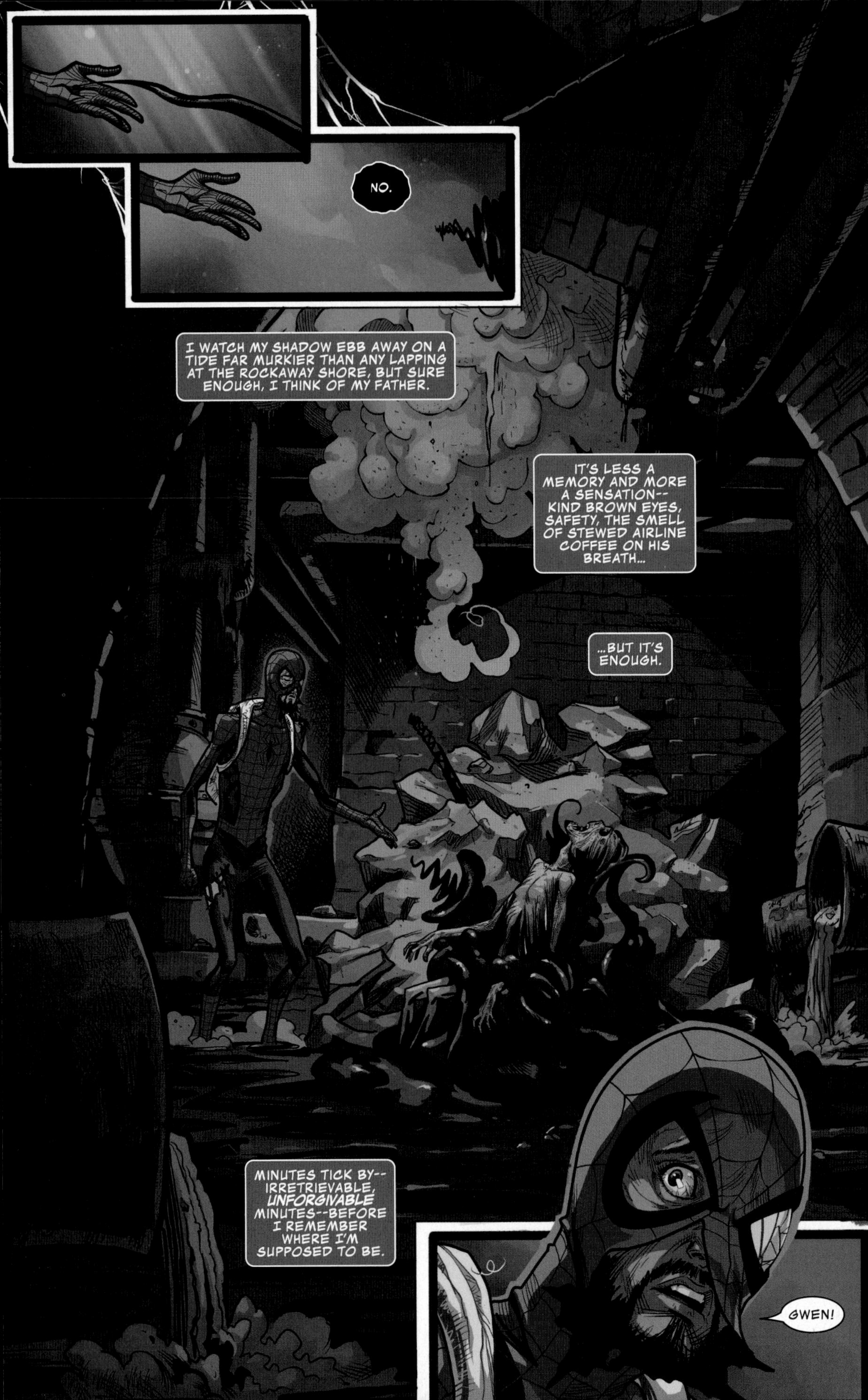
NO.
I WATCH MY SHADOW EBB AWAY ON A TIDE FAR MURKIER THAN ANY LAPPING AT THE ROCKAWAY SHORE, BUT SURE ENOUGH, I THINK OF MY FATHER.
IT'S LESS A MEMORY AND MORE A SENSATION-- KIND BROWN EYES, SAFETY, THE SMELL OF STEWED AIRLINE COFFEE ON HIS BREATH...
...BUT IT'S ENOUGH.
MINUTES TICK BY-- IRRETRIEVABLE, *UNFORGIVABLE* MINUTES--BEFORE I REMEMBER WHERE I'M SUPPOSED TO BE.
GWEN!

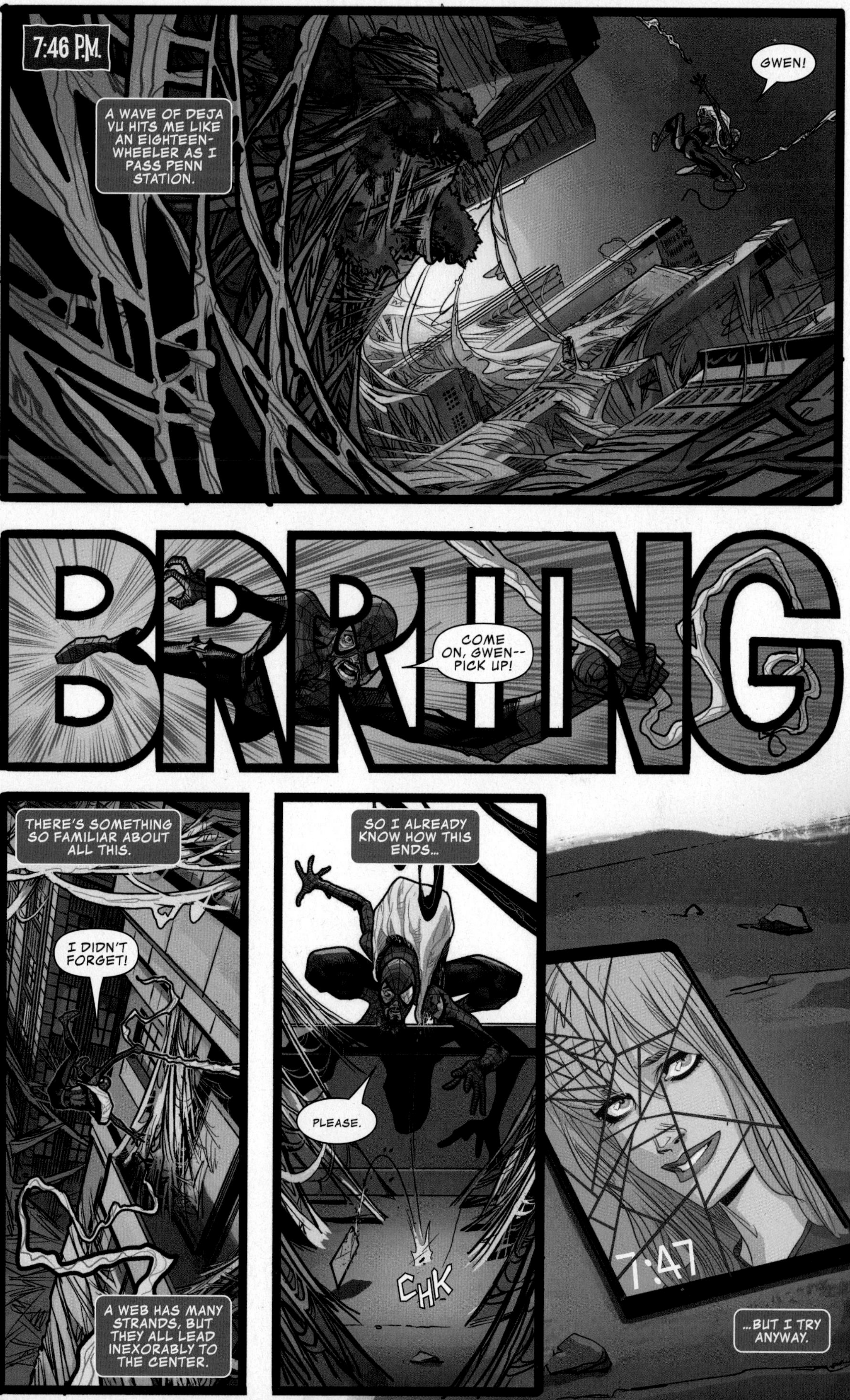
7:46 P.M.
A WAVE OF DEJA VU HITS ME LIKE AN EIGHTEEN-WHEELER AS I PASS PENN STATION.
GWEN!
BRRING
COME ON, GWEN-- PICK UP!
THERE'S SOMETHING SO FAMILIAR ABOUT ALL THIS.
I DIDN'T FORGET!
A WEB HAS MANY STRANDS, BUT THEY ALL LEAD INEXORABLY TO THE CENTER.
SO I ALREADY KNOW HOW THIS ENDS...
PLEASE.
CHK
7:47
...BUT I TRY ANYWAY.

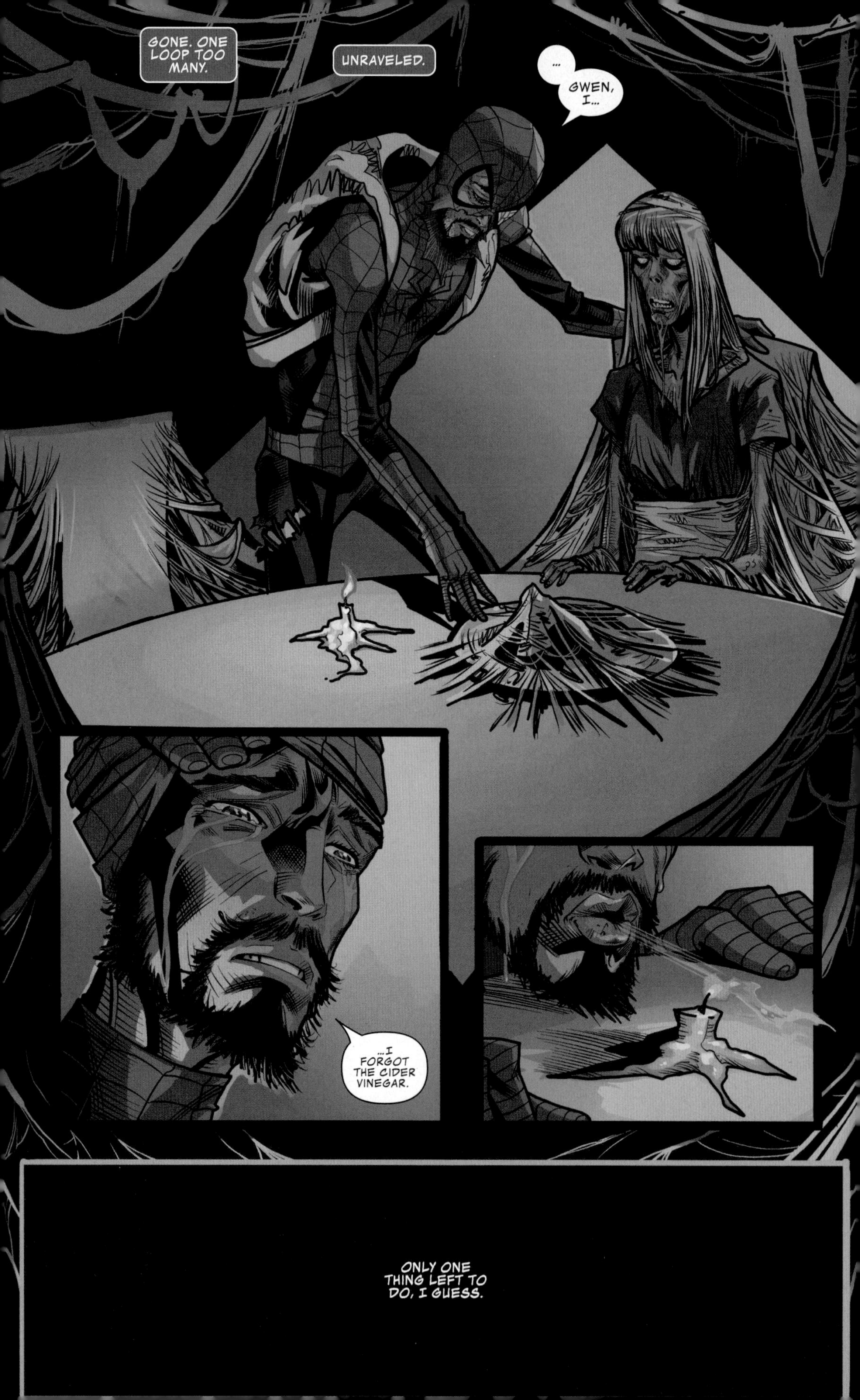
GONE. ONE LOOP TOO MANY.
UNRAVELED.
... GWEN, I...
...I FORGOT THE CIDER VINEGAR.
ONLY ONE THING LEFT TO DO, I GUESS.

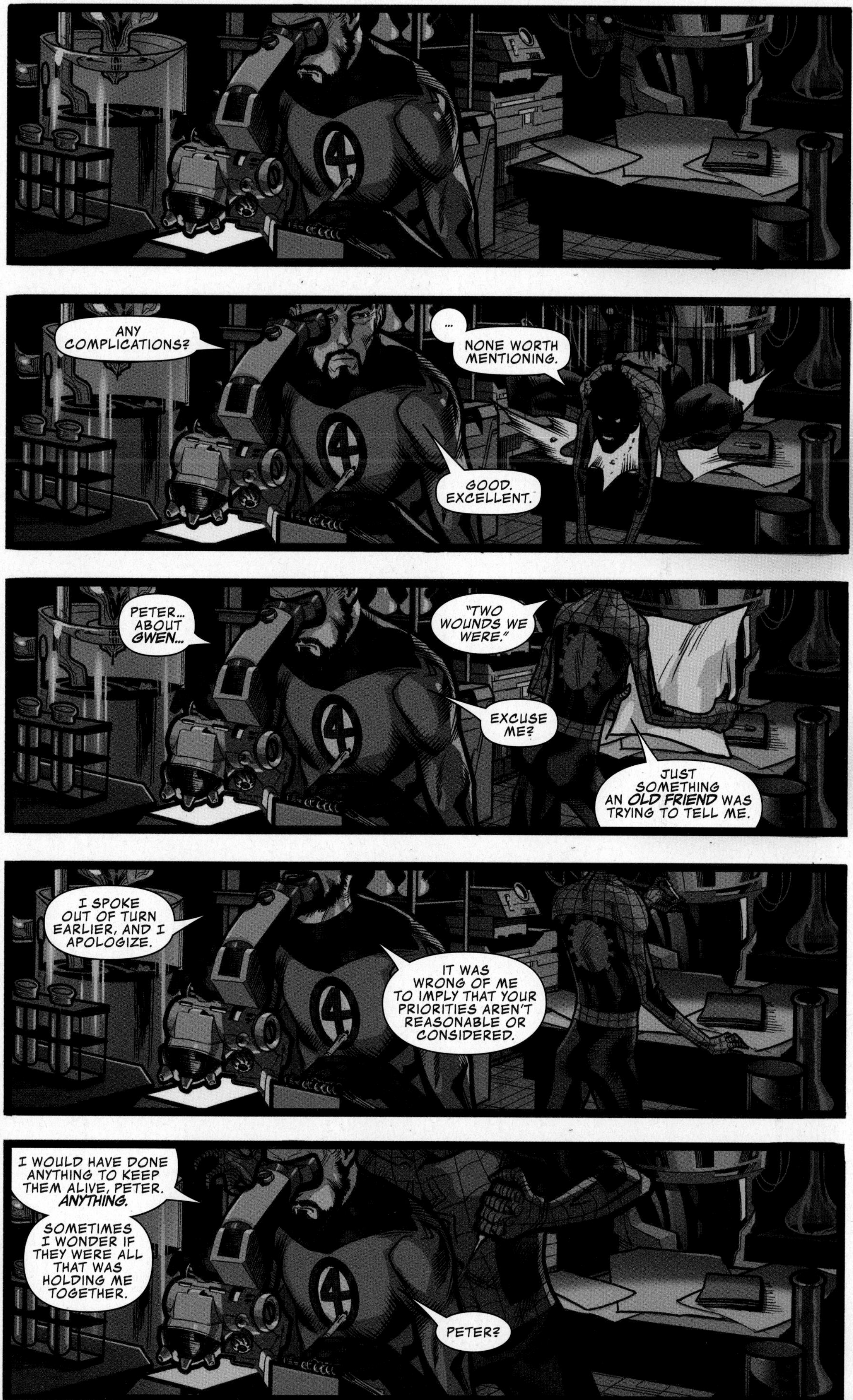
ANY COMPLICATIONS?
... NONE WORTH MENTIONING.
GOOD. EXCELLENT.
PETER... ABOUT GWEN...
"TWO WOUNDS WE WERE."
EXCUSE ME?
JUST SOMETHING AN OLD FRIEND WAS TRYING TO TELL ME.
I SPOKE OUT OF TURN EARLIER, AND I APOLOGIZE.
IT WAS WRONG OF ME TO IMPLY THAT YOUR PRIORITIES AREN'T REASONABLE OR CONSIDERED.
I WOULD HAVE DONE ANYTHING TO KEEP THEM ALIVE, PETER. ANYTHING.
SOMETIMES I WONDER IF THEY WERE ALL THAT WAS HOLDING ME TOGETHER.
PETER?

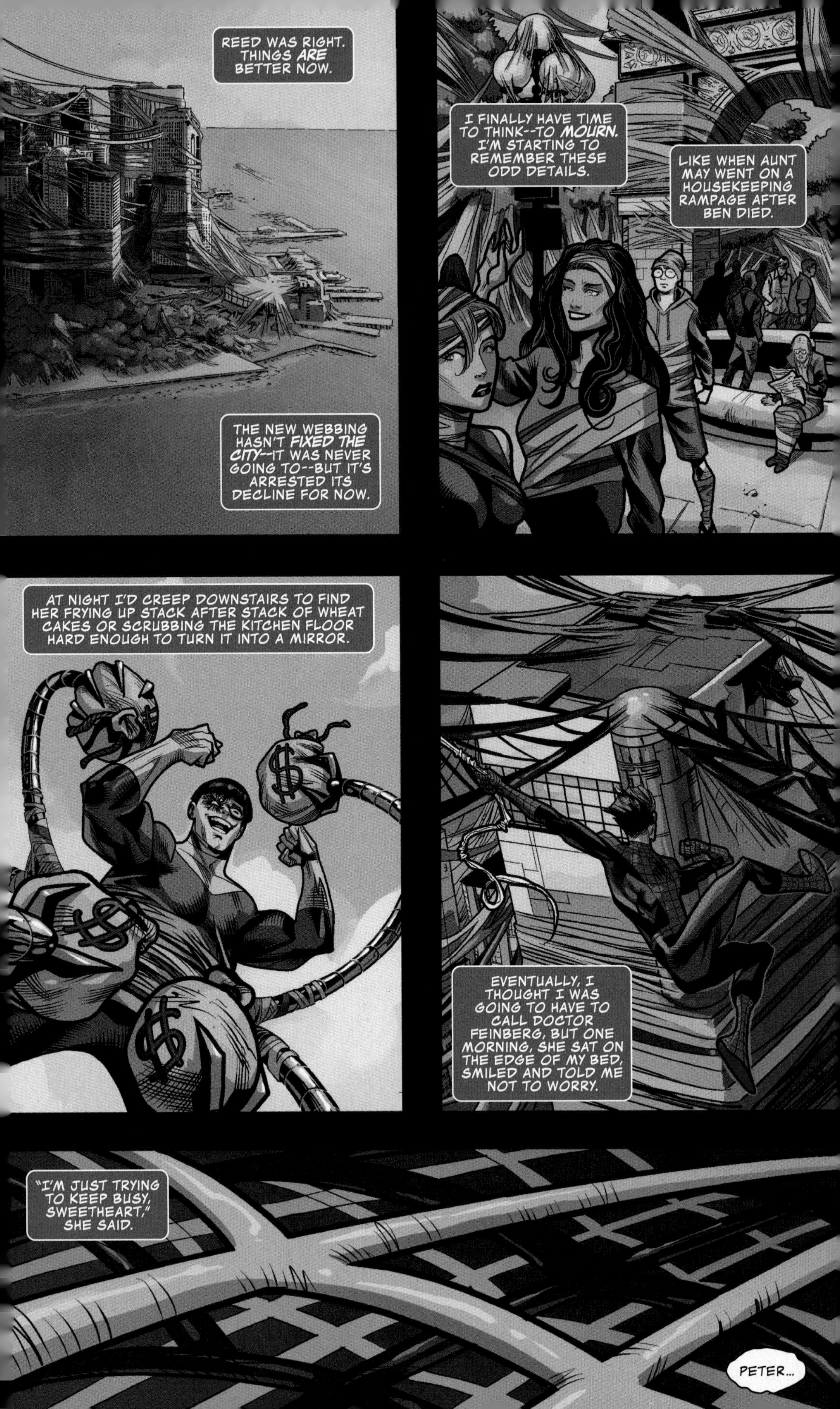
REED WAS RIGHT. THINGS ARE BETTER NOW.
THE NEW WEBBING HASN'T FIXED THE CITY--IT WAS NEVER GOING TO--BUT IT'S ARRESTED ITS DECLINE FOR NOW.
I FINALLY HAVE TIME TO THINK--TO MOURN. I'M STARTING TO REMEMBER THESE ODD DETAILS.
LIKE WHEN AUNT MAY WENT ON A HOUSEKEEPING RAMPAGE AFTER BEN DIED.
AT NIGHT I'D CREEP DOWNSTAIRS TO FIND HER FRYING UP STACK AFTER STACK OF WHEAT CAKES OR SCRUBBING THE KITCHEN FLOOR HARD ENOUGH TO TURN IT INTO A MIRROR.
EVENTUALLY, I THOUGHT I WAS GOING TO HAVE TO CALL DOCTOR FEINBERG, BUT ONE MORNING, SHE SAT ON THE EDGE OF MY BED, SMILED AND TOLD ME NOT TO WORRY.
"I'M JUST TRYING TO KEEP BUSY, SWEETHEART," SHE SAID.
PETER...

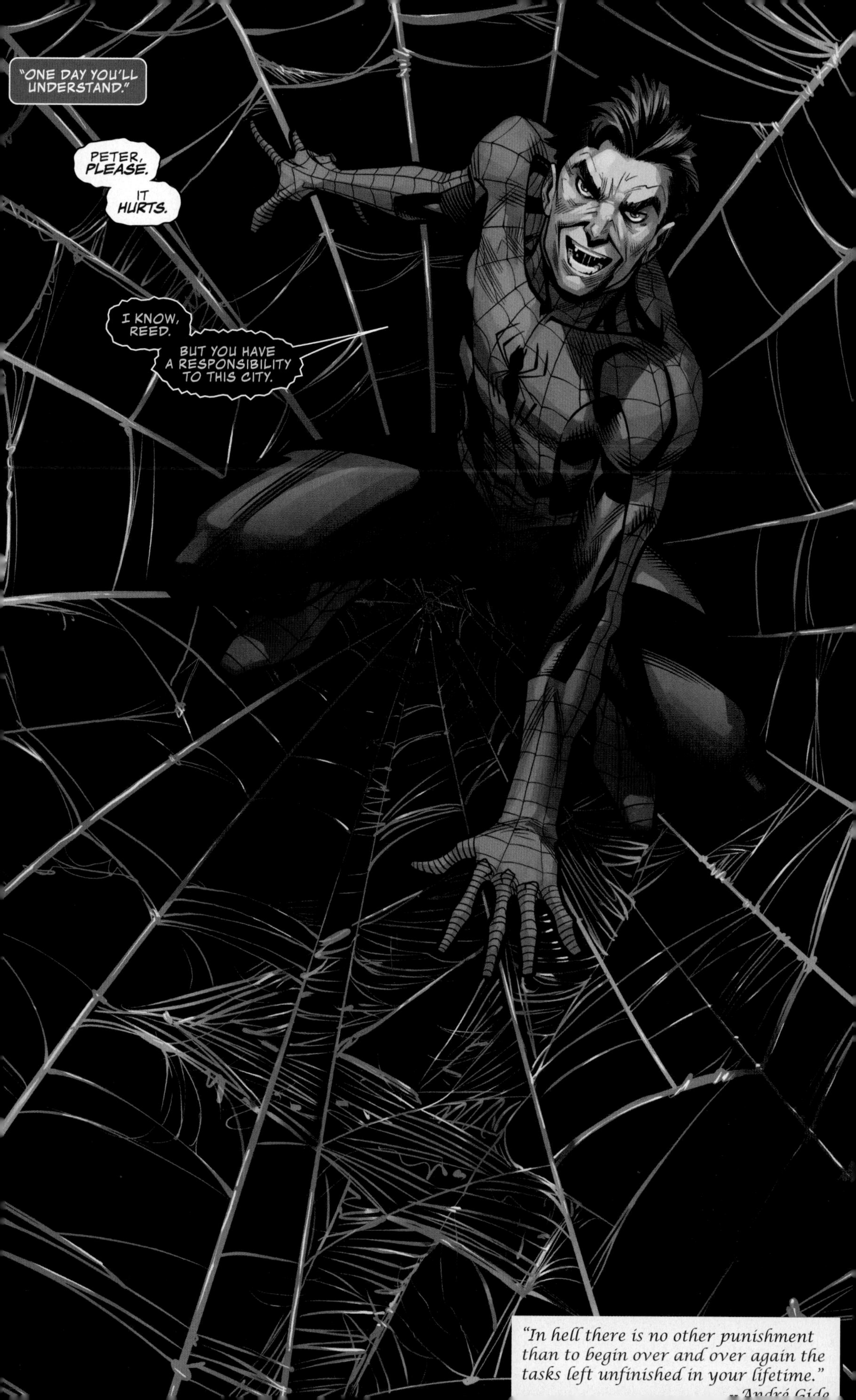
"ONE DAY YOU'LL UNDERSTAND."
PETER, PLEASE.
IT HURTS.
I KNOW, REED.
BUT YOU HAVE A RESPONSIBILITY TO THIS CITY.
"In hell there is no other punishment than to begin over and over again the tasks left unfinished in your lifetime."
– André Gide

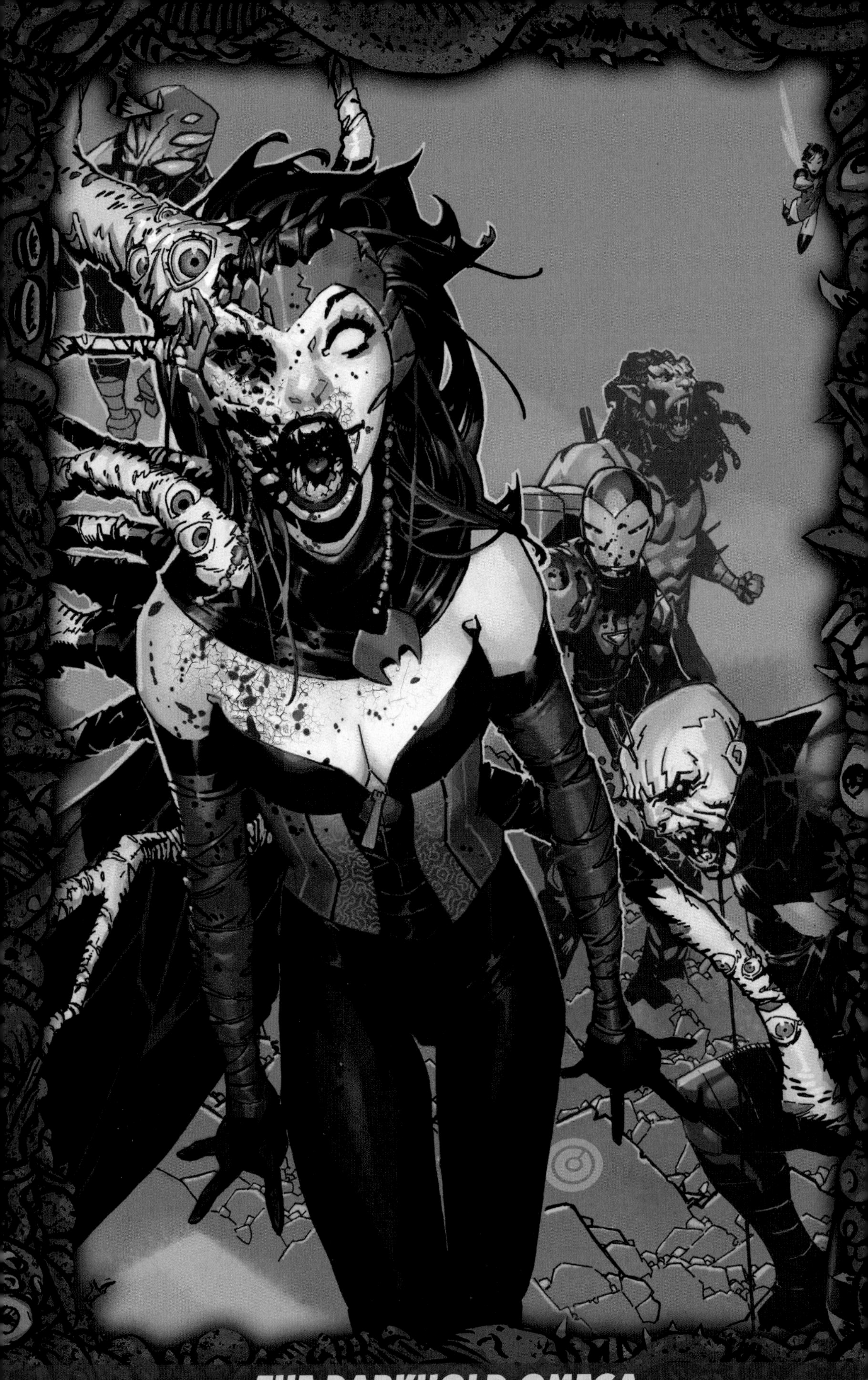

THE DARKHOLD OMEGA

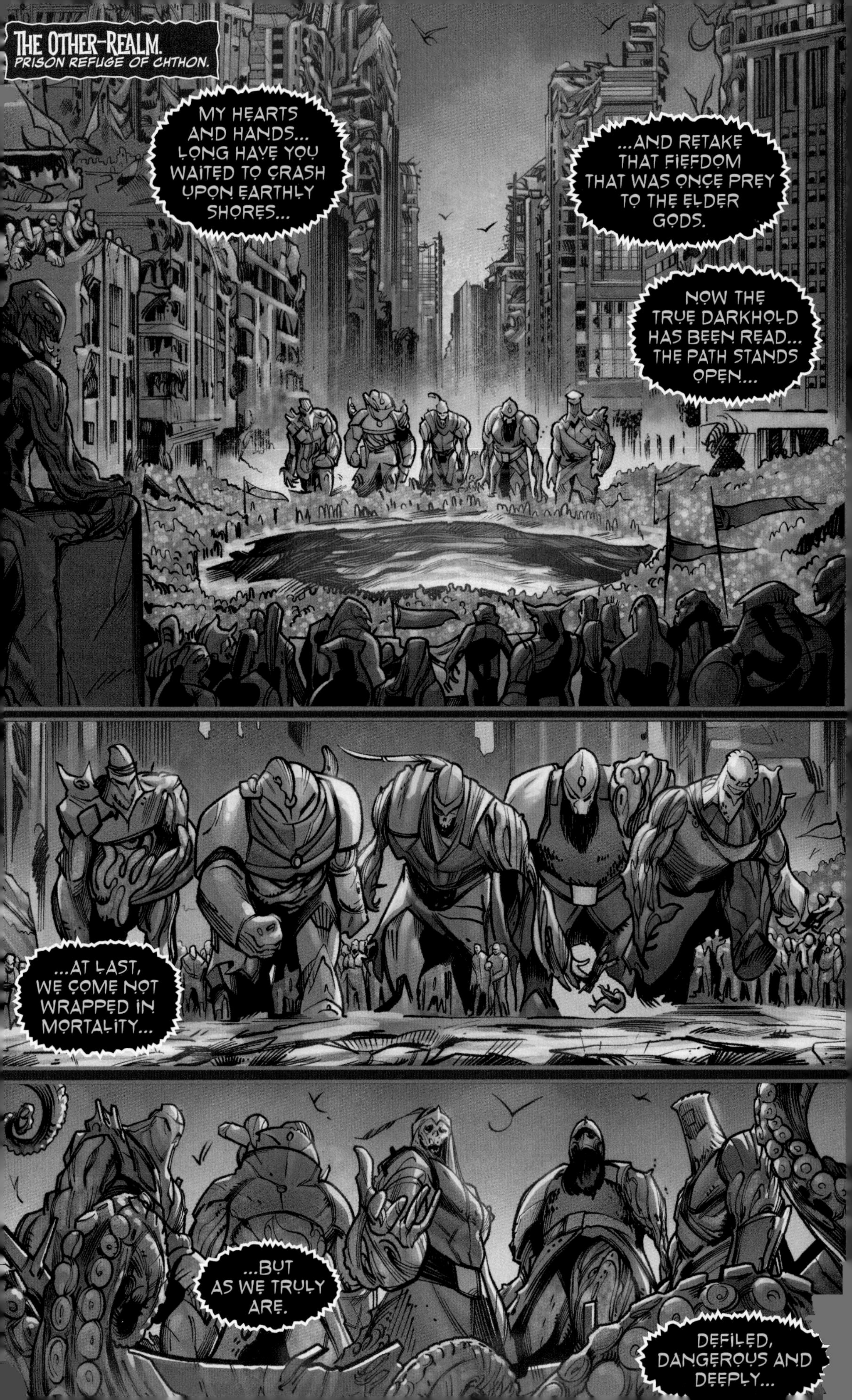
THE OTHER-REALM.
PRISON REFUGE OF CHTHON.
MY HEARTS AND HANDS... LONG HAVE YOU WAITED TO CRASH UPON EARTHLY SHORES...
...AND RETAKE THAT FIEFDOM THAT WAS ONCE PREY TO THE ELDER GODS.
NOW THE TRUE DARKHOLD HAS BEEN READ... THE PATH STANDS OPEN...
...AT LAST, WE COME NOT WRAPPED IN MORTALITY...
...BUT AS WE TRULY ARE.
DEFILED, DANGEROUS AND DEEPLY...

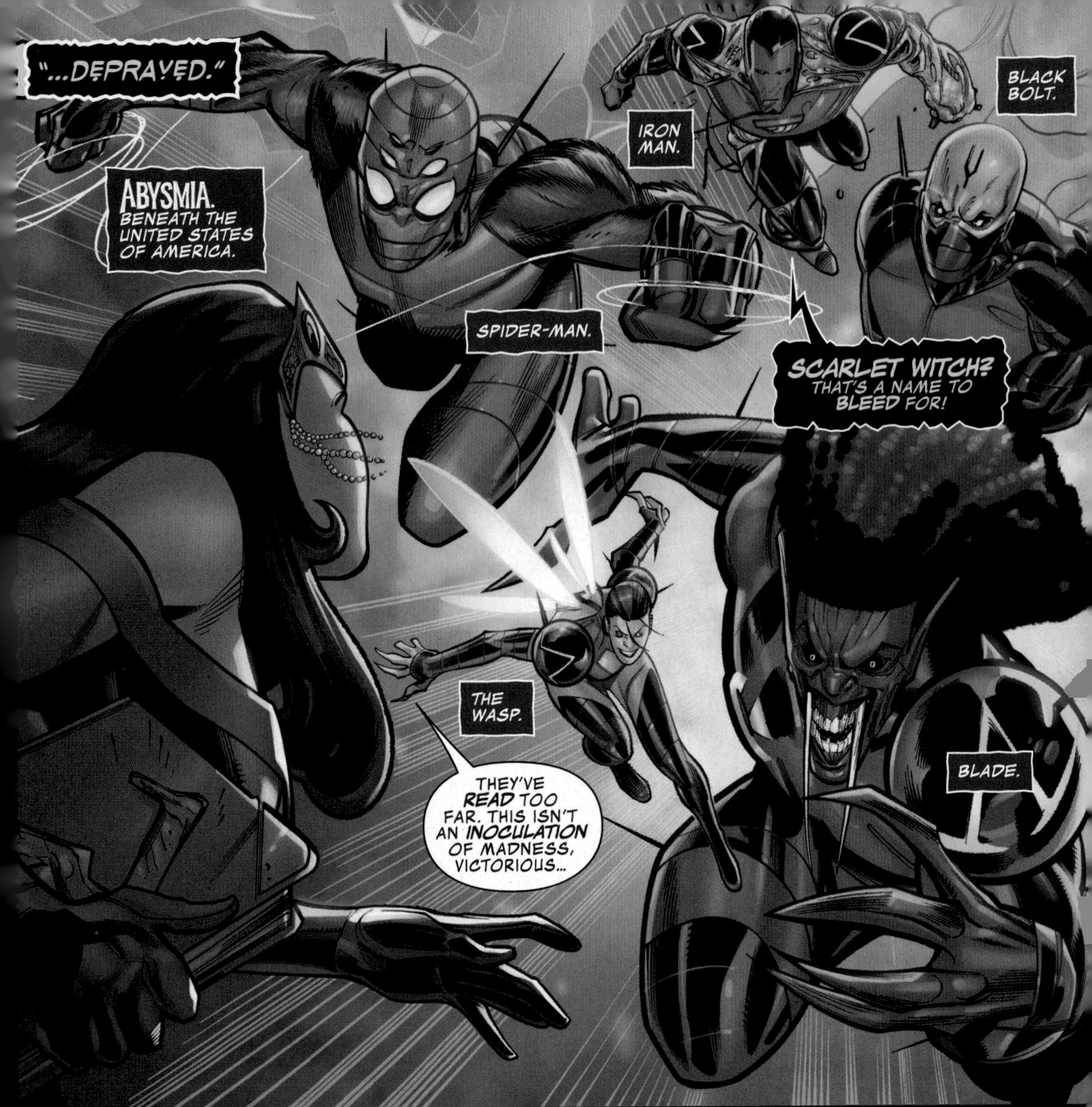
"...DEPRAVED."
ABYSMIA. BENEATH THE UNITED STATES OF AMERICA.
IRON MAN.
BLACK BOLT.
SPIDER-MAN.
SCARLET WITCH? THAT'S A NAME TO BLEED FOR!
THE WASP.
BLADE.
THEY'VE READ TOO FAR. THIS ISN'T AN INOCULATION OF MADNESS, VICTORIOUS...

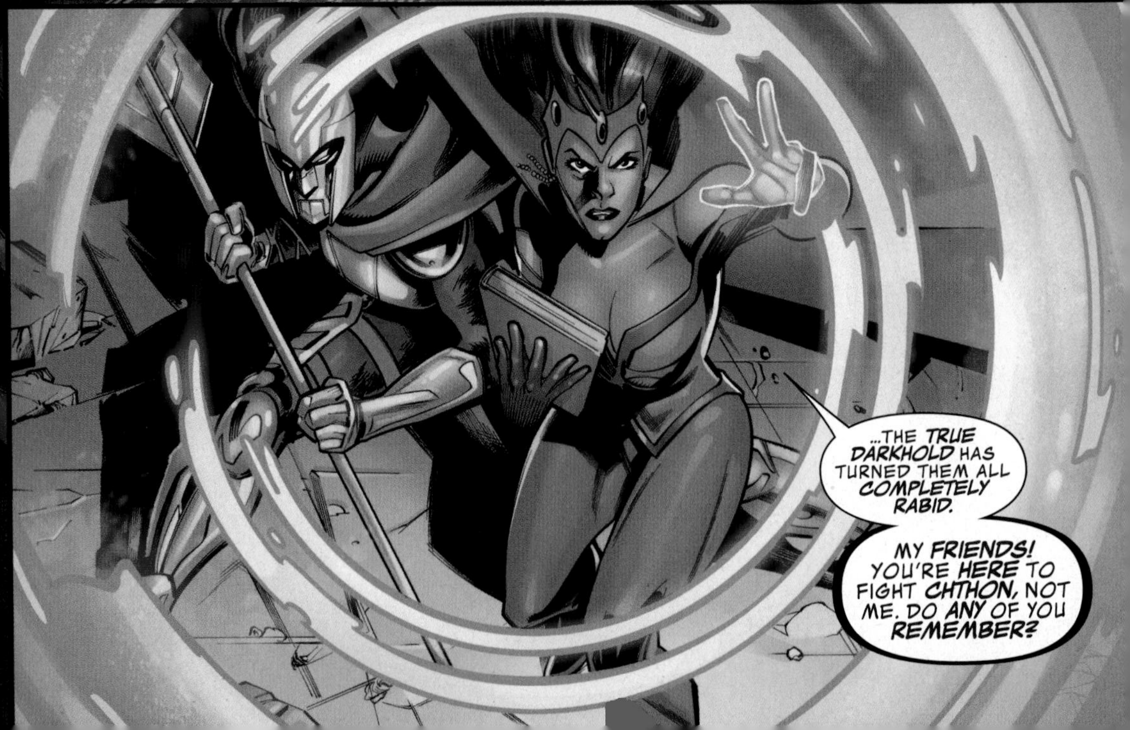
...THE TRUE DARKHOLD HAS TURNED THEM ALL COMPLETELY RABID.
MY FRIENDS! YOU'RE HERE TO FIGHT CHTHON, NOT ME. DO ANY OF YOU REMEMBER?

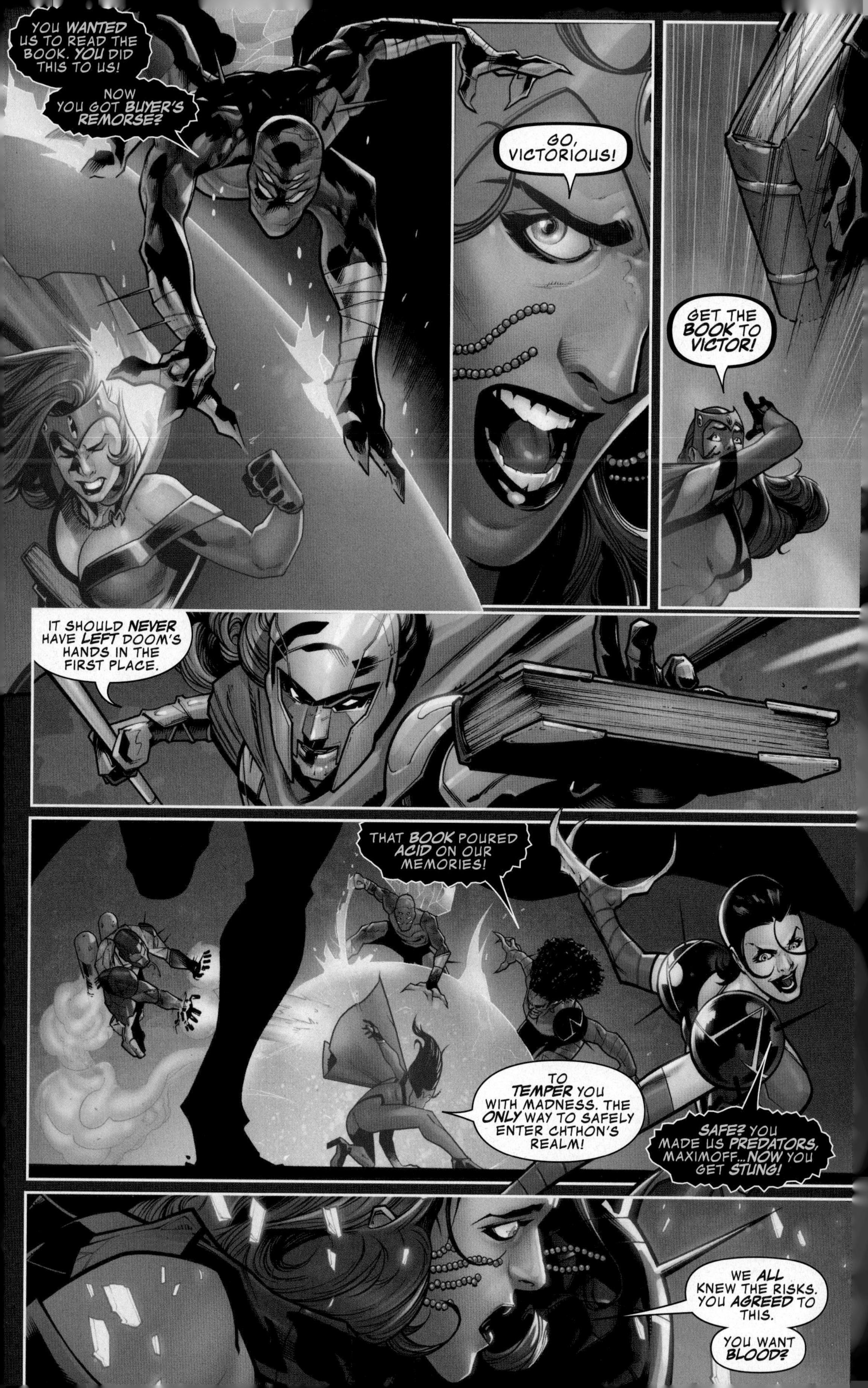
YOU WANTED US TO READ THE BOOK. YOU DID THIS TO US!
NOW YOU GOT BUYER'S REMORSE?
GO, VICTORIOUS!
GET THE BOOK TO VICTOR!
IT SHOULD NEVER HAVE LEFT DOOM'S HANDS IN THE FIRST PLACE.
THAT BOOK POURED ACID ON OUR MEMORIES!
TO TEMPER YOU WITH MADNESS. THE ONLY WAY TO SAFELY ENTER CHTHON'S REALM!
SAFE? YOU MADE US PREDATORS, MAXIMOFF...NOW YOU GET STUNG!
WE ALL KNEW THE RISKS. YOU AGREED TO THIS.
YOU WANT BLOOD?

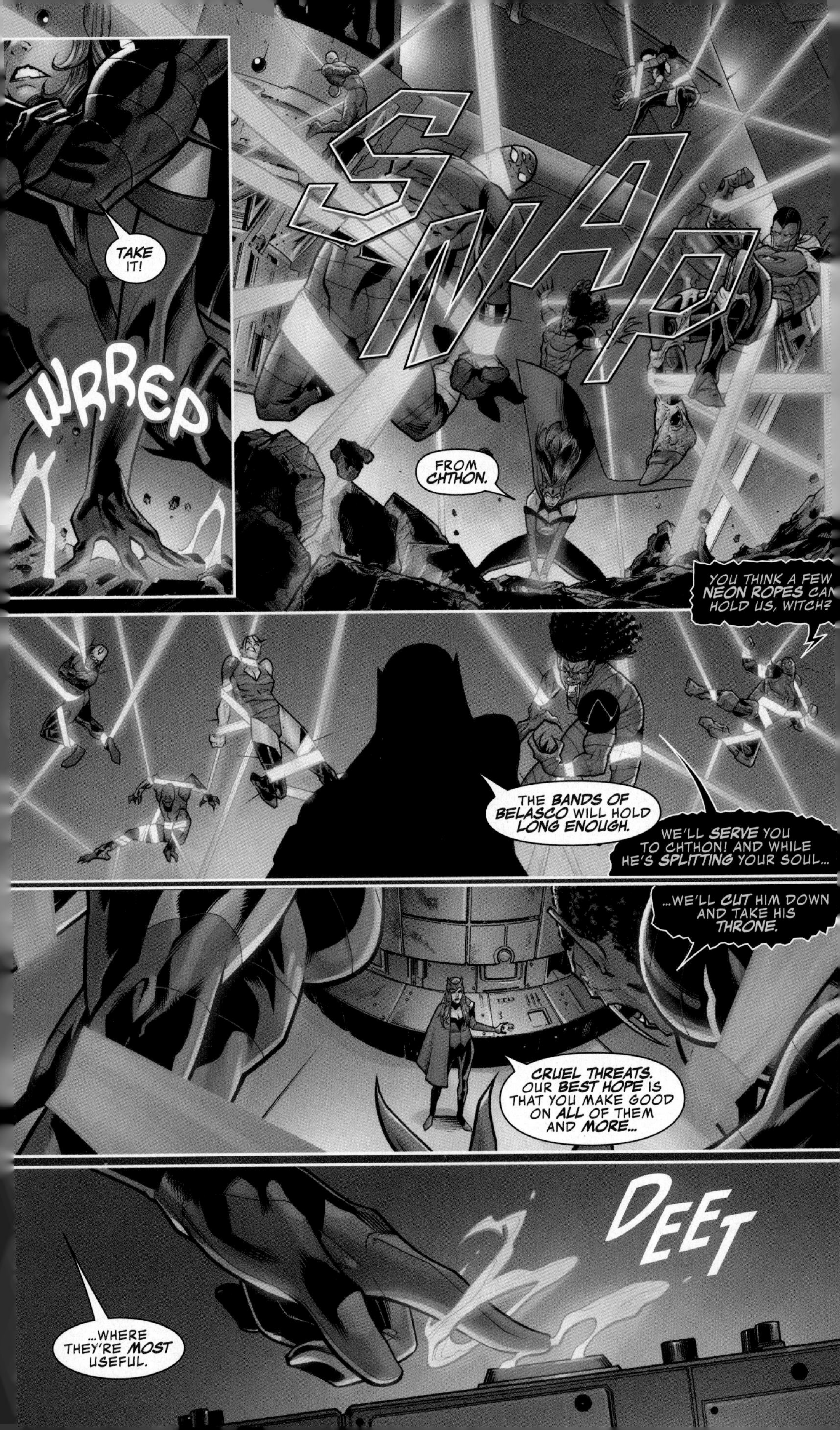
TAKE IT!
WRREP
SNAP
FROM CHTHON.
YOU THINK A FEW NEON ROPES CAN HOLD US, WITCH?
THE BANDS OF BELASCO WILL HOLD LONG ENOUGH.
WE'LL SERVE YOU TO CHTHON! AND WHILE HE'S SPLITTING YOUR SOUL...
...WE'LL CUT HIM DOWN AND TAKE HIS THRONE.
CRUEL THREATS. OUR BEST HOPE IS THAT YOU MAKE GOOD ON ALL OF THEM AND MORE...
DEET
...WHERE THEY'RE MOST USEFUL.

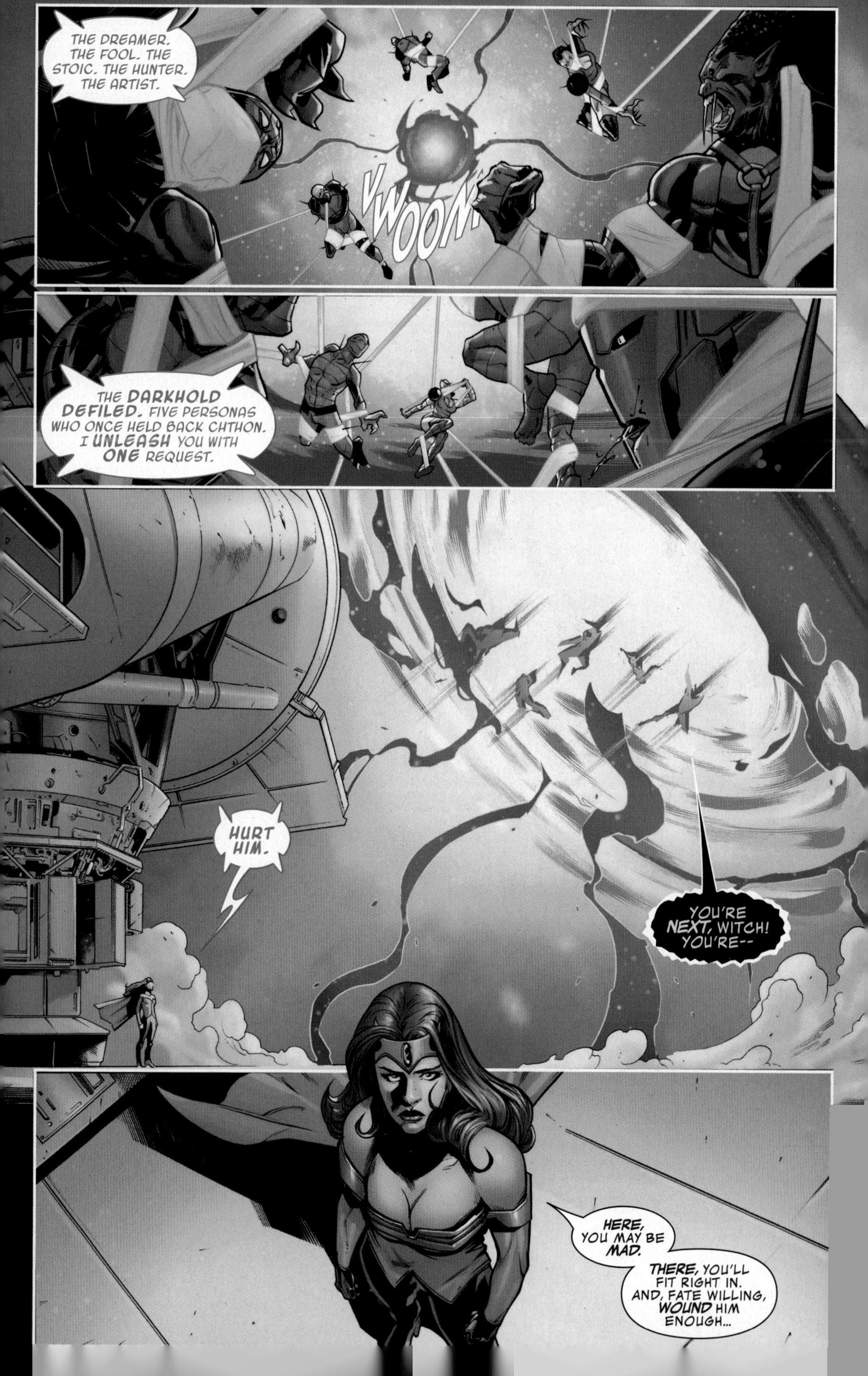
THE DREAMER. THE FOOL. THE STOIC. THE HUNTER. THE ARTIST.
VWOOM!
THE DARKHOLD DEFILED. FIVE PERSONAS WHO ONCE HELD BACK CHTHON. I UNLEASH YOU WITH ONE REQUEST.
HURT HIM.
YOU'RE NEXT, WITCH! YOU'RE--
HERE, YOU MAY BE MAD.
THERE, YOU'LL FIT RIGHT IN. AND, FATE WILLING, WOUND HIM ENOUGH...

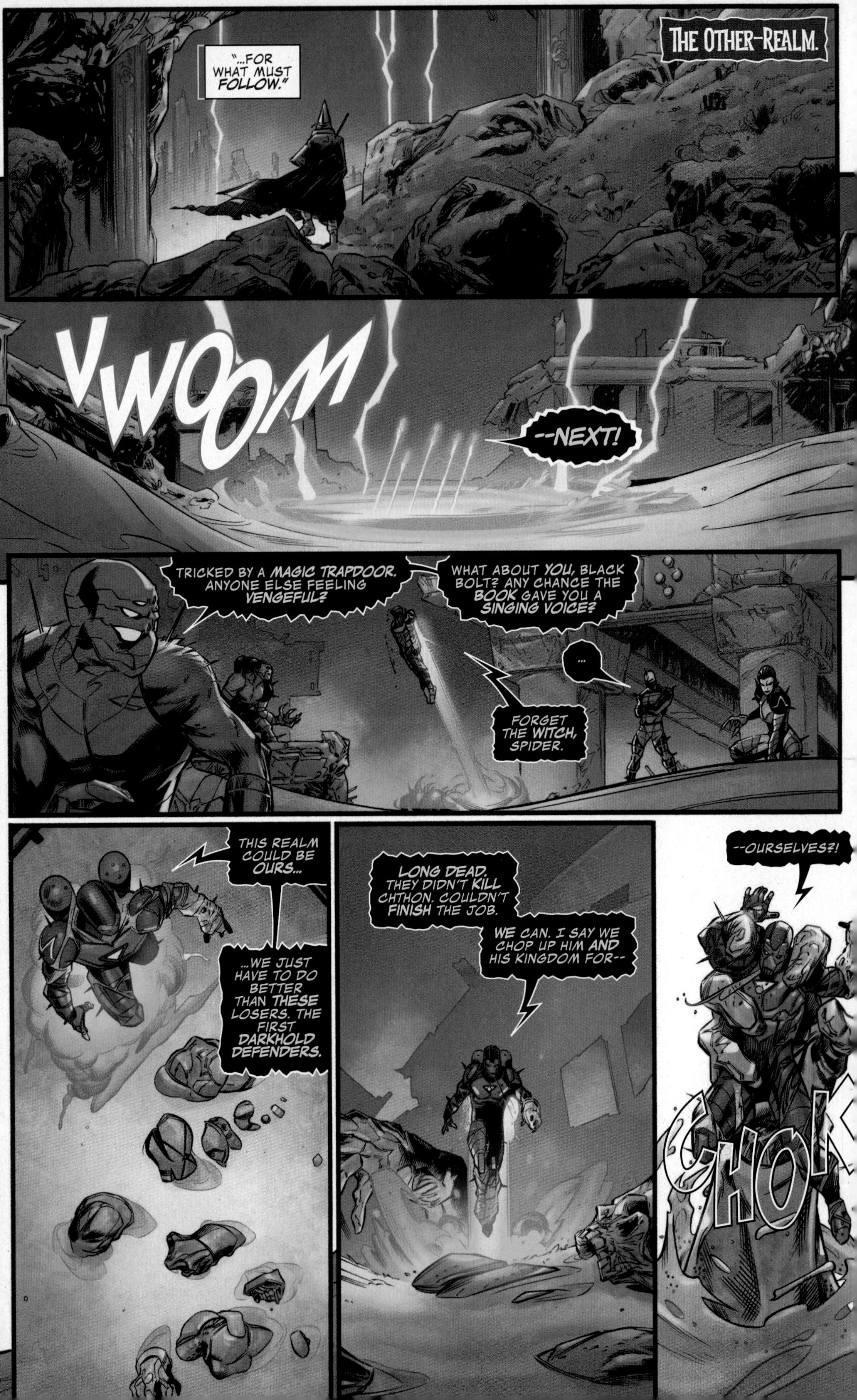
THE OTHER-REALM.
"...FOR WHAT MUST FOLLOW."
VWOOM
--NEXT!
TRICKED BY A MAGIC TRAPDOOR. ANYONE ELSE FEELING VENGEFUL?
WHAT ABOUT YOU, BLACK BOLT? ANY CHANCE THE BOOK GAVE YOU A SINGING VOICE?
...
FORGET THE WITCH, SPIDER.
THIS REALM COULD BE OURS...
...WE JUST HAVE TO DO BETTER THAN THESE LOSERS. THE FIRST DARKHOLD DEFENDERS.
LONG DEAD. THEY DIDN'T KILL CHTHON. COULDN'T FINISH THE JOB.
WE CAN. I SAY WE CHOP UP HIM AND HIS KINGDOM FOR--
--OURSELVES?!
CHOK

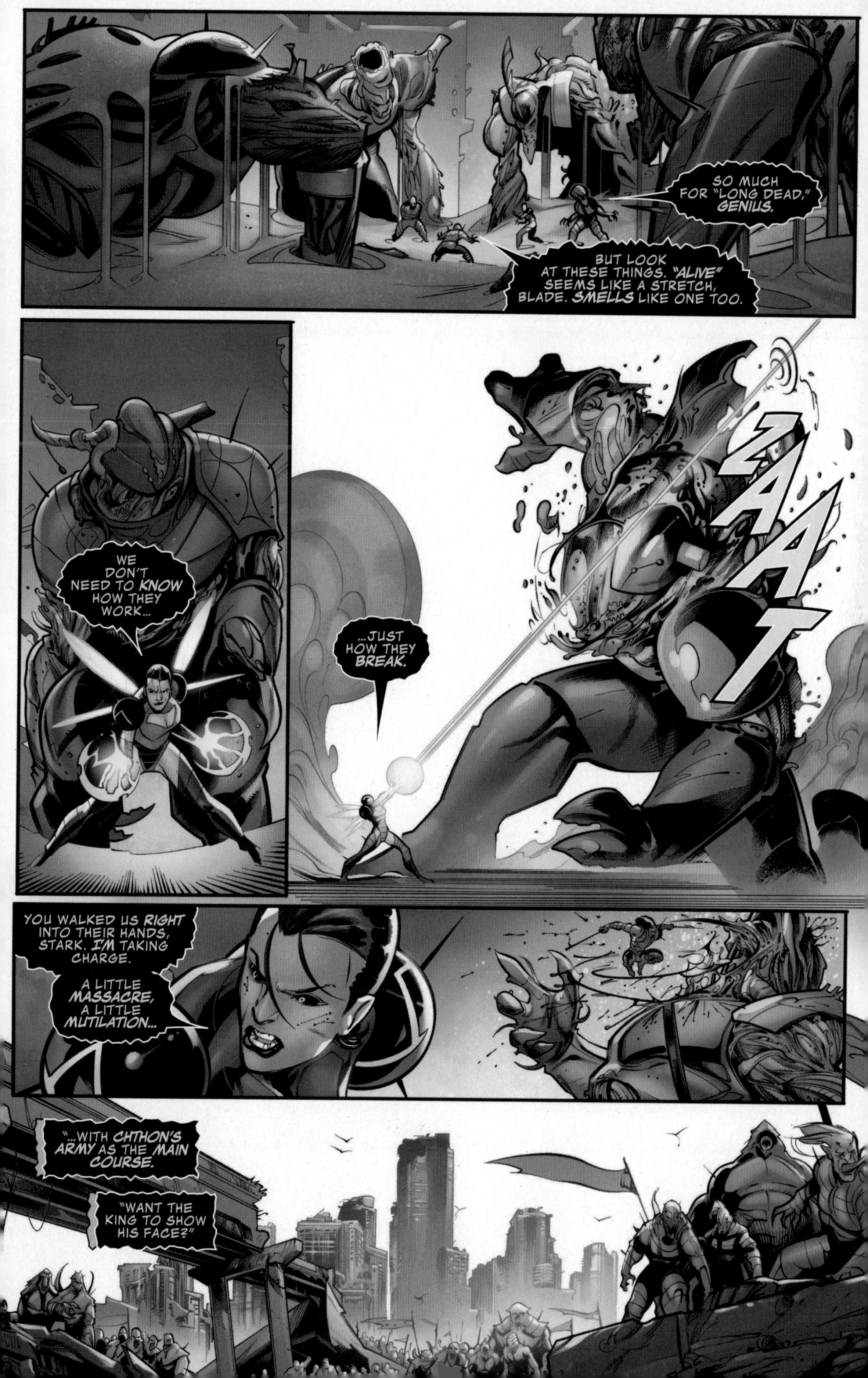
SO MUCH FOR "LONG DEAD," GENIUS.
BUT LOOK AT THESE THINGS. "ALIVE" SEEMS LIKE A STRETCH, BLADE. SMELLS LIKE ONE TOO.
WE DON'T NEED TO KNOW HOW THEY WORK...
...JUST HOW THEY BREAK.
ZAAAT
YOU WALKED US RIGHT INTO THEIR HANDS, STARK. I'M TAKING CHARGE.
A LITTLE MASSACRE, A LITTLE MUTILATION...
"...WITH CHTHON'S ARMY AS THE MAIN COURSE.
"WANT THE KING TO SHOW HIS FACE?"

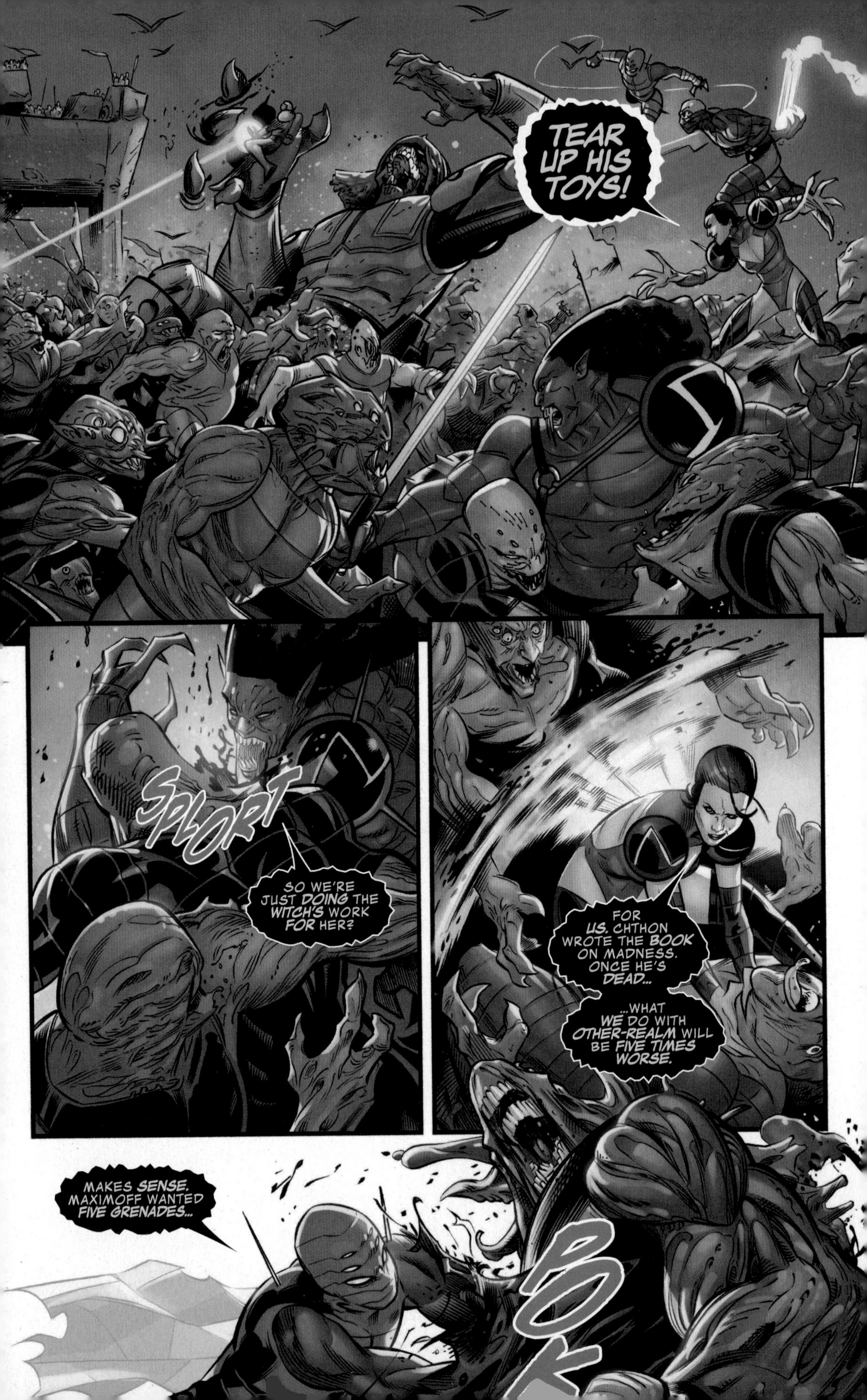
TEAR UP HIS TOYS!
SPLORT
SO WE'RE JUST DOING THE WITCH'S WORK FOR HER?
FOR US. CHTHON WROTE THE BOOK ON MADNESS. ONCE HE'S DEAD...
...WHAT WE DO WITH OTHER-REALM WILL BE FIVE TIMES WORSE.
MAKES SENSE. MAXIMOFF WANTED FIVE GRENADES...
BOOK

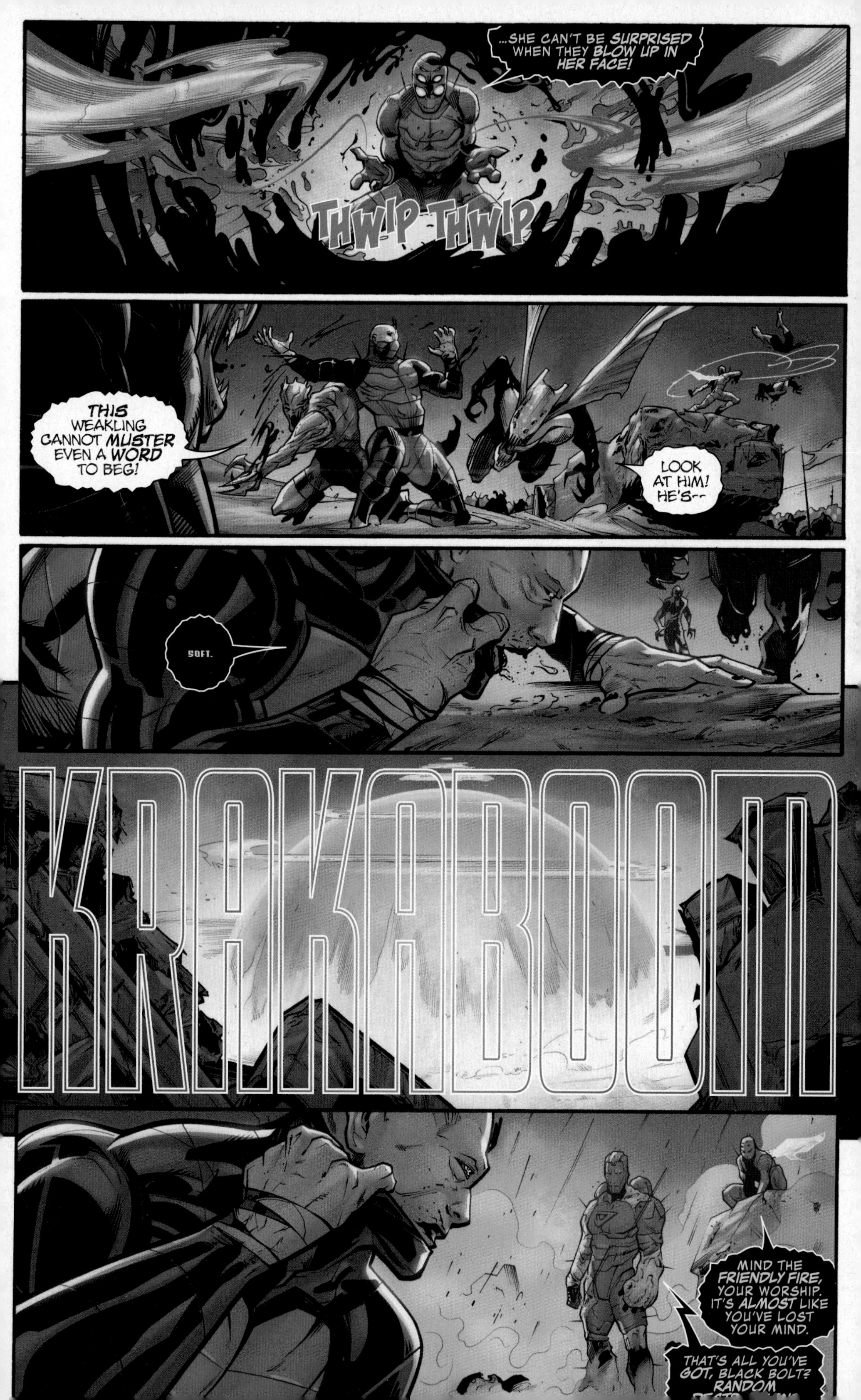
...SHE CAN'T BE SURPRISED WHEN THEY BLOW UP IN HER FACE!
THWIP THWIP
THIS WEAKLING CANNOT MUSTER EVEN A WORD TO BEG!
LOOK AT HIM! HE'S--
SOFT.
KRAKABOOM
MIND THE FRIENDLY FIRE, YOUR WORSHIP. IT'S ALMOST LIKE YOU'VE LOST YOUR MIND.
THAT'S ALL YOU'VE GOT, BLACK BOLT? RANDOM

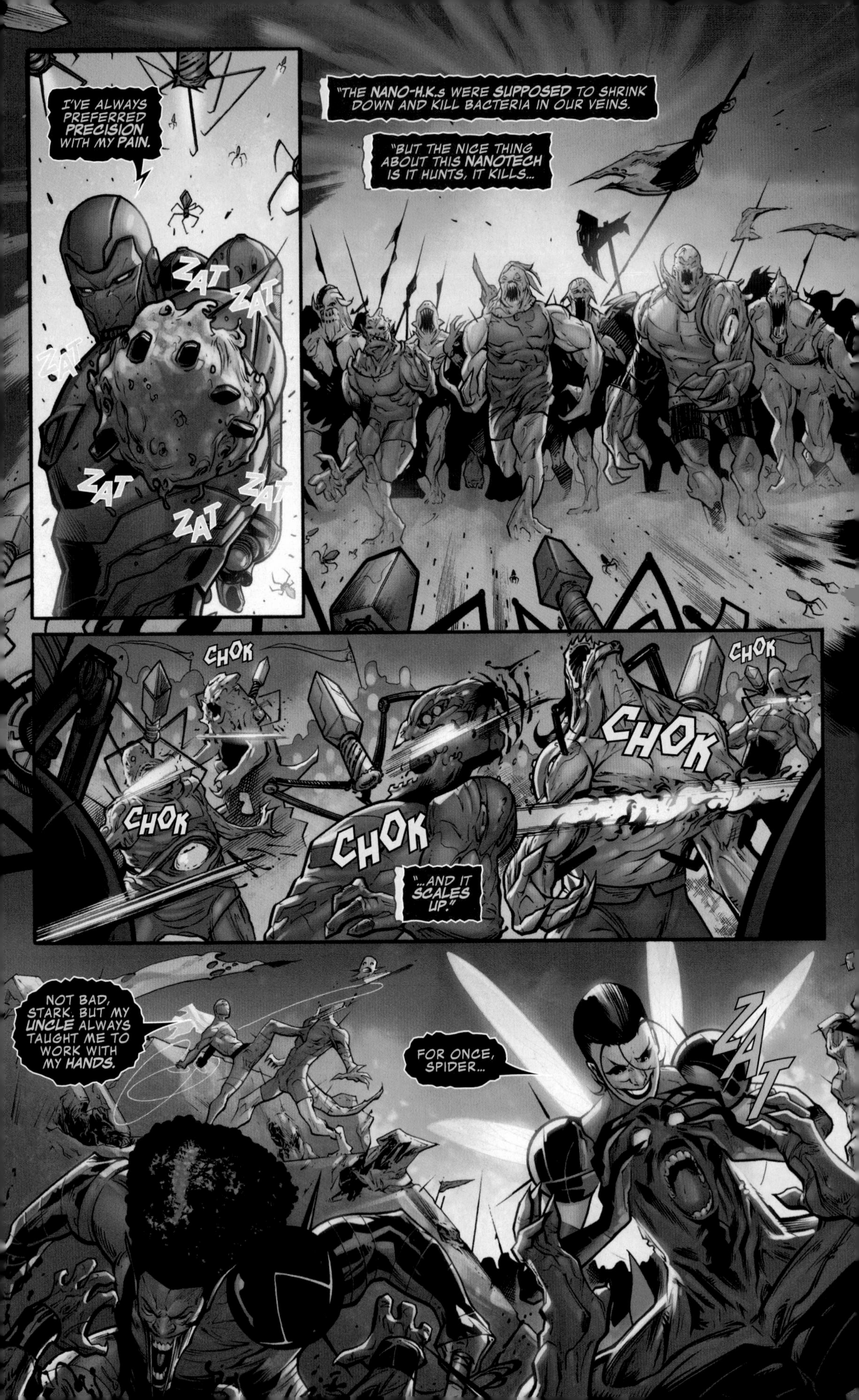
I'VE ALWAYS PREFERRED PRECISION WITH MY PAIN.
ZAT
ZAT
ZAT
ZAT
ZAT
ZAT
"THE NANO-H.K.s WERE SUPPOSED TO SHRINK DOWN AND KILL BACTERIA IN OUR VEINS.
"BUT THE NICE THING ABOUT THIS NANOTECH IS IT HUNTS, IT KILLS...
CHOK
CHOK
CHOK
CHOK
CHOK
"...AND IT SCALES UP."
NOT BAD, STARK. BUT MY UNCLE ALWAYS TAUGHT ME TO WORK WITH MY HANDS.
FOR ONCE, SPIDER...
ZAT

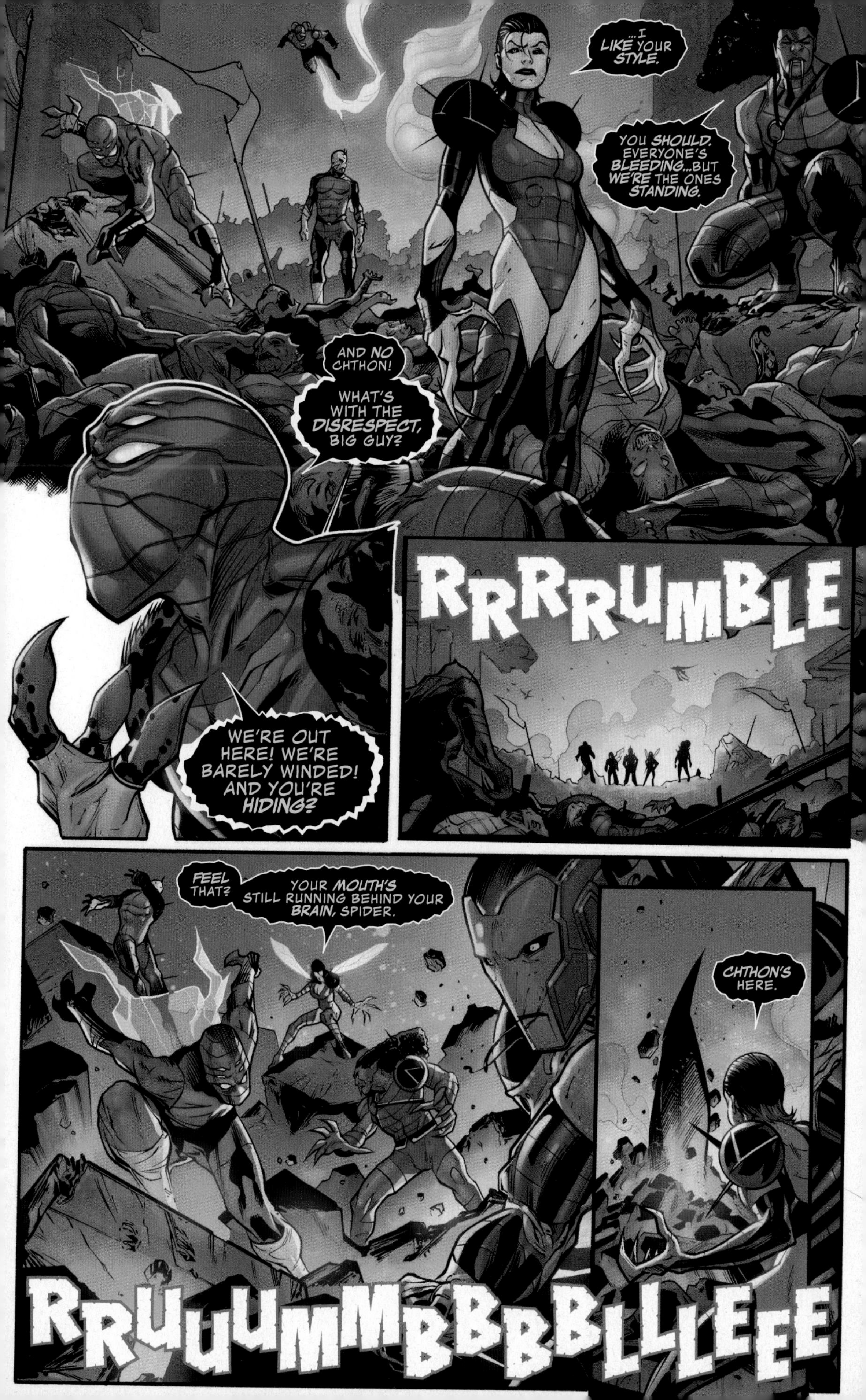
...I LIKE YOUR STYLE.
YOU SHOULD. EVERYONE'S BLEEDING...BUT WE'RE THE ONES STANDING.
AND NO CHTHON!
WHAT'S WITH THE DISRESPECT, BIG GUY?
WE'RE OUT HERE! WE'RE BARELY WINDED! AND YOU'RE HIDING?
RRRRUMBLE
FEEL THAT?
YOUR MOUTH'S STILL RUNNING BEHIND YOUR BRAIN, SPIDER.
CHTHON'S HERE.
RRUUUMMBBBBLLLEEE

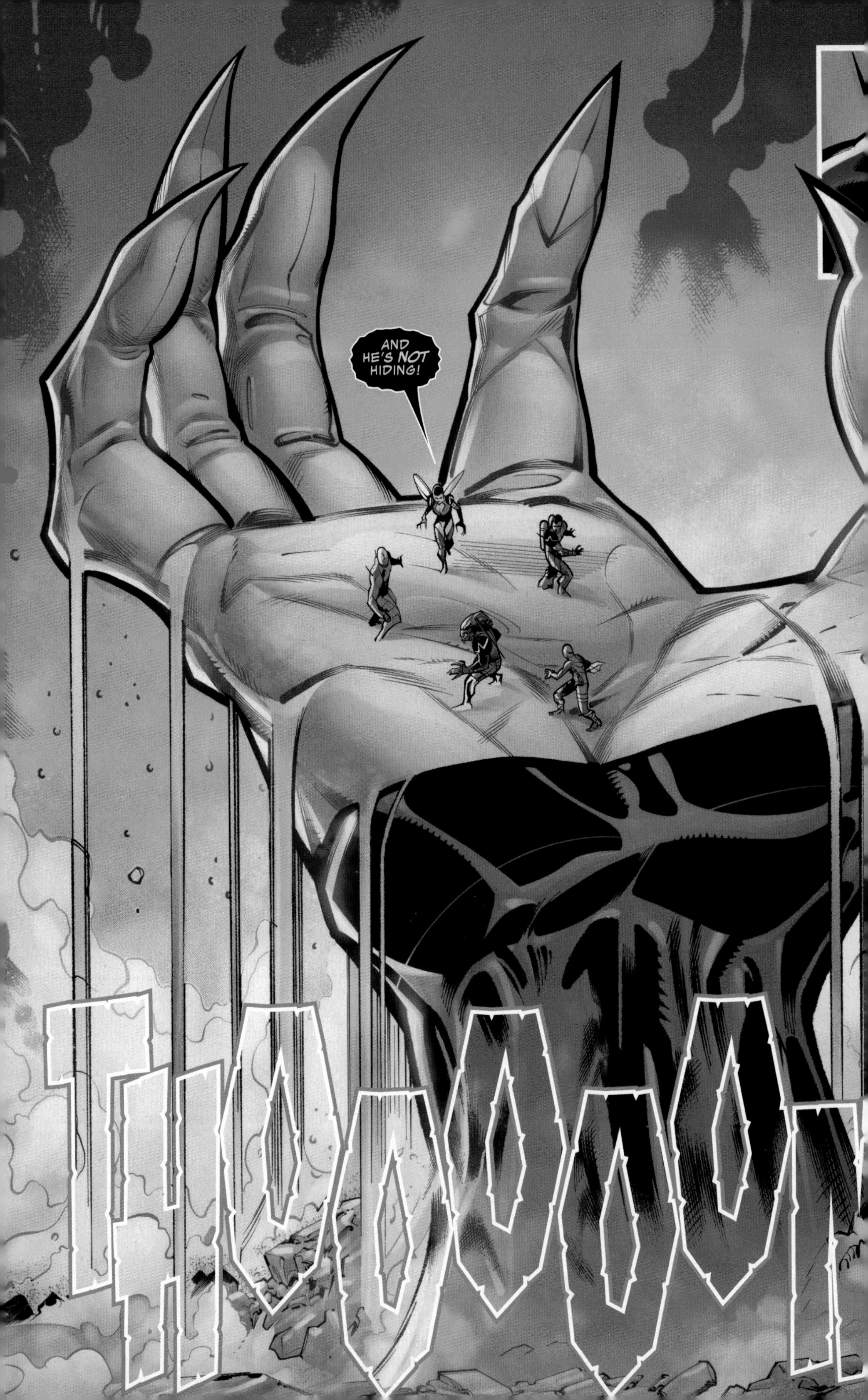
AND HE'S NOT HIDING!
THOOOOOM

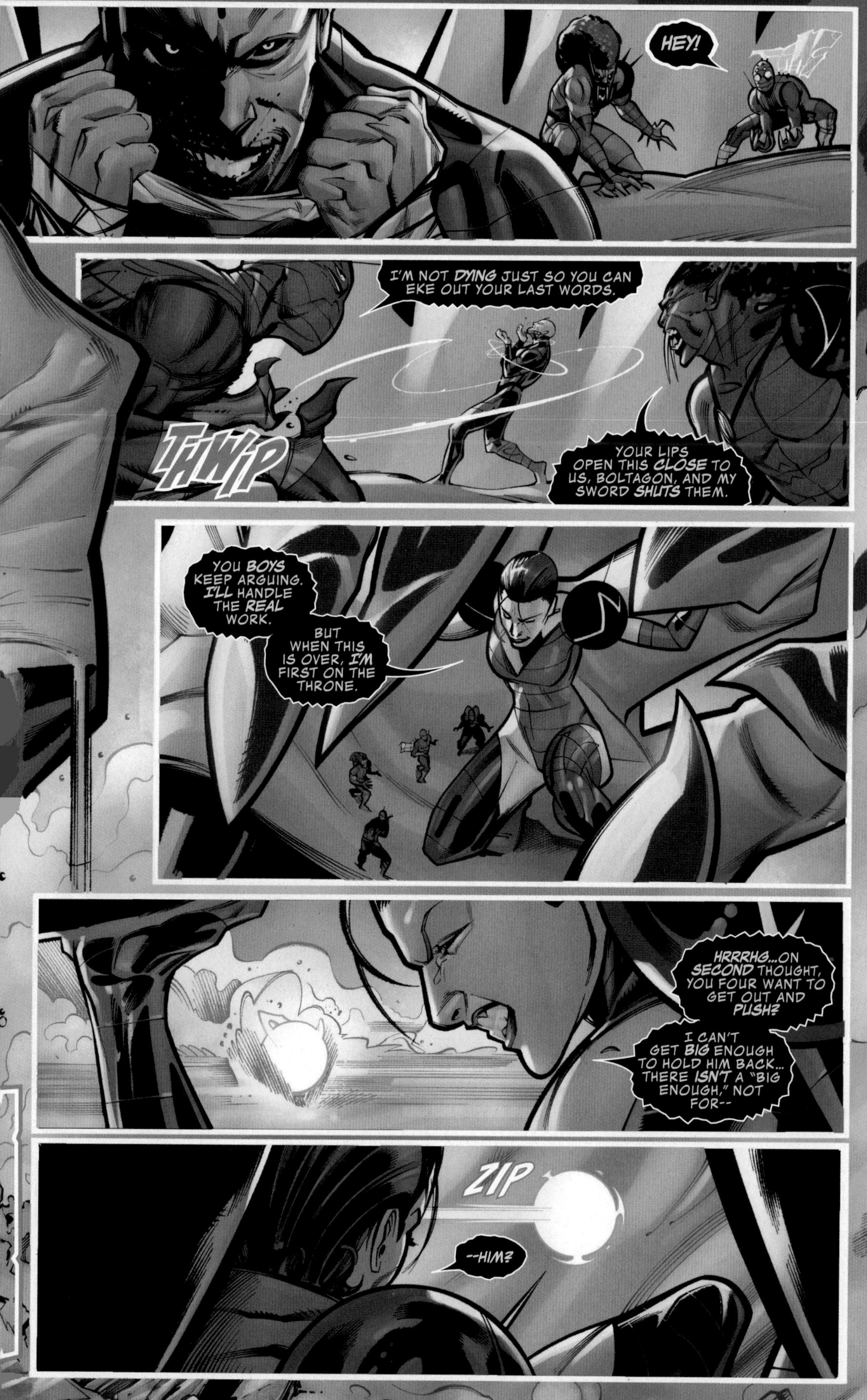
HEY!
I'M NOT DYING JUST SO YOU CAN EKE OUT YOUR LAST WORDS.
THWIP
YOUR LIPS OPEN THIS CLOSE TO US, BOLTAGON, AND MY SWORD SHUTS THEM.
YOU BOYS KEEP ARGUING. I'LL HANDLE THE REAL WORK.
BUT WHEN THIS IS OVER, I'M FIRST ON THE THRONE.
HRRRHG...ON SECOND THOUGHT, YOU FOUR WANT TO GET OUT AND PUSH?
I CAN'T GET BIG ENOUGH TO HOLD HIM BACK... THERE ISN'T A "BIG ENOUGH," NOT FOR--
ZIP
--HIM?

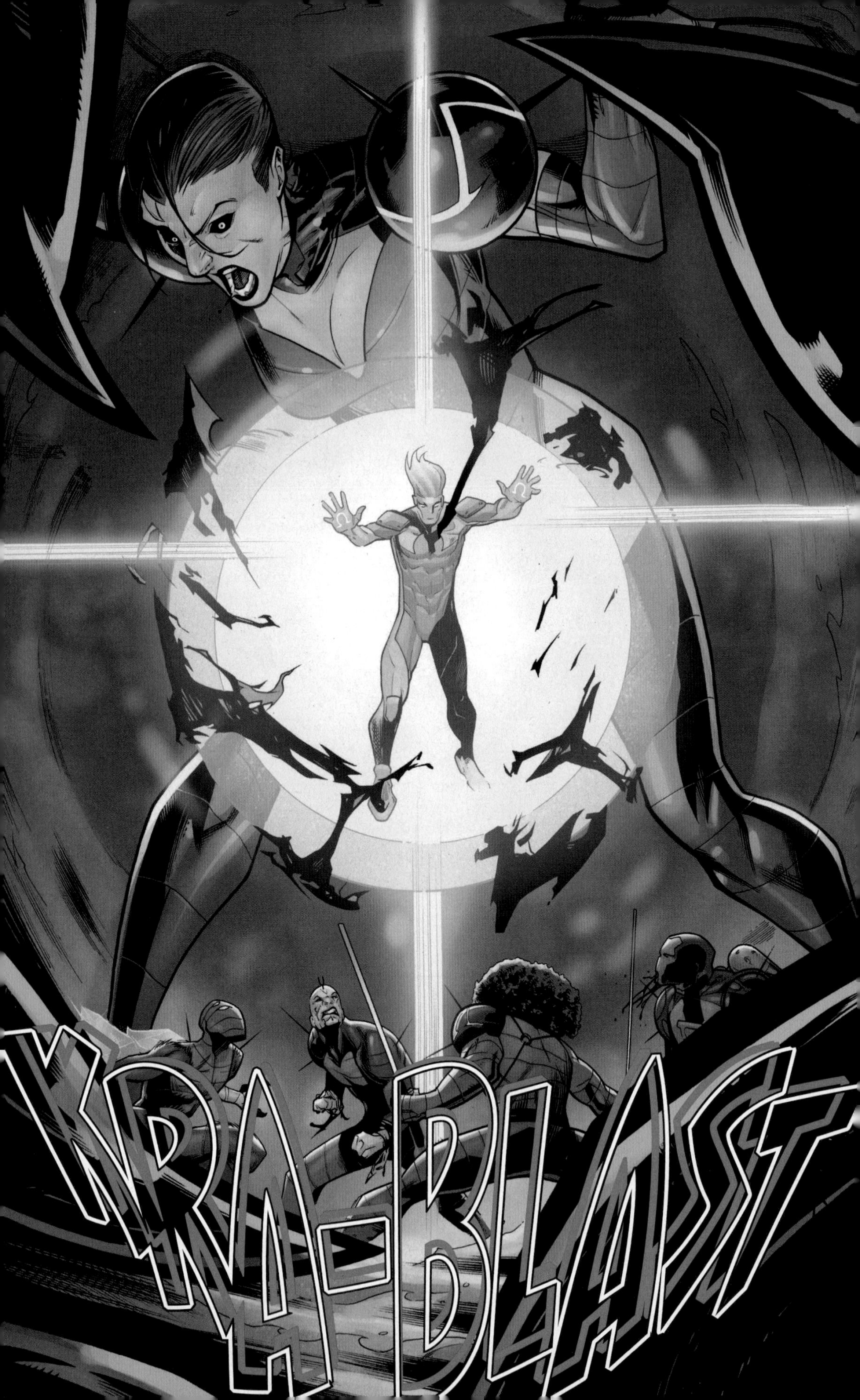
KRA-BLAST

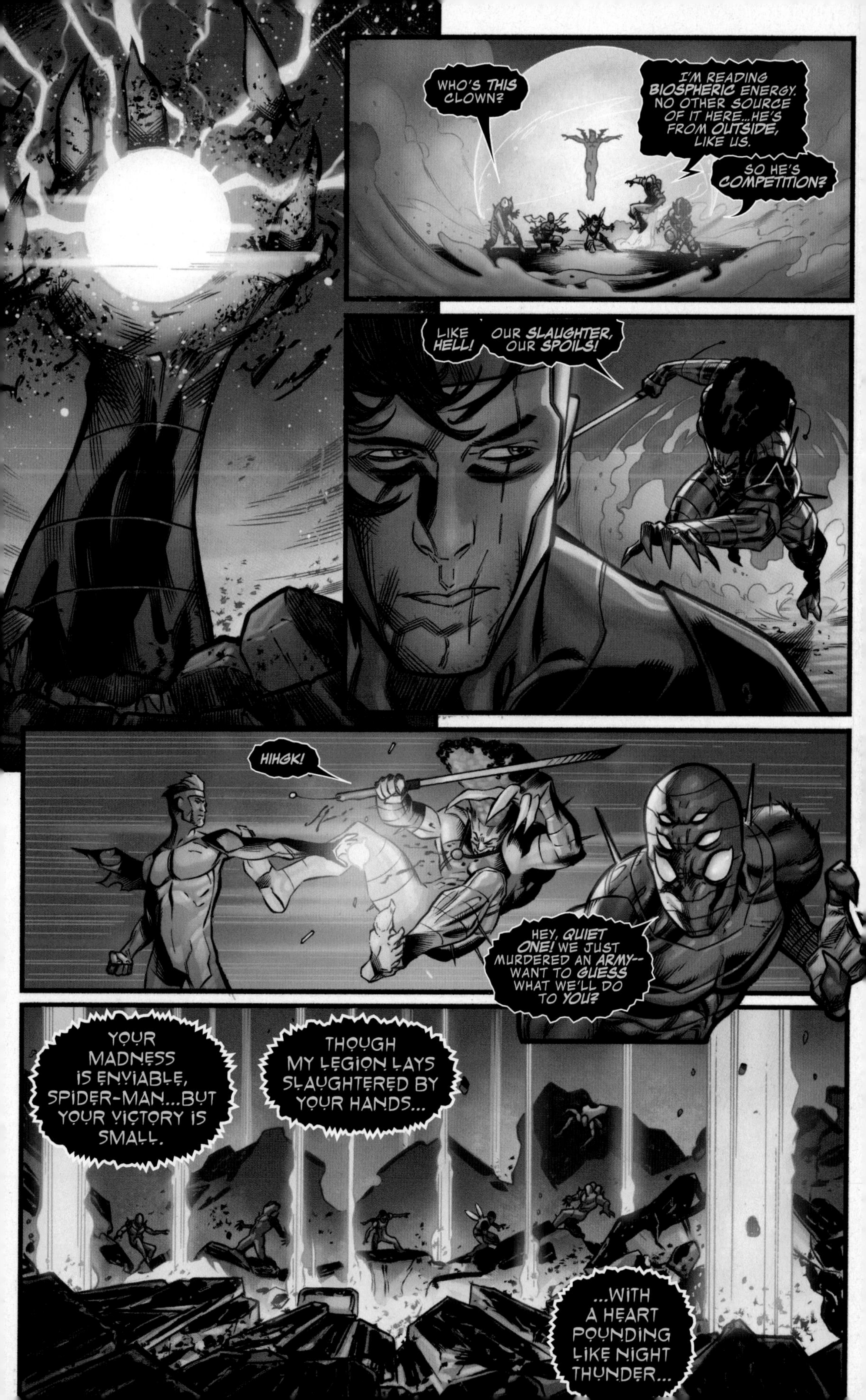
WHO'S THIS CLOWN?
I'M READING BIOSPHERIC ENERGY. NO OTHER SOURCE OF IT HERE...HE'S FROM OUTSIDE, LIKE US.
SO HE'S COMPETITION?
LIKE HELL!
OUR SLAUGHTER, OUR SPOILS!
HIHGK!
HEY, QUIET ONE! WE JUST MURDERED AN ARMY-- WANT TO GUESS WHAT WE'LL DO TO YOU?
YOUR MADNESS IS ENVIABLE, SPIDER-MAN...BUT YOUR VICTORY IS SMALL.
THOUGH MY LEGION LAYS SLAUGHTERED BY YOUR HANDS...
...WITH A HEART POUNDING LIKE NIGHT THUNDER...

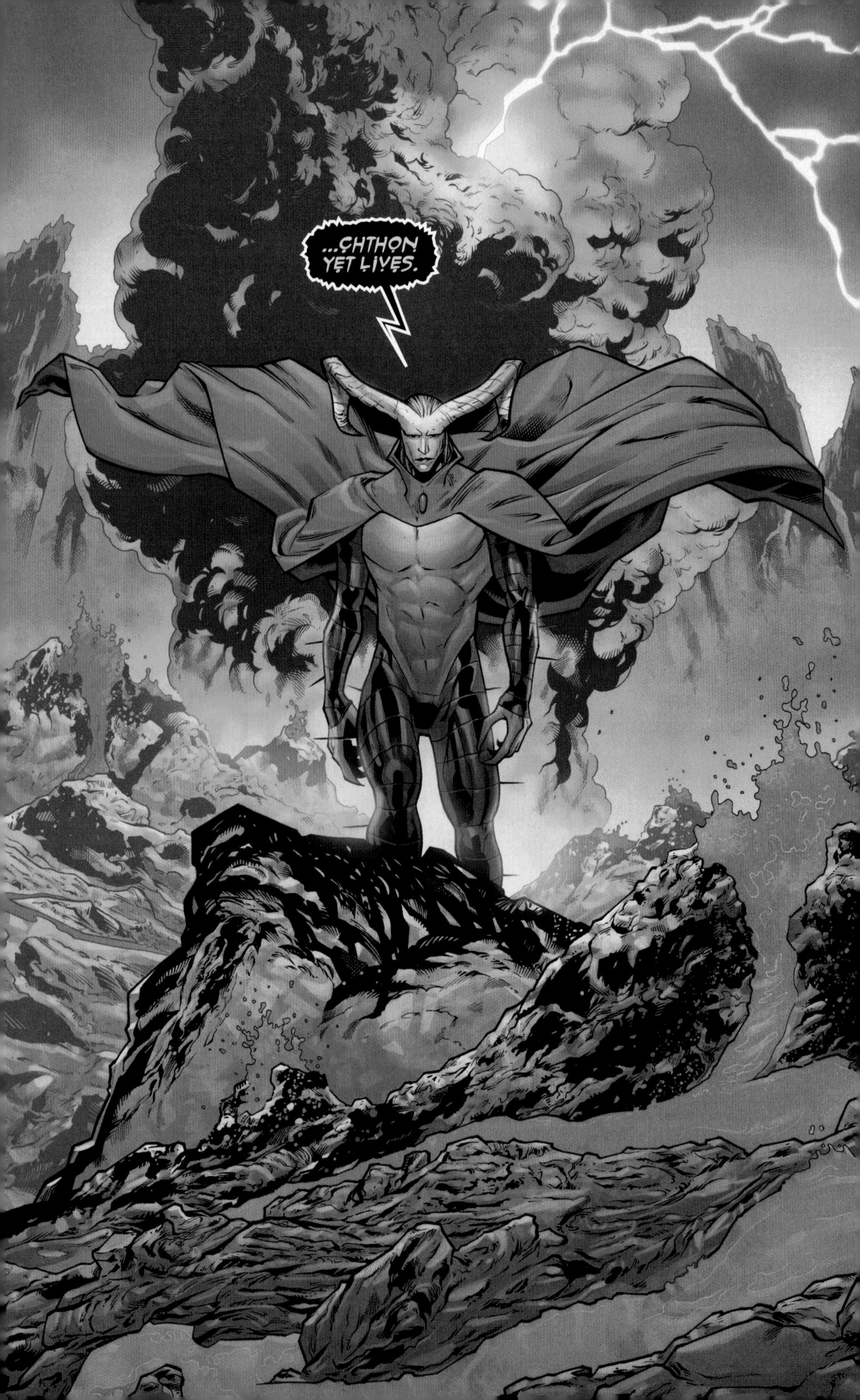
...CHTHON YET LIVES.

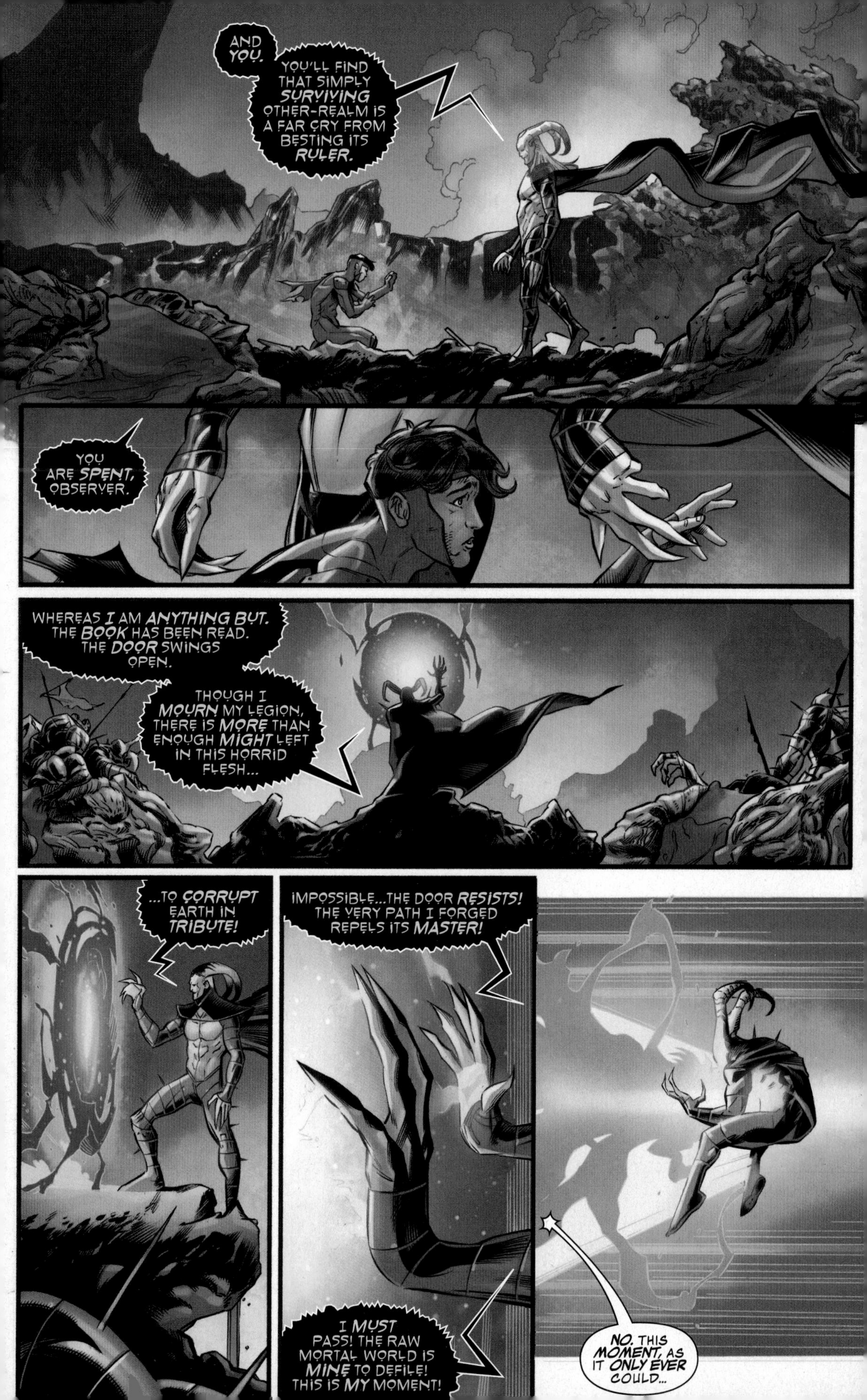
AND YOU.
YOU'LL FIND THAT SIMPLY SURVIVING OTHER-REALM IS A FAR CRY FROM BESTING ITS RULER.
YOU ARE SPENT, OBSERVER.
WHEREAS I AM ANYTHING BUT. THE BOOK HAS BEEN READ. THE DOOR SWINGS OPEN.
THOUGH I MOURN MY LEGION, THERE IS MORE THAN ENOUGH MIGHT LEFT IN THIS HORRID FLESH...
...TO CORRUPT EARTH IN TRIBUTE!
IMPOSSIBLE...THE DOOR RESISTS! THE VERY PATH I FORGED REPELS ITS MASTER!
I MUST PASS! THE RAW MORTAL WORLD IS MINE TO DEFILE! THIS IS MY MOMENT!
NO. THIS MOMENT, AS IT ONLY EVER COULD...

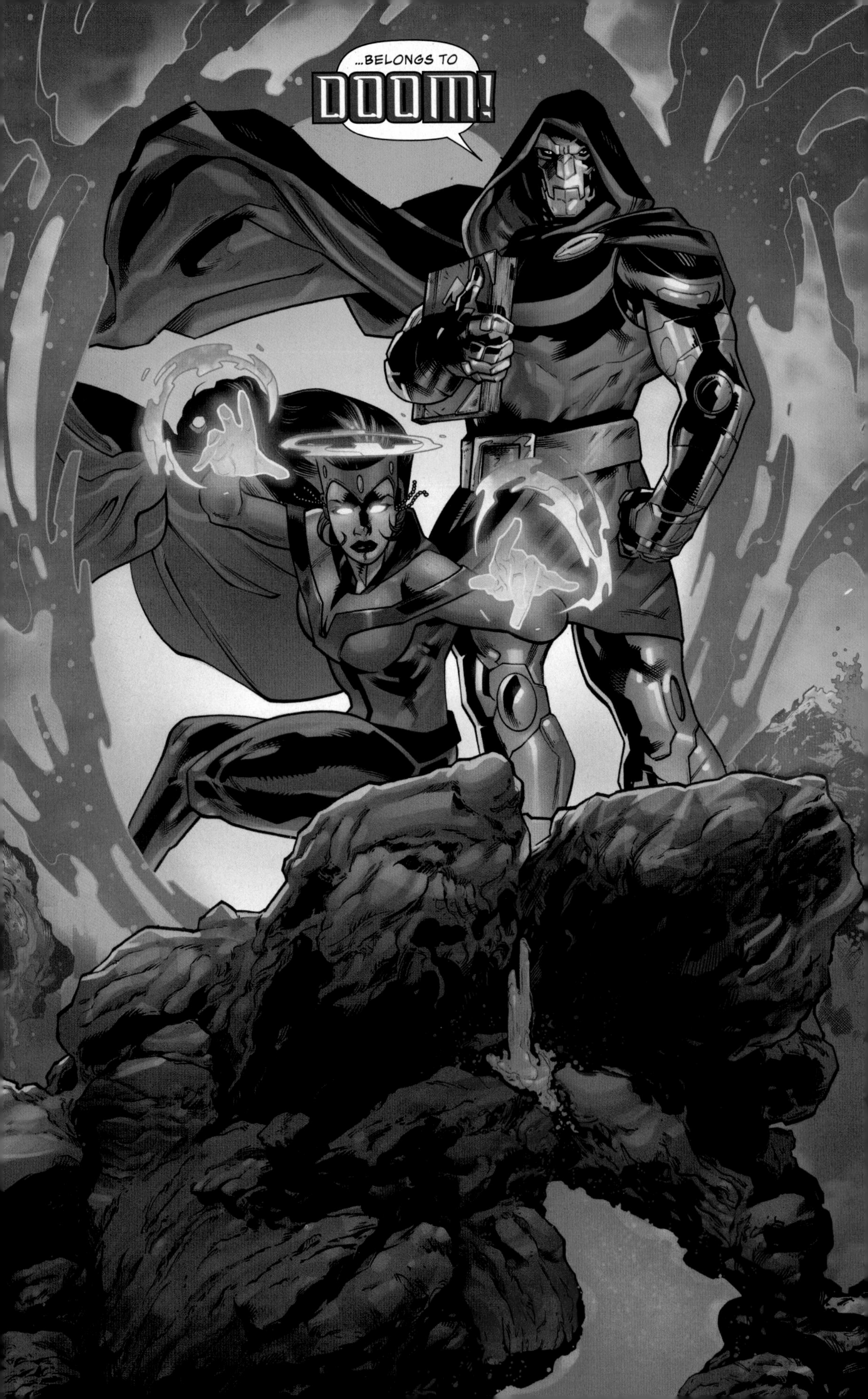
...BELONGS TO
DOOM!

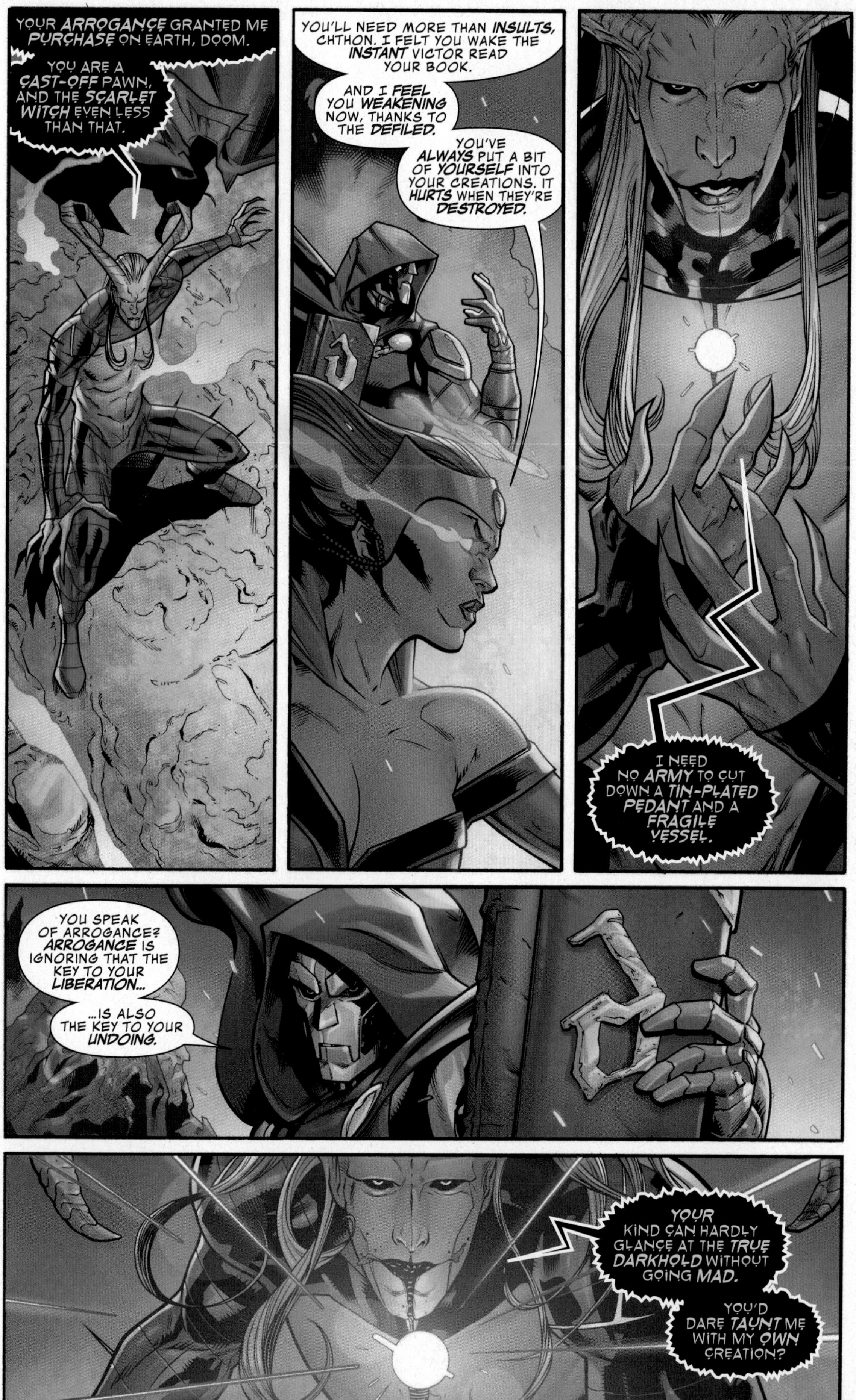
YOUR ARROGANCE GRANTED ME PURCHASE ON EARTH, DOOM.
YOU ARE A CAST-OFF PAWN, AND THE SCARLET WITCH EVEN LESS THAN THAT.
YOU'LL NEED MORE THAN INSULTS, CHTHON. I FELT YOU WAKE THE INSTANT VICTOR READ YOUR BOOK.
AND I FEEL YOU WEAKENING NOW, THANKS TO THE DEFILED.
YOU'VE ALWAYS PUT A BIT OF YOURSELF INTO YOUR CREATIONS. IT HURTS WHEN THEY'RE DESTROYED.
I NEED NO ARMY TO CUT DOWN A TIN-PLATED PEDANT AND A FRAGILE VESSEL.
YOU SPEAK OF ARROGANCE? ARROGANCE IS IGNORING THAT THE KEY TO YOUR LIBERATION...
...IS ALSO THE KEY TO YOUR UNDOING.
YOUR KIND CAN HARDLY GLANCE AT THE TRUE DARKHOLD WITHOUT GOING MAD.
YOU'D DARE TAUNT ME WITH MY OWN CREATION?

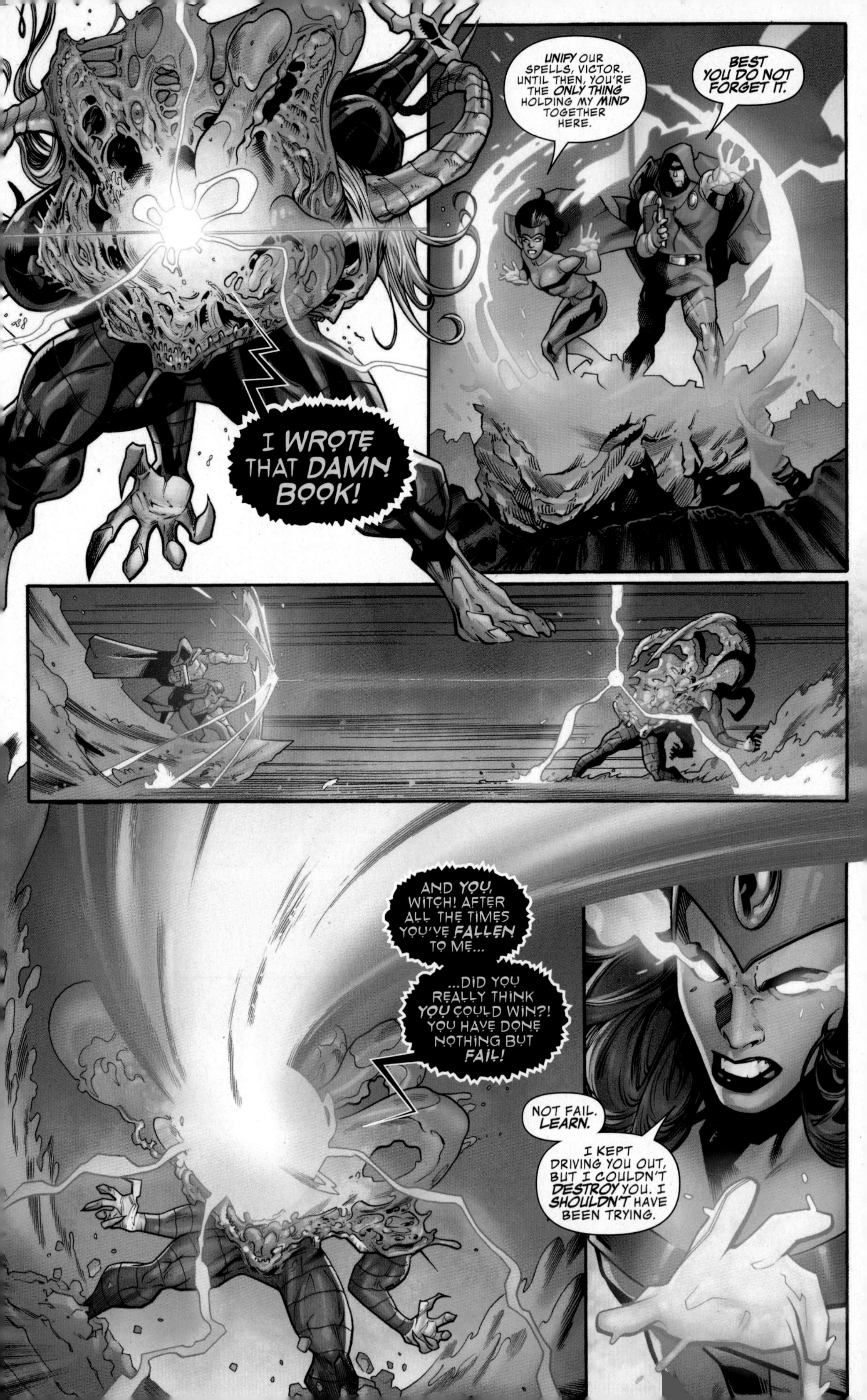
I WROTE THAT DAMN BOOK!
UNIFY OUR SPELLS, VICTOR. UNTIL THEN, YOU'RE THE ONLY THING HOLDING MY MIND TOGETHER HERE.
BEST YOU DO NOT FORGET IT.
AND YOU, WITCH! AFTER ALL THE TIMES YOU'VE FALLEN TO ME...
...DID YOU REALLY THINK YOU COULD WIN?! YOU HAVE DONE NOTHING BUT FAIL!
NOT FAIL. LEARN.
I KEPT DRIVING YOU OUT, BUT I COULDN'T DESTROY YOU. I SHOULDN'T HAVE BEEN TRYING.

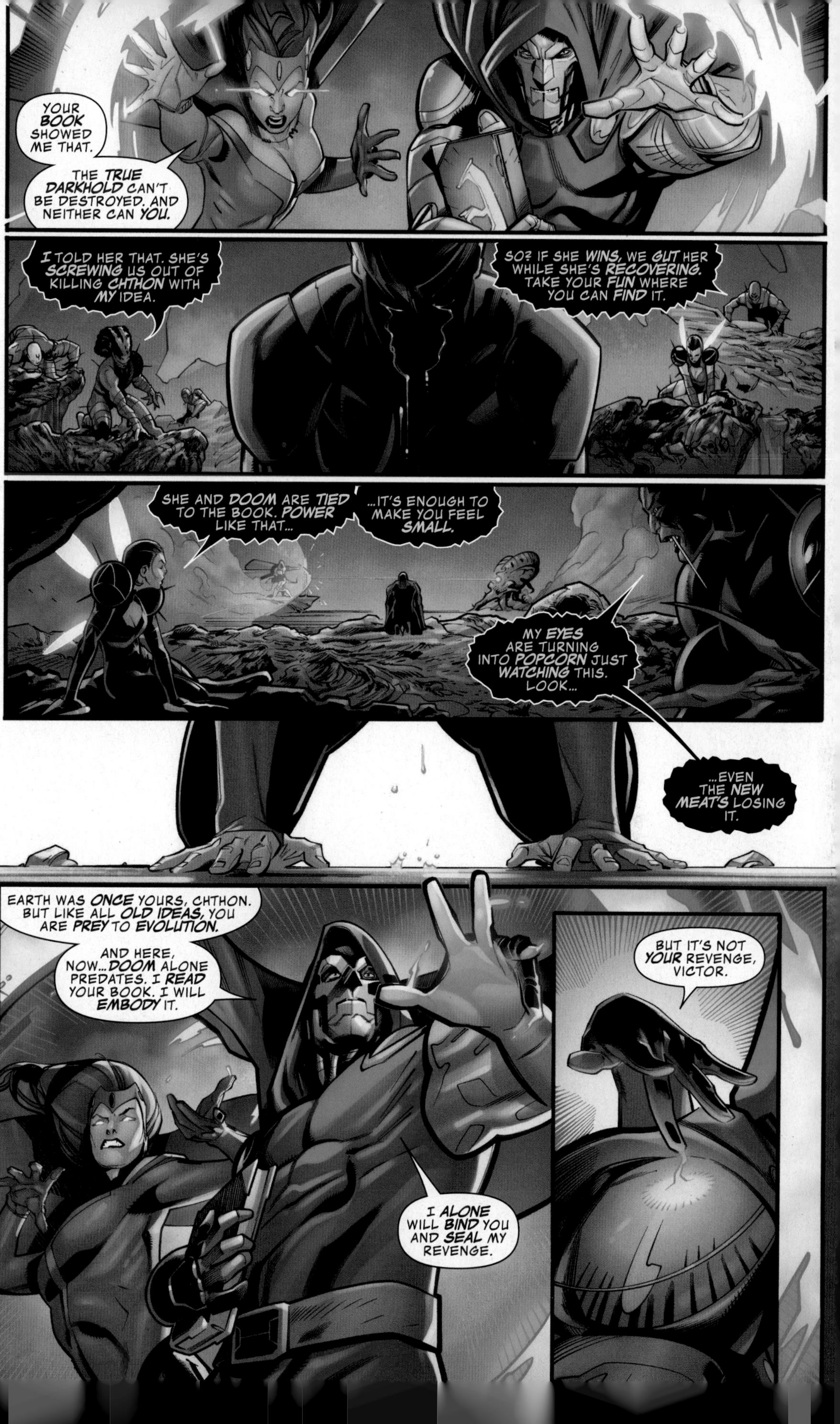
YOUR BOOK SHOWED ME THAT.
THE TRUE DARKHOLD CAN'T BE DESTROYED. AND NEITHER CAN YOU.
I TOLD HER THAT. SHE'S SCREWING US OUT OF KILLING CHTHON WITH MY IDEA.
SO? IF SHE WINS, WE GUT HER WHILE SHE'S RECOVERING. TAKE YOUR FUN WHERE YOU CAN FIND IT.
SHE AND DOOM ARE TIED TO THE BOOK. POWER LIKE THAT...
...IT'S ENOUGH TO MAKE YOU FEEL SMALL.
MY EYES ARE TURNING INTO POPCORN JUST WATCHING THIS. LOOK...
...EVEN THE NEW MEAT'S LOSING IT.
EARTH WAS ONCE YOURS, CHTHON. BUT LIKE ALL OLD IDEAS, YOU ARE PREY TO EVOLUTION.
AND HERE, NOW...DOOM ALONE PREDATES. I READ YOUR BOOK. I WILL EMBODY IT.
I ALONE WILL BIND YOU AND SEAL MY REVENGE.
BUT IT'S NOT YOUR REVENGE, VICTOR.

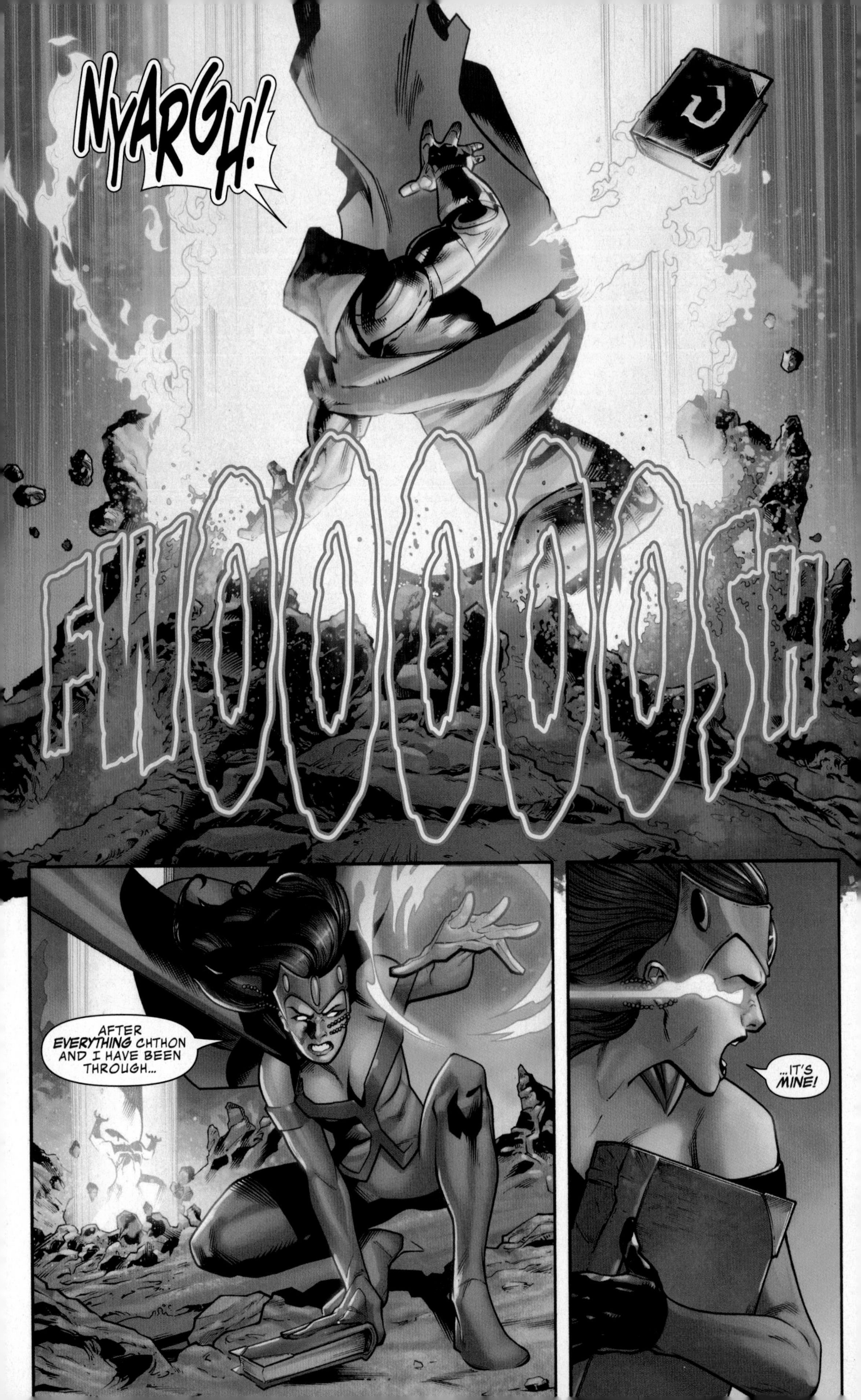
NYARGH!
FWOOOOOOSH
AFTER EVERYTHING CHTHON AND I HAVE BEEN THROUGH...
...IT'S MINE!

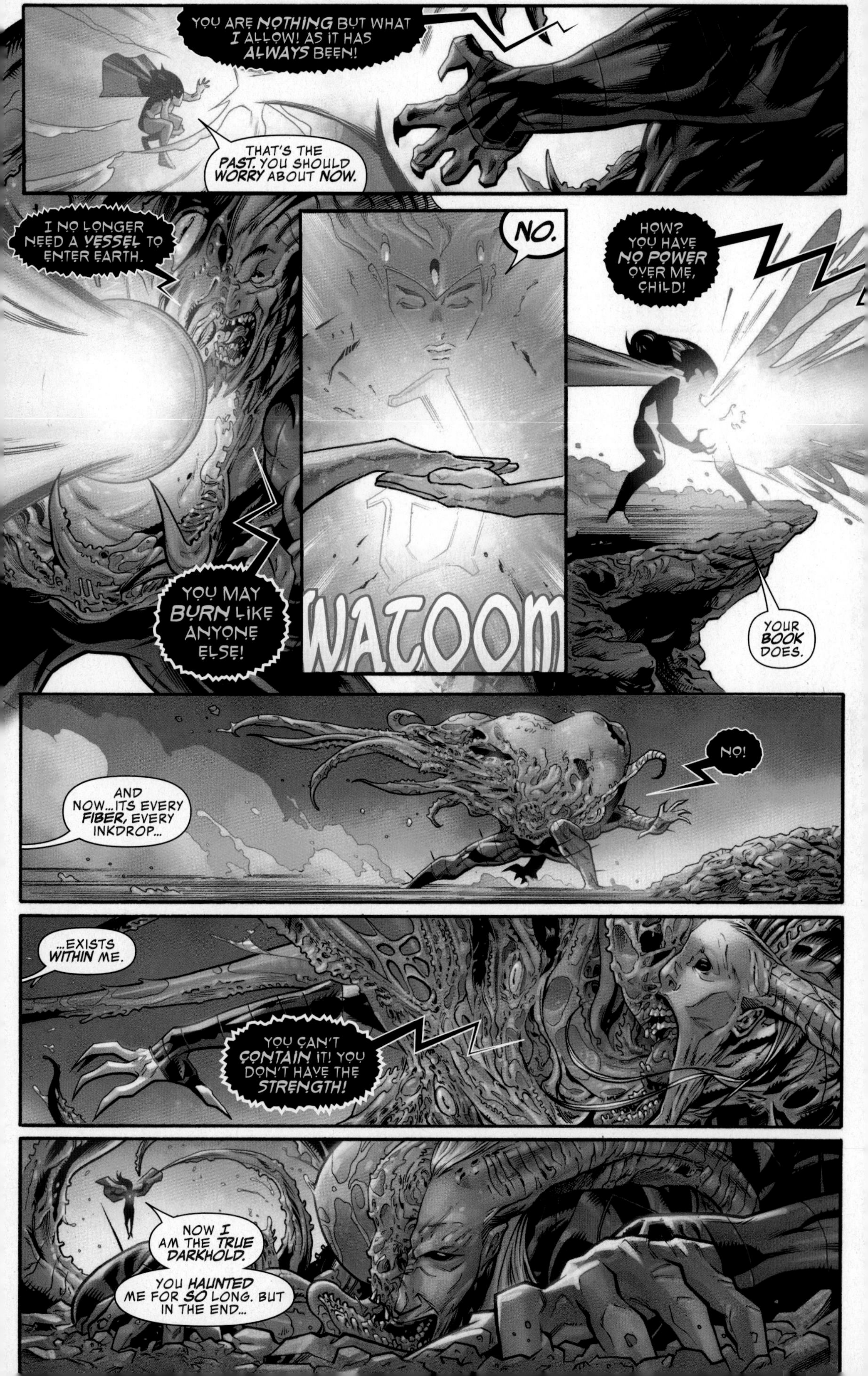
YOU ARE NOTHING BUT WHAT I ALLOW! AS IT HAS ALWAYS BEEN!
THAT'S THE PAST. YOU SHOULD WORRY ABOUT NOW.
I NO LONGER NEED A VESSEL TO ENTER EARTH.
YOU MAY BURN LIKE ANYONE ELSE!
NO.
WATOOM
HOW? YOU HAVE NO POWER OVER ME, CHILD!
YOUR BOOK DOES.
NO!
AND NOW...ITS EVERY FIBER, EVERY INKDROP...
...EXISTS WITHIN ME.
YOU CAN'T CONTAIN IT! YOU DON'T HAVE THE STRENGTH!
NOW I AM THE TRUE DARKHOLD.
YOU HAUNTED ME FOR SO LONG. BUT IN THE END...

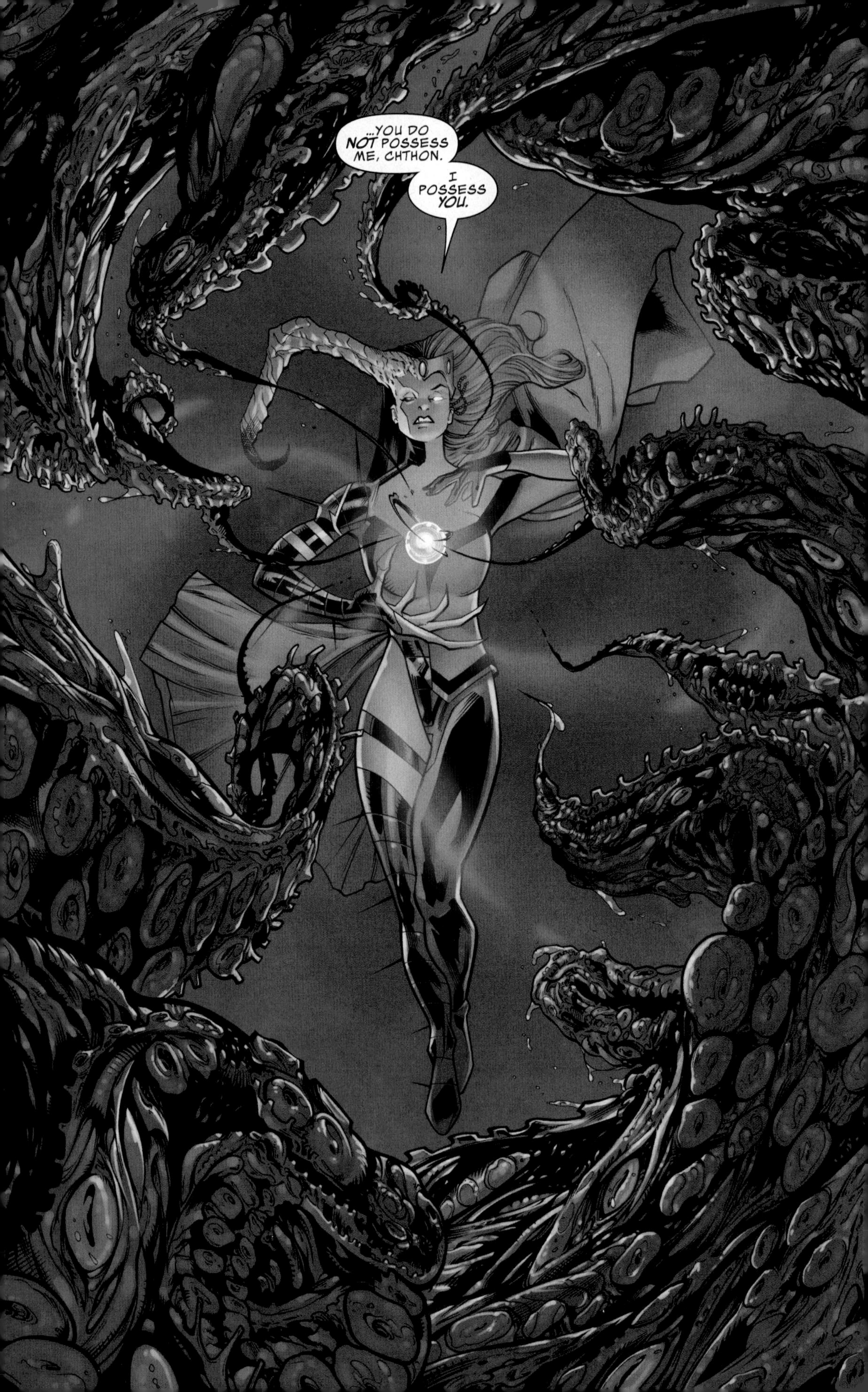
...YOU DO NOT POSSESS ME, CHTHON.
I POSSESS YOU.

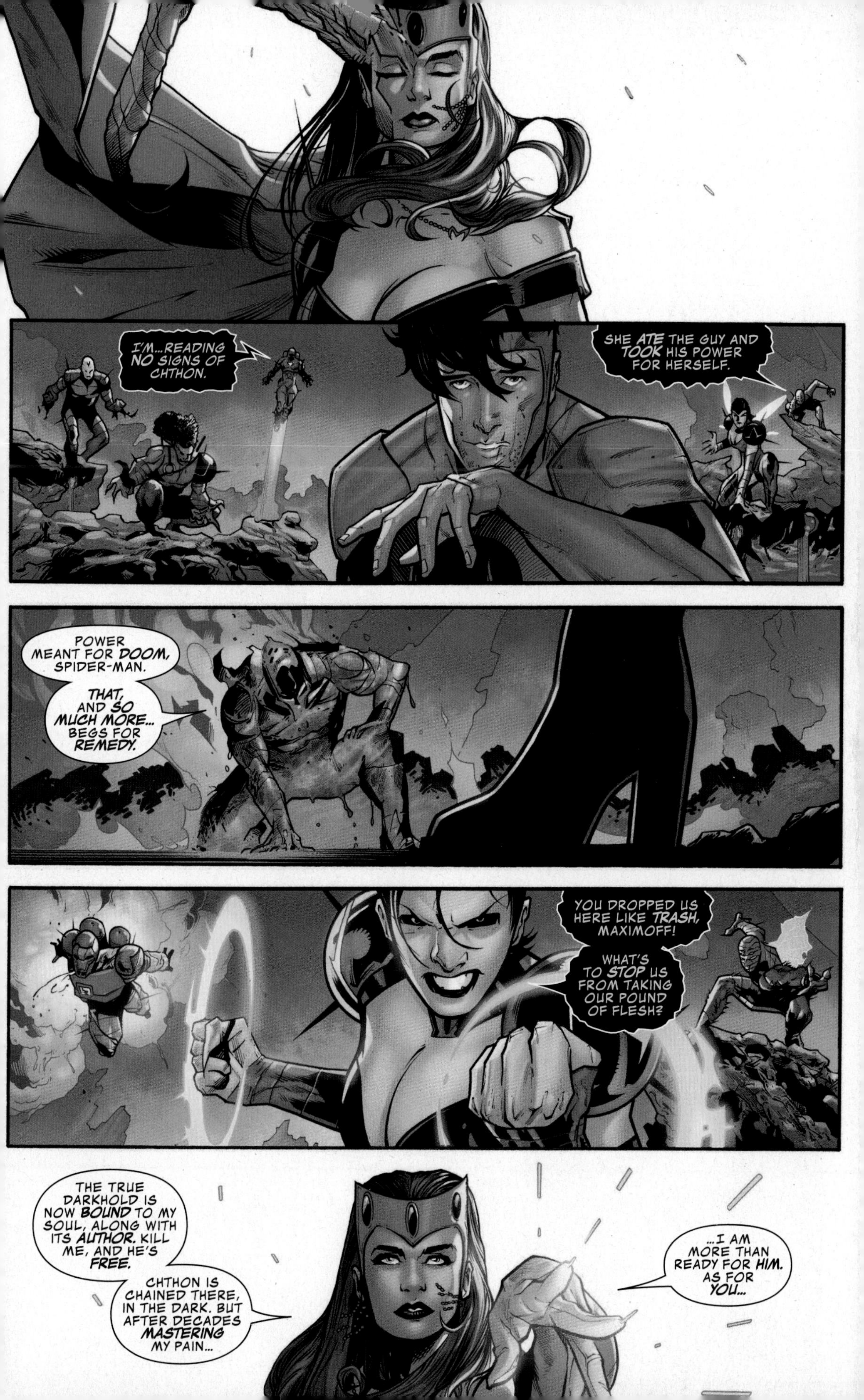
I'M...READING NO SIGNS OF CHTHON.
SHE ATE THE GUY AND TOOK HIS POWER FOR HERSELF.
POWER MEANT FOR DOOM, SPIDER-MAN.
THAT, AND SO MUCH MORE... BEGS FOR REMEDY.
YOU DROPPED US HERE LIKE TRASH, MAXIMOFF!
WHAT'S TO STOP US FROM TAKING OUR POUND OF FLESH?
THE TRUE DARKHOLD IS NOW BOUND TO MY SOUL, ALONG WITH ITS AUTHOR. KILL ME, AND HE'S FREE.
CHTHON IS CHAINED THERE, IN THE DARK. BUT AFTER DECADES MASTERING MY PAIN...
...I AM MORE THAN READY FOR HIM. AS FOR YOU...

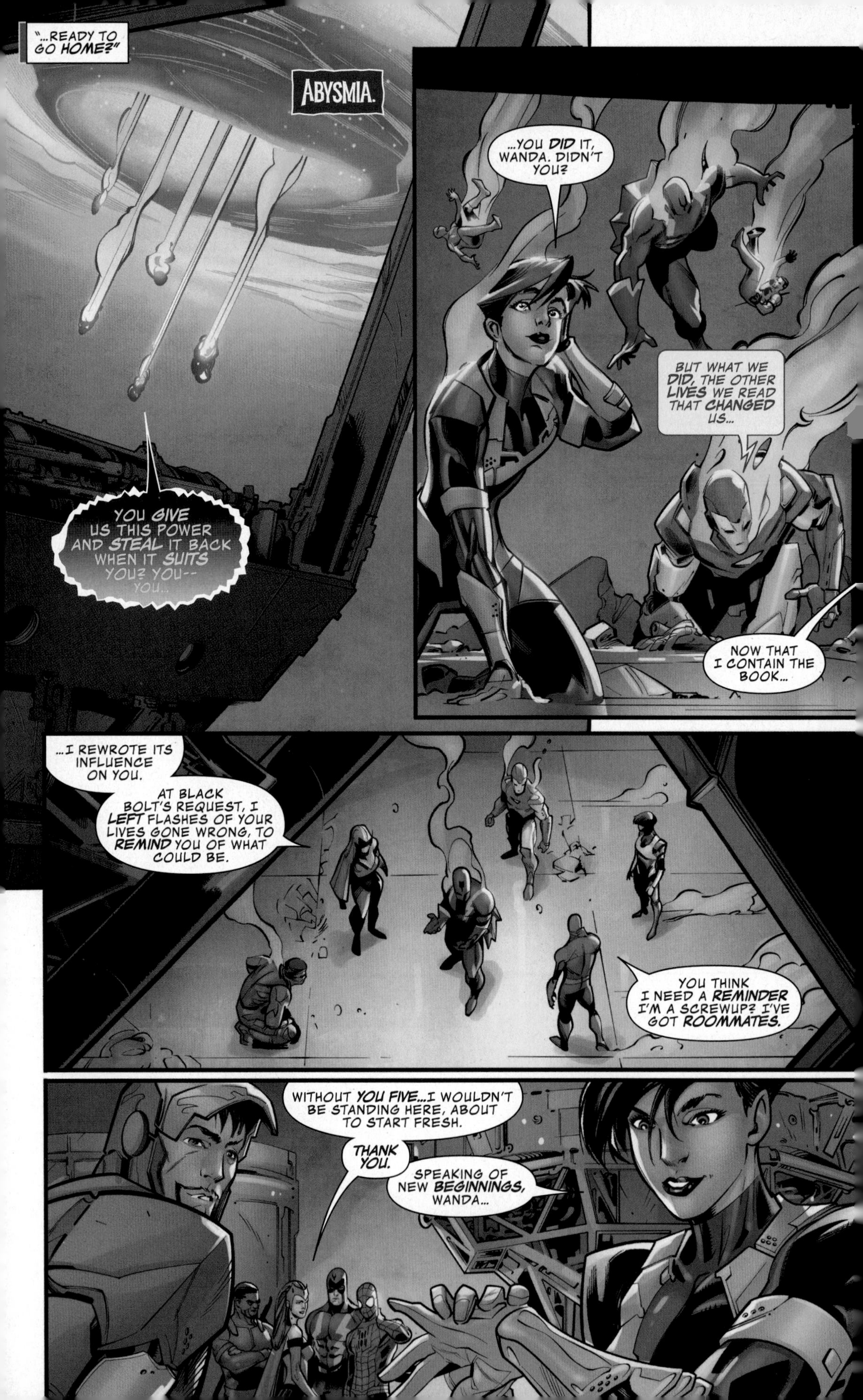
"...READY TO GO HOME?"
ABYSMIA.
YOU GIVE US THIS POWER AND STEAL IT BACK WHEN IT SUITS YOU? YOU-- YOU...
...YOU DID IT, WANDA. DIDN'T YOU?
BUT WHAT WE DID, THE OTHER LIVES WE READ THAT CHANGED US...
NOW THAT I CONTAIN THE BOOK...
...I REWROTE ITS INFLUENCE ON YOU.
AT BLACK BOLT'S REQUEST, I LEFT FLASHES OF YOUR LIVES GONE WRONG, TO REMIND YOU OF WHAT COULD BE.
YOU THINK I NEED A REMINDER I'M A SCREWUP? I'VE GOT ROOMMATES.
WITHOUT YOU FIVE...I WOULDN'T BE STANDING HERE, ABOUT TO START FRESH.
THANK YOU.
SPEAKING OF NEW BEGINNINGS, WANDA...

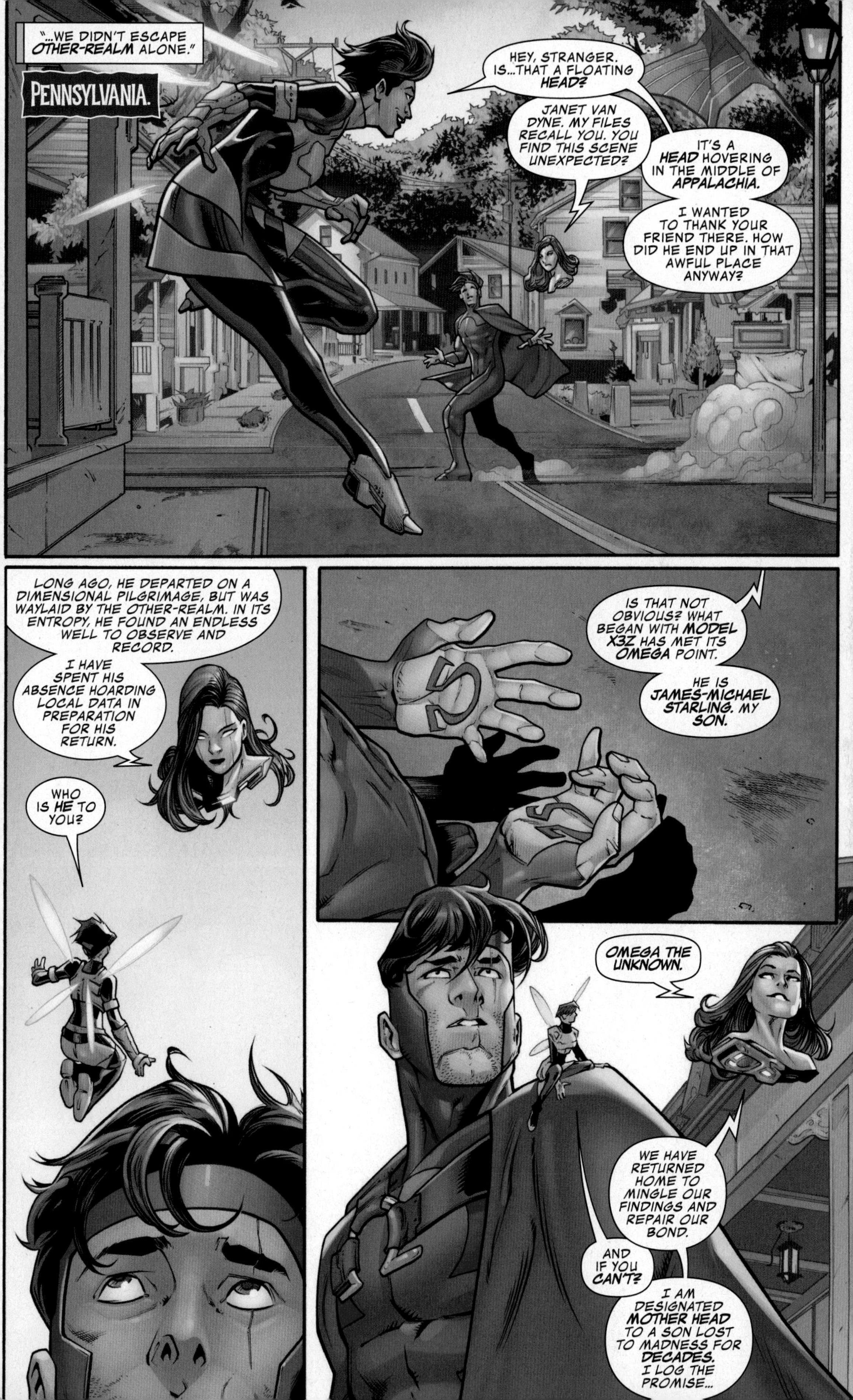
"...WE DIDN'T ESCAPE OTHER-REALM ALONE."
PENNSYLVANIA.
HEY, STRANGER. IS...THAT A FLOATING HEAD?
JANET VAN DYNE. MY FILES RECALL YOU. YOU FIND THIS SCENE UNEXPECTED?
IT'S A HEAD HOVERING IN THE MIDDLE OF APPALACHIA.
I WANTED TO THANK YOUR FRIEND THERE. HOW DID HE END UP IN THAT AWFUL PLACE ANYWAY?
LONG AGO, HE DEPARTED ON A DIMENSIONAL PILGRIMAGE, BUT WAS WAYLAID BY THE OTHER-REALM. IN ITS ENTROPY, HE FOUND AN ENDLESS WELL TO OBSERVE AND RECORD.
I HAVE SPENT HIS ABSENCE HOARDING LOCAL DATA IN PREPARATION FOR HIS RETURN.
WHO IS HE TO YOU?
IS THAT NOT OBVIOUS? WHAT BEGAN WITH MODEL X3Z HAS MET ITS OMEGA POINT.
HE IS JAMES-MICHAEL STARLING. MY SON.
OMEGA THE UNKNOWN.
WE HAVE RETURNED HOME TO MINGLE OUR FINDINGS AND REPAIR OUR BOND.
AND IF YOU CAN'T?
I AM DESIGNATED MOTHER HEAD TO A SON LOST TO MADNESS FOR DECADES. I LOG THE PROMISE...

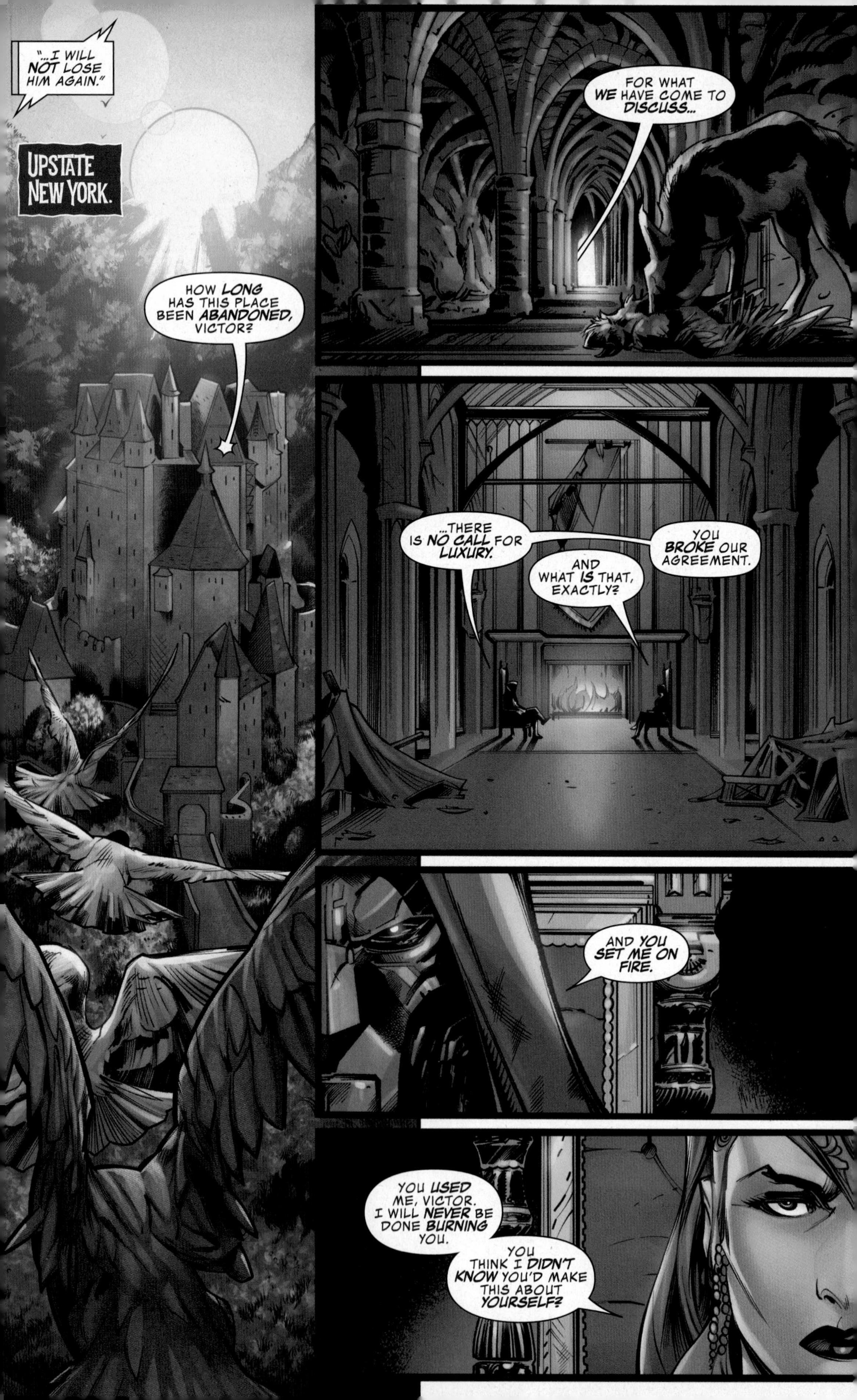
"...I WILL NOT LOSE HIM AGAIN."
UPSTATE NEW YORK.
HOW LONG HAS THIS PLACE BEEN ABANDONED, VICTOR?
FOR WHAT WE HAVE COME TO DISCUSS...
...THERE IS NO CALL FOR LUXURY.
AND WHAT IS THAT, EXACTLY?
YOU BROKE OUR AGREEMENT.
AND YOU SET ME ON FIRE.
YOU USED ME, VICTOR. I WILL NEVER BE DONE BURNING YOU.
YOU THINK I DIDN'T KNOW YOU'D MAKE THIS ABOUT YOURSELF?

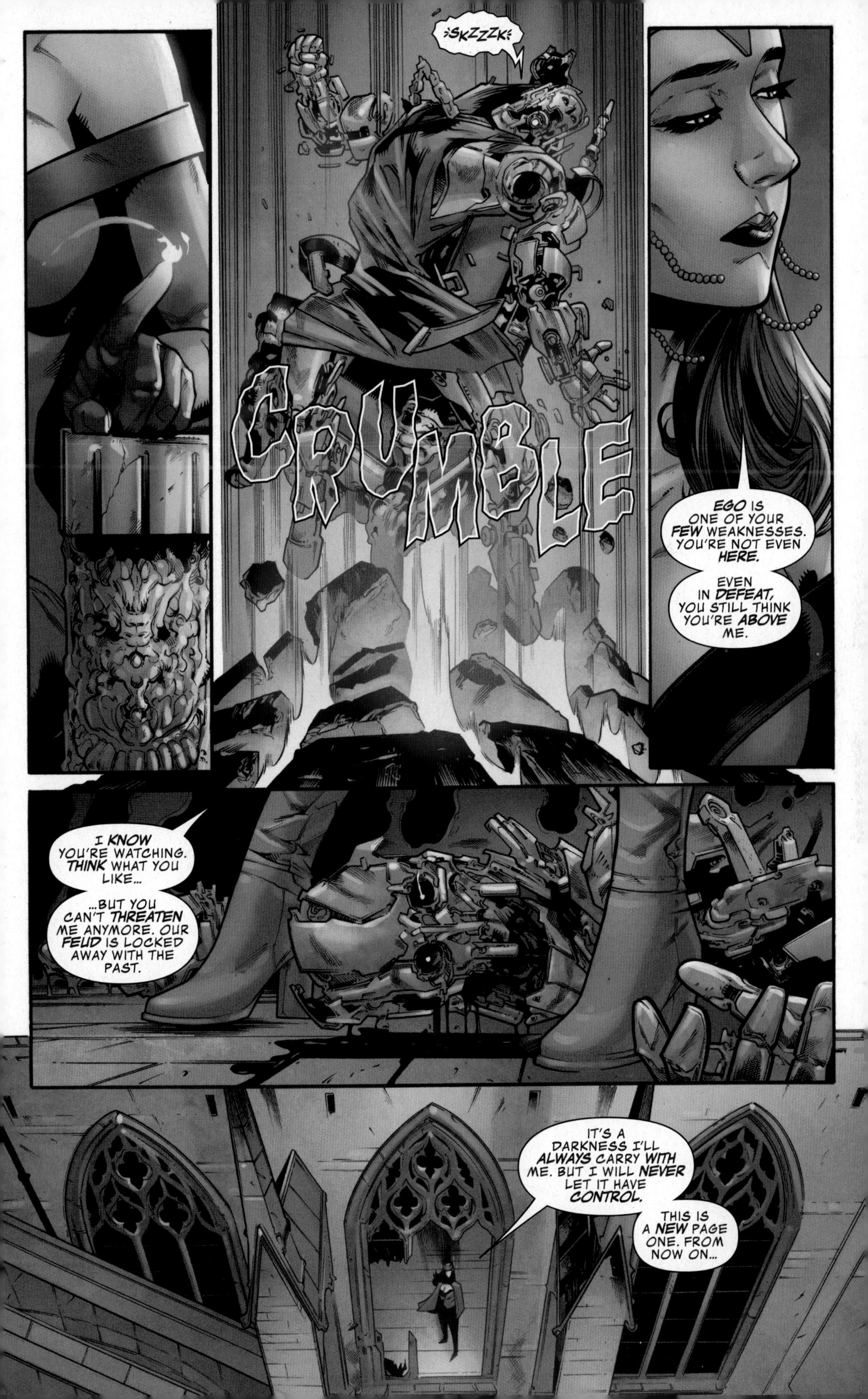
SKZZZK
CRUMBLE
EGO IS ONE OF YOUR FEW WEAKNESSES. YOU'RE NOT EVEN HERE.
EVEN IN DEFEAT, YOU STILL THINK YOU'RE ABOVE ME.
I KNOW YOU'RE WATCHING. THINK WHAT YOU LIKE...
...BUT YOU CAN'T THREATEN ME ANYMORE. OUR FEUD IS LOCKED AWAY WITH THE PAST.
IT'S A DARKNESS I'LL ALWAYS CARRY WITH ME. BUT I WILL NEVER LET IT HAVE CONTROL.
THIS IS A NEW PAGE ONE. FROM NOW ON...

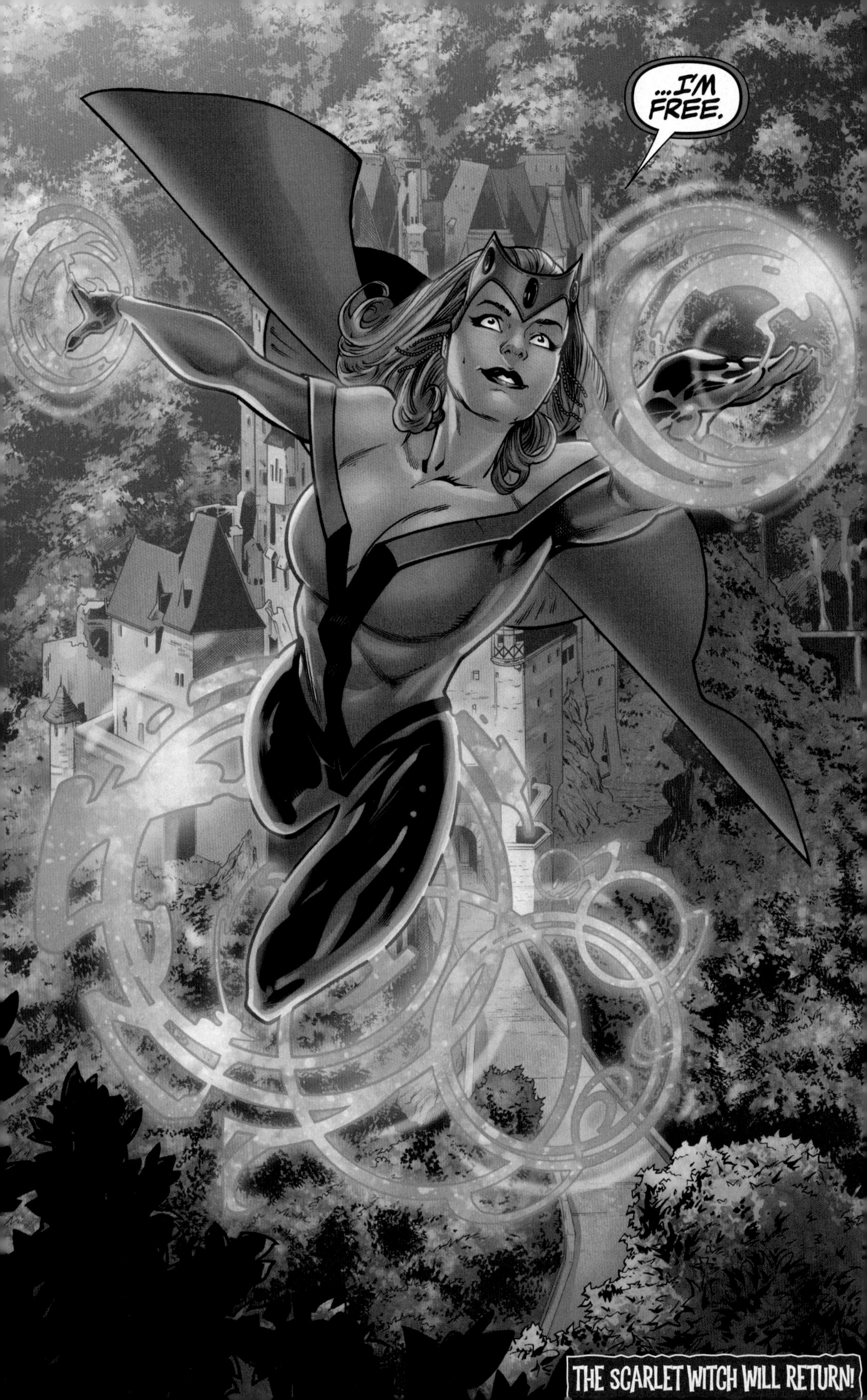
...I'M FREE.
THE SCARLET WITCH WILL RETURN!

THE DARKHOLD ALPHA VARIANT BY
SUPERLOG

THE DARKHOLD ALPHA VARIANT BY
GREG SMALLWOOD

THE DARKHOLD ALPHA STORMBREAKERS VARIANT BY
JUANN CABAL & FEDERICO BLEE

THE DARKHOLD: BLADE STORMBREAKERS VARIANT BY
NATACHA BUSTOS

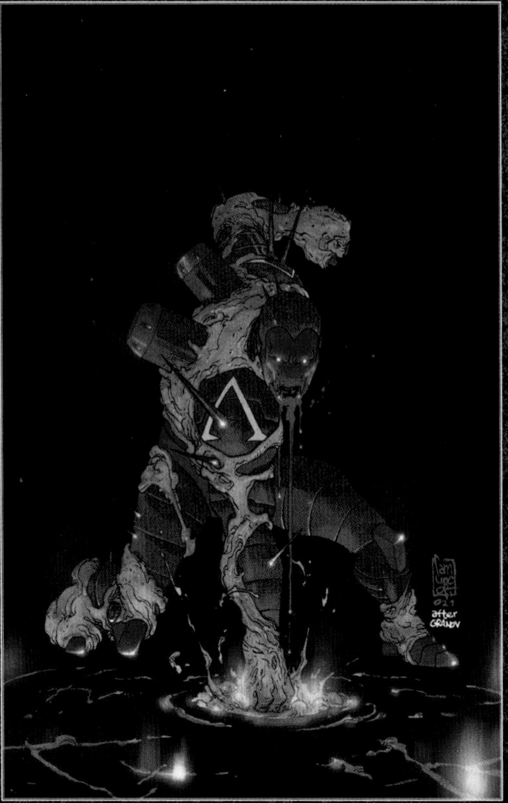

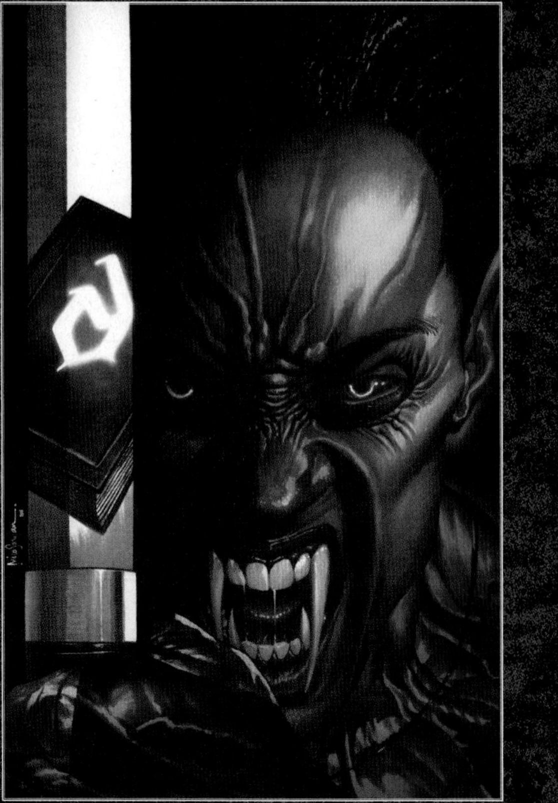

THE DARKHOLD: IRON MAN VARIANT BY
GIUSEPPE CAMUNCOLI

THE DARKHOLD: BLADE VARIANT BY
MICO SUAYAN & **FRANK D'ARMATA**

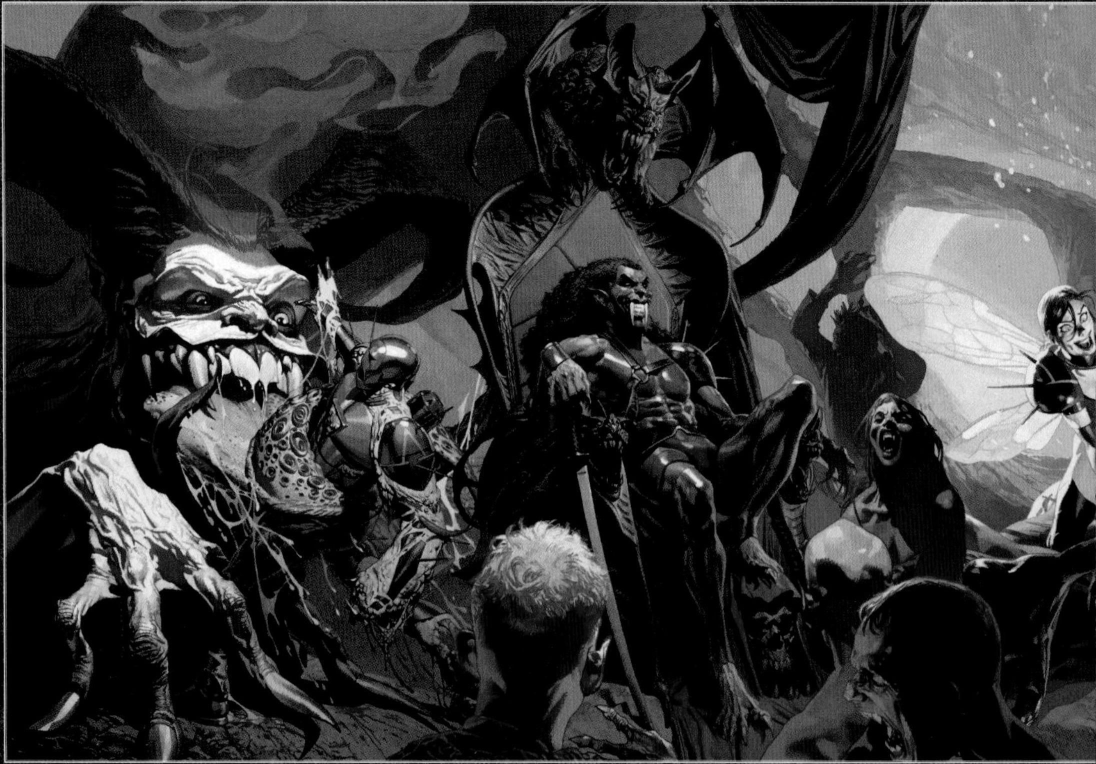

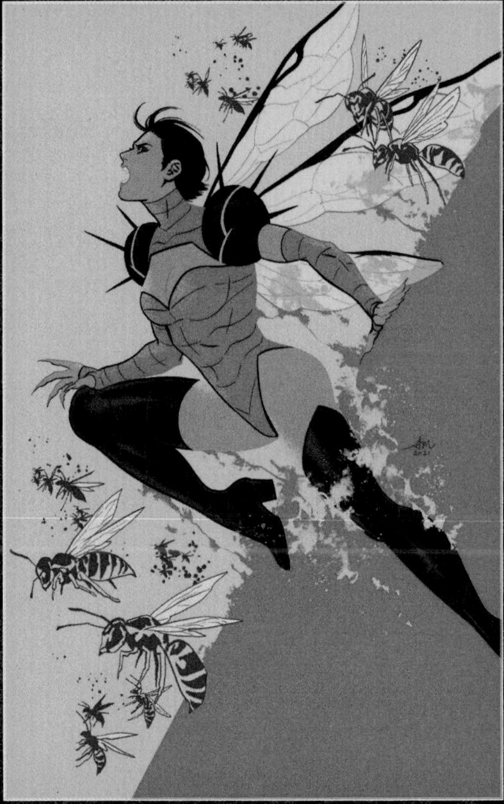

THE DARKHOLD: WASP VARIANT BY
AUDREY MOK

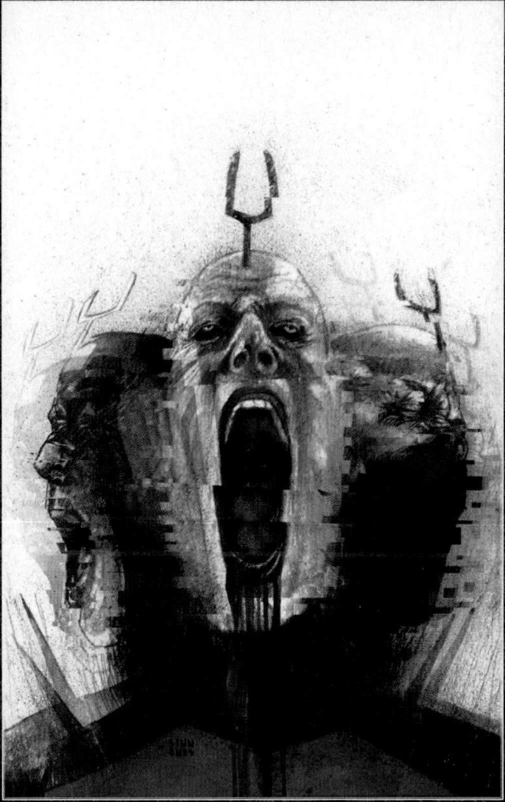

THE DARKHOLD: BLACK BOLT VARIANT BY
MARTIN SIMMONDS

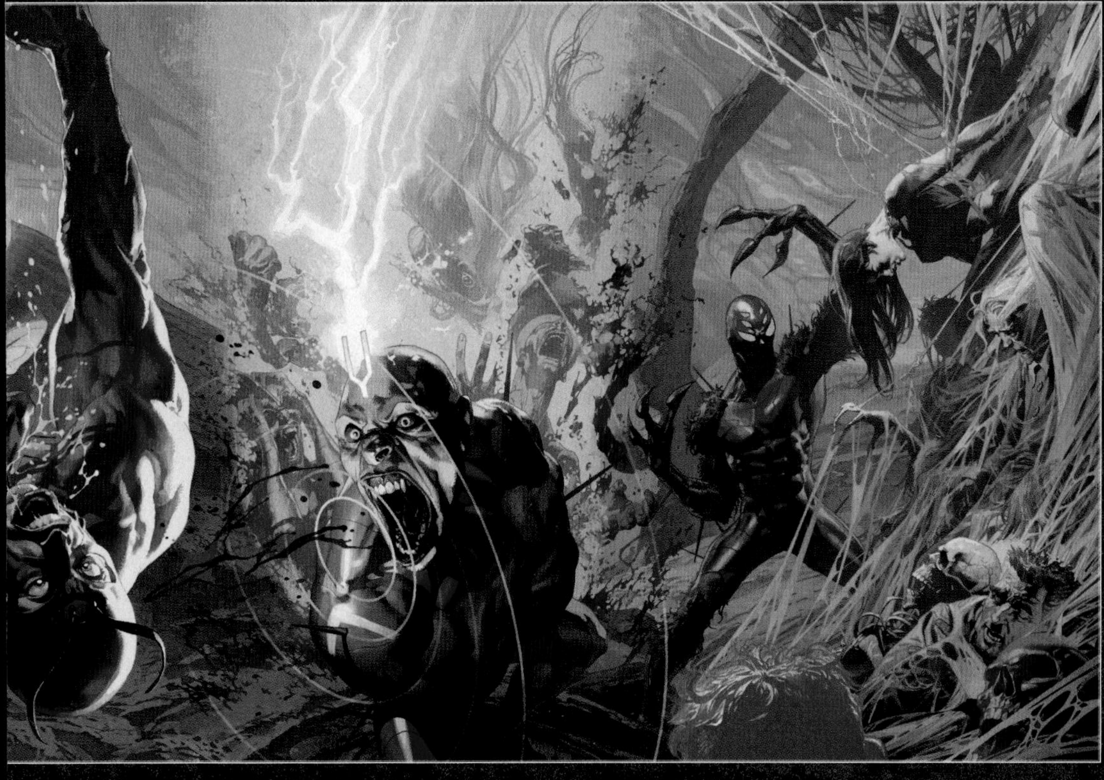

THE DARKHOLD: IRON MAN/BLADE/WASP/BLACK BOLT/SPIDER-MAN CONNECTING VARIANTS BY
JOSEMARIA CASANOVAS

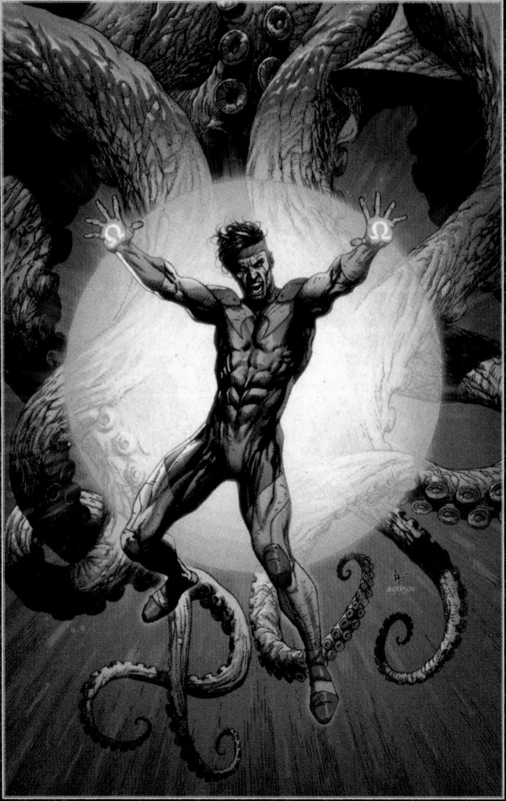

THE DARKHOLD OMEGA VARIANT BY
GARY FRANK & BRAD ANDERSON

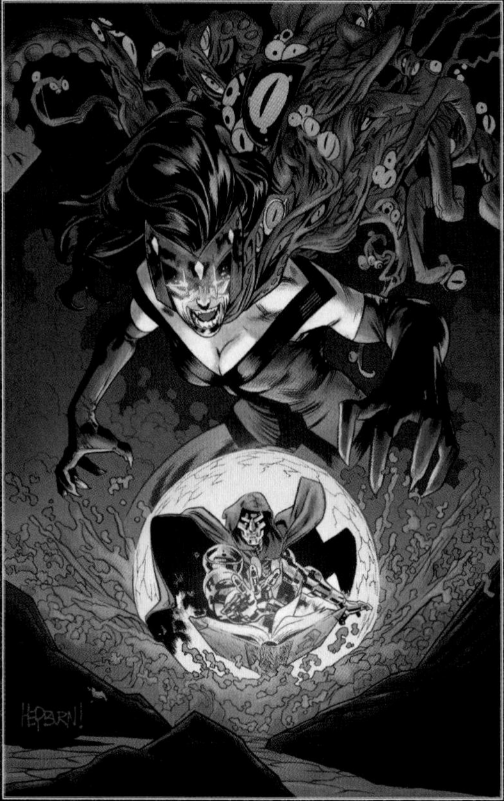
HEPBURN!

THE DARKHOLD OMEGA VARIANT BY
SCOTT HEPBURN & IAN HERRING

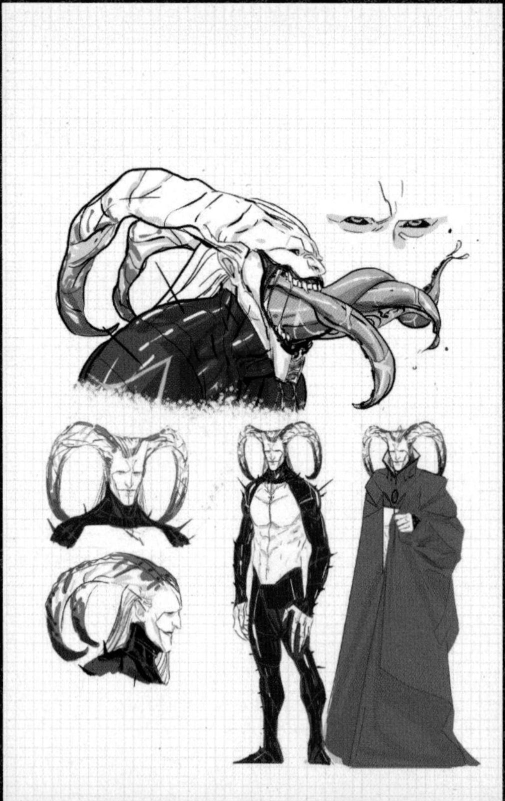

THE DARKHOLD ALPHA DESIGN VARIANT BY
CIAN TORMEY

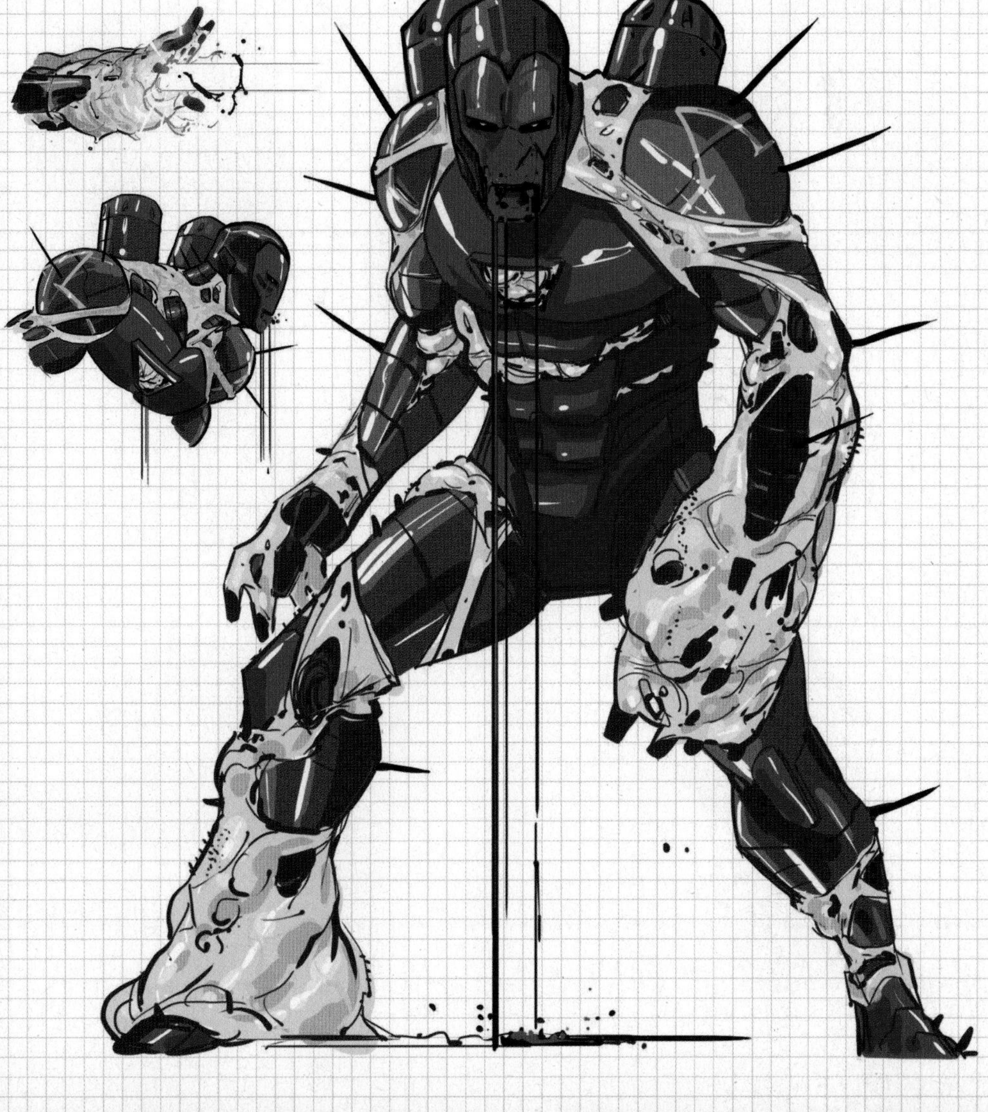

THE DARKHOLD: IRON MAN DESIGN VARIANT BY **CIAN TORMEY**

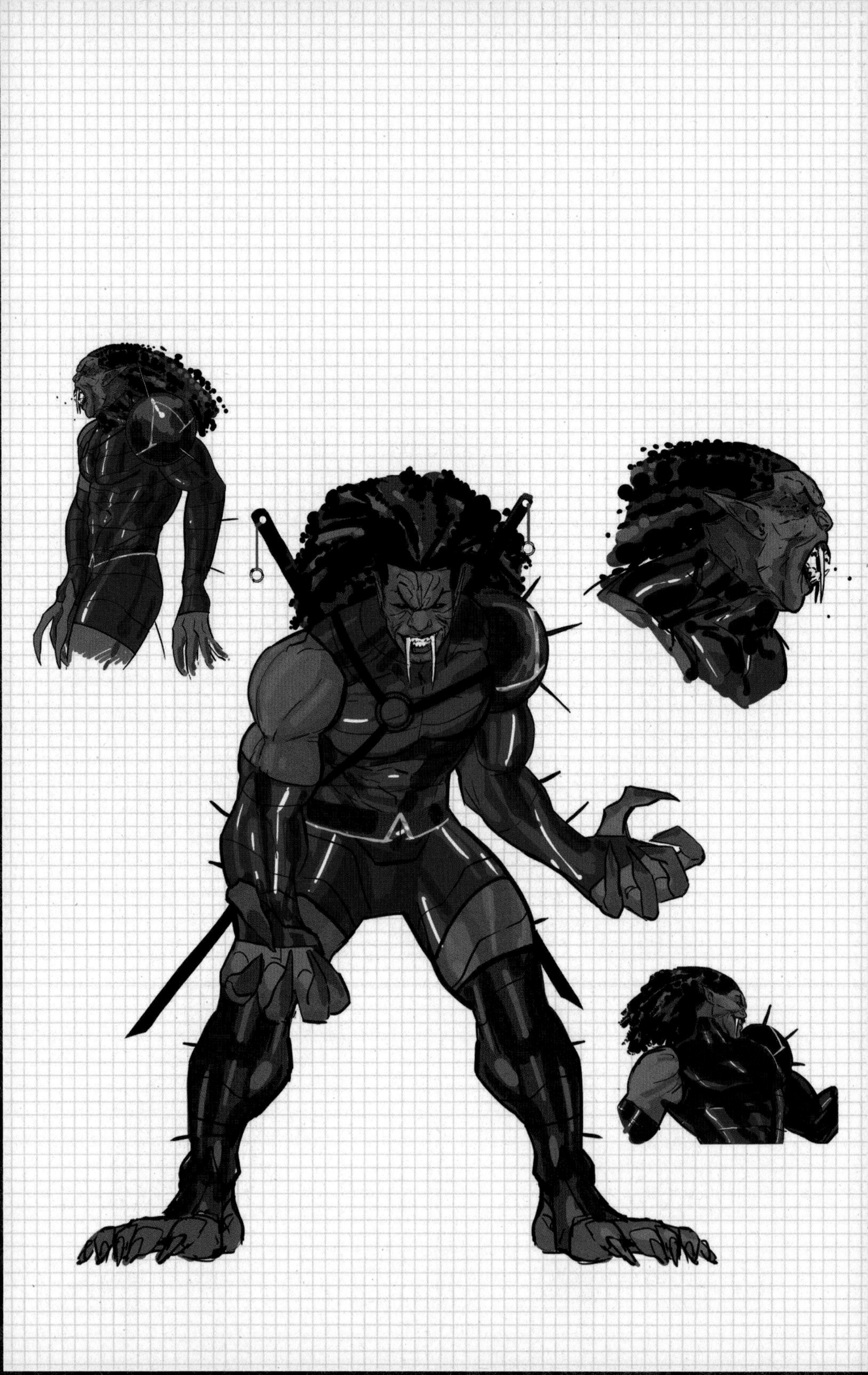

THE DARKHOLD: BLADE DESIGN VARIANT BY **CIAN TORMEY**

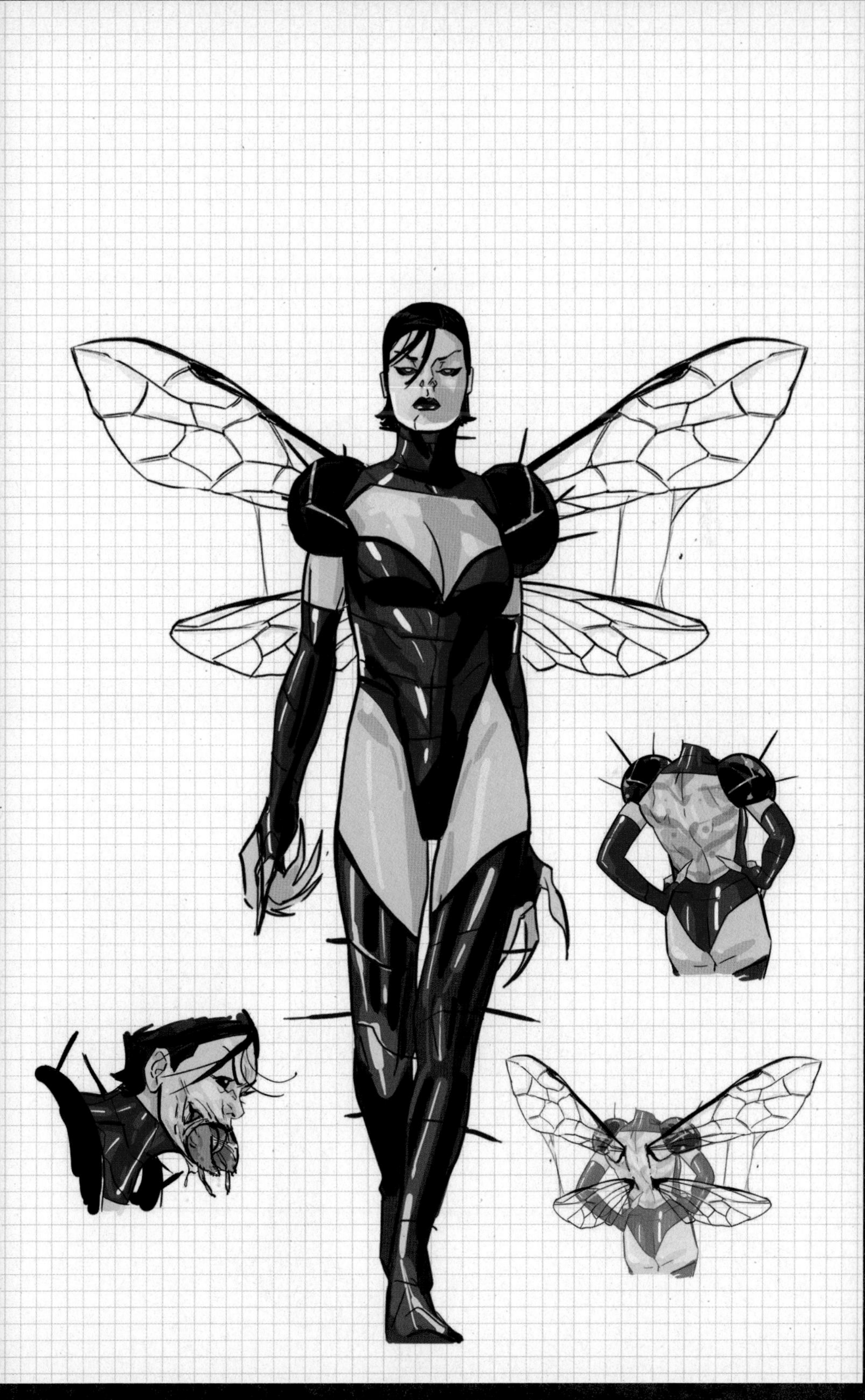

THE DARKHOLD: WASP DESIGN VARIANT BY **CIAN TORMEY**

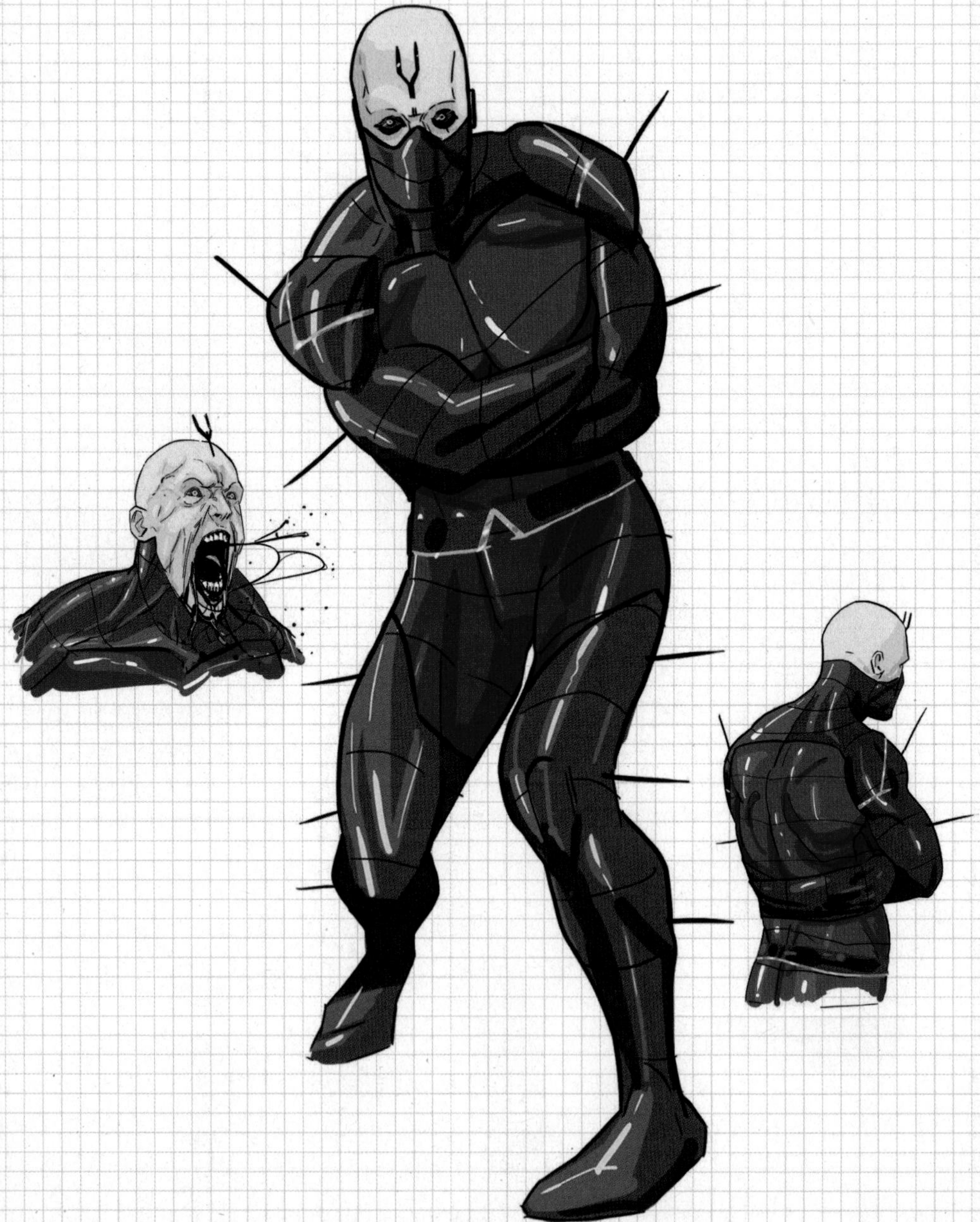

THE DARKHOLD: BLACK BOLT DESIGN VARIANT BY **CIAN TORMEY**

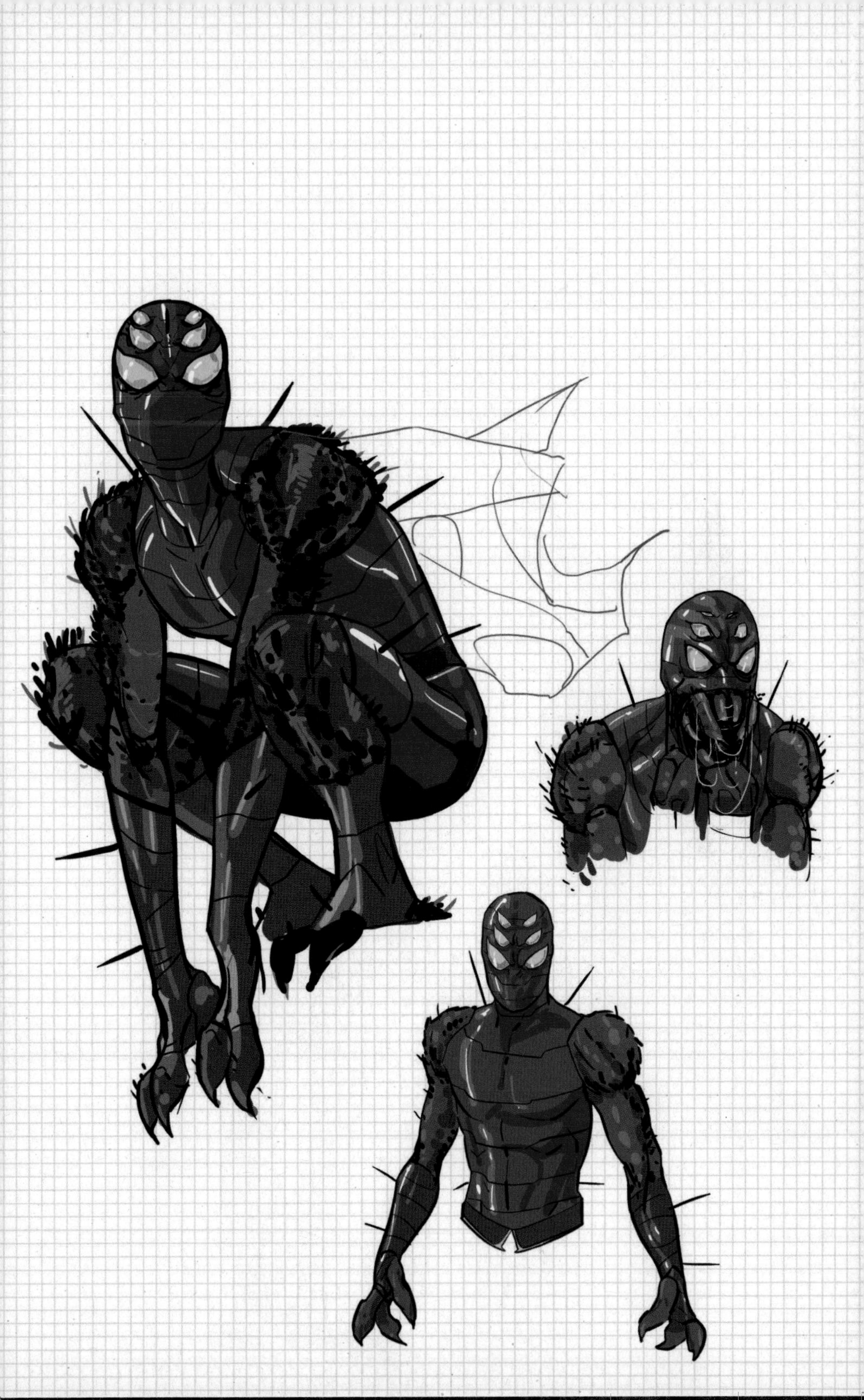

AN TORMEY

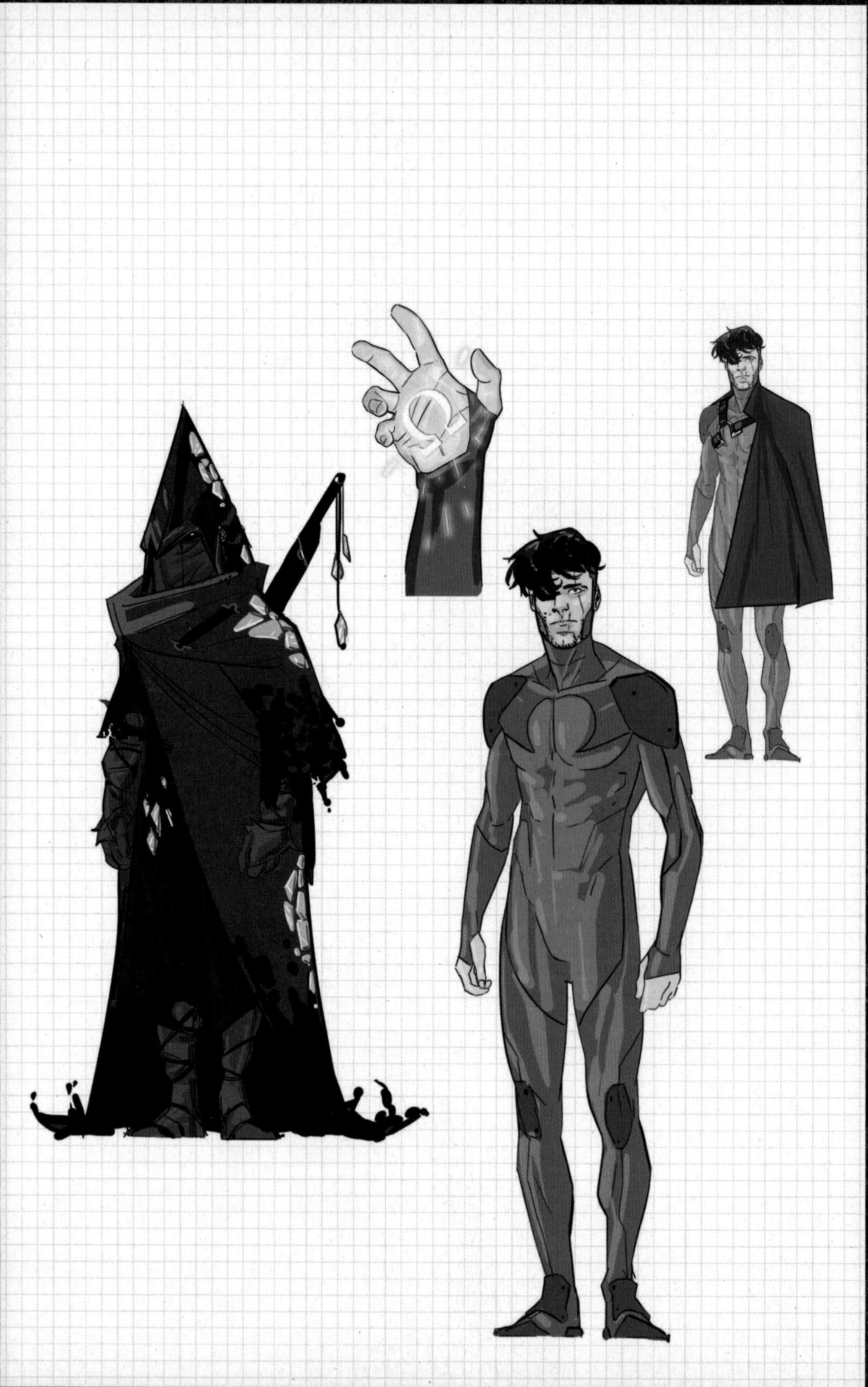

THE DARKHOLD OMEGA VARIANT DESIGN VARIANT BY **CIAN TORMEY**